RICHES, POVERTY, AND THE FAITHFUL

In the book of Revelation, John appeals to the faithful to avoid the temptations of wealth, which he connects with evil and disobedience within secular society. New Testament scholars have traditionally viewed his somewhat radical stance as a reaction to the social injustices and idolatry of the imperial Roman cults of the day. Mark D. Mathews argues that John's rejection of affluence was instead shaped by ideas in the Jewish literature of the Second Temple period which associated the rich with the wicked and viewed the poor as the righteous. Mathews explores how traditions preserved in the *Epistle of Enoch* and later Enochic texts played a formative role in shaping John's theological perspective. This book will be of interest to those researching poverty and wealth in early Christian communities, and the relationship between the traditions preserved in the Dead Sea Scrolls and the New Testament.

MARK D. MATHEWS is Teaching Elder and Senior Pastor at Bethany Presbyterian Church in Oxford, PA. He is a member of the Society of Biblical Literature and of Tyndale House Fellowship.

SOCIETY FOR NEW TESTAMENT STUDIES

MONOGRAPH SERIES

General editor: Paul Trebilco

154

RICHES, POVERTY, AND THE FAITHFUL

SOCIETY FOR NEW TESTAMENT STUDIES

MONOGRAPH SERIES

Recent titles in the series

131. *Ancient Rhetoric and Paul's Apology*
     FREDERICK J. LONG

132. *Reconstructing Honor in Roman Philippi*
     JOSEPH H. HELLEMAN

133. *Theological Hermeneutics and 1 Thessalonians*
     ANGUS PADDISON

134. *Greco-Roman Culture and the Galilee of Jesus*
     MARK A. CHANCEY

135. *Christology and Discipleship in the Gospel of Mark*
     SUZANNE WATTS HENDERSON

136. *The Judaean Poor and the Fourth Gospel*
     TIMOTHY J. M. LING

137. *Paul, the Stoics, and the Body of Christ*
     MICHELLE LEE

138. *The Bridegroom Messiah and the People of God*
     JOCELYN MCWHIRTER

139. *The Torn Veil*
     DANIEL M. GURTNER

140. *Discerning the Spirits*
     ANDRÉ MUNZINGER

141. *The Sheep of the Fold*
     EDWARD W. KLINK III

142. *The Psalms of Lament in Mark's Passion*
     STEPHEN P. AHERNE-KROLL

143. *Cosmology and Eschatology in Hebrews*
     KENNETH L. SCHENCK

144. *The Speeches of Outsiders in Acts*
     OSVALDO PADILLA

145. *The Assumed Authorial Unity of Luke and Acts*
     PATRICIA WALTERS

146. *Geography and the Ascension Narrative in Acts*
     MATTHEW SLEEMAN

147. *The Ituraeans and the Roman Near East*
     E. A. MYERS

148. *The Politics of Inheritance in Romans*
     MARK FORMAN

149. *The Doctrine of Salvation in the First Letter of Peter*
     MARTIN WILLIAMS

150. *Jesus and the Forgiveness of Sins*
     TOBIAS HÄGERLAND

151. *The Composition of the Gospel of Thomas*
     SIMON GATHERCOLE

152. *Paul as an Administrator of God in 1 Corinthians*
     JOHN K. GOODRICH

153. *Affirming the Resurrection of the Incarnate Christ*
     MATTHEW D. JENSEN

Riches, Poverty, and the Faithful

Perspectives on Wealth in the Second Temple Period
and the Apocalypse of John

MARK D. MATHEWS

 CAMBRIDGE
UNIVERSITY PRESS

CAMBRIDGE UNIVERSITY PRESS
Cambridge, New York, Melbourne, Madrid, Cape Town,
Singapore, São Paulo, Delhi, Mexico City

Cambridge University Press
The Edinburgh Building, Cambridge CB2 8RU, UK

Published in the United States of America by Cambridge University Press, New York

www.cambridge.org
Information on this title: www.cambridge.org/9781107018501

© Mark D. Mathews 2013

First published 2013

Printed and bound in the United Kingdom by the MPG Books Group

A catalogue record for this publication is available from the British Library

Library of Congress Cataloguing in Publication data
Mathews, Mark D., 1964–
Riches, poverty, and the faithful : perspectives on wealth in the Second Temple period
and the Apocalypse of John / Mark D. Mathews.
    pages   cm. – (Society for New Testament Studies monograph series ; 154)
Includes bibliographical references and index.
ISBN 978-1-107-01850-1
1. Wealth – Biblical teaching.   2. Bible. N.T. Revelation – Criticism, interpretation, etc.
3. Dead Sea scrolls.   4. Jewish religious literature – History and criticism.   I. Title.
BS2825.6.W37M38   2013
228'.06 – dc23   2012025994

ISBN 978-1-107-01850-1 Hardback

CONTENTS

Acknowledgements   *page* ix
List of abbreviations   xi

PART I   INTRODUCTION   1

1 **The question of wealth in the Apocalypse**   3
   1.1 The problem   3
   1.2 Scholarly approaches to wealth in the New Testament   5
   1.3 Scholarly approaches to the Apocalypse   10
   1.4 The concept of wealth in relation to the faithful   30
   1.5 Methodological approach   32

PART II THE LANGUAGE OF WEALTH AND
   POVERTY, RICH AND POOR, IN THE
   SECOND TEMPLE PERIOD   35
   Introduction   35

2 **Dead Sea Scrolls: non-sectarian Aramaic documents**   42
   2.1 *Aramaic Levi Document*   42
   2.2 Early Enoch tradition   44
   2.3 Summary of Aramaic traditions   60

3 **Dead Sea Scrolls: non-sectarian Hebrew documents**   63
   3.1 Wisdom of Ben Sira (Sirach)   63
   3.2 *Mûsār l^e Mēvîn* (4QInstruction)   80
   3.3 *Two Spirits Treatise* (1QS 3:13–4:26)   90

4 **Dead Sea Scrolls: sectarian Hebrew documents**   92
   4.1 *Damascus Document* (DD)   92
   4.2 *Community Rule* (1QS)   100
   4.3 *War Scroll* (1QM)   110
   4.4 *Pesher Habakkuk* (1QpHab)   112
   4.5 *Hodayot* (1QHa)   115
   4.6 Summary of Hebrew traditions   119

5   Other Jewish literature   121
  5.1   Wisdom of Solomon   121
  5.2   *The Similitudes* (*1 Enoch* 37–71)   126
  5.3   *Eschatological Admonition* (*1 Enoch* 108)   129
  5.4   *Sibylline Oracles*   131
  5.5   Preliminary conclusions   137

**PART III   WEALTH, POVERTY, AND THE
            FAITHFUL COMMUNITY IN THE
            APOCALYPSE OF JOHN**   141
            Introduction   141

**6   The language of wealth and poverty in the Seven
      Messages: Rev 2–3**   144
  6.1   The Seven Messages   144

7   The present eschatological age: Rev 4–6   167
  7.1   The inauguration of the eschatological age   167
  7.2   Worthy is the Lamb to receive wealth   170
  7.3   Breaking the seven seals   175
  7.4   The third rider   178
  7.5   A voice from the midst of the throne   182

8   Buying and selling in Satan's World: Rev 12–13, 18   185
  8.1   The mark of the Beast   185
  8.2   The function of myth and tradition in Rev 12–13   189
  8.3   The climax of economic critique: Rev 18   197
  8.4   Wealth and the faithful: Rev 18:4–5   198
  8.5   Wealth and Babylon   202
  8.6   Excursus: the use of merchant and sailor imagery in
         Jewish traditions   204
  8.7   A theology of wealth in the Apocalypse   216

9   Conclusions   219

  Bibliography   225
  Index of passages   247
  Index of authors and topics   267

ACKNOWLEDGEMENTS

This book would not have been possible without the help of so many special people. First, I would like to thank my thesis supervisor, Professor Loren T. Stuckenbruck, for his unwavering support and extreme patience throughout this research project. He has challenged me in so many ways to stretch myself and expand my categories and has produced in me a great appreciation for excellence in scholarship. I would also like to thank my secondary supervisor, Dr William Telford, for his meticulous reading of my work and many corrections and suggestions throughout the research process. Thanks are also due to Professor Robert Hayward for reading my work on the Aramaic and Hebrew texts from Qumran and for his helpful observations. In addition, I would like to thank Dr Stephen Barton and Dr John Court for a very rigorous, yet gracious viva and for their engaging conversation and suggestions for future research. A special note of gratitude also goes to Princeton Theological Seminary for making arrangements for housing, for allowing me access to Speer and Luce libraries after our return to the US, and for granting me study space in the Ph.D. study suite. It was there that the final draft of the book was written.

I owe my deepest gratitude, however, to those who laboured silently and made the research process ultimately possible. I would like to thank my father-in-law, Ray Reichenbach, for his continued financial support throughout my academic career, without whom I would never have made it to the level of doctoral studies. Thanks are also due the Panacea Society for providing a doctoral research grant during my time in Durham. I would also like to acknowledge our church family at Park Cities Presbyterian Church in Dallas, Texas for their prayerful and financial support.

It would have been next to impossible to write this book without the extremely generous support of Don and Charlotte Test in Dallas, to whom I am especially grateful. They took an interest in my research early on and not only committed fully to supporting us during our time in Durham but also became very dear and special friends in the process. A very special thanks to both of you. You are exceptional people, unusually generous, exceedingly wise, and a real breath of fresh air! You have ultimately made this experience possible and my entire family and I are eternally grateful.

Most importantly, I thank my precious family for their incredible support, encouragement, and quiet frustration when I was so often locked away in my study. To Raina, Grace, and Sara, who often heard, 'Not now, honey, Daddy has work to do', and seldom complained. But most of all I thank my wife Aimee, truly my greatest friend in all the world. You have so graciously and courageously held me up during some very difficult and stressful times. You always encouraged and never complained and when the world laughed at my decision to answer a new direction in life you stood by me like a true, faithful friend. I only hope I can live long enough to repay the loyalty and love you have shown me, though I am not sure that would be possible. It is to you, Aimee, that this book is dedicated.

ABBREVIATIONS

AARTTS	American Academy of Religion Texts and Translations Series
AB	*Astronomical Book*
ABD	*Anchor Bible Dictionary*
ABRL	Anchor Bible Reference Library
AGAJU	Arbeit zur Geschichte des Antiken Judentums und des Urchristentums
ALD	*Aramaic Levi Document*
AmAnth	*American Anthropologist*
ANRW	*Aufstieg und Niedergang der römischen Welt*, ed. Wolfgang Haase and Hildegard Temporini (Berlin and New York: de Gruyter, 1992)
ANYAS	Annals of the New York Academy of Sciences
AOAT	Alter Orient und Altes Testament
AOW	*Apocalypse of Weeks*
AR	*Archiv für Religionswissenschaft*
ASV	American Standard Version
ASTI	*Annual of the Swedish Theological Institute*
ATANT	Abhandlungen zur Theologie das Alten und Neuen Testaments
ATLABS	American Theological Library Association Bibliography Series
ATSI	*Annual of the Swedish Theological Institute*
BAIU	*Bulletin de l'Alliance Israélite Universelle*
BDAG	Walter Bauer, *A Greek–English Lexicon of the New Testament and Other Early Christian Literature*, 3rd edn. Rev. and ed. Frederick William Danker (University of Chicago Press, 2000)
BDF	F. Blass and A. Debrunner (eds), *A Greek Grammar of the New Testament and Other Early Christian Literature* (University of Chicago Press, 1961)

BECNT	Baker Exegetical Commentary on the New Testament
BETL	Bibliotheca Ephemeridum Theologicarum Lovaniensium
BFCT	Beiträge zur Förderung christlicher Theologie
Bib	*Biblica*
BJS	Brown Judaic Studies
BJSUCSD	Biblical and Judaic Studies, University of California San Diego
BNTC	Black's New Testament Commentaries
BOW	*Book of the Watchers*
BR	*Biblical Research*
BTB	*Biblical Theology Bulletin*
BVB	Beiträge zum Verstehen der Bibel
BZAW	*Beihefte zur Zeitschrift für die alttestamentliche Wissenschaft*
BZNW	*Beiheft zur Zeitschrift für die neutestamentliche Wissenschaft*
CBCOT	Cambridge Bible Commentaries on the Old Testament
CBOTS	Conectica Biblica Old Testament Series
CBQ	*Catholic Biblical Quarterly*
CBQMS	Catholic Biblical Quarterly Monograph Series
CCWJCW	Cambridge Commentaries on Writings of the Jewish and Christian World 200 BC to AD 200
CD	Cairo Genizah MSS
CEJL	Commentaries on Early Jewish Literature
CHCS	Croom Helm Classical Studies
CRINT	Compendia Rerum Iudaicarum ad Novum Testamentum
DCLS	Deuterocanonical and Cognate Literature Studies
DCLY	Deuterocanonical and Cognate Literature Yearbook
DD	*Damascus Document*
DJD	Discoveries in the Judaean Desert
DNEBT	Die Neue Echter Bibel Themen
DSD	*Dead Sea Discoveries*
DSS	Dead Sea Scrolls
DSSHAG	James H. Charlesworth, Frank M. Cross, et al. (eds.), *The Dead Sea Scrolls: Hebrew, Aramaic, and Greek Texts with English Translations*, 6 vols. Princeton Theological Seminary Dead Sea Scrolls Project (Tübingen: J. C. B. Mohr (Paul Siebeck), 1994)

DSSR	Donald W. Parry and Emanuel Tov (eds.), *The Dead Sea Scrolls Reader*, 6 vols. (Leiden: Brill, 2003–5)
DTTBYML	Marcus Jastrow (ed.), *A Dictionary of the Targumim, the Talmud Babli and Yerushalmi, and the Midrashic Literature with an Index of Scriptural Quotations* (New York: Pardes Publishing House, 1950)
EB	Études bibliques
EDSS	Lawrence H. Schiffman and James C. Vanderkam (eds), *Encyclopedia of the Dead Sea Scrolls*, 2 vols (New York: Oxford University Press, 2000)
EJ	Études juives
EMML	Ethiopian Manuscript Microfilm Library
EQ	*Evangelical Quarterly*
ESV	English Standard Version
Eth.	Ethiopian
EUS	European University Studies
Exp	*The Expositor*
FOTL	The Forms of the Old Testament Literature
FRLANT	Forschungen zur Religion und Literatur des Alten Neuen Testaments
GAP	Guides to Apocrypha and Pseudepigrapha
GBSOTS	Guides to Biblical Scholarship Old Testament Series
GDNES	Gorgias Dissertations, Near East Series
GKC	Wilhelm Gesenius, *Gesenius' Hebrew Grammar*, 2nd edn (Oxford: Clarendon Press, 1983)
HA	Handbuch der Altertumwissenschaft
HALOT	Ludwig Koehler and Walter Baumgartner, *The Hebrew and Aramaic Lexicon of the Old Testament*, trans. M. E. J. Richardson, 2 vols (Leiden: Brill Academic Publishers, 2002)
HDHL	Historical Dictionary of the Hebrew Language
HNT	Handbuch zum Neuen Testament
HSM	Harvard Semitic Monographs
ICC	International Critical Commentary
IDB	George Arthur Buttrick, *Interpreter's Dictionary of the Bible*, 5 vols. (New York: Abingdon Press, 1961)
IEJ	*Israel Exploration Journal*
Int	*Interpretation*
JA	*Journal Asiatique*
JBL	*Journal of Biblical Literature*
JJS	*Journal of Jewish Studies*

JQR	*Jewish Quarterly Review*
JSJSup	Supplements to the Journal for the Study of Judaism
JSNT	*Journal for the Study of the New Testament*
JSNTSup	Journal for the Study of the New Testament, Supplement Series
JSOT	*Journal for the Study of the Old Testament*
JSOTSup	Journal for the Study of the Old Testament, Supplement Series
JSP	*Journal for the Study of the Pseudepigrapha*
JSPSup	Journal for the Study of the Pseudepigrapha, Supplement Series
JTS	*Journal of Theological Studies*
JU	Judentum und Unwelt
KKNT	Kritisch-exegetischer Kommentar über das Neue Testament
LNTS	Library of New Testament Studies
LSJ	Henry George Liddell and Robert Scott (eds), *A Greek–English Lexicon*, 9th edn (Oxford: Clarendon Press, 1996)
LSTS	Library of Second Temple Studies
LXX	Septuagint
MHUC	Monographs of the Hebrew Union College
MM	J. H. Moulton and G. Milligan, *Vocabulary of the Greek Testament*, rev. edn (Peabody, MA: Hendrickson, 1997)
MNTC	Moffat New Testament Commentary
MNTS	McMaster New Testament Studies
MSupHACA	Mnemosyne Supplements, History and Archaeology of Classical Antiquity
MT	Masoretic text
NASB	New American Standard Bible
NCBC	New Century Bible Commentary
NEBT	Die Neue Echter Bibel Themen
NET	New English Translation
NICOT	New International Commentary on the Old Testament
NICNT	New International Commentary on the New Testament
NIDOTTE	Willem VanGemeren (ed.), *New International Dictionary of Old Testament Theology and Exegesis*, 5 vols (Grand Rapids, MI: Zondervan, 1997)
NIGTC	New International Greek Testament Commentary
NIV	New International Version

NLT	New Living Translation
NovTest	*Novum Testamentum*
NRSV	New Revised Standard Version
NSBT	New Studies in Biblical Theology
NSKAT	Neuer Stuttgarter Kommentar Altes Testament
NT	New Testament
NTD	Das Neue Testament Deutsch
NTM	New Testament Message
NTOA	Novum Testamentum et Orbis Antiquus
NTS	*New Testament Studies*
OT	Old Testament
OTNT	Ökumenischer Taschenbuchkommentar zum Neuen Testament
OTP	James H. Charlesworth (ed.), *The Old Testament Pseudepigrapha* (Garden City, NY: Doubleday, 1983)
PLIAJS	Philip L. Lown Institute of Advanced Judaic Studies
RB	*Revue biblique*
RBL	*Review of Biblical Literature*
RevBib	*Revue biblique*
RevQ	*Revue de Qumran*
RGW	Religions in the Graeco-Roman World
RhetRev	*Rhetoric Review*
RS	Religion and Society
SBL	Society of Biblical Literature
SBLDS	Society of Biblical Literature Dissertation Series
SBLEJL	Society of Biblical Literature. Early Judaism and its Literature
SBLMS	Society of Biblical Literature Monograph Series
SBLSCSS	Society of Biblical Literature Septuagint and Cognate Studies Series
SBLSP	Society of Biblical Literature Seminar Papers
SBLSS	Society of Biblical Literature Symposium Series
SBT	Studies in Biblical Theology
ScripHier	*Scripta Hierosolymitana*
SCSS	Septuagint and Cognate Studies Series
SDSSRL	Studies in the Dead Sea Scrolls and Related Literature
SIL	Summer Institute of Linguistics
SILPL	Summer Institute of Linguistics Publications in Linguistics
SIS	Studies in Interactional Sociolinguistics
SNT	Studien zum Neuen Testament
SocAn	*Sociological Analysis*

SocRel	*Sociology of Religion*
SPB	Studia Post-Biblica
SPS	Sacra Pagina Series
SPSHS	Scholars Press Studies in the Humanities Series
SPSJCO	The Second Princeton Symposium on Judaism and Christian Origins
STDJ	Studies on the Texts of the Desert of Judah
StPB	Studia Post-Biblica
SUNT	Studien zur Umwelt des Neuen Testaments
SVTP	Studia in Veteris Testamenti Pseudepigrapha
TAB	The Aramaic Bible
TANZ	Texte und Arbeiten zum neutestamentlichen Zeitalter
TBN	Themes in Biblical Narrative
TDNT	G. Kittel and G. Friedrich (eds), *Theological Dictionary of the New Testament*, trans. G. W. Bromiley, 10 vols (Grand Rapids, MI: Eerdmans, 1964–76)
TDOT	G. J. Botterweck and H. Ringgren (eds), *Theological Dictionary of the Old Testament*, trans. J. T. Willis, G. W. Bromiley, and D. E. Green, 17 vols (Grand Rapids, MI: Eerdmans, 1974–2006)
TNIV	Today's New International Version
T-S	Taylor-Schechter
T-S AS	Taylor-Schechter Additional Series
TSAJ	Texte und Studien zum Antiken Judentum
TST	*Two Spirits Treatise*
TUGAL	Texte und Untersuchengen zur Geschichte der altchristlichen Literatur
TynBul	*Tyndale Bulletin*
UBSHS	United Bible Societies Handbook Series
UTPSS	University of Texas Press Slavic Series
VTest	*Vetus Testamentum*
VTSup	Supplements to Vetus Testamentum
WBC	Word Biblical Commentary
WUNT	*Wissenschaftliche Untersuchungen zum Neuen Testament*
ZNW	*Zeitschrift für die neutestamentliche Wissenschaft und die Kunde älteren Kirche*

All biblical and otherwise ancient citations in this volume follow the *SBL Handbook of Style*.

PART I

Introduction

1

THE QUESTION OF WEALTH IN THE APOCALYPSE

1.1 The problem

For you say, 'I am rich (πλούσιός εἰμι) and have acquired great wealth (πεπλούτηκα), and need nothing,' yet you do not realize that you are the one who is miserable and pitiful and poor (πτωχὸς) and blind and naked. (Rev 3:17)

The text above illustrates the theological problem to be considered in relation to the Johannine Apocalypse. One might suppose that this passage reflects only a concern for certain attitudes towards wealth. Yet, in contrast to the circumstances portrayed in the missive to Smyrna, 'I know your tribulation and poverty, yet you are rich' (2:9), it seems as if the writer values their impoverished state over a lifestyle of wealth as depicted in Laodicea. A similar tone can be detected among the other churches as well. Philadelphia, for example, is said to have 'few resources' and shares with Smyrna the absence of any call for repentance.[1] In addition, the 'teaching of Balaam' (2:14), as some commentators suggest, includes what the author regarded as an excessive interest in wealth and could be a reference to greed as shown in later traditions.[2] John's primary opponent Jezebel is explicitly connected with the rich whore Babylon through the language of sexual immorality (πορνεύω) and deceit (πλανάω), which in chapters 17–18 is associated with economic activity (Rev 2:20–3; 17:2–6; 18:3–4, 23; cf. 13:14–17). The author's disdain for wealth among the churches is so great that he can unambiguously say that the poor are rich while those enjoying economic success are poor. Commentators have struggled to make sense of this juxtaposed

---

[1] The phrase μικρὰν ἔχεις δύναμιν in 3:8 can be taken as 'you have few resources'; *BDAG*, p. 263 (cf. Rev 18:3).

[2] 2 Pet 2:15; Jude 11; Philo, *Mos.* 1:294–9; Josephus, *Ant.* 4:126–30; *m. 'Abot* 5:19–22; *Tg.* Num 24:14; *Midr. Rab.* Num 20:23. See Charles, *Revelation*, vol. I, p. 63; Harrington, *Revelation*, p. 61; Fiorenza, *Vision*, p. 56; see also Ginzberg, *Legends of the Jews*, vol. II, pp. 764–5; Vermès, *Scripture and Tradition*, pp. 127–77.

language suggesting a spiritual interpretation, yet these studies offer little support for such conclusions and avoid the difficult issue; the lack of repentance for the poor and the sharp calumniation of the rich seems to indicate that John associates faithfulness with one's economic status.

The arrogant speech attributed to the rich in the passage cited above (3:17) functions further to denigrate the wealthy and draw associations with Babylon (18:7) in the only other place where this device occurs.[3] In the vilification of Babylon's wealth, which is developed most extensively in chapter 18, a prophetic word simultaneously exhorts and warns the faithful in relation to the Roman Empire: 'Come out of her, my people, lest you take part in her sins, lest you share in her plagues' (18:4). Taken together with the harsh censure of wealth in the seven messages and the praise of poverty, this passage encourages us to consider whether the author is calling his audience to withdraw completely from the present economic system.[4]

The language of Revelation 18 has been examined in detail for its many allusions to the Hebrew Bible, in particular the oracles against the nations of Tyre and Babylon in the prophetic tradition (Isa 13, 23; Jer 50–1; Ezek 27). Yet a transformation of the language by the author is evident in his explicit denunciation of riches. Those who have dealt with this text in light of the biblical tradition have identified this transformation, though without an analysis or explanation that accounts for this shift. Commentators have sought to explain the radical reshaping of these OT texts as the author's interpretation of these traditions in light of his present socio-historical circumstances. Yet, these studies have produced a wide variety of speculation, none of which has dealt directly with the author's almost categorical rejection of wealth or explained his correlation between faithfulness and poverty. This leads to the question of the present study: To what degree can we say that John's portrayal of the faithful Christian community is informed by more recent Jewish interpretive traditions related to wealth in the Second Temple period? The harsh denigration of wealth and praise of poverty in the seven messages goes beyond any critique found in the Hebrew Bible. This encourages us to advance additional questions, which are subsidiary to the first. Is John's language of wealth conventional, and, if so, with what traditions is he in contact? Moreover, is the 'idea' contained in this language traditional? We ask this in an attempt to ascertain the extent to which we can understand John's perspective on wealth as a whole. We must also inquire as

---

[3] See discussion in section 6.1, below, pp. 55–6; 161–3.
[4] Yarbro Collins, 'Revelation 18', p. 202.

to John's strategy in relation to 'how' he uses this wealth language in an effort to move his recipients to a particular resolution of what it means to be faithful. To what extent is faithfulness in the Christian community, as portrayed by John, inconsistent with the accumulation of wealth? We will further ask to what degree we can say John's use of traditional perspectives in Scripture and developments of early Jewish literature legitimized or strengthened his attempt to impose his perspective on the communities he is addressing. The need for research that answers these questions in relation to the Book of Revelation becomes clearer when considered in view of the current state of scholarly research on the topic of wealth in the NT.

1.2 Scholarly approaches to wealth in the New Testament

There is no shortage of books that seek to provide a 'Christian' perspective of wealth, though these are frequently written on a popular level. Less abundant are those volumes that take a scholarly approach to the subject. These studies underscore the degree to which scholars have either (1) been reticent or unable to fit John's perspective on wealth into a systematic treatment of the subject or (2) have underestimated the value of its contribution to the discussion of wealth in the NT.

Hengel produced a helpful, yet brief, volume that traces the idea of possessions among the faithful community from the Hebrew Bible into the early church.[5] He correctly notes the presence of apocalyptic themes in John's critique of the wealth of Rome. However, this treatment of the subject does not have as its aim to produce a coherent view of John's perspective on wealth, nor does he endeavour to synthesize the material in order to find a unified point of view on wealth as a whole. In line with his aims, he does not provide any insight into what traditions in the Second Temple period might reflect the author's apocalyptic critique of wealth in Rev 18. Rather, he rightly concludes that a homogenous outlook on wealth in the early church cannot be deduced.[6]

Blomberg attempts to provide a 'biblical' theology of riches from a Christian perspective.[7] While this volume includes discussions of wealth in the Hebrew Bible and the Second Temple period, there is no engagement with how these traditions have shaped John's view of wealth. Rather, his emphasis is on the *Sitz im Leben* of the texts, in which reactions to historical events drive the interpretation. Consequently, the Apocalypse

---

[5] Hengel, *Property and Riches*. [6] *Ibid.*, p. 84.
[7] In Blomberg, *Poverty nor Riches*. See also González, *Faith and Wealth*.

of John plays no role in this assessment or, for that larger role, does not factor into what one would consider in regard to the larger question of wealth and poverty and biblical theology. More importantly, the emphasis is on a systematic understanding of the teachings of Jesus and Paul, with the Apocalypse being relegated to a chapter entitled 'The Rest of the New Testament'.

Hoppe's 2004 volume on poverty in the Bible deals with the language of 'the poor' from a socio-historical perspective, yet lacks any discussion of the poverty of Smyrna (Rev 2:9), and provides only a cursory treatment of the metaphorical poverty attributed to the church at Laodicea.[8] In the chapter entitled 'New Testament', the writer divides the material into three categories: Gospels, Paul, and 'Other Books', providing only a brief discussion of John's Apocalypse. More recently, Berges and Hoppe have offered a discussion on the perspectives of wealth in the Old and New Testaments.[9] While noting especially distinctive features between the Old and New Testaments, there is no attempt to account for these differences by placing them in conversation with traditions from the Second Temple period or their possible impact on the NT writers.

More specialized studies on wealth and poverty in the NT are frequently focused on either Luke-Acts or the epistle of James,[10] while others seek to demonstrate a coherent view of the teachings of Jesus.[11] Thus the state of scholarship concerning John's view of wealth in the Apocalypse has been almost entirely neglected.[12] This is seen most recently in a contribution by Regev in which he compares the social approaches to wealth and sectarianism of Qumran with the early Christian communities. Given the apocalyptic nature of the documents related to the Qumran community and the sectarian nature of John's communication to the seven churches, it is surprising, since both demonstrate a decided

---

[8] Hoppe, *No Poor Among You*, pp. 163–5.   [9] Berges and Hoppe, *Arm und Reich*.

[10] Metzger, *Consumption and Wealth*; Pilgrim, *Good News to the Poor*; Gillman, *Possessions and the Life of Faith*; Phillips, *Reading Issues of Wealth*; Gradl, *Zwischen Arm und Reich*; Takatemjen, *The Banquet is Ready*; Bosch, *Good News for the Poor*; Stanford, 'Their Eyes They Have Closed?'; Krüger, *Jakobusbrief als prophetische Kritik der Reichen*; Maynard-Reid, *Poverty and Wealth in James*; Maier, *Reich und Arm*; Kelly, 'Poor and Rich in the Epistle of James'.

[11] Schmidt, *Hostility to Wealth*; Poulain, *Jésus et la richesse d'après Saint-Luc*; Mealand, *Poverty and Expectation*; Heuver, *Teachings of Jesus Concerning Wealth*.

[12] Two volumes make no mention of the Book of Revelation in their treatment of the theme of wealth: Countryman, *The Rich Christian in the Church* and Wheeler, *Wealth as Peril and Obligation*.

concern over wealth, that the author does not include in his comparison the Johannine Apocalypse.[13] One recent volume, however, has been devoted to the topic, having as its focus 'heavenly wealth'.[14] Royalty's point of departure is the internal struggle between John and the rival prophetess Jezebel, who promotes a decadent lifestyle that includes assimilation into the dominant culture and eating meat sacrificed to Roman idols.[15] In order to establish his prophetic authority, John presents Jesus in terms of wealth since this was the 'preeminent symbol of power in antiquity'.[16] In doing so, he underscores the significance of the 'high status' wealth of heaven in contrast to the 'low status' commercial wealth of Jezebel and Babylon/Rome. Royalty argues that John portrays Christ as a moral philosopher and maintains that wealth imagery in the Apocalypse is best located within Greco-Roman literature and culture. This study, although groundbreaking, raises a number of finer points, which will merit attention throughout the present work. For now, however, it is appropriate to discuss larger questions that emerge from Royalty's study.

First, Royalty may be too quick to dismiss the importance of traditional Jewish sources. While he identifies John's 'excessive' use of language from the Hebrew Bible, he contends that his recipients would have been unfamiliar with these traditions and would have failed to recognize the multilayered intertextuality. He states, 'it is unlikely that his urban Greek audience had the scriptural knowledge to hear the allusions . . . The audience would have been more knowledgeable about Greco-Roman culture, in which they lived, than the Hebrew prophets, whom they may have never read.'[17] Moreover, he asserts that John 'deconstructs' the authority of his prophetic sources through a series of 'strong misreadings'.[18] Although he recognizes how much John reconfigures any Jewish traditions he may have received, including the Hebrew Bible, his thesis is overstated. Undoubtedly, Greco-Roman culture is in the air, but this emphasis is one-sided. On the contrary, the earliest church viewed itself as Jewish and its attachment to ancient Jewish traditions vis-à-vis

---

[13] Regev, 'Wealth and Sectarianism', pp. 211–29.

[14] Royalty, *Streets of Heaven*. Adela Yarbro Collins and Richard Bauckham have both contributed helpful articles pertaining to John's language of wealth (see section 1.3). Here I draw attention to the fact that only one volume has been dedicated solely to the study of wealth in John's Apocalypse.

[15] See also Duff, *Who Rides the Beast?* He also argues that John's primary concern is the internal struggle within the churches and deals with wealth as a subsidiary issue.

[16] *Ibid.*, p. 38.   [17] Royalty, *Streets of Heaven*, pp. 18–19.   [18] *Ibid.*, p. 243.

Christian apocalypses and testaments argues against this notion.[19] Moreover, the writer's use of prophetic speech forms, names of biblical characters to denigrate opponents, and the apocalyptic idiom argue strongly against the idea that John would not expect his readers to understand this language. It seems idiosyncratic for an author to communicate to an audience through a medium of expression that he or she knows they will not recognize.[20] Royalty rightly notes the writer's development and reshaping of biblical traditions in formulating his own message. However, his contention that this in some way undermines the authority of the Hebrew Bible and is the basis for looking to Greco-Roman sources for our understanding of the Apocalypse does not compel.

Second, Royalty's arrangement of his texts for analysis is overly schematic. He compares only four of his five primary texts for examination in John's Apocalypse (1:12–16; 4:2–11; 17–18; 21–2) with ancient Jewish literature and concludes that John's strategy lies in Greco-Roman sources. This is further illustrated by the way he then focuses only on Greco-Roman sources when discussing Rev 2:9 and 3:17. The Greco-Roman context, which has purportedly shaped John's language of wealth, is then located in Stoic ideas, though Royalty recognizes that the language of the text itself agrees with Cynic philosophy.[21] According to Royalty, the imagery of Christ clothed in a long robe and golden sash (1:13) 'would evoke Stoic attitudes towards wealth' as *adiaphora*.[22] More generally, in his analysis of wealth texts from Revelation in comparison to Jewish literature, he focuses only on wealth imagery, i.e. golden crowns and jewels, and not on John's language of riches (πλοῦτος) or the accumulation of wealth (πλουτέω).

---

[19] John's concern over 'those who say they are Jews but are not' suggests some degree of self-identity as the true Jews (Rev 2:9; 3:9). For a discussion concerning the definitive split between Christianity and Judaism, see Dunn, *Parting of the Ways*, pp. 301–29; Alon, *Jews in their Land*, pp. 288–307. For a discussion about the possible Christian provenance of pseudepigraphal literature, see Davila, *Provenance of the Pseudepigrapha*; de Jonge, *Pseudepigrapha of the Old Testament*; Elgvin, 'Jewish Christian Editing', 278–304.

[20] e.g. manna, Jezebel, Balaam, twelve tribes of Israel, new Jerusalem, priestly descriptions of Jesus, reference to Jesus as the lamb slain (Passover), Temple, priests. The antagonism between the Synagogue of Satan and the churches of Smyrna and Philadelphia and those who call themselves Jews but are not underscores the author's expectation that his audience was not only familiar with Old Testament traditions but considered themselves to be the true Jews. It is beyond the scope of this book to argue for either the Christian or Jewish nature of the Apocalypse. However, for a discussion of the apocalyptic aspects of the Book of Revelation, see Aune, *Apocalypticism*, pp. 150–74. See also n. 93, below.

[21] Royalty, *Streets of Heaven*, pp. 162–3.   [22] *Ibid.*, p. 123.

Finally, and more importantly, Royalty's focus on the non-Jewish, Greco-Roman world could not produce a sustained engagement with the literature of the Hebrew Bible or other ancient Jewish literature. While he does offer a limited discussion of *1 Enoch* and the *Sibylline Oracles*, other literature, such as documents from the Dead Sea Scrolls and related texts, is not explored. An example of his limited involvement in these texts is evidenced by the absence of any protracted discussion of the negative language of wealth in the *Epistle of Enoch* and its similarity to the Apocalypse, although he recognizes its presence and cites a very significant text (*1 Enoch* 97:8–10).[23] Rather, he maintains that the pejorative tone against the rich in the *Epistle of Enoch* has no connection with the Apocalypse because 'there is no such universal condemnation of wealth in Revelation'.[24]

Royalty's conclusions contrast prima facie with what the text of Revelation portrays as an almost categorical rejection of wealth. Apart from the Lamb's worthiness to receive riches and the gold and jewel-laden new Jerusalem, nothing positive can be said about John's portrayal of wealth on earth in the present age. In addition, a discussion of the call for the faithful to 'Come out' in the critique of the wealth of Rome (18:4) is entirely absent. Rather, he concludes that wealth imagery functions to maintain and increase status in the same way that it functions in the aristocratic Greco-Roman culture.[25] The author's contrasting perspectives on wealth function to establish his prophetic authority over Jezebel and other rivals, which, according to Royalty, is the primary aim of the author. This emphasis, correct as it is, nonetheless leads to a conclusion that John's calls for action in the Apocalypse are 'few' and 'vague'.[26] The result of his analysis does not do justice to the numerous imperatives that are directed to the Christian community throughout the Apocalypse.[27]

In relation to the present study, the most important of these imperatives are John's admonitions to repent (2:5, 16, 21–2; 3:3, 19) and to 'Come out' (18:4). Thus, Royalty's study does not provide an answer for how John expects the faithful to respond to his message or what form their repentance is to take. The textual evidence that ties the seven messages with the critique of Babylon in chapter 18 and the subsequent call to

---

[23] Charles identified this passage as a parallel to Rev 3:17. Charles, *Book of Enoch*, p. xcvii.

[24] Royalty, *Streets of Heaven*, p. 57.   [25] *Ibid.*, p. 245.   [26] *Ibid.*, p. 128.

[27] The seven messages contain twenty such imperatives: 2:5, 7, 10–11, 16–17, 25, 29; 3:2–3, 6, 11, 13, 19, 22. See also 13:9, 18; 14:7; 18:4; 22:17.

'Come out' suggests John's perspective on wealth for the faithful community cannot be understood without making this connection. Royalty's focus on wealth imagery to formulate an argument based on status honour in the Greco-Roman world leaves aside the problem John seems to be concerned with more directly; how is wealth to be negotiated in relation to the faithful community? This emphasis, in conjunction with his limited engagement with Jewish apocalyptic literature outside the canon of the Hebrew Bible, elicits the need in NT scholarship for a reading of John's language of wealth in the Apocalypse that takes these issues into account. The scope, limitations, and the approach adopted by such a study might be best formulated in light of previous approaches to the Book of Revelation. Since the communities John addresses lived in the Greco-Roman world of Asia Minor a discussion of those scholars who have focused on the social world of the Roman Empire is warranted.

1.3   Scholarly approaches to the Apocalypse

From the perspective of the social world

The following overview shall consider recent studies that attempt to locate John's language and imagery within the historical setting of Roman Asia Minor. While the topic of wealth is implicit in most of the secondary literature, those who focus on it explicitly are rare. One such investigation engages the issue indirectly by focusing on the economic environment of Asia Minor, particularly with the intersection between the economy and the Roman imperial cults.[28]

Kraybill takes as his point of departure the seer's critique of merchant shippers in Rev 18:1–19, which provides the basis for a historical reconstruction of political oppression and an increasingly stronger presence of the imperial cults among trade guilds. From here, he retrogresses back onto the vision of the beasts in Rev 13 the writer's focus on Christian involvement in trade and trade networks in first-century Asia Minor.[29]

---

[28] Kraybill, *Imperial Cult and Commerce.*

[29] More recent scholarship has shown that trade guilds or *collegia* were not the equivalent of medieval trade guilds, nor did they perform 'regulatory or protective functions', but were more interested in the social lives of its members (Aune, *Revelation 1–5*, p. 186; vol. II, p. 768; see also Malherbe, *Social Aspects*, p. 88). These social groups were unique organizations characterized by a fraternal or familial construct, administratively functioning as a 'mini-society' or 'small city' (Perry, *The Roman Collegia*, p. 78). This fraternal aspect also involved religious ceremonies. The majority of evidence available for the maritime guilds comes from Peutoli and Ostia, both of which were port cities on the western coast of Italy. Epigraphic evidence suggests that trade guilds began to flourish in the Empire

The study assumes the literal language of wealth in 3:17 and properly connects it with the censure of wealth in chapter 18. Moreover, it recognizes the call to "Come out" in 18:4, and correctly identifies this as a demand to cut all commercial and economic ties with Rome.[30] According to Kraybill, the 'intersection of cult and commerce' creates active participation in idolatry, which is the basis of John's concern. Thus, he calls Christians 'to sever or avoid *economic and political ties* with Rome' because of the 'unholy allegiance to an emperor who claimed to be divine'.[31] In turn, this withdrawal creates a situation of persecution and economic difficulty. Since only some had already withdrawn from participation, John's response is directed both to the social injustices being experienced by the faithful and the idolatry of those who continue.

To the extent that Christians had 'ready access to ships, docks, and guild halls that serviced Rome's enormous appetite', Kraybill argues that they *could have* been involved in the maritime trade.[32] While he admits there is scant evidence to support this idea, his approach necessitates the reconstruction of a historical setting that accounts for it.[33] Intrinsically, then, John's concern is not with wealth *per se* but with the much broader issue of idolatry.[34]

---

during the second and third centuries CE. It is not until the late third and into the fourth and fifth centuries CE that the state became involved in the operations of these guilds, which ultimately led to their downfall. Thus, it is anachronistic to speak of trade guilds acting as trade unions, as such, or having been well developed and thoroughly permeated by the imperial cults as early as the first century CE. One can assume, however, that such associations did exist in first century Asia Minor. An Egyptian papyrus attests an association of salt traders in 47 CE, of which one can see the blending of economic and religious spheres in the life of the group. This helps to establish the likelihood of *collegia* existing on a broader scale in the first century. However, it provides no evidence of participation under duress but merely reflects an agreement made between its members (Meijer and van Nijf, *Trade, Transport and Society*, p. 75; see also Harland, *Associations, Synagogues, and Congregations*, pp. 161–73). The extent to which Kraybill proposes these associations were well established is unconvincing. More importantly, the interrelation of the imperial cult and the guilds is suspect.

[30] See also Yarbro Collins, 'Revelation 18', p. 202; contra Beale, *Revelation*, p. 898, who states it would 'contradict the essence of Christian calling to witness to the world'. Yet, 'witness' in the Apocalypse seems to have an entirely different meaning, not least a different outcome than Beale seems to be suggesting (cf. Rev 6:9; 11:3, 7; 12:11; 14:3; 17:6; 20:4).

[31] Kraybill, *Imperial Cult and Commerce*, p. 17 (emphasis mine).   [32] *Ibid.*, p. 16.

[33] If the Apocalypse can be given a Neronian date, it is unlikely that such an infiltration would have occurred at that time. See Wilson, 'Domitianic Date', pp. 587–95.

[34] This same approach is taken by David deSilva who argues that John's concern over wealth and economic participation among the Christian community was fostered by the close relationship of idolatry and commerce in the Roman economic system. He critiques Royalty's thesis that the primary source of conflict in the churches is a power struggle with the prophetess Jezebel. In doing so, he rightly points out John's concern with the church's

Kraybill sets up his study by taking what he calls 'the majority opinion of modern scholarship' that John's primary concern is with socioreligious pressure being applied to Christians by the imperial cult.[35] Coupled with the growing pressure on Christians to become more involved in cult worship, this created a situation of religious tension in which Christians had to negotiate their involvement in the economic activity of trade guilds against an attempt to remain faithful. He states, 'The cult so threatened Christians that John thought some would soon die for refusing to participate.'[36] He tempers this statement by suggesting that other Christians felt an internal desire to participate and consequently reaped the economic benefits of doing so.[37]

While Kraybill provides a way into the study of wealth in the Apocalypse, there are limitations to his argument that should be delineated. First, how descriptive can we say the language of merchants and sailors is in chapter 18? Does this imagery demonstrate a real concern over merchant shippers or has the language simply been brought forward from the prophetic text from which the author has borrowed? The lack of any mention of merchants and shippers elsewhere in the Apocalypse points to the latter.[38] Second, and most obvious, the assumption that imperial cults are at the forefront of the author's concerns creates an interpretive scheme whereby the texts are held hostage to this reconstruction of history. One cannot completely discard the importance of the social setting to the text, yet Kraybill's emphasis on the larger social world overlooks the explicit internal conflict between rival teachers that is clearly reflected

---

assimilation into the culture and the need to formulate an identity associated with loyalty to the Lamb and not based on economic prosperity. While both are correct to some degree, the latter seems to reflect John's more immediate concern. deSilva, *Seeing Things John's Way*, pp. 58–63, 69–72.

[35] Kraybill's view is largely based on the vision of the two beasts in Rev 13 and manifests itself in a variety of interpretations. See below, pp. 192–6 for a review of the history of interpretations of this passage.

[36] Kraybill, *Imperial Cult and Commerce*, pp. 26–7.

[37] These somewhat opposing ideas concerning the imperial cults reflect the general indecision about the degree to which they were in any way involved in the function of trade guilds or forced Christian participation in worship in the first century CE. As will be discussed below, there is little agreement that the situation of Roman Asia Minor reflected any widespread persecution toward Christians or that the imperial cults forced worship in and through trade guilds or associations. For arguments that dismiss a Domitianic persecution, see Thompson, *Apocalypse and Empire*, pp. 95–115; Wilson, 'Domitianic Date', pp. 587–95. See also Ulrich, 'Euseb, *HistEccl* III', pp. 269–89; Harland, *Associations, Synagogues and Congregations*, pp. 239–64; Kloppenberg and Wilson (eds.), *Voluntary Associations*, pp. 1–15; Price, *Rituals and Power*, pp. 123–6, 220–22.

[38] For a detailed discussion of this possibility see the Excursus in section 8.6, below: 'The use of merchant and sailor imagery in Jewish traditions'.

in the seven messages, in which a concern over imperial cults is absent.[39] In light of this internal dispute, the author may be advancing a more comprehensive theological claim while a focus on imperial cults assumes the Apocalypse reflects an *ad hoc* response to a socio-historical crisis limited to time and space. The difference is significant. Third, taking chapter 18 as his point of departure engenders an approach where this passage informs earlier texts that relate to wealth (2:9; 3:17; 13:17). Working with the assumption that Rev 18 reflects a concern for Christian involvement in idolatrous trade guilds, Kraybill reflects back onto chapter 13 and the seven messages John's concern that seafarers and merchants in the church are his primary audience.

Finally, his proposal is also compromised by the absence of any mention of idolatry in the message to the rich in Laodicea or in the entirety of chapter 18 where John's most severe attack on wealth occurs. While he rightly points out the importance of the two beasts in chapter 13, his suggestion that they 'provide the key to understanding Revelation as a whole' is overstated.[40] The displacement of his key texts into a pre-determined order does not provide a reading in which the language of wealth develops in its normal linear fashion; that is, the way the recipients would have heard it. John's reformulation of language and images throughout the Apocalypse indicates that the development of certain motifs is purposeful. Consequently, Kraybill's reading does not consider the development or rhetorical function of John's many uses of the term 'rich' (πλοῦτος), or the idea of accumulating wealth (πλουτέω); nor does he explicate how these terms are contrasted with the language of 'poverty' (πτωχεία) (2:9, 3:17–18; 18:3, 7, 15, 19). If the writer is primarily speaking to merchant shippers, in what way does the Apocalypse function to other members of the faithful community? Kraybill's reading is too limited in this respect. However, if he is correct in his conclusion that John is calling his readers to separate from the economic system of the Empire, he does not provide an answer for how the traditional language and motifs John incorporated into the text may have legitimized this appeal. Moreover, it is not clear whether this refers only to those who are shippers or anyone involved in commerce.

[39] See Royalty, *Streets of Heaven*, pp. 27–38; Aune, *Revelation 1–5*, p. cxxxii; Prigent, *Apocalypse of St John*, p. 151; Yarbro Collins, *Crisis and Catharsis*, pp. 74–5; deSilva, *Seeing Things John's Way*, pp. 30–1.

[40] Commentators generally regard the throne-room vision as the most significant text for understanding the Apocalypse as a whole. See Fiorenza, *Vision*, p. 58; Boring, *Revelation*, p. 109; Caird, *Revelation*, pp. 74–5; Achtemeier, 'Rev 5:1–14', 284–5; Johns, *Lamb Christology*, pp. 159–60.

Steven Friesen provides a more helpful way of understanding John's discourse of imperial worship in his thematic study of imperial cults.[41] Rather than a reaction to economic participation in trade guilds, Friesen asserts that John's communication is more theological, at least in contrast to the dominant discourse of the Empire. John rejects the use of Greco-Roman myth that provides the cosmology of the cultic system and replaces it with Jewish mythic traditions that support the authority of the Kingdom of God and the slaughtered Lamb.[42] Here Friesen offers the correct balance between cosmology and eschatology in the Apocalypse. He maintains that John is concerned with establishing the true structure of the universe in contrast to the Greco-Roman cosmology that was built on emperor worship. He rightly identifies John's strategy to portray the present age as one ruled temporarily by Satan, until the consummation of the kingdom is realized in the new Jerusalem. This depicts the imperial cults and the Roman Empire as a masquerade of the true kingdom on earth. In addition, he notes the forty-two months where Satan rules 'is spent either in deception or endurance; it does not belong to the time of eternal dominion'.[43] How the present age is to be viewed by the faithful community is a crucial concern to the present study and it is here that Friesen encourages additional research along these lines.

Friesen detects John's use of the prophetic tradition in his critique of Rome in Rev 18 and notes the transformation of language relating to wealth and merchants, yet he provides no explanation for this shift. Moreover, he views the critique in Rev 18 not simply as a rejection of Rome and its wealth but a rejection of empire.[44] He states, 'So, in John's text, imperial cults are not an aberration; they are a fitting manifestation of imperialism.'[45] Here Friesen raises our sights from the level of imperial cults to empire as a whole. The present study wishes to consider further whether in John's text we might say imperialism itself is not an aberration but a fitting manifestation of the present evil age ruled by Satan. If so, then John's cosmology can inform our understanding of how he perceives wealth in relation to the faithful community in the present age.

Friesen's study does not include the possibility that John's communication stems from the dispute reflected in the seven messages. Like Kraybill, there is little discussion as to how the missives relate to the

---

[41] Friesen, *Imperial Cults*; also, *Twice Neokoros* and 'Satan's Throne, Imperial Cults', pp. 351–73.

[42] Friesen does not suggest that John rejects mythic literary traditions. Rather, he is referring to the myth of emperor worship within the context of the imperial cult.

[43] Friesen, *Imperial Cults*, p. 164.   [44] *Ibid.*, p. 208.   [45] *Ibid.*, pp. 208–9.

overall message of the Apocalypse or how John's language of rich and poor in the seven messages intersects with the writer's portrayal of the imperial cults. Friesen rightly points out that John provides a contrasting image of what faithfulness to the Lamb looks like against the imperial system. His study emphasizes John's rejection of the imperial system and his portrayal of the universe in a way that establishes the absolute authority of God. Moreover, God and the Lamb are the only ones worthy to be worshipped in contrast to the idolatrous human emperor worship practiced in the imperial cults. However, Friesen comes short of describing what that looks like. In what way could John oppose the visible system of the imperial cults? Did he simply provide a theological argument that legitimized the one over the other? If so, how do proposals that suggest John is moving his audience to a more concrete resolution fit into this scheme? The calls for repentance in the seven messages and the cry to 'Come out' in Rev 18:4 suggest John expects some form of response from his recipients. If the imperial cults are the expected manifestation of the wicked imperial system, how does faithfulness manifest itself in relation to the faithful community? When he suggests that the readers establish their identity not from the centre of the Greco-Roman world but from the margins, from the periphery of the Empire, we might ask, what does that entail?

Friesen correctly asserts that John's concern is with the faithful enduring in the present age. In that sense loyalty, obedience, and worship are what identify the faithful. Yet, as he indicates, these are the same characteristics that identify the faithful in the imperial cults. What marks the faithful community for John is suffering in contrast to the easy lifestyle that obedience and worship in the Roman system provides. It is here that the present study seeks to take Friesen's study forward and ascertain whether John proposes a visible way to distinguish the two. In what way are the faithful to suffer? Does this include a complete rejection of wealth and commerce? This is along the lines of Kraybill's proposal of withdrawal from trade guilds, though Friesen's emphasis on obedience and worship points further to issues of loyalty, which is a more comprehensive perspective. Moreover, he includes in John's communication the idea that his critique is driven by more than socio-historical circumstances; that is, John's communication is shaped by his world view. To what extent is John's communication to the churches moving them towards a greater degree of loyalty to the Lamb? Additionally one might ask whether, in John's mind, the imperial cults pose as great a threat to this loyalty as material possessions. Friesen offers no explanation for John's language of wealth to the churches nor does he make the connection between the letters and the denigration of wealth in chapter 18.

Fiorenza takes a historical-critical approach to the Book of Revelation, yet also engages literary-critical analyses. In doing so, she also finds the social background of the Apocalypse to be one of persecution and difficulty for Christians in the tyrannical reign of Domitian.[46] Thus, the language of tribulation and suffering reflects the actual circumstances of some of the recipients. In addition, the 'mythopoeic' language of the Apocalypse is the writer's construction of an 'alternative world' that encourages Christians to persevere in light of their present persecution.[47] The denigration of wealth in Rev 18 is a socio-political critique of the social injustices of the Empire carried out on Christians who are poor and marginalized. As a poetic-rhetorical work John tries to 'elicit emotions, identities, and reactions while simultaneously persuading and motivating his readers to "act right;" that is, to maintain loyalty in the face of persecution and possible death'.[48]

If the seven churches have such different circumstances, some suffering persecution while others are rich and self-sufficient, how does the message of enduring suffering apply to the latter? Fiorenza maintains that the Laodicean church, and others who held a similar position, may have aligned themselves with Paul (Rom 13:1–7) or Peter (1 Pet 2:17), both of whom emphasize honouring the emperor and did not see this as compromise. She does, however, appreciate that the promises of eschatological blessing are only made to the poor and not the rich,[49] yet provides no explanation for the theological implications of this distinction. To what degree can we say that John links the economic status of the addressees to their eschatological salvation? Fiorenza comes close to answering this question when commenting on the symbolic vision of the 144,000:

> While the vision and audition highlight the election of those who are with the Lamb on Mount Zion, an accurate interpretation stresses that their actions and lives are the preconditions for such eschatological salvation.[50]

According to Fiorenza, the sealing of the 144,000 has the same rhetorical function as the call to 'Come out' in Rev 18:4. She sees this as a metaphor for the eschatological exodus of salvation for remaining faithful under the persecution of the idolatrous Empire. Yet, the prophetic call includes

---

[46] Fiorenza, *Vision*, pp. 17, 193. Cf. Thompson, *Apocalypse and Empire*, pp. 129–32.
[47] Fiorenza, *Justice and Judgment*, pp. 187–8.   [48] *Ibid.*, p. 187.
[49] Fiorenza, *Vision*, p. 57.   [50] Fiorenza, *Justice and Judgment*, p. 191.

the suggestion that those who do not 'Come out' will be guilty of 'participating in her sins' (18:4). It seems unlikely that those who had been persecuted so violently would have to be urged to leave. In what way would a refusal on the part of those who had already been so faithful result in an active participation in Babylon's sins? It seems more likely that some form of socio-economic or even physical separation is in mind. Fiorenza's insistence of a setting of socio-economic persecution is driven by an eschatological focus. Theories of widespread persecution have generally been rejected, at least to the degree proposed in her study.[51] To what extent this can be attested in Asia Minor may be even more difficult to prove since the more widely known instances under Nero and Claudius took place in Rome.[52] It is now understood that Christians probably experienced a relatively peaceful existence in the Roman world, some even realizing considerable socio-economic success (Acts 16:14; Tim 16:17; Rev 3:17),[53] yet this does not preclude episodes of sporadic, localized persecution. Her suggestion that the poetic language of the Apocalypse functioned to stir emotions and reactions in order to move the audience to 'act right' is correct. However, in the absence of any widespread, programmatic persecution, the question then becomes, in what way does John want his readers to act?

A different approach is taken by Yarbro Collins, who argues that John is responding to a 'perceived crisis'.[54] Although she, like Kraybill, thinks John is admonishing Christians to renounce participation and involvement in trade guilds, she does so without the underlying persecution theory. More importantly to the present study, she highlights the nature of John's attack against the Roman Empire by stating:

> [T]he book of Revelation is not simply a product of a certain social situation, not even a simple response to circumstances. At root it is a *particular religious view of reality*, inherited in large part, which is the framework within which John interprets

---

[51] See Thompson, *Apocalypse and Empire*, pp. 27–8. See also Wilson, 'Domitianic Date', pp. 587–605 (esp. 597–8); Jones, *Emperor Domitian*, pp. 114–17; Southern, *Domitian: Tragic Tyrant*, pp. 114–17; Friesen, *Imperial Cults*, pp. 143–5.

[52] Tacitus, *Ann.*, 15.44.

[53] Wilken, *Christians*, p. 16; Duff, *Who Rides the Beast?*, pp. 24–30; Verner, *Household of God*, p. 184. For discussions of the various socio-economic levels in the Pauline literature, see Meeks, *First Urban Christians*, pp. 51–73; Theissen, *Social Setting of Pauline Christianity*, pp. 69–119.

[54] Yarbro Collins, *Crisis and Catharsis*, pp. 84–107; Hanson, *Dawn of Apocalyptic* (1979), pp. 9–10 has been very influential in the modern understanding that apocalypses arise out of situations of crisis and this idea is still pervasive in much of NT scholarship.

his environment. The book of Revelation is thus a product of the *interaction between a kind of pre-understanding and the socio-historical situation* in which John lived.[55]

The italicized text underscores the focal point of the present study, which goes undeveloped in Yarbro Collins's study; how does the author's theological pre-understanding of what the present age should reflect intersect with his expectations for the Christian communities in relation to wealth? Even still, Yarbro Collins goes beyond Fiorenza's mythopoeic language and recognizes John is building his argument on received traditions. At the same time, she maintains an emphasis on the socio-historical situation with less attention given to John's 'pre-understanding'. She contends that the Christian community is experiencing 'relative deprivation' and felt marginalized in the shadow of the excessive wealth and power of the Roman Empire. Thus, John's communication is viewed from a socio-political perspective. According to Yarbro Collins, the excessive wealth of the Empire would have created in John and his readers, feelings of envy and resentment.[56] Thus, the Apocalypse serves as anti-Roman propaganda that functions psychologically to deal with these feelings of antipathy. Like Kraybill, she contends that wealth is not rejected by John but is presented as evil in order to control these feelings of hostility and resentment.

In dealing with the issue of wealth, Yarbro Collins takes as her point of departure the critique of Rome in chapter 18. She compares this text to the Sibylline Oracles, which likewise contain anti-Roman propaganda.[57] She then examines the censure of wealth in the seven messages and states:

> He [John] criticized the Laodiceans' reliance on their wealth because it was evidence of their lack of zeal. Wealth was one of Rome's faults in John's eyes, presumably because Roman leaders and allies were felt to possess it at the expense of others. The vision of the new Jerusalem shows that John did not view wealth as evil in itself; he saw it as one of the blessings of salvation to be granted in the future.[58]

Yarbro Collins makes the very astute observation that John views wealth as a future blessing for the faithful. What, then, does this have to say about wealth in the present age? She suggests that John advocates a detachment

---

[55] Yarbro Collins, *Crisis and Catharsis*, pp. 106–7 (italics added).

[56] For a fuller expression of the resentment of Christians toward the wealth of Babylon see Lawrence, *Apocalypse*, pp. 210–11.

[57] Yarbro Collins, *Crisis and Catharsis*, pp. 122–3.   [58] *Ibid.*, p. 134.

from wealth and values even more a life of poverty.[59] Thus John is moving toward some level of 'social exclusivism'.[60] At the same time, she insists that this does not include a complete separation like the Qumran community, though she offers no explanation for what this exclusivism might include. More importantly, there is no consideration for how the author could propose such a radical position to his audience. How does John arrive at these conclusions? On what basis can he suggest to his readers/hearers that poverty is the mark of the faithful Christian community? Since John's position involves withdrawal from the economic system, it should be asked how, according to Yarbro Collins, this would resolve feelings of resentment. Since some in the church were already realizing economic success, an impoverished state would only increase this hostility. In addition, the voice of the Laodicean church does not give any indication of envy or resentment. Rather, they seem to be quite content in their circumstances. While there may have been some resentment within the churches themselves, the degree to which John would impose such a radical imposition on his readers simply to quell feelings of envy is to be questioned. We might also ask how we can reconcile the call for repentance in the seven messages with those who refuse to repent throughout the Apocalypse and are consequently destroyed. While Yarbro Collins's work is quite helpful in moving us beyond viewing the Apocalypse as merely an ad hoc response to socio-historical circumstances, there seems to be more at stake than the psychological process of catharsis.

Richard Bauckham likewise takes Rev 18 as his point of departure and maintains that John's critique of Babylon's wealth reflects a reaction to the excessive commercial trade of the Empire and its violent impact on her subjects. Like Yarbro Collins, he notes the voice of anti-Roman propaganda as seen in the *Sibylline Oracles*, though he attributes John's language largely to the prophetic tradition.[61] Bauckham makes the connections between the seven messages and the call to 'Come out', and rightly notes this is a call for separation. Yet this radical perspective on wealth cannot be found in the *Sibylline Oracles'* anti-establishment propaganda, nor can it be fully seen in the prophetic tradition. Thus, like Yarbro Collins, he leaves open the question of which received traditions inform this perspective.

While Leonard Thompson does not treat the issue of wealth or discuss the relevant texts of this thesis, his literary-critical approach stands in sharp contrast to proponents of the historical-critical method. Thompson

[59] *Ibid.*, p. 158.   [60] *Ibid.*, p. 127.
[61] Bauckham, *Climax of Prophecy.* See also below, p. 28.

argues that apocalyptic literature, not least the book of Revelation, is not dependent upon any form of crisis, perceived or real. His detailed analysis of previous interpretations based on Domitian's tyrannical reign and persecution theories indicates that a reconstruction of the social setting is not the best method of interpreting the language of the Apocalypse. Rather, the crisis is revealed *through* the text in the revelatory knowledge of the seer. Thompson goes one step beyond Yarbro Collins's idea of 'perceived crisis' by demonstrating the social function *of* an apocalypse as opposed to how the perceptions of crises work *in* social situations.[62] In other words, John takes up the apocalyptic idiom to make a theological statement to his readers in language and traditions that they share in order to provide an understanding of 'what the *whole* world is like, which includes an understanding of how Christians relate to other Christians, to other groups in the cities of Asia, and, more generally, to public social events'.[63] In doing so, he has transformed the dominant discourse of public knowledge into a symbolic universe that portrays the world in a way that moves the readers to become sectarian, though able to maintain a cosmopolitan existence.[64] That the literary convention of an apocalypse is used to communicate to John's readers apart from any crisis highlights the importance of considering other apocalyptic Jewish traditions in understanding how the shared language might have helped to legitimize John's perspective of wealth.

Thompson notes that the boundaries John creates in the text are soft. For example, in this symbolic universe, good and evil are contrasted and are yet shown to exist within the same sphere. While humans exist on the earthly plane, demons in the underworld and God and his angels in heaven, they are shown to cross over into other spheres of existence throughout the text. This strategy, according to Thompson, is used by John to call the faithful to a 'cosmopolitan sectarianism' by demonstrating how the faithful can live within passable boundaries in their own culture without being compromised.[65] Yet, John critiques the wealth of the church and Rome while portraying the throne room and new Jerusalem in language of gold and precious gems and the Lamb as worthy to receive wealth. So, while Thompson suggests the boundaries John creates are marked yet soft and passable he does not explain the antithetical *attitudes* that distinguish wealth on the earth from that in heaven and the eschaton. In addition, he offers no discussion concerning the prophetic call to' Come

---

[62] Thompson, *Apocalypse and Empire*, p. 28.   [63] *Ibid.*, p. 33.
[64] *Ibid.*, p. 176–97.   [65] *Ibid.*, p. 192.

out' (18:4) since chapter 18 is missing entirely in his volume. How can the faithful be both cosmopolitan and sectarian when they are specifically commanded to separate? Although Thompson is correct in identifying imagery that crosses boundaries within the literary world of the text, he does not take seriously the sharp distinctions between the faithful and the wicked in terms of wealth language.

To summarize, these studies underscore the general disagreement among scholars who take the social world of Roman Asia Minor as their point of departure. Some read Revelation in light of widespread persecution (Fiorenza, Kraybill), while others see only localized periods of harassment (Friesen). Some contend John's language of wealth is driven by feelings of resentment and envy as a perceived crisis (Lawrence, Yarbro Collins), while still others see no crisis at all (Thompson). These same studies find disagreement regarding the degree to which John reacts to economic participation in relation to the imperial cults and trade guilds. Some argue that cults forced worship on Christians through guilds, while others provide a more comprehensive view that points to no involvement from the top, only localized pressure to participate in feasts, celebrations, and civic events.

The uncertainty that emerges from the approaches adopted in the literature reviewed above reinforces how little we can know about what John is reacting to in the social world of the Empire. And while these studies offer reasonable possibilities, the degree of influence the Roman Empire is given in shaping John's message far outweighs the consideration of how received traditions have impacted the author's world view.[66] Furthermore, as Royalty and Duff have pointed out, the catalyst for John's message could be linked more closely to the conflict within the churches rather than within the larger social world, though assimilation into the latter may have been the underlying issue. The present study wishes to take seriously the prophetic rivalry between John and Jezebel, as well as other rival teachers in the churches. In doing so, it will consider the degree to which John's message is a theological response shaped by his world view in which the Roman Empire becomes the *object* of John's critique and not the *subject*. The importance of received traditions to this approach makes it necessary to consider the work of scholars who have focused on the writer's use of traditions in the Hebrew Bible.

---

[66] See Stuckenbruck, *Angel Veneration*, p. 39, who also highlights the importance of the shared pre-understanding of the symbols used by John and its effectiveness in his communication.

From the perspective of the Hebrew Bible

The Book of Revelation is replete with biblical allusions and John's language of wealth is frequently caught up in the issue of his use of OT prophetic traditions, some of which are evident in key passages that deal with wealth (4:1–11; 6:1–8; 13:1–18; 18:1–24).[67] Since the approach to be outlined below is shaped by John's exploitation of antecedent traditions, it is important to discuss scholarly approaches to his use of the Hebrew Bible. Studies on 'intertextuality' between Revelation and the biblical tradition usually take one of two basic approaches, each of which we will examine: (1) in relation to the OT prophetic tradition from a broad perspective, and (2) John's use of particular prophetic books.

From the broader prophetic tradition

Since the mid nineteenth century, only four scholarly studies have been devoted entirely to the use of the OT in the Apocalypse.[68] A few important articles have been published on the subject in the time between von Schlatter, *Das alte Testament in der johanneischen Apokalypse* (1912), Beale, *The Use of Daniel in Jewish Apocalyptic Literature and in the Revelation of St John* (1984), and Moyise, *The Old Testament in the Book of Revelation* (1999).[69] However, for the sake of brevity, I will focus largely on the work of G. K. Beale and Steve Moyise, who reflect the most

---

[67] There is significant disagreement on the total number of Old Testament allusions in the Apocalypse. The following demonstrates this disparity: The UBS[4] lists 392, while NA[27] lists over 600. The variance among individual scholars ranges from 250 (Charles, *Revelation*, vol. I, pp. lxviii–lxxxi), to almost 1,000 (van der Waal, *Openbaring*, pp. 174–241). For a more detailed list, see Fekkes, *Isaiah and Prophetic Traditions*, p. 62. This variance suggests counting allusions may be less fruitful than simply recognizing John's use of Old Testament and other Jewish traditions as a mine for his language and imagery without slavishly following any particular text. Cf. Rev 3:17 and Hos 12:8; Rev 18 and Isa 13, 23; Jer 50–1; Ezek 27.

[68] Lücke, *Einleitung in die Offenbarung* (1848), who looks to Daniel as the influence for the apocalyptic nature of the Book of Revelation; von Schlatter, *Das alte Testament in der johanneischen Apokalypse*, who deals with the subject from the perspective of the genre of apocalypse; Moyise, *Old Testament in the Book of Revelation*; and Beale, *John's Use of the Old Testament* (1998). R. H. Charles also discusses John's use of the Old Testament but in order to ascertain his dependence on a Hebrew or Aramaic source. He dismisses the author's dependence on the LXX or any other version (Charles, *Revelation*, vol. I, p. lxvi). A more recent treatment examines the intertextuality of literary units in the Apocalypse. See Aune, *Apocalypticism*, pp. 120–49.

[69] Vanhoye, 'L'Utilisation du livre d'Ézéchiel', 436–76; Trudinger, 'Old Testament in the Book of Revelation', 82–8; see also Köstenberger, 'The Use of Scripture', pp. 230–54, though he is largely dependent on the work of Beale.

current streams of discussion on the topic as a whole. Beale's most recent treatment is largely a defence of the critiques of his earlier work in which he argued that the Apocalypse was to be understood 'ultimately within the framework of Daniel 2'.[70] He further contends that certain passages in the Book of Revelation are a midrash of Daniel 7 and 10. His understanding of NT use of the OT is centred on the hermeneutical principle that the context of the original subtext (OT) informs significantly the meaning of the new context (NT).[71] In particular, he contends that John is interpreting the Daniel 7 *prophecy* of the son of man and the saints in a way that shows *fulfilment* in the suffering Lamb and Christians, respectively.[72]

His initial aim is to determine when the author is 'consciously' or 'unconsciously' alluding to the OT.[73] According to Beale, this is determined by clear OT allusions, clusters of allusions, and structural features. Yet, these categories can be somewhat subjective, which is borne out in the variety of attempts to distinguish them. For example, Beale maintains that the structure of the Apocalypse is largely influenced by Daniel, while Goulder and Vanhoye argue the same for the book of Ezekiel.[74] Moreover, the great variance in the number of actual allusions underscores the subjectivity of this method. To be sure, it is difficult to substantiate the claim that the clustering of allusions belonging to one particular tradition implies a heightened conscious effort to signal to the readers the original context of that tradition over others, if at all. The dichotomy that Beale presents in relation to conscious and unconscious effort is unnecessary since it is reasonable to assume that the author was conscious of everything he wrote and the traditions with which he was in contact. More importantly, assessing whether the author is simply borrowing prophetic language or interpreting it is a difficult task, and only further lends itself to subjectivity.

Moyise, on the other hand, takes a more moderate position. Like Beale, he recognizes that some sense of correspondence between traditions is tactical on the part of the writer and that:

> The task of intertextuality is to explore how the source text continues to speak through the new work and how the new work forces new meanings from the source text.[75]

---

[70] Beale, *Use of Daniel*, p. 277.

[71] Beale, *John's Use of the Old Testament*, pp. 126–8.

[72] Beale, *Use of Daniel*, p. 297.   [73] See Beale, *Revelation*, pp. 319–21.

[74] Goulder, 'Cycle of Prophecies', pp. 342–67.

[75] Moyise, *Old Testament in Revelation*, p. 111.

This quote highlights the primary difference in goals between Moyise and Beale. The former is concerned with the hermeneutics of how we are to understand the use of the OT in Revelation while the latter has a predetermined hermeneutic that drives the research.[76] While Beale's approach recognizes that some relationship exists between text and subtext, the majority of emphasis in his study is given to the source text. Moyise, on the other hand, appreciates the tension between the Apocalypse and the OT allusions since many of them appear to be used without regard to the original context. This tension, he states, is where the meaning of Revelation resides.[77] Thus, the OT and the Apocalypse share similar language, imagery, and style, though without importing the original context into the new text on every occasion. The approaches of Beale and Moyise, while offering insightful ideas for evaluating the hermeneutical principles employed by John, also indicate the limited scope of intertextuality with which both work since they press their discussions toward a dominant subtext. These constraints are highlighted best by Aune in his intertextual reading of the Apocalypse:

> The modern critic, on the other hand, can never become fully aware of the range of ancient responses to the Apocalypse for the simple reason that many (perhaps even most) of the precursor texts which the ancient reader would have assumed have been lost and are consequently unknown to us.[78]

When we consider the significance of this statement alongside the possibility of oral traditions that also circulated, it becomes possible to suggest that limiting the study of received traditions in the Apocalypse to the OT is overly reductionistic. This neglects the possibility that (1) other traditions outside the Hebrew Bible may also be incorporated into a text, or that (2) other traditions, which were also widely circulated and used similar language and imagery, also play a role in John's communicative aims. This substantiates the need for a more comprehensive discussion.

Fiorenza rightly identifies the degree to which scholars view John's hermeneutic is ultimately bound up in their view of the role of NT prophets. She asserts that the author never introduces the OT material with any formulaic quotation such as 'it is written' or 'this was to fulfil the Scripture' nor does he ever quote any OT text directly.[79] Rather, John

---

[76] See the critique by Yarbro Collins, 'Review of *The Use of Daniel*', pp. 734–5.

[77] Moyise, *Old Testament in Revelation*, p. 138.

[78] Aune, *Apocalypticism*, p. 121.

[79] Fiorenza, *Justice and Judgment*, p. 135.

uses language and imagery from the Hebrew Bible, Jewish apocalyptic literature, ancient Near Eastern mythology, and the Jesus tradition in an eclectic fashion to form his own visions and message.[80] Thus, attention should be drawn to the distinction between Christian homily and exegesis, which coincides with Beale's and Moyise's emphasis on interpretation and exposition, and Christian prophecy that is concerned with the announcement of salvation and judgement.[81] Even still, she is overly dependent on the writer's socio-historical circumstances in determining the meaning behind his language of wealth, which was shown above to lead to a variety of opposing conclusions. However, her understanding of John's 'anthological' use of traditions presses the conversation away from 'literary dependence' towards a consideration of the degree to which the language, imagery, and ideas evident in the Apocalypse reveal a certain theological world view that the author possesses that has been shaped by received traditions. It also requires that we consider more comprehensively the traditions that have shaped his theology.

Specialized studies of the prophetic tradition

Moyise's conclusions are largely dependent upon and follow along the same lines as the study of Jean-Pierre Ruiz.[82] He too understands the intertextual relationship between the subtext and the text and focuses on reader-response criticism. This literary connection, according to Ruiz, underscores John's expectation that his readers will read the 'texts within the texts'; that is, he has reactualized the prophetic passages through a Christian rereading of the Jewish Scriptures.[83] Ruiz seeks to demonstrate how the unity of Rev 16:17–19:10 is reflected in the prophetic reappropriation of the metaphors Prostitute, Beast, and Babylon, which are held in contrast with the Bride, Lamb, and new Jerusalem. He argues that the enemies of God portrayed in the Hebrew Bible have been reactualized as the now present enemy of Rome and its idolatrous system of worship. In doing so, he emphasizes how John reshapes antecedent traditions that he shares with his audience to portray Rome as the harlot Babylon in a way that they would understand. His study highlights the importance of John's use of traditional language to communicate his message without seeing these images as 'fulfilment' of prophecy.

---

[80] *Ibid.*, p. 136.
[81] *Ibid.*, p. 137. See also Müller, *Prophetie und Predigt*, pp. 237–9.
[82] Ruiz, *Ezekiel in the Apocalypse.*   [83] *Ibid.*, p. 520.

Fekkes, on the other hand, focuses on John's use of Isaiah, though he tends more towards Beale's understanding of intertextual relationships.[84] Fekkes's approach to the Apocalypse is straightforward intertextuality between biblical traditions and is evident in his claim that 'John's use of previous prophetic and apocalyptic traditions is "almost" *exclusively limited to the OT*'.[85] Yet he also acknowledges that John does 'adopt shared apocalyptic traditions not found in the OT'.[86] John's conflation of multiple traditions to form new visions also leads Fekkes to conclude that his 'use of the OT may sometimes be determined less by special books than by particular themes or traditions in which he has an interest'.[87] Fekkes sees John as a continuum of the OT prophets and understands his use of OT traditions to be interpretive in the sense of promise and fulfilment.[88]

Like Fekkes, Mazzaferri argues that John is a Christian prophet and the Apocalypse is predictive prophecy. He also states, 'Apocalyptic sources do not evince the slightest generic intent, and are employed so sporadically and superficially that they would hardly be missed if deleted.'[89] One can detect that he is concerned with how the Apocalypse functions as a genre, a method the present study avoids. His treatment of 'classical' prophecy is helpful, though he tries too hard to make a clear distinction between prophecy and apocalyptic in the Book of Revelation. John is a prophet, though he calls himself a servant.[90] The book claims to be 'prophecy' yet is also an 'apocalypse'. Concerning the latter, it is a 'full-blown apocalypse'[91] according to scholarly consensus, a position Mazzaferri rejects completely.[92] At the same time, it is Christian prophecy.

Even if we agree with Mazzaferri that its generic intent is primarily prophetic, to underplay the apocalyptic language and imagery is not helpful in determining John's purposes. In particular it is salient to note

---

[84] Fekkes, *Isaiah and Prophetic Traditions*.

[85] *Ibid.*, p. 38 (italics added).   [86] *Ibid.*, n. 48.

[87] *Ibid.*, p. 74; contra Kiddle, *Revelation*, pp. xxvii–xxxiii, who, although he acknowledges John has incorporated traditions outside the Old Testament, does not think a study of them will provide anything significant.

[88] For a similar approach, see Farrer, *Rebirth of Images*, pp. 13–22.

[89] Mazzaferri, *Genre of Revelation*, p. 379.

[90] The present study sees John as a prophet from a circle of early Christian prophets (Rev 22:9). For further discussions concerning authorship, see Yarbro Collins, *Crisis and Catharsis*, pp. 25–50; Aune, *Revelation 1–5*, pp. xlvii–lv; deSilva, *Seeing Things John's Way*, pp. 31–4.

[91] Collins, *Apocalyptic Imagination*, p. 269.

[92] Mazzaferri, *Genre of Revelation*, pp. 257–8.

Mazzaferri's dichotomy of the conditionality of prophecy and determinism in apocalyptic. He is correct in pointing out the calls for repentance among the seven messages, though the apocalyptic section (4:1–22:9) is strongly deterministic in relation to the earth dwellers. This group is frequently referred to as those who do not repent and are set as a foil for the faithful. Yet, their fate is sealed since the faithful have been written in the Lamb's book of life since before the foundation of the world (13:8; 17:8). As difficult as it is to reconcile, the Book of Revelation is both prophetic and apocalyptic.[93] However, the importance of the Apocalypse is not its form but its content.[94] Thus, John's purpose has less to do with getting the wicked to repent than it does with distinguishing the righteous from the wicked. What form that takes has yet to be determined but will be an underlying question throughout the present study.

As already mentioned, Beale proposes that John is largely dependent on the book of Daniel for his language and imagery. He takes as his point of departure the priority of Daniel in relation to all apocalyptic literature, both Jewish and Christian, from the Second Temple period.[95] This approach and subsequent conclusions are a result of an a priori assumption of an early date for Daniel.[96] His study focuses on the influence of Daniel in chapters 1, 4–5, 13, and 17 of the Apocalypse.

---

[93] John Collins and the SBL Genres Project Apocalypse Group in 1979 proposed the following definition: '"Apocalypse" is a genre of revelatory literature with a narrative framework, in which a revelation is mediated by an otherworldly being to a human recipient, disclosing a transcendent reality which is both temporal, insofar as it envisages eschatological salvation, and spatial, insofar as it involves another supernatural world' (*Apocalypse: The Morphology of a Genre*, p. 9). Naturally, the discussion of genre classification for Revelation is complex. Some have attempted to categorize the Apocalypse as either apocalyptic (Collins, *Apocalyptic Imagination*, p. 269; Wikenhauser, *Introduction to the New Testament*, pp. 544–6; Charlesworth, *New Testament Apocrypha and Pseudepigrapha*, p. 27) or a book of prophecy, or at least that it should be classified within the genre of prophecy (Caird, *Revelation*, pp. 9–11; Fiorenza, *The Apocalypse*, pp. 18–20; Mounce, *Revelation*, pp. 1–8. See also Hahn, 'Die Sendschreiben der Johannesapokalypse', pp. 357–94; Müller, *Prophetie und Predigt*, pp. 47–104; Hill, *New Testament Prophecy*, pp. 70–93; Aune, *Prophecy in Early Christianity*, pp. 274–87). The present study does not overvalue any classification of the Apocalypse in the sense that it becomes the overriding focus. Rather, it recognizes the apocalyptic nature of the original edition (4:1–22:9) and the prophetic characteristics of the later expansions (1:1–3:22; 22:10–21). See Roloff, *Revelation*, p. 8.

[94] Beasley-Murray, 'Biblical Eschatology II', p. 275.

[95] Beale, *Use of Daniel*, p. 327. See, however, Stuckenbruck, 'Formation and Re-Formation of Daniel', pp. 101–30.

[96] Beale, *Use of Daniel*, p. 67. However, traditions related to Daniel among the Dead Sea Scrolls indicate it is unlikely that we can even talk about a priority of Daniel in relation to these Second Temple traditions. See Stuckenbruck, 'Formation and Re-Formation of Daniel', pp. 129–30.

Bauckham also gives preference to John's reliance on the OT, though he recognizes the apocalyptic tradition in which John participates.[97] In four case studies he points out traditions that Rev 18 shares with other Jewish apocalypses yet he maintains the primary significance of canonical sources. However, like Beale and Moyise, Bauckham can say:

> Its relation to the non-canonical apocalypses is different from its relation to the Old Testament. The latter forms a body of literature which John expects his readers to know and explicitly to recall in detail while reading his own work . . . In the case of the non-canonical apocalypses, on the other hand, the relationship is such that we cannot be sure that John knew any particular apocalypse or expected his readers to do so.[98]

This statement is problematic since we cannot know what John expected of his readers based on a distinction of canonical and non-canonical sources. And, while we cannot know whether John knew of any particular apocalypse, the fact that he writes in the apocalyptic idiom suggests the likelihood may not be as limited as Bauckham is suggesting. Moreover, this assumes that John has limited himself to a certain genre (apocalypse) outside of the Hebrew Bible, an idea driven by his thesis that chapter 18 reflects political resistance literature. Consequently, he only considers Jewish apocalypses that criticize Rome, which limits his analysis to the *Sibylline Oracles*.

Through the theme of wealth and poverty, the present study will seek to demonstrate how traditions other than so-called non-canonical apocalypses may inform John's perspective. On the one hand, Bauckham's emphasis on known forms of discourse is a helpful observation and one the present study will consider. On the other hand, his overemphasis on an anti-Roman polemic raises certain questions. In light of the critique of wealth and praise of poverty in the seven messages, can John's perspective on wealth be limited to Rome or is he more interested in how the faithful negotiate wealth? Is his message an ad hoc response to Rome's social injustices or is his view of wealth in the Apocalypse more comprehensive?[99] Bauckham's understanding of Rev 18 as 'political resistance literature' assumes that Rome is the source of John's overall critique of wealth.

---

[97] Bauckham, *Climax of Prophecy*, pp. ix–xvii; 38–91.   [98] *Ibid.*, p. xi.

[99] See Provan, 'Foul Spirits, Fornication and Finance', 81–100 who asks similar questions of Bauckham's limitation of Babylon to Rome.

In summary, these studies focus primarily on John's use of the Hebrew Bible, though there remains disagreement over the hermeneutical principle he employed and which of the prophets is his primary source. However, this approach can become overly subjective when one considers the degree to which John radically reshapes and mixes antecedent traditions together to form new visions. Consequently, studies that seek to highlight one prophetic tradition as John's primary source are forced and provide limited evidence for lifting one tradition over another. In addition, these studies have either limited the data to canonical sources or follow generic guidelines that exclude the possibility that John is in contact with other Jewish apocalyptic traditions. However, to the degree that a variety of texts concerned with wealth were circulating during this period, it is worth considering whether John was in conversation with or demonstrates some familiarity with traditions that were already in vogue in his time.

Charles is one of a few scholars who took seriously John's contact with traditions outside the Hebrew Bible and did not colour his work with canonical concerns.[100] He felt John's engagement with other Jewish traditions was so significant that he could state, 'without a knowledge of the Pseudepigrapha it would be impossible to understand our author'.[101] Prigent also observes the importance of the Jewish roots outside the OT that influenced the theology of John.[102] He notes in particular the importance of the extensive publication of the Dead Sea Scrolls for aiding our understanding of traditions and theological concepts that were being circulated during the Second Temple period. To this end, Catherine Murphy has published a significant monograph dealing with the topic of wealth in the Dead Sea Scrolls and the Qumran community.[103] This provides the impetus for considering how traditions related to wealth, and the rich and poor during the Second Temple period may inform John's perspective. While the scholars mentioned in this section do not have as their primary interest wealth and poverty in the Apocalypse, my reading wants to affirm the general direction of inquiry they have taken. It is not necessary for me to contest that John uses the prophetic tradition significantly since these studies have already demonstrated that he does. It is also not necessary for me to provide an analysis of John's use of the OT prophets in and of themselves, though some discussion will be warranted. Rather, I wish to consider a wider range of possibilities

---

[100] His work is marked by a sharp dichotomy between Jewish and Christian traditions.
[101] Charles, *Revelation*, vol. I, p. ixv.   [102] Prigent, *Apocalypse*, pp. 22–36.
[103] Murphy, *Wealth in the Dead Sea Scrolls*.

having established the need to have a more comprehensive discussion. In addition, my emphasis will not be on locating particular texts that John is dependent upon for his language. Rather, I wish to consider whether the language of wealth in the Apocalypse shares similar attitudes, language, and imagery that were already circulating in the Second Temple period that may have been formative in shaping the author's world view. It is necessary at this point to clarify the meaning of the term 'wealth' and the primary aim of study.

1.4   The concept of wealth in relation to the faithful

While the present study is concerned with how the language of wealth is used in Jewish apocalyptic texts from the Second Temple period and the Johannine Apocalypse, and in particular how these terms relate to the 'faithful community', it is important to take into account the wider symbolic implications of the concept of wealth in the ancient world. Wealth in the ancient world is not limited to money or movable goods but can also be reflected symbolically in honour, wisdom, power, and right relationships within the wider social matrix. The social world of early Christianity and for that matter the entirety of the Second Temple period would have viewed the desired commodities of life such as food, land, health, honour, and power; that is, their 'total environment', as 'finite in quantity and always in short supply'. In other words, they would have viewed their world as a limited good society.[104] Unlike modern Western thought, in which all goods are potentially unlimited and our ability to gain them rests with the producer, the idea of limited good meant that the increase of one's position, status, wealth, or any other commodity through short-term transactions, would come at the expense of another and would ultimately tear at the fabric of the long-term maintenance of honour within the larger cosmic and social order.[105]

In the largely agrarian or peasant societies of the first century most people would be concerned more with maintaining their inherited status than with acquiring excess goods or seeking achievement.[106] One's

---

[104] Foster, 'Peasant Society', p. 296; See also Malina, 'Limited Good and the Social World', p. 167.

[105] Parry and Bloch, *Money and the Morality of Exchange*, pp. 24–5 note that the displacement of these two transactional orders in which 'the individual involvement in the short-term cycle will become an end in itself and is no longer subordinated to the reproduction of the larger cycle . . . evokes the strongest censure'.

[106] Malina, *New Testament World*, p. 103.

honour would be of more value in that society than would be the individual accumulation of riches at another's expense. Those who are unable to maintain their inherited status in an honourable way as a result of sickness, displacement, debt, accidental injury, or death, could be viewed as 'poor,' and this would have the implication of being 'socially ill-fated'.[107] Those who have been born into or inherited a life of abundance must maintain their honour within society through rituals of exchange that maintain their status, not only in an economic sense of being 'rich', but also in a social sense as being honourable. Thus patron–client relationships are established in which those of higher status maintain their honour by providing benefits to clients, while those clients reciprocate by giving praise and other forms of support to their benefactors.[108]

In a limited-good society the great majority of people would be neither poor nor rich in the sense of financial assessment, but would be considered relatively equal with regard to their inherited status or lineage.[109] Those who would seek to become 'rich' through the acquisition of money or capital would be viewed as dishonourable if this activity should occur at the expense of another. Thus the categories of 'poor' and 'rich' in the ancient world would reflect those who, on the one hand, have fallen victim to circumstances that prevent them from maintaining their inherited status, and, on the other hand, those who pursue the individual accumulation of riches and may be willing to compromise the cosmic and social order for personal gain.

In the case of the present study the goal is not so much to consider how people lived in relation to wealth or in determining the social implications of exchange mechanisms, though these will become evident as the texts are discussed. The primary aim is to ask whether the documents in question provide any coherent theological perspective with regard to the expectation of the promise of material blessing in the Deuteronomistic tradition for what is deemed the 'faithful community'. Thus, although 'wealth' may indeed be reflected in symbolic representations of wisdom, power, relationships, and applications of covenant fidelity, I am particularly interested in determining whether traditions in the Second Temple period have shaped what John expects is possible for the faithful Christian community. Stated differently, is material blessing or affluence to be expected as a feature of the present age for the faithful?

---

[107] *Ibid.*, p. 106.   [108] Mott, 'The Power of Giving and Receiving', pp. 61–4.
[109] Malina, *New Testament World*, p. 106.

1.5   Methodological approach

The analysis of the secondary literature above makes it possible now to outline the approach adopted by the present study. Previous research has attempted to locate the reason for John's critique of wealth within the social world of the Roman Empire, yet with no concrete agreement or satisfactory explanation for his radical perspective. For this reason I have chosen to adopt a tradition-historical approach.[110] Previous studies that have taken this approach have (1) limited the possibility of received traditions to the canon of the Hebrew Bible or Jewish apocalypses (Moyise, Beale, Bauckham), (2) considered John's use of wealth 'imagery' in relation to Greco-Roman traditions and not the language of affluence in Jewish apocalyptic literature or the Dead Sea Scrolls (Royalty, Duff), and/or (3) focused on John's critique of wealth in relation to Rome and not in relation to expectations for the faithful community (Yarbro Collins, Duff, Bauckham, Royalty). This highlights the need for an examination of wealth and poverty language in Jewish and apocalyptic literature that demonstrates a decided concern for how material wealth is to be negotiated among the faithful.

Moreover, in contrast to those who have considered the Book of Revelation and its intertextual relationship with the OT, I am taking a thematic intertextual approach in order to ascertain whether it is possible to suggest that John is in conversation with traditions that reflect a similar perspective on wealth. I will do so with the following questions in mind. How is the possession of wealth negotiated theologically in these texts? Is the language of wealth used figuratively or literally, and in either case to what does it refer? To what degree can we say that the texts containing this wealth language are concerned with the correction of injustices or a reversal of fortunes? The study will also be sensitive to whether a tradition of interpretation can be found in this literature that is being taken up in the Apocalypse.

In the first phase of the study texts from Qumran will be investigated in the following order. (1) Non-sectarian documents discovered among

---

[110] In essence, this is an exercise in historical theology; that is, a history of ideas. Certainly the label of historical theology is usually kept within the domain of church history. However, in terms of historical theology the present study wants to consider the various traditions that were circulating in the Second Temple period that may have influenced John's world view and the perspective he imposes on his readers. For more on the value of a tradition-historical approach in New Testament scholarship, see Morgan and Barton, *Biblical Interpretation*, pp. 92–132.

the Qumran Dead Sea Scrolls (DSS) that are preserved in Aramaic that help us to understand the use of wealth language within the broader scope of Second Temple Judaism. This will include the earliest Enochic traditions – *Fall of the Watchers*, *Apocalypse of Weeks*, and the *Epistle of Enoch* – as well as the *Aramaic Levi Document*. (2) Non-sectarian texts preserved in Hebrew. These texts include Ben Sira, *Mûsār lᵉMēvîn* (4QInstruction), and the *Two Spirits Treatise*. (3) Next, sectarian documents will be examined to see how the communities of Qumran used this language to define the boundaries of faithfulness and community life in relation to wealth. These documents will include *Damascus Document*, *Community Rule*, *War Scroll*, *Pesher Habakkuk*, and *Hodayot*. (4) Finally, other Jewish literature composed in Greek, which was not preserved in the Qumran caves will be examined, that includes Wisdom of Solomon, *Similitudes* (*1 Enoch* 37–71), *Eschatological Admonition* (*1 Enoch* 108), and the third *Sibylline Oracle*.

Previous studies that have attempted to explain John's perspective on wealth frequently take as their point of departure the harsh critique of Rome in chapter 18 and then read back into other texts a socio-political agenda or a connection to the Imperial cults and trade guilds. Other studies highlight the writer's concern with wealth among the churches without, however, drawing the connection with the critique of Rome's riches in chapter 18. This analysis makes it possible to propose reading the language of wealth in the Book of Revelation in the order that it occurs. In doing so, it may be possible to surmise whether the writer develops the topic of wealth throughout the Apocalypse in a way that imposes upon its readers a more programmatic, comprehensive approach for the faithful community.

In section 3, I will examine the Second Temple texts collectively against the language of wealth and poverty in the Apocalypse. First, the letters to the churches in Rev 2–3 will be considered in light of the many references, both explicit and implicit, to wealth and poverty (2:4, 5, 9, 13, 14, 20; 3:4, 8, 17–18). Next, the throne-room vision and its references to gold and precious jewels will be examined along with the reference of wealth in relation to the Lamb (Rev 4–5). In this same chapter, the third horseman will be explored in view of the economic symbol of balancing scales that he holds in his hand. Following this, we will investigate the language of the rich and poor in chapter 13 along with references to buying and selling in relation to the beast. Finally, chapter 18 will be analysed for its many references to wealth. In addition, we will also examine the connections between the language of wealth in 18:1–24 and the letters to the churches, especially as they relate to the call to "Come out" in 18:4. Conclusions will follow that focus on how it is possible to speak about John's perspective with regard to the possession of wealth within the Christian community and to what degree this view is informed by antecedent traditions.

PART II

The language of wealth and poverty, rich and poor, in the Second Temple period

Introduction

Because this study is one of historical theology; that is, a history of theological perspectives, it is necessary to consider what kinds of traditions were circulating during the Second Temple period with which John of the Apocalypse may have been familiar. This will assist in answering the questions: to what extent does the message of John about wealth reflect views expressed in any of these texts and is it possible to determine those views of which he may have been critical? Thus the present chapter will provide an overview that helps the reader understand ideas reflected in current Jewish traditions that demonstrate a concern over wealth that were circulating during the Second Temple period. This analysis will elucidate the ways in which different communities thought theologically about the relationship between the faithful community and affluence.

Second Temple Judaism was both unified and complex in that there were basic elements that various groups held as foundational,[1] though their interpretations of sacred Jewish traditions sometimes varied greatly.[2] For this reason, an examination of various documents within the Second Temple period is

---

[1] For a discussion of this issue, one that reflects the extremes of the argument, see Sanders, *Paul and Palestinian Judaism*, and the subsequent review by Neusner, *Ancient Judaism: Debates and Disputes*, pp. 127–41, 195–230. See also Neusner, *Rabbinic Judaism*, pp. 7–23. The present study wishes to take a more balanced approach since the literature from the period reflects a variety of theological interpretations of how the faithful exercise obedience and worship to God; that is, they seek to answer the question, 'What is it that really constitutes Israel?', Newsom, *Self as Symbolic Space*, p. 4. See also Dunn, *Parting of the Ways*, pp. 24–47; Metso, 'Shifts in Covenantal Discourse', pp. 497–512.

[2] See Talmon, 'The Internal Diversification of Judaism', 16–43; Green, 'Ancient Judaism', pp. 293–310. See also Schiffman, 'Jewish Sectarianism', pp. 1–46 and *Understanding Second Temple Judaism*, pp. 4–5, who suggests

warranted. Moreover, since there are a variety of interpretive traditions related to peripheral issues such as wealth, it is appropriate methodologically to examine each text in its own right. In doing so, I will heed the caution of Cohen, who warns against being either 'unifiers' or 'separators' in relation to academic studies of Second Temple Judaism.[3] His warning is against viewing Second Temple Judaism as either overly unified or diverse. He encourages a balanced position, stating, 'the two approaches are complementary rather than contradictory, and a fully convincing interpretation of the material will require some attention to each'.[4] Thus, the present study is encouraged to consider (1) what fundamental theological premise various groups might be considering when speaking about wealth, and (2) whether the different texts reflect distinctive views about this theological premise – in particular, how they view affluence in relation to what they consider the faithful community. The former requires some discussion now, while the latter can be determined only after an analysis of the material.

As the elect people of God, however that was interpreted among the many coteries within Judaism, the thread of Deuteronomistic theology was fundamental to all.[5] In addition to inheriting the land, peace, and freedom from political domination, the faithful were also promised material blessing. This blessing was expressed in the form of agrarian abundance and bountiful progeny (Deut 28:3–11) as well as silver and gold (Deut 8:16). Most important to the present study is how obedience becomes closely tied with economic prosperity in

more unity than diversity. See also Cohen, *Maccabees to the Mishnah*, pp. 12–14, who points out the diversity in the interpretive traditions, while maintaining that the Jews were viewed largely by outsiders as a unified group. However, the present study also wants to take seriously how they distinguished themselves in relation to one another.

[3] Cohen, 'Modern Study of Ancient Judaism', pp. 55–73; Sarason, 'Response', 74–9 largely agrees with Cohen but stresses the need to examine texts on their own terms in a nuanced fashion since the evidence overall is limited.

[4] Cohen, 'Modern Study of Ancient Judaism', p. 62. The focus of our study is not on how people lived in relation to wealth historically or what conditions brought about economic disparity, though this will come into play throughout the study. Rather, the emphasis is on how the language of wealth is used in various documents and what theological expectations these texts reveal concerning wealth and the faithful community.

[5] I am speaking in particular about a theology of retribution as articulated in the blessings and curses of Deut 28–31. See Weinfeld, *Deuteronomic School*, pp. 307–19.

the blessings and curses of the Deuteronomistic tradition and how this idea is interpreted, or assumed, in the Second Temple texts.

A theology of retribution would have brought into question the piety of faithful Jews who did not enjoy the economic success of the rich, upper-class leaders of the nation whose affluence could be seen as the sign of God's blessing. This visible manifestation of God's favour among those who were considered by some to be corrupt (2 Macc 4:10–17) and the disparity in economic circumstances between the minority upper class and the masses became an issue through which rival sects sought to identify themselves and defend their piety. It is against this backdrop that wealth is to be examined. Attention will be given to Jewish apocalyptic literature, since (1) this material has not been seriously considered in previous studies of Revelation, and (2) John writes in the apocalyptic idiom. Special interest will be given to how groups with an apocalyptic world view attempt to negotiate wealth. The distinction of literature as 'apocalyptic' requires a brief discussion.

In speaking about apocalyptic literature I am not focused on, nor concerned with, the genre 'apocalypse'. These are to be distinguished since the latter represents a genre of literature identified according to function and features.[6] Only some of the documents considered in this thesis are apocalypses. In addition, I do not consider all of the communities behind the documents in question to reflect a historical movement of apocalypticism, though some may.[7] Rather, I am speaking of a 'corpus of literature . . . that can be called "apocalyptic" at least in an extended sense'.[8] Thus I use the term as an adjective to describe the nature of the texts in question. Stone's definition suffices to describe the texts in the present study:

---

[6] See Collins's definition of an apocalypse in *Apocalypse: The Morphology of a Genre*, above, Chapter 1, n. 93. See also Aune, 'Problem of Genre', pp. 65–96 and *Revelation 1–5*, pp. lxxvii–lxxxii, who places emphasis on form, function, and content; see also Hellholm, 'Problem of Apocalyptic Genre', pp. 13–64, who combines form, function, and content with a 'syntagmatic' approach.

[7] See Koch, *Rediscovery of Apocalyptic*, pp. 28–33; Hanson, 'Apocalypticism', 27–34. For a more helpful discussion that highlights the difficulty of defining these terms so concretely, see Collins, *Apocalyptic Imagination*, pp. 12–14.

[8] Collins, *Apocalyptic Imagination*, p. 3. All of the texts discussed in this section with the exception of Sirach and Wisdom of Solomon are included in Collins's discussion.

'apocalyptic' or 'apocalypticism' should be regarded
as a pattern of thought, primarily eschatological in
character, typifying some apocalypses and also a number of works belonging to other genres of literature
belonging to the period of the Second Temple.[9]

However, this definition should be qualified, since it overem-
phasizes the eschatological aspect of the literature. This is best
corrected by Rowland:

Apocalyptic is as much involved in an attempt to understand things *as they are now* as to predict future events.
The mysteries of heaven and earth and the real significance of contemporary persons and events in history
are also the dominant interests of the apocalypticists.
There is thus a concern with the world above and its
mysteries as a means of explaining human existence
in the present. Apocalyptic has a vertical dimension
which is just as important as any predictions made
about the future.[10]

Rowland's emphasis on the cosmology of apocalyptic literature
is especially helpful since it reorients our thinking towards the
ethical implications of the knowledge of heavenly mysteries and
the eschatological consequences of one's actions.

I would also like to distinguish between 'apocalyptic' literature and the idea that apocalypses always arise out of crises.[11]
While the earliest apocalypses were most likely produced during times of socio-historical difficulties, the continued use of the
apocalyptic idiom over an extended period of time and in a variety of socio-historical circumstances suggests that it may have
simply become an 'inherited medium of expression'.[12] Since
many of the texts under investigation are not formal apocalypses, an emphasis on the crisis aspect of the genre would not be
helpful.[13] It would also be unwise to take a referential approach

---

[9] Stone, 'Apocalyptic Literature', p. 394. See also Hanson, *Dawn of Apocalyptic*, pp. 427–44.

[10] Rowland, *Open Heaven*, p. 2 (italics added).

[11] Hanson's *Dawn of Apocalyptic* reflects the classical representation of this
position.

[12] Stuckenbruck, *Angel Veneration*, p. 40; see also Charlesworth, 'Apocalypse of John', pp. 23–4.

[13] The *Apocalypse of Weeks* can be considered an apocalypse, though a study
of the historical setting is of little value as will be shown below.

in order to ascertain historical information about economic life on the ground since apocalyptic literature is more expressive and symbolic.[14] Rather, an emphasis on the sociological function of the idiom may be more helpful in understanding the use of wealth language in these texts. Newsom has rightly stated:

> apocalyptic is an 'outsider' discourse: not a language of the oppressed but a language of those who *elect* a stance of marginality and seek to use that marginal status to find a place in the cultural conversation.[15]

It is from this perspective that we will evaluate the texts below. To what degree does the language of wealth reflect certain theological ideas that may be a response to rival interpretations or may mirror what is taken for granted in the dominant cultural conversation? How does the language of wealth function in establishing or legitimizing these theological views? This can also be understood against the backdrop of texts that are not apocalyptic yet still demonstrate a decided concern over wealth. For that reason, I have included two documents in the discussion that are not considered apocalyptic.

Wisdom of Ben Sira and Wisdom of Solomon are not apocalyptic, though the latter contains apocalyptic elements in the Eschatological Book. The former represents traditional sapiential literature and the passages related to wealth are so numerous that one would be remiss not to include it in the discussion. The latter also contains eschatological concerns and speaks of wealth in relation to the faithful, though it is not formally considered apocalyptic. However, due to its date in the latter part of the Second Temple period and its popularity in early Christianity, its inclusion in the discussion is warranted.

The material is ordered in a way that will allow us to consider what traditions provide the pool of ideas that may have given rise to similar motifs in later literature. In doing so, the discussion begins with non-sectarian documents discovered among the Qumran Dead Sea Scrolls that are preserved in Aramaic. This will include the earliest Enochic traditions – *Fall of the Watchers*, *Apocalypse of Weeks*, and the *Epistle of Enoch* – as well as the *Aramaic Levi Document*. These documents, preserved in

---

[14] Collins, *Apocalyptic Imagination*, p. 17.
[15] Newsom, *Self as Symbolic Space*, p. 48 (italics added).

the Qumran caves, were collected and copied at the site, though they are not productions of the Qumran community. It is necessary to make this distinction since not every document found at the site found complete agreement with the ideas expressed by the community in the sectarian productions.[16] In addition, it helps to establish ideas about wealth that were circulated more widely than the information found in the sectarian documents. The discussion continues with an analysis of non-sectarian texts preserved in Hebrew. This will include Ben Sira, *Mûsār lᵉMēvîn* (4QInstruction), and the *Two Spirits Treatise*.

This will be followed by an examination of wealth language in the sectarian literature of the DSS. Earlier DSS scholars tended to divide the Qumran material between biblical and non-biblical texts, the latter of which were regarded as sectarian texts.[17] This approach has been largely abandoned and more recent scholarship provides a clearer distinction, though there is some disagreement concerning the qualifications of a sectarian document.[18] The present study follows the work of Devorah Dimant and Armin Lange who make this distinction based on sectarian terminology.[19] Within this category, only texts that demonstrate a concern over wealth are discussed, all of which are generally accepted as sectarian:[20] *Damascus Document, Community Rule, War Scroll, Pesher Habakkuk,* and *Hodayot.*

[16] Smith, 'The Dead Sea Sect', pp. 347–8.

[17] See Dupont-Sommer, *Essene Writings*, pp. 8–20. See also Vermès, *Dead Sea Scrolls*, pp. 41–73. Surprisingly, the current software programs offered by both Accordance and Bibleworks also divide the material into two modules: Dead Sea Scrolls Biblical Manuscripts and Qumran Sectarian Manuscripts. The latter includes many texts that are obviously not sectarian.

[18] See Jokiranta, '"Sectarianism" of the Qumran "Sect"', pp. 223–39 (esp. 236–8). See also Davies, 'A "Groningen" Hypothesis', pp. 521–41 (esp. 521–6); Newsom, '"Sectually Explicit" Literature', pp. 167–87.

[19] Dimant, 'The Qumran Manuscripts: Contents and Significance', in Dimant and Schiffman, *Time to Prepare the Way*, pp. 24–58 (esp. 27–36). Also Dimant, 'Library of Qumran', pp. 170–6; Dimant, 'Qumran Sectarian Library', in Stone, *Jewish Writings of the Second Temple Period*, pp. 483–550; Lange, *Weisheit und Prädestination*, pp. 127–8, who argues that the *Two Spirits Treatise* is not a Qumran document based on terminology. Cf. Stegemann, 'Die Bedeutung der Qumranfunde', p. 511.

[20] Stegemann, Dimant, and Newsom include *Damascus Document, Community Rule, War Scroll*, the pesherim, and the *Hodayot* as sectarian documents. See also Wassen and Jokiranta, 'Groups in Tension', pp. 205–45.

Finally, other Jewish literature not preserved in the Qumran caves that were composed in Greek is analysed.[21] These include Wisdom of Solomon, later additions to the Enoch tradition, which include the *Similitudes* and *Eschatological Admonition*, as well as the third Jewish *Sibylline Oracle*. The discussion of each document begins with brief introductory material that establishes the available manuscript evidence and the approximate date of composition. In the case of the DSS, some documents are part of manuscript traditions that developed over time and may be important in understanding how issues related to wealth evolved within the community. Where these traditions differ in a way that directly affects a document's view of wealth in the relevant passages, a discussion of its importance will be provided. Otherwise, it can be assumed that, although information has been provided on the various manuscript traditions, no variant exists that affects the discussion.

The presentation of the material in this chapter is the last stage of a process that involved several steps. I have isolated every text within the documents listed above that deals with the language of wealth, poverty, the rich and poor, as well as other economic references. I have completed a thorough analysis of each passage, commenting on them and noting the development of patterns and making observations. I acknowledge the great complexity of these many documents, not least the DSS material, and in the initial phases of examination have taken seriously the shape of the material, and the way in which it has been preserved. However, certain patterns and dominant points of view have emerged from the texts during this analysis, which have allowed the discussion to be streamlined somewhat and the material is being offered based on these patterns. In addition, since the material related to the Dead Sea community presents a variety of literary and theological concerns, other scholars are cited who provide a much more thorough investigation of the finer points of interest that are subsidiary to the present study.

---

[21] Two manuscripts from Qumran contain portions of Ben Sira (2Q18; 11Q5) and a number of fragments were discovered at Masada. This is discussed in detail below.

2

DEAD SEA SCROLLS: NON-SECTARIAN
ARAMAIC DOCUMENTS

2.1   *Aramaic Levi Document*

Aramaic Levi Document (ALD) is contained in two fragments found in the
Cairo Genizah in 1896 consisting of one complete leaf and one partial leaf
(Cambridge University Library MS T-S 16.94),[1] as well as one other leaf
(MS Heb c 27 fo. 56[r–v]), which is housed in the Bodleian Library.[2] These
manuscripts are dated prior to the turn of the first millennium CE.[3] The
former two were published in 1900 by Pass and Arendzen and the latter by
Cowley and Charles in 1907.[4] The document is also found in manuscripts
from caves 1 and 4 of Qumran: 1Q21; 4Q213, 213a, 213b; 4Q214, 214a,
214b. The dates range from 150 to 151 BCE.[5] The Genizah manuscripts
largely agree with the Qumran material, although two of the cave 4
manuscripts (4Q214a, 4Q214b) preserve different recensions from the
'dominant text'.[6] The document itself can be dated to the late third century
or early second century BCE, based on: (1) palaeographic evidence of
the Qumran manuscripts, (2) a reference in the *Damascus Document*

---

[1] I would like to extend thanks to the Taylor-Schechter Genizah Research Unit at
Cambridge University Library for granting me access to this manuscript during my research.

[2] Pass and Arendzen, 'Fragment of an Aramaic Text', 651. For a description of the
different manuscripts, see Drawnel, *Aramaic Wisdom Text*, pp. 21–43.

[3] T-S 16.94 are dated prior to 1000 CE. See Beit-Arié, *Makings of the Medieval Hebrew
Book*, p. 83; Greenfield and Stone, 'Aramaic Testament of Levi', p. 216. The Bodleian
Library manuscript is dated from the end of the ninth to the beginning of the tenth century
CE; Drawnel, *Aramaic Wisdom Text*, pp. 29–30.

[4] Greenfield, Stone, and Eshel, *Aramaic Levi Document*, pp. 1–2.

[5] *Ibid.*, 4. For a detailed discussion, see Stone and Greenfield, 'First Manuscript',
pp. 257–81; 'Second Manuscript', pp. 1–15; 'Third and Fourth Manuscript', pp. 245–
59; 'Fifth and Sixth Manuscript', pp. 271–92. See also Drawnel, *Aramaic Wisdom Text*,
pp. 21–43.

[6] Greenfield, Stone, and Eshel, *Aramaic Levi Document*, p. 8. There are also three Greek
fragments found on Mt Athos (E, E 2,3, and E 18,2) (Athos, MS Koutloumousiou 39, cat.
No. 3108; MS Koutloumousiou 39, fos. 201[v]–202[r]; MS Koutloumousiou 39, fos. 205[v]–
207[r], respectively). These have been dated to the eleventh century based on the minuscule
text. For a discussion of these manuscripts, see Drawnel, *Aramaic Wisdom Text*, p. 31.

(CD 4:15), which is dated to the second century BCE, and (3) the textual development demonstrated in the various recensions preserved among the cave 4 material. However, Drawnel offers a convincing argument that it should be dated at the end of the fourth or beginning of the third centuries BCE.[7]

ALD is not the same as the Greek *Testament of Levi* nor is it an Aramaic version of that work, though contact between the documents is evident.[8] Moreover, in contrast to *Testament of Levi*, *ALD* does not appear to be a testament.[9] It places a high regard on the priesthood, attributing both priestly and royal language to Levi, and emphasizes the purity of the levitical priestly line. It provides one text that deals with wealth that includes parallels in the Qumran materials as well as the Greek *Testament of Levi*:

> And they seat him on the seat of honour in order to hear his wise
> words. Wisdom is a great wealth of honour (glory) for those
> familiar with it and a fine treasure (סימא) to all who acquire (קנה)
> it. If there will come mighty kings and a great army and cavalry
> accompanied by chariots – and they will seize the possessions
> (נכסים) of the land and country and will plunder the wealth (הון)
> which is in them, (yet) the treasure (אוצר) house of wisdom they
> will not plunder. And they will not find its hidden places and
> they will not enter its gates,[[10]] and will not [] its go[o]d things
> [and will not] be able to conquer its walls [] and will not [and will
> not] see its treasure. (*ALD* 13:10–12) [par. 4Q213 i 1:19–ii 2:1;
> T. Levi 13:1–9][11]

Here Levi teaches his progeny the importance of seeking after wisdom, which metaphorically is 'treasure' (סימא).[12] The word קנה 'acquire' occurs in the biblical tradition as a commercial term meaning 'to purchase',[13] though it is also used in the sapiential literature to denote the acquisition of wisdom.[14] Placed in poetic parallelism to ידע it figuratively denotes the

[7] Drawnel, *Aramaic Wisdom Text*, pp. 63–75 (esp. 67). So also Milik, *Books of Enoch*, p. 24.

[8] Greenfield, Stone, and Eshel, *Aramaic Levi Document*, pp. 14–17.

[9] Drawnel, *Aramaic Wisdom Text*, pp. 85–96.

[10] The Genizah text ends here and what follows is reconstructed from 4Q213.

[11] Translation taken from Greenfield, Stone and Eshel, *Aramaic Levi Document*, pp. 105–7.

[12] This term has the same meaning as אוצר. *HALOT*, pp. 1.23–4, 751. This is attested in Sir 40:18b where MS B reflects אוצר while B mg. attests סימא.

[13] *NIDOTTE*, vol. III, p. 941.

[14] Prov 1:5; 4:5, 7; 15:32; 16:16; 17:16; 18:15; 19:8; 23:23; Sir 51:23–5.

process of learning.[15] At the same time, the dissemination of wisdom in *ALD* comes only through the priestly line of Levi, and its mantic nature is evident in the heavenly ascent (4:1–8) and implicit in his reference to Joseph (13:1). Levi is warned to avoid fornication (פחז) and harlotry (זנות) (6:3) and is given instructions on maintaining the purity of the priestly office (6–10). Thus, the intended audience is encouraged to view themselves as the righteous community who are privy to this knowledge.

In the biblical tradition, learned wisdom is frequently compared to precious metals and stones (Job 28:12–19; Prov 3:5; 8:10–11; 16:16; 20:15; cf. 4Q525), and the one who gains wisdom also acquires and maintains material wealth. While *ALD* attests that wisdom is a treasure, it does not include any expectation of material wealth for its readers. Rather, it emphasizes a life of loyalty to God by means of living according to the heavenly wisdom (13:1–3). While there is no explicit critique of wealth in this passage, the contrast between the armies who pursue riches but are unable to find wisdom (13:11–12) provides an early testimony of an implicit contrast between the acquisition of wisdom and the pursuit of wealth. There is also a loose connection between this warning and the admonition to avoid sexual immorality.

2.2   Early Enoch tradition

Book of the Watchers

The *Book of the Watchers* (BOW) contains fundamental theological motifs that reflect the core material of the Enochic traditions as a whole. This document consists of five sections: (1) Introductory Oracles (1–5), (2) *The Fall of the Watchers* (6–11), (3) Enoch's prophetic commission (12–16), (4) First Heavenly Journey (17–19), and (5) Second Heavenly Journey (20–36). Of interest to the present study are *The Fall of the Watchers* and Enoch's prophetic commission. In the former, two fallen angel myths are incorporated into one story.[16] First, the Shemihazah myth tells the story of rebellious angels who take human wives and produce giant offspring. These giants engage in violent acts against the human race as they seek to satiate their enormous appetites and desires. Second, the angel Asael teaches humankind heavenly secrets including metallurgy, by which they produce weapons of war and jewellery, and teaches them about precious stones, jewels, and cosmetics (8:1–2).

---

[15] Drawnel, *Aramaic Wisdom Text*, p. 340.

[16] Newsom, '1 Enoch 6–19', pp. 313–14. She notes that there may be three traditions that underlie the Watchers myth. See also Nickelsburg, 'Apocalyptic and Myth', pp. 399–400.

The result of this knowledge was great violence on the face of the earth, for which reason all sin is attributed to Asael (10:7). Consequently, he and the other rebellious angels are bound in darkness until the final judgement,[17] while the bastard offspring of the Watchers are destroyed in the flood. Thus, God cleanses the earth from all iniquity and an age is envisioned in which God 'opens the store chamber of heaven' upon the righteous (*1 Enoch* 11:1–2), language taken from the blessings of the Deuteronomistic tradition (Deut 28:16). Later traditions, however, continue the story.[18] Because the bastard offspring are both spirit and fleshly beings, when their bodies are destroyed, their spirits continue to dwell on the earth and torment mankind (*1 Enoch* 15:8–12). Yet, they too will be given over to destruction, though not until the final judgement (*1 Enoch* 16:1–2). Thus, the story of the Watchers provides an explanation for the wickedness and violence in the world by stating that both the secrets revealed to mankind and the demon spirits continue to multiply evil on the earth in the present age. Although God has dealt decisively with the wicked offspring and the fallen angels, the present age marks a time where the results of this forbidden relationship persist in causing violence and sin in the world.

The Fall of the Watchers (6–11) narrative represents some of the earliest Enochic traditions.[19] In addition, chapters 6–19 form the core material of BOW as a whole (1–36).[20] As part of the larger unit, it is dated to the middle of the third century BCE,[21] although the traditions contained therein can be dated even earlier.[22] The document is attested in Aramaic in the Qumran manuscripts 4Q201–2, 4Q204–6, and XQpapEn ar.[23] These manuscripts are dated from the first half of the second century to the late first century BCE. It should be noted that the Aramaic fragments represent only a few words of material, none of which comprises an entire column or line of text.[24] I have listed the Enochic corpus under

[17] See *1 Enoch* 86:1–4; *Jub.* 4:15; *Tg.* Ps.-*Jon.* Gen 6:2; *T. Reub.* 5; *Ps.-Clem. Hom.* 8:11–15. For a discussion of these various traditions, see Nickelsburg, *A Commentary on the Book of 1 Enoch: Chapters 1–36; 81–108* (henceforth *1 Enoch 1*), pp. 194–6.

[18] See Yoshiko Reed, *Fallen Angels*, pp. 58–83.

[19] Milik, *Books of Enoch*, p. 25; Newsom, '1 Enoch 6–19', p. 312; Stone, 'Book of Enoch', p. 484.

[20] Stuckenbruck, *1 Enoch 91–108*, p. 8; Knibb, *Essays on the Book of Enoch*, p. 18; Vanderkam, *Growth of an Apocalyptic Tradition*, p. 114; Charles, *Book of Enoch*, pp. 249–51.

[21] Nickelsburg, *1 Enoch 1*, p. 7.

[22] Stuckenbruck, *1 Enoch 91–108*, p. 8. See also Stone, 'Book of Enoch', p. 484.

[23] Nickelsburg, *1 Enoch 1*, 9–10. See also Knibb, *Essays on the Book of Enoch*, pp. 44–8. Knibb does not include 1Q19bis.

[24] Knibb, *Essays on the Book of Enoch*, p. 47.

Aramaic manuscripts not because the Dead Sea fragments provide any complete extant portions of the passages under consideration. Rather, I do so in order to demonstrate the age of the traditions and the pool of ideas attested in them. In doing so, it allows us to consider the possibility of chronological reception of these traditions in later works. The wide popularity of the Enoch traditions, especially the BOW, warrants a discussion of the degree to which ideas about the individual accumulation of riches may have been received in subsequent writings.

> Asael taught men to make swords of iron and breastplates of bronze. He revealed to them the metals of the earth and how to fashion jewellery and silver into bracelets for women. He taught them about antimony and about making eye shadow, and about all kinds of precious stones, and about coloured dyes. And the world was changed. The result was great wickedness on the earth. Men committed fornication and went astray, becoming corrupt in all their ways.   (*1 Enoch* 8:1–2)[25]

This text provides the foundational acts of the Watchers that are further developed in later Enochic traditions. References to silver bracelets, precious stones, jewellery made from the metals of the earth, and coloured dyes underscore a concern over affluence. These items of luxury would have been most prevalent among the wealthiest people. In the Hebrew Bible, this language is used to denounce the pride of the women of Jerusalem who are adorned with bracelets, jewellery, and fine garments (Isa 3:16–24; Ezek 23:40–2). Two Aramaic terms are preserved in 4Q202 1 ii:28 that relate to eye paint. The verb כחל refers to 'painting one's eyes' while צדיד refers to antimony or eye shadow.[26] These are also attested in Ezek 23:40; *Tg.* 2 Kgs 9:30 and *Tg.* Jer 4:30 in which the concept of painting eyes occurs only in relation to wicked women.[27] It is the last act performed by Jezebel just prior to her death.

An interest in oppression and violence is also evident in the formulation of weapons, an idea that is further developed in later Enochic traditions that calumniate (1) the accumulation of silver and gold (*1 Enoch* 52:7; 94:7; 97:8–10) in order to gain power, (2) the decadent lifestyles of the rich (*1 Enoch* 98:2), and (3) fashioning idols (*1 Enoch* 65:6–8; 99:6). This view of precious stones, jewellery, and eye make-up in connection with the origin of evil indicates that the writer(s) view(s) the outward display

---

[25] All translations are taken from Olson, *Enoch*, unless otherwise noted.
[26] *DTTBYML*, vol. I, pp. 618, 629.   [27] Thompson, 'Eye Paint', p. 202.

of an affluent lifestyle as quintessential to the corruption of humankind. This is confirmed by the statement, 'and the world was changed'.[28]

A contrast is implied between heavenly wisdom and false teaching in the BOW. The angels are condemned for sharing secrets of heaven with humankind, while Enoch receives wisdom during his heavenly ascent, in both the BOW and the *Astronomical Book* (AB).[29] The instruction of the fallen angels encourages humankind to become involved with items related to wealth, i.e., precious stones, jewellery, and gold, which lead to violence and an excessive lifestyle. Enoch's wisdom involves cosmological secrets that encourage faithfulness and endurance by emphasizing the consequences of actions in the afterlife. In addition, the progeny of the angels are referred to as the בני זנותא 'sons of fornication' (τοὺς τῆς υἱοὺς πορνείας) (*1 Enoch* 10:9). While the Hebrew Bible often associates luxurious items with violence[30] and oppression, the connection with sexual immorality appears to be a new development.[31] The biblical tradition also speaks of fornication in relation to covenant unfaithfulness and idolatry but not wealth.[32]

> In those days I will open the store chambers of blessing which are in heaven so that I may send them down upon the earth, upon the works and labours of the sons of men. Peace and Truth will be united through all the days and all generations of eternity.   (*1 Enoch* 11:1)[33]

The distance implied between the seventy generations that the Watchers are bound and the Final Judgement points to an interim period in which the spirits of the bastard offspring continue to wreak havoc on humankind and lead them astray from worshipping God (*1 Enoch* 15:8–9; 19:1). This distance, taken together with the phrase 'In those days', implies an eschatological blessing for the righteous who suffer in this

---

[28] This statement is attested in *1 Enoch* 86:2. For a discussion of the textual difficulty in this text, see Knibb, *Ethiopic Book of Enoch*, p. 81. Nickelsburg does not include this statement in his translation, *1 Enoch 1*, p. 188. See also Olson, *Enoch*, p. 34.

[29] See Reed, 'Heavenly Ascent, Angelic Descent', pp. 47–66; Newsom, '1 Enoch 6–19', p. 319.

[30] Job 20:19; Pss 17:14; 62:10; Prov 11:16; 28:16; Isa 3:12; 10:2; Jer 5:27; 17:11; 51:13; Ezek 22:5, 9; Amos 4:1; Obad 13; Hab 2:6; Zeph 1:9.

[31] Sir 34:21–7; *1 Enoch* 94:6–95:2; 95:4–7; 97:8–10; 99:11–16; 2 Macc 3:10; *Sib. Or.* 2:56; CD 4:11–18; 6:16–17; 8:4–9; 19:16–21; 1QS 4:9–11; 10:18–19; 11:1–2; 1QpHab 1:7–8; 6:1; 8:11–12, 15; 9:4–7; 1QHa 10:32–4; 18:22–5; 4Q390 2 i:8–10; 4Q397 14–21:5; Luke 3:14; Jas 2:6; Rev 2:9; 18:3.

[32] Jer 3:8, 9; 13:22, 27; Ezek 16:32; 23:37; Hos 3:1; 4:12, 15; Mal 3:5.

[33] While this line is not extant in the cave 4 material, the context in which they occur is, which also alludes to the hope of eschatological blessing (4Q204 1 v:7).

present age. Just as the giants destroyed the produce of mankind and carried out violence against them, in the future God will restore their previous losses and will bring about conditions of peace and truth. Language of the Deuteronomistic promise of blessing can be detected:

> The LORD will open for you his rich storehouse, the heavens, to give the rain of your land in its season and to bless all your undertakings. You will lend to many nations, but you will not borrow.   (Deut 28:12)

Both passages emphasize God's blessing of agrarian abundance, though the Enochic text promises peace to those who are experiencing tribulation in the present age. In that sense the present order is viewed in terms that denote tribulation and deception. The fixed judgement of the wicked and the promise of a future reward for the faithful indicate that in the earliest Enochic traditions a postponement of the Deuteronomistic blessing can already be detected.

> [F]urthermore, before this happens, you will witness the destruction of your beloved ones with all of their sons and their possessions (קנין). You will not have these to enjoy; rather, they will fall before you by the sword of destruction.   (*1 Enoch* 14:6)

This passage could reflect the earliest attestation of the wicked and possessions in the Enochic tradition. However, a reconstruction of the text proves problematic. The translation by Nickelsburg lacks the reference to possessions; 'you will see the destruction of your sons, your beloved ones; and that you will have no pleasure in them'.[34] This follows the Greek τὴν ἀπώλειαν τῶν υἱῶν ὑμῶν τῶν ἀγαπητῶν. Black reads, 'and all their sons and their flocks', which suggests a form of possessions.[35] Isaac renders the phrase, 'and you will not have their treasures'.[36] However, Milik translates, 'and of (their) possessions'.[37] Olson and Milik's extended readings are dependent upon the presence of קנה in 4Q202 i:6:9 and 4Q204 i:6:16, of which both manuscripts are very fragmented.

The 'beloved ones' are the giant offspring that were born to human women that have brought oppression and violence on others since their birth (*1 Enoch* 7:2–6; 9:8–9; see the Book of Giants at 1Q23 9+14+15:2–5; 4Q531 1:1–6; 4Q203 4:3–6; 8:7–15). The reference to 'their sons' indicates the children of the bastard offspring, thus the grandsons of the

---

34 Nickelsburg, *1 Enoch 1*, p. 251.   35 Black, *Book of Enoch*, p. 33.
36 Isaac, 'Enoch', p. 20.   37 Milik, *Books of Enoch*, p. 193.

Watchers are also in view.[38] This may be a veiled reference to those whom the author(s) think(s) are currently practising the teachings of the Watchers. If the extended reading is preferred, the text implies a critique of the accumulation of wealth and an extravagant lifestyle by including the destruction of possessions in the judgement.

The term (קִנְה) indicates property that has been acquired and the destruction of both the wicked and their possessions is echoed in later Enochic traditions (*1 Enoch* 98:2–3).[39] This may indicate an awareness of the reference to property here (*1 Enoch* 8:1–2) as it further develops the sins committed through the forging of jewellery and make-up. The connection between the deviant knowledge passed on by Asael and the subsequent destruction of the giants and their possessions becomes paradigmatic for later announcements of judgement against wealthy, wicked oppressors (*1 Enoch* 97:10; 98:2–3; 100:6).

Apocalypse of Weeks (AOW)

This document is an independent unit (*1 Enoch* 93:1–10; 91:11–17)[40] within the overall text of the *Epistle of Enoch* (*1 Enoch* 91–105). Though originally a separate work later incorporated into the Enochic tradition, it is not attested independent of the *Epistle* in either the DSS or the Ethiopic tradition.[41] It is preserved among the Dead Sea fragments in 4Q212, which based on palaeographic evidence can be dated to the middle of the first century BCE.[42] If we consider the reference to AOW in *Jub.* 4:18, we can establish a *terminus ante quem* somewhere in the early 160s BCE.[43] Moreover, the lack of any reference to Antiochene persecution would indicate a date somewhere before the Maccabean period, possibly around 170 BCE.[44] At best a date somewhere in the first third of the second century BCE can be surmised.[45]

The AOW provides an account of world history using a well-established tradition of dividing history into time periods of seven and

---

[38] Black, *Book of Enoch*, p. 146.

[39] *HALOT*, vol. II, pp. 1111–12. See also *DTTBYML*, vol. II, p. 1391.

[40] For a detailed discussion of the proper placement of the texts in questions, see Stuckenbruck, *1 Enoch 91–108*, pp. 49–52. See also Olson, 'Recovering the Original Sequence', pp. 69–94.

[41] Stuckenbruck, *1 Enoch 91–108*, p. 49.   [42] *Ibid.*, p. 50.

[43] Nickelsburg, *Jewish Literature*, pp. 73–4.

[44] Knibb, 'Apocalypse of Weeks', p. 217.

[45] Nickelsburg, *1 Enoch 1*, pp. 440–1; Vanderkam, *Growth of an Apocalyptic Tradition*, pp. 142–9; Black, *Book of Enoch*, p. 288; Stuckenbruck, *1 Enoch 91–108*, pp. 60–2.

ten weeks.[46] The seventh week probably represents the author's time, while weeks 8–10 are yet future. An explicit reference to wealth occurs in the passage concerning the eighth week.

> After that the eighth week will come: the week of righteousness in which all the righteous will be given a sword so that they may execute a righteous judgment on all the wicked, who will be delivered into their hands. And as that week reaches its close, they will gain riches (נכסין) righteously. And the royal Temple of the Great One will be built in splendour for all generations forever.   (*1 Enoch* 91: 12–13)

This text is attested in 4Q212 1 iv:17, where the phrase 'they will gain riches righteously' is fully intact. Whether this text denotes a reversal of fortunes in the sense that the righteous will receive material wealth in the eschaton is determined by how one understands the term 'riches' (נכסין). It can describe material wealth such as jewellery, silver and gold items from the Temple, one's general possessions, as well as agrarian goods such as grain.[47] The contrast between righteous wealth in the future age and the portrayal of the wicked as rich sinners shows that the writer(s) categorically reject(s) wealth as a feature of the present age for the faithful community.[48] Whether the righteous obtain the wealth of wicked sinners in a complete reversal of fortunes is not clear. However, this clearly denotes a postponement of the Deuteronomistic promise of blessing.

The Epistle

This section of the *Epistle of Enoch* is contained in *1 Enoch* 92:1–5 and 93:11–105:2. Its attestation in 4Q204 and 4Q212 provides a *terminus ad quem* of the middle to late first century BCE, while its use of the earlier BOW provides a *terminus a quo* of the late third century BCE.[49] Possible references to the *Epistle* as a whole in *Jubilees* places it somewhere

---

[46] Nickelsburg, *1 Enoch 1*, p. 440. See also Collins, *Apocalyptic Imagination*, p. 50.

[47] *HALOT*, vol. I, p. 699; *DTTBYML* vol. II, p. 911; Porten and Yardeni, *Textbook of Aramaic Documents*, A4.7:12–13; A4.7:16; B2.9:12; B3.3:11; C1.1:66. See also Beyer (ed.), *Die aramäischen Texte*, vol. I, p. 637, vol. II, p. 441. Stuckenbruck asserts that domestic and agricultural abundance are in view here rather than jewels and precious metals, *1 Enoch 91–108*, p. 136.

[48] Cf. *1 Enoch* 94:6–11; 96:5; 98:7–10; 102:9–10.

[49] Stuckenbruck, *1 Enoch 91–108*, p. 214.

in the middle of the second century.[50] The absence of allusions to the Maccabean revolt further suggests that the various parts of the *Epistle* were written prior to this event.[51]

The body of the *Epistle* consists of eight woe oracles situated within three discourses.[52] The first (*1 Enoch* 94:6–100:6), which contains six woe oracles, demonstrates a decided concern over wealth obtained by unjust means. The second discourse (*1 Enoch* 100:7–102:3) deals with divine judgement, while the third (*1 Enoch* 102:4–104:8) attempts to answer the question of theodicy. Six of the eight passages in the present section occur within the first discourse.

> Woe to those who build their houses with sin, for they will be overthrown from their entire foundation and they will fall by the sword. And (woe to) those who accumulate gold and silver: in the judgment they will be quickly destroyed. (*1 Enoch* 94:7)[53]

The building metaphor here and in the preceding verse (*1 Enoch* 94:6; cf. 99:13) describing the oppressive activity of the rich is contrasted with the building of the eschatological Temple in the AOW (*1 Enoch* 91:13). In the biblical tradition, 'building a house' frequently refers to the construction of the Temple.[54] However, it also occurs in relation to establishing one's family or dynasty.[55] The background for the passage is Jeremiah 22:13: 'Woe to the one who builds his house not in righteousness' (הוי בנה ביתו בל צדק). This text refers to Jehoiakim building his palace by oppression, using forced, slave labour. In the present text it could reflect confiscation of land by the rich in connection with judges who take bribes.[56] Consequently, Nickelsburg reads, 'those who acquire gold and silver *in judgment* will quickly perish'.[57] However, Stuckenbruck rightly notes, 'the force of the invectives against the rich among

---

[50] *Jub.* 4:19; 7:29; 10:17. See Vanderkam, *Textual and Historical Studies*, pp. 231–41, who dates the work after the Maccabean revolt.

[51] Nickelsburg, *Jewish Literature*, p. 72 dates it in the early 160s BCE. See also Wacholder, *Dawn of Qumran*, pp. 41–2, who prefers a date before the Maccabean revolt. So also Stuckenbruck, *1 Enoch 91–108*, p. 215.

[52] Stuckenbruck, *1 Enoch 91–108*, pp. 188–90; Nickelsburg outlines the material in six discourses rather than three: *1 Enoch 1*, p. 421.

[53] Translation taken from Stuckenbruck, *1 Enoch 91–108*, pp. 262–3.

[54] This usage occurs 63 times in 1 Kgs, 61 times in 2 Chr, 28 times in 1 Chr, and 23 times in Nehemiah. Jenni and Westermann, *Theological Lexicon*, vol. I, p. 245.

[55] Deut 25:9; Ruth 4:11; 1 Sam 2:35; 2 Sam 7:27; 1 Kgs 11:38; 1 Chr 17:10, 25; Ps 127:1; Prov 14:1; 24:3; Job 22:23; Jer 18:9; 31:28; Amos 9:11.

[56] Nickelsburg, 'Riches, the Rich, and God's Judgment', vol. II, p. 526.

[57] Nickelsburg, *1 Enoch 1*, p. 460. Cf. Olson, *Enoch*, p. 229 (italics added).

the woes that follow reflects more than a mere conditional criticism of wealth'.[58] The allusions to the reversal of fortunes mentioned in the eighth week of AOW suggest the same; that is, a categorical rejection of wealth. Four elements are present in both texts: judgement, a sword, riches, and the building metaphor. In the eighth week, the righteous will be given a sword to carry out judgement on the wicked. In the present verse the wicked will 'fall by the sword' and will be destroyed in 'the judgement'. In addition, the faithful will receive riches righteously in contrast to the unjust accumulation of wealth by the wicked, at which time the Temple will be 'built' in splendour.

If the denigration of wealth in the *Epistle* is more comprehensive, the use of language from the prophetic tradition may simply function to align the opponents with the wicked from Israel's past. This would allow the writer(s) to stand in the line of the biblical prophets and evoke similar judgements against the rich of his (their) own day. In doing so, it is assumed that those who are rich have obtained their wealth in the same manner as rich oppressors mentioned in the prophetic tradition. Thus, 'building their houses through sin' could be a metaphorical parallel to the literal 'accumulating gold and silver' (cf. Job 22:23–5).[59] The lack of an additional 'woe' between these two lines indicates they are placed in synonymous parallelism.

> Woe to you rich ones, for you have trusted in your wealth. However, you will have to depart from your wealth since in the days of your wealth you did not remember the Most High. You have committed blasphemy and iniquity and you have been prepared for the day of bloodshed, for the day of darkness, and for the great day of judgment.   (*1 Enoch* 94:8–9)[60]

Here the address in the second person provides the 'first direct denunciation of the rich in the *Epistle*'.[61] The crimes for which they are guilty are placing trust in their riches and not remembering God, which in the biblical tradition is a flagrant breach of covenantal faithfulness:[62]

> Be careful not to say, 'My own ability and skill have gotten me this wealth.' You must remember the Lord your God, for he is the one who gives ability to get wealth . . . if you do this he will confirm his covenant that he made by oath to your ancestors,

---

[58] Stuckenbruck, *1 Enoch 91–108*, p. 263.   [59] Nickelsburg, *1 Enoch 1*, p. 461.
[60] Stuckenbruck, *1 Enoch 91–108*, p. 256.   [61] *Ibid.*, p. 263.
[62] Cf. Pss 49:6; 52:7; 62:10; Prov 11:28; Job 8:13–14; 15:31; 31:23–8; Jer 9:23; 48:7; 49:4.

even as he has to this day. Now if you forget the Lord your God at all and follow other gods, worshiping and prostrating yourselves before them, I testify to you today that you will surely be annihilated.   (Deut 8:17–19)

The judgement promised in the Deuteronomistic tradition is evoked in the Enochic text. Stuckenbruck has pointed out that the expression 'have been prepared' (*delwāna konkemu*) is a *passivum divinum*: 'God is at work in preparing judgement while the rich gather their wealth' (cf. *1 Enoch* 98:10; 99:6).[63] Thus the woe oracle functions to point out the breach of covenant fidelity and to provide a formal announcement of judgement. The lack of any call for repentance on the part of the sinners indicates the certainty of their judgement. They are told, 'Give up any hope that you will be saved' (*1 Enoch* 98:10), and 'no remedy will be available to you, thanks to your sin' (*1 Enoch* 95:4). This draws on the paradigm developed in the Watchers myth in which the fallen angels are unable to be restored (*1 Enoch* 14:4–7) and they, along with their offspring, have a day of judgement that is fixed. These woe oracles function rhetorically to announce officially the destruction of the rich and provide a written testimony that will be used against the sinners in the final judgement (*1 Enoch* 96:4, 7; 97:7).[64]

The allusion to the Deuteronomistic warning against self-glorification indicates that the rich opponents are being associated with those who are in breach of covenant fidelity. This may arise from a concern that the opponents are in some way equating their wealth with the sign of God's material blessing.

Woe to you sinners for your riches give you the appearance of righteousness but your hearts convict you of being sinners, and this fact will serve against you – a testament to your evil deeds!   (*1 Enoch* 96:4)

This text reflects the pinnacle of an engagement with the problem of theodicy and is the first and most explicit indication that the writer(s) is (are) debating a Deuteronomistic theology of wealth in relation to the opponents.[65] The contrast is between what one can perceive by appearances in the present and the cosmological and eschatological realities disclosed in Enoch's heavenly journey. Outward, visible blessing is the mark of the faithful in the biblical tradition, while poverty and oppression

---

[63] Stuckenbruck, *1 Enoch 91–108*, p. 265.   [64] *Ibid.*, p. 197.
[65] *Ibid.*, p. 297; Nickelsburg, *1 Enoch 1*, p. 471.

are the signs that Israel is under the covenant curses.[66] While this text, or the *Epistle* as a whole, does not reject a Deuteronomistic theology of wealth, it challenges the validity of material blessing as a tangible sign of covenant obedience in the present age, in light of its postponement (*1 Enoch* 91:13).[67]

> Woe to you who devour the very finest of the wheat and drink wine from large bowls, but trample down the lowly in your might.   (*1 Enoch* 96:5)

While this is the only occurrence in which the Enochic community is referred to as 'the lowly', it is not the only text that 'defines the objects of oppression by their social status'.[68] Rather, the language of food consumption implies not only the high status of the rich but also that their excessive lifestyles come as a result of the oppression of the poor (cf. *1 Enoch* 102:9).[69] The critique concerning their level of indulgence can be seen in the description of 'devouring' wheat and drinking wine from 'large bowls'. This language is influenced by Amos 5:11 and 6:6 respectively:

> Therefore because you trample on the poor (דל, πτωχοί) and take from them levies of grain, you have built houses of hewn stone, but you shall not live in them; you have planted pleasant vineyards, but you shall not drink their wine.   (Amos 5:11)

> who drink wine from bowls, and anoint themselves with the finest oils, but are not grieved over the ruin of Joseph!
>   (Amos 6:6)

The absence of any other reference to the Enochic community as 'lowly' or 'poor' in the *Epistle* indicates that the term functions here as a description of the activities of the sinners as influenced by the prophetic tradition. However, given the extensive language that refers to the opponents as rich, it is reasonable to assume that they may have viewed themselves in terms of being poor.[70] In either case, the message is clear. Even if the Enochic community was not destitute or experiencing the kind of oppression depicted in Amos, the author certainly perceives a relative

---

[66] Deut 8:7–10; 11:13–14; 28:2–14; Prov 10:15, 22; 14:20, 24; 22:4. Cf. Deut 28:15–68.

[67] Nickelsburg, 'Torah and the Deuteronomic Scheme', pp. 233–4; Stuckenbruck, *1 Enoch 91–108*, p. 297. Cf. Dillman, *Das Buch Henoch*, p. 308.

[68] Nickelsburg, *1 Enoch 1*, p. 471.   [69] Stuckenbruck, *1 Enoch 91–108*, p. 298.

[70] *Ibid.*, p. 300.

deprivation in relation to the community's opponents. By aligning himself with the prophetic tradition he is also able to associate the opponents with the wicked from Israel's past, thus refuting any notion that their wealth is the result of covenant obedience (cf. Deut 15:11).

> Woe to you who gain gold and silver unjustly (οὐκ ἀπὸ δικαιοσύνης) and say, 'We have grown very wealthy (πεπλουτήκαμεν) and have amassed possessions, and we have acquired everything that we desire. Now let us do whatever we wish, for we have hoarded silver in our treasure storerooms and lots of good things in our houses.' But they will be poured out of there like water! You are deceived, for your riches (πλοῦτος) will not last. Rather they will quickly (ταχὺ) take flight from you for you have amassed all of it unjustly (ἀδίκως) and you will be given over to a great curse.   (*1 Enoch* 97:8–10)

Here the writer(s) employ(s) the use of imputed speech to refute what he perceives are wrong attitudes about wealth held by the opponents. Reported speech finds its roots in ancient historiography but is also a feature of ancient Jewish and early Christian texts.[71] The topic is frequently divided into the two very broad categories of direct and indirect speech. Imputed or attributed speech is marked by the use of a second or third person verb of speaking, followed by a phrase in the first person. When this occurs with a present tense verb followed by a present form of 'to be' it is referred to as *belief awareness attribution*.[72] In such cases, the speech is not simply a historical account of what someone said, but assigns to a person a belief or viewpoint that the writer regards as their defining characteristic, at least with regard to the subject matter of the text in which the speech is reported. Moreover, it becomes somewhat theatrical in that the one reporting the speech takes on the role of the original speaker and portrays them in a stereotypical fashion.[73] What follows is typically the reality of the statement in question. Here the rich are deceived because they think their wealth is sufficient and will

---

[71] Isa 29:15; 47:8; Jer 2:23, 35; 13:22; 21:13; 42:13–14; Ezek 18:25; Amos 7:16; Hab 2:6; Mal 1:4; 2:17; 3:8. There are also occurrences in Pss 10:13; 35:25; Prov 24:12. Cf. Sir 5:1; 11:18–19; Wis 2:1–11; 2 Esd 10:12–13; Matt 3:9; Luke 3:8; John 8:52; Rom 2:2; Rev 3:17; 18:7.

[72] Larson, *Reported Speech*, pp. 102–3. See also Holt and Clift, *Reporting Talk*, pp. 184–5.

[73] Wiersbicka, 'Direct and Indirect Discourse', pp. 273–87. See also Holt and Clift, *Reporting Talk*, p. 47.

last forever. The biblical background is found in the Deuteronomistic tradition: 'Be careful not to say, "My power and the might of my own hand have gotten me this wealth"' (Deut 8:17). A similar occurrence in the first person is found in the prophetic tradition:

> A trader, in whose hands are false balances, he loves to oppress. Ephraim boasts, 'I am very rich! I have become wealthy! In all that I have done to gain my wealth, no one can accuse me of any offence that is actually sinful.'   (Hos 12:8–9)

The shift from the singular in these traditions to the first person plural 'we' in the Enochic tradition indicates the writer's categorical denunciation of the rich. The prophetic tradition calumniates a self-sufficient attitude (Jer 9:23–4) and links the rich with those who are in breach of covenant faithfulness. While the opponents themselves make no mention of how they amassed their fortunes, at the beginning and the end of the soliloquy the writer(s) attribute(s) it to unjust means. The indictment 'not from righteousness' (οὐκ ἀπὸ δικαιοσύνης) mirrors the phrase in the AOW (*1 Enoch* 91:13) in which the faithful gain riches 'righteously' (בקשוט יקנון נכסין) (4Q212 1 iv:17).

The writer(s) refute(s) the arrogant claim by stating that their riches will be taken from them 'quickly' (ταχύ), which most likely derives from Prov 23:5: 'When your eyes light upon it, it is gone; for suddenly it takes wings to itself, flying like an eagle toward heaven.' Yet in the biblical text it is the pursuit of riches that is decried and not unjust gain. Moreover, the biblical tradition maintains a positive perspective on wealth and simply denotes the temporality of riches and warns against trusting in them. In the Enochic text the critique is personalized and functions as a prophetic announcement of judgement categorically to denounce 'the rich'. In relation to the Deuteronomistic tradition, the use of imputed speech places the rich sinners squarely outside the purview of the faithful community and explicitly denies the possibility that their wealth is the result of covenant obedience.

> For you men will deck yourselves out with beautiful adornments more than women and with lovely colours more than girls, in royalty, magnificently, and with authority. (They will have to eat gold and silver for food and pour these out for water within their houses! And this because they are utterly lacking in knowledge and wisdom). And so you will be destroyed along with your

possessions, your glory, your honour. And in shame and in slaughter and in great poverty, their spirit will be thrown into a fiery furnace.   (*1 Enoch* 98:2–3)[74]

The language of beautification can be found in the *Fall of the Watchers* (*1 Enoch* 8:1–2) in which Asael taught humans about eye make-up, jewellery, and coloured-dyes. Similar language here indicates that the writer is making a connection between the pre-diluvian humans, who followed Asael's teaching, and his present opponents. The figurative portrayal of gold and silver in such abundance as food and water demonstrates the excessive lifestyle that the writer(s) is (are) critiquing. Yet the fate of the rich is the same as the progeny of the wicked angels; they are to be destroyed along with their possessions (*1 Enoch* 14:6).

The writer(s) associate(s) the opponents again with breaches of covenant fidelity in portraying them as cross-dressers (Deut 22:5), and the highest levels of society are most likely in view.[75] A contrast is made between having an abundance of gold and silver and being devoid of knowledge. This coincides with the situation reflected in the seventh week of the AOW (*1 Enoch* 93:9–10). The question for the present text is whether (a) their lack of knowledge is a result of their wealth, or (b) they lose their wealth (98:2b) because they lack understanding. The Ethiopic text reads 'on account of this', referring back to the wealth in the previous verse, suggesting (a) is the best option. The Greek reads, 'because they do not have knowledge and understanding' ([διὰ τὸ μ]ὴ ἐπιστήμην αὐτοὺς μηδὲ φρόνησιν μηδεμίαν [ἔχειν]), expressing cause.[76] The Ethiopic reading is to be preferred for the following reasons. (1) The context suggests that the reference to the wicked in terms of such excessive wealth is to heighten the expectation of the destruction of their possessions, which (2) is eschatological and could not take place if they lose their wealth before the Day of Judgement. Thus a complete eschatological reversal of fortunes is in view in the threefold contrast between wealth, glory, honour, and shame, slaughter, and great poverty. This coincides with the activities in the eighth week (*1 Enoch* 91:12–13). (3) The knowledge that these people lack is that their riches cannot save them at the time of judgement (*1 Enoch* 100:6).[77] Therefore, they continue in their present lifestyle trusting in riches, only to be destroyed on the Day of Judgement.

---

[74] The last line is taken from Stuckenbruck, *1 Enoch 91–108*, pp. 329–34. Olson lacks the phrase 'and in great poverty'.

[75] Stuckenbruck, *1 Enoch 91–108*, pp. 330–1; Nickelsburg, *1 Enoch 1*, p. 475.

[76] Stuckenbruck, *1 Enoch 91–108*, p. 334.

[77] *1 Enoch* 100:6 does not imply a universal salvation as much as it does a universal understanding of the message of the *Epistle*.

> Observe the sea captains who sail upon the sea. Their ships are tossed by the waves and shaken by tempests. Distressed, and battered by the storm, they are afraid and jettison all their goods and possessions into the sea, for they have forebodings in their hearts: the sea will swallow them up and they will perish in it!   (*1 Enoch* 101:4–5)

This text offers the reader an analogy of proper response to God and possessions. The preceding verses (*1 Enoch* 101:1–3) begin with an imperative to 'consider' (κατανοέω) the works of God in order to have a proper fear or reverence for him. Another imperative is provided at the beginning of the present text: 'Observe' (ὁράω), offering an analogy in terms the audience would clearly understand, ships and sailors.[78] Thus, together these two imperatives are directed at the same audience, the children of men, who are the sinners addressed in *1 Enoch* 100:10–13. Four ideas are present in this text that concur with ideas already proposed by the writer: (1) goods and possessions, (2) the testimony of one's heart, (3) proper response in light of imminent destruction, (4) understanding and wisdom.

The readers would understand the severity of the situation since this imagery is found in the biblical tradition (Jon 1:5). A sailor's cargo is his livelihood and the loss of such would mean financial ruin. Yet according to what we find in Jonah, even the idolatrous sailors were afraid (יִרְא) and parted with their possessions in light of impending doom. In the Enochic tradition, the sea captains throw their livelihood overboard out of 'foreboding in their hearts' (ὑποπτεύουσιν ἐν τῇ καρδίᾳ αὐτῶν). This could allude to the language in *1 Enoch* 96:4 where it is said that the hearts of the wicked convict them and will testify against them. In contrast to the ship captains, however, the wicked (*1 Enoch* 96:4) make no effort to listen to their hearts and thus the parable does not serve as a polemic in calling the unrighteous to repent.[79] Rather, it represents an appropriate response to God in light of coming destruction, something even the righteous are indirectly warned to consider. Moreover, it highlights the irreversible consequences of associating with the sinners whose fate is already sealed.

---

[78] The Ethiopic reads 'kings of the ships' while the Greek reads 'sea captains'. Working from Hallévi's proposal of a Hebrew dependence, it has been proposed that the Ethiopic translator, having direct access to the Aramaic text, mistook מלכי ('kings of') for מלחי ('sailors of'). There is no extant Aramaic parallel among the DSS material and the Greek reading is to be preferred. Knibb, *Ethiopic Book of Enoch*, vol. II, p. 236. See also J. Hallévi, 'Rédaction primitive du livre d'Énoch', p. 392.

[79] Stuckenbruck, *1 Enoch 91–108*, p. 479.

The analogy goes one step further, however, by explicitly pointing out a correct response to God with regard to possessions. In light of the persistent concern over wealth in the *Epistle*, this parable seems to tie together the previous points the author has been making. It especially seems to echo the concern in *1 Enoch* 98:2–3 where the rich are viewed as devoid of the ability to make a proper decision regarding wealth and, as a consequence, will be destroyed. The Greek text has the shorter reading that includes only 'knowledge' (ἐπιστήμη), while the Ethiopic reads knowledge and wisdom, using the same two terms as 98:3 (*temhert wa-tebaba*). While the Greek text is to be preferred and refers to general knowledge that even sea-creatures possess,[80] the expansion in the Ethiopic text may indicate that a later scribe or redactor included the dual use of terms in order to draw the same connection made in *1 Enoch* 98:3; that is, although the rich have general knowledge, their wealth precludes them from receiving revealed knowledge. In either case, the message is still clear: sinners do not fear God despite imminent destruction and thus continue to trust in and love their possessions more than God. This reveals a lack of wisdom and the certainty of judgement for those who accumulate wealth.

> Woe to the sinners who have died! Whenever you die in the wealth of your sins your peers will say this concerning you, 'Blessed are the sinners! They have seen all their days and now they have died prosperous and wealthy. They saw no trouble or slaughter during their lifetimes and they have died in honour. During their lives judgment did not occur against them.' (*1 Enoch* 103:5–6)

This is the last of eight woe oracles announcing judgement against the wicked, although this text is addressed to the wicked dead. Here again the writer(s) use(s) indirect speech to expose the misperception of the wicked who suppose the fate of the rich and poor is the same after death (*1 Enoch* 102:6–11). In the present life, the sinners enjoy what a Deuteronomistic theology of wealth suggests belongs to the righteous, while the faithful experience what appears to be the covenant curses (*1 Enoch* 103:10–13).[81]

---

[80] Charles, *Book of Enoch*, p. 252; Nickelsburg, *1 Enoch 1*, p. 508; Stuckenbruck, *1 Enoch 91–108*, p. 481. Cf. Black, *Book of Enoch*, p. 310; Olson, *Enoch*, p. 245.

[81] Charles, *Book of Enoch*, p. 256; Nickelsburg, *1 Enoch 1*, p. 523; Argal, *1 Enoch and Sirach*, p. 189; contra Stuckenbruck, *1 Enoch 91–108*, p. 533.

The Greek does not include the phrase 'died in the wealth of their sins', which is extant only in the Ethiopic.[82] It does not reflect dying in the abundance of one's sins, but rather dying in 'sinful wealth'.[83] This implies that their wealth came at the expense of the righteous. Moreover, it emphasizes the same concern of theodicy addressed in *1 Enoch* 96:4. The sinners view life only from the present, only by what they see, and, according to the present circumstances, they are enjoying the sign of God's blessing. Under these circumstances the recipients would most likely see themselves as being under the Deuteronomistic curses of the covenant (Deut 28–31). By use of imputed speech the writer(s) also refute(s) the present understanding of his (their) own community: 'We had hoped to become the head but have become the tail' (cf. Deut 28:13, 44), 'We have abandoned the hope of safely surviving' (cf. Deut 28:29).[84] It is this world view that the *Epistle* seeks to correct. The writer(s) appeal(s) to the mysteries of heaven and swear(s) that he has 'read the tablets of heaven' in order to provide a more comprehensive, cosmological understanding of the universe and the nature of the present age (*1 Enoch* 103:1–2).

The refutation that follows (*1 Enoch* 103:3–4) envisions a complete eschatological reversal of fortunes.[85] The righteous are assured that their circumstances will be even better than what the sinners are presently experiencing and that the wicked will experience great distress and suffering in Sheol. In traditional language of the prophetic oath formula, the writer(s) swear(s) that the righteous will be vindicated and the wicked will be judged (*1 Enoch* 104:1–3). Thus the faithful are encouraged not to become companions of the wicked rich, even though they are strong and prosperous (*1 Enoch* 104:6). By remaining distant from them, they will instead become companions of the hosts of heaven, which reflects a categorical rejection of the rich in the present age.

2.3   Summary of Aramaic traditions

The *ALD* reflects a very early tradition that does not explicitly calumniate wealth but contrasts the pursuit of riches with the acquisition of revealed

---

[82]   See Nickelsburg, *1 Enoch 1*, p. 514, who argues this is a gloss. See also Stuckenbruck, *1 Enoch 91–108*, pp. 529, 533.

[83]   Nickelsburg, *1 Enoch 1*, p. 524.

[84]   Cf. *1 Enoch* 103:9–14; Deut 28:25–6, 33, 38–42, 44–5, 48, 51, 62, 64–6; Dillman, *Das Buch Henoch*, p. 322. See also Stuckenbruck, *1 Enoch 91–108*, p. 548.

[85]   Nickelsburg, *1 Enoch 1*, p. 522; Charles, *Book of Enoch*, p. 256.

wisdom. The BOW, which is dated in the third century BCE, or even earlier, along with the AOW and the *Epistle*, which are dated in the early part of the second century BCE, reflect the earliest Jewish traditions that explicitly calumniate the rich and provide a rich supply of formative traditions relating to affluence and the righteous. Utilizing both sapiential and prophetic language, BOW links wealth language and imagery to the problem of evil and the origins of sin. The BOW contrasts the instruction of the fallen angels that leads to violence and oppression with the heavenly wisdom offered to the righteous, which leads to life and blessing. Yet the Enochic text offers some hope for a future restoration and blessing, which is absent in *ALD*.

The *Epistle* reshapes earlier Enochic traditions and places the culpability of sin on human beings, and provides a sharper critique of the rich. Like the biblical prophets, the writer(s) make(s) the connection between wealthy oppressors and sinners, though a significant shift in the prophetic language is evident. (1) In the biblical tradition the term 'the rich' is primarily a sapiential label used both positively and negatively[86] and is used in the prophets to refer to those who oppress the righteous.[87] In the *Epistle* it is used categorically to describe the wicked. (2) The judgement brought on Israel for its injustice to the poor in the prophetic tradition was designed to bring about repentance and restore the nation and thus maintains a hope for material blessing in the present age. However, the judgement of the wicked rich in the *Epistle* is placed in an eschatological context and their judgement is certain with no chance for repentance. The prophetic announcements in the *Epistle* function as a formal testimony to the deeds of the wicked while simultaneously warning the faithful community of the irreversible consequences of associating with the rich. (3) The prophetic tradition envisions a correction of injustices while the Enochic tradition looks for a reversal of fortunes. The prophets Isaiah and Amos critique the wicked leadership of Israel that abuse those without power. When they are taken into captivity it is in view of an eventual restoration of the nation during which time these social injustices will be expunged. The Enochic tradition views the present age as a time of wickedness and testing until the culmination of the eighth week when the wicked will be destroyed along with their possessions and the

---

[86] Job 34:19; Prov 10:15; 14:20; 18:11, 23; 22:2, 7, 16; 28:11; Qoh 5:12; 10:6, 20; Sir 8:2; 10:22, 30; 13:18–23.

[87] Isa 3:15; 10:2; Jer 2:34; Lam 4:13; Ezek 16:49; Amos 2:6–7; 4:1; 5:11–12; 8:4, 6; Hab 2:4; 3:14; Zech 7:9–10. See also Jer 5:5; 9:23; Mic 6:12.

righteous will be vindicated and will receive their deserved reward for faithfulness.

While these texts do not critique wealth per se they do clearly calumniate the affluent and postpone any expectation of material blessing for the faithful to the eschaton. In that regard they are clear that wealth is not a feature of the present age for the faithful community.

3

DEAD SEA SCROLLS: NON-SECTARIAN
HEBREW DOCUMENTS

3.1 Wisdom of Ben Sira (Sirach)

This document, also known as Sirach and Ecclesiasticus, was written by a wisdom teacher who presents himself as Yeshua ben El-azar ben Sira some time in the first quarter of the second century BCE.[1] The discovery of six Hebrew manuscripts in the Cairo Genizah in 1896, as well as two manuscripts from Qumran (2Q18; 11Q5)[2] and several fragments at Masada[3] helped to establish Hebrew as the original language of the document. In total, there are nine extant Hebrew manuscripts of Ben Sira.[4]

Sirach was translated into Greek by his grandson late in the second century BCE.[5] The document enjoyed wide circulation in the Second Temple period and was considered authoritative by some Jews, which is demonstrated by the stichometric manuscripts found at both Qumran and Masada. This scribal practice is also attested in texts that were later added to the canon of the Hebrew Bible.[6] It was included in the

---

[1] Skehan and Di Lella, *Wisdom of Ben Sira*, p. 9. If Ben Sira's description of the high priest Simon (50:1–21) is a reference to Simon II, this would provide a *terminus a quo* of 196 BCE, since he is described as a past figure. In addition, the lack of any mention of the radical reforms by Antiochus IV provides a *terminus ad quem* of 175 BCE; Williams, 'Date of Ecclesiasticus', pp. 563–5. Wright III, 'Book of Ben Sira', in *EDSS*, p. 91; Reiterer, 'Review of Recent Research', in Beentjes, *Book of Ben Sira in Hebrew*, p. 37; Scoggins, *Sirach*, pp. 18–20; Gilbert, 'Methodological and Hermeneutical Trends', p. 7.

[2] See Baillet, Milik, and de Vaux, *Les 'Petites Grottes' de Qumrân*, vol. I, pp. 75–7.

[3] See Yadin, *Ben Sira Scroll*.

[4] MS A Sir 3:6–7:29 (T-S 12.863, T-S 12.864), MS B Sir 10:19–11:10 (T-S 12.871), MS C Sir 3:14–18, 21–2; 41:16; 4:21; 20:22–3; 4:22–3 (T-S 12.867), MS D Sir 36:24–38:1 (*BAIU*, Paris), MS E Sir 32:16–34:1 (ENA 3597), MS F Sir 31:24–32:7; 32:12–33:8 (T-S AS 213.17) 2Q18 Sir 6:14–15, 20–31 (Jerusalem), 11QPs^a Sir 51:13–20, 30b (Jerusalem), Masada Scroll assorted portions of *Sir* 39–44 (Jerusalem), Beentjes, *Book of Ben Sira in Hebrew*, pp. 13–19. For the present study, where it is relevant, I rely on the edition by Beentjes.

[5] Skehan and Di Lella, *Wisdom of Ben Sira*, p. 135.

[6] *Ibid.*, p. 20. See also Nickelsburg, *Jewish Literature*, pp. 62–3.

LXX and is extant in the great uncial codices Vaticanus, Sinaiticus, and Alexandrinus, which provide the basis for the text (GR I). Other Greek manuscripts contain an extended version known as (GR II).[7] Ben Sira is considered an apocryphal book by both Jews and Protestant Christians but deuterocanonical by the Roman Catholic Church and is placed among the wisdom texts of the Old Testament. While the issue of its canonicity may be debated, its popularity, wide circulation, and importance to Jewish traditions in the Second Temple period are not. Thus it is vital to a thorough study of wealth and poverty in this period.

The document follows closely traditional Jewish wisdom from the Hebrew Bible. The author holds the Temple cult and the priesthood in high regard (Sir 7:29–31; 35:1–12; 44–45),[8] which marks a sharp contrast with the Enochic tradition that is indifferent towards the Second Temple.[9] In addition, Ben Sira makes what is taken by some commentators as a veiled critique of the value placed on hidden wisdom in the Enochic tradition (Sir 1:1–10; 3:21–5). Whether this critique can be isolated to that tradition alone we cannot know. However, the text does reflect a rejection of speculative wisdom in general, which places it at odds with the Enochic and other apocalyptic traditions. The wisdom Ben Sira offers is not exclusive to the prophet or sage but is accessible to all human beings, most of all to those who love and obey God.[10] Like Proverbs, Ben Sira offers a number of texts that deal with the topic of wealth and poverty.

Prior to an analysis of the passages, a few comments are necessary concerning the differences in vocabulary between the Hebrew texts and the Greek translation. The variety of terms used to describe the poor in the Greek text reflects the descriptive references in the Hebrew, albeit not in a consistent way. Generally, Ben Sira uses the terms דל and עני to refer to the poor, although the terms אביון, מסכן, and רש are also employed. In the Hebrew Bible עני is frequently used in a technical sense to refer to those who are dispossessed.[11] Moreover, its use indicates persons who have been afflicted by some cause outside of themselves or who have been wrongfully impoverished due to exploitation.[12] Ben Sira, however,

---

[7] See Gilbert, 'Methodological and Hermeneutical Trends', pp. 3–4.

[8] Nickelsburg, *Jewish Literature*, pp. 53–4. See also Zsengellér, 'Does Wisdom Come from the Temple?', pp. 135–49.

[9] Nickelsburg, *1 Enoch 1*, pp. 54–5.

[10] Beentjes, 'Full Wisdom', p. 152.   [11] *NIDOTTE*, vol. III, p. 455.

[12] Ex 3:7; 41:31; Deut 16:3; 26:7; 2 Kgs 14:26; Ps 9:12; 22:24; Prov 15:15; 22:22; 30:14; 31:5, 9, 20; Job 10:15; 24:4, 9, 14; 29:12; 30:16, 27; 34:28; 36:8, 15, 21; Isa 3:14; 10:2.

does not see this group as destitute since they have a roof under which they can live (Sir 40:23) and engage in some form of employment, though earning only enough to live day-by-day (Sir 31:4). The term דל is used to refer to the poor, yet they too are not indigent since they are able to offer sacrifices (Ex 30:15; Lev 14:21). It also denotes one who is weak or unimportant (Judg 6:15). Ben Sira employs the term fifteen times in various ways. It refers to the needy (Sir 4:4), the wise poor (Sir 10:23, 30; 11:1), the poor as a social class distinct from the rich (Sir 13:2), as prey for the rich (Sir 13:3, 19), as the unimportant in relation to the rich (Sir 13:22, 23), and as those whose prayers are heard by God (Sir 35:21). These various terms are generally translated by the grandson with the Greek terms πτωχός and ταπεινός, which are used synonymously throughout the document.[13]

The term עשיר is used to refer to both riches (Sir 3:17; 10:30, 31; 11:14, 18; 13:24; 14:3; 30:16, 19) and the rich (Sir 13:2, 3, 17–23; 19:1; 30:14; 31:1, 3; 32:1). The word הון is used always in reference to wealth (Sir 6:14; 8:2; 10:27; 31:3; 38:11). Other terms that refer to riches and the rich are, חיל, חרוץ, and טובה. The term עשיר is always translated with the Greek πλοῦτος or its cognates. The other terms are translated most commonly with the word χρῆμα. Of the fifty-two references to the rich and riches, forty-seven of them are translated with these two terms, fifteen by χρῆμα and thirty-two by πλοῦτος. The translation technique utilized by Ben Sira's grandson may indicate that the language of wealth, riches, and poverty had come to have more rhetorical value in later traditions and did not require the subtleties demonstrated in the Hebrew Ben Sira.[14] Throughout this section both the Hebrew text and Greek translation will be considered and variances between the two will be discussed in order to demonstrate the way in which some ideas concerning wealth were developing during the Second Temple period.

Since the Greek text translates some words synonymously and uses primarily πτωχός and ταπεινός to refer to poverty and the poor, and πλοῦτος or πλούσιος to refer to the rich and riches, as well as χρῆμα for wealth, it is to be assumed that unless otherwise noted this is the case throughout this portion of the study. Thus, when the words 'poor' and 'poverty' in the English translation are not marked, πτωχός or ταπεινός is the underlying Greek term. Likewise, when 'rich' or 'riches' are unmarked, πλοῦτος,

[13] Wright, 'Discourses of Riches', p. 560. See also Asensio, 'Poverty and Wealth', pp. 152–7.

[14] Wright, *No Small Difference*, p. 249, rightly indicates that Ben Sira's grandson sought to produce a translation, not a mechanical reproduction of his grandfather's work.

πλούσιος or χρῆμα are the underlying term. Other significant terms that are important to the study will be marked and discussed.

Wealth as responsibility

> My son, do not deprive the poor of their livelihood or turn away from the eyes of the needy (ἐπιδεής). Do not grieve the soul of the hungry nor anger one who is downtrodden. Do not trouble the heart of the desperate and do not turn away from giving to the needy (προσδέομαι). Do not reject a petitioner in distress and do not turn your face away from the poor. Do not turn your eyes away from a beggar (δέομαι) and give no man a reason to curse you; for if in the ache of his bitterness he curses you, his Maker will hear his prayer.   (Sirach 4:1–6)[15]

The teaching here is focused on how to live among the poor, indicating that Ben Sira and his students were most likely not poor themselves.[16] Poverty is presented as a possibility even for the faithful, yet this condition appears to be short lived and not one that they can remain in if they are diligent (Sir 11:17; 21–22). Three times in the passage an admonition is given not to turn away from the needy, using δέομαι or its cognates, suggesting the background for this idea may be Deut 15:7–8. The LXX reads:

> If there is among you anyone in need (ἐνδεής), a member of your community in any of your towns within the land that the Lord your God is giving you, do not be hard-hearted or tight-fisted towards your needy (ἐπιδέομαι) neighbour. You should, rather, open your hand, willingly lending enough to meet the need (ἐπιδέομαι), whatever it may be.   (Deut 15:7–8)

This term (ἐνδεής) refers specifically to those who ask for something in a pleading way.[17] It can refer to asking something from God in petition, though here it relates to those who are socially marginalized and seek help. This would remind the readers that if one expects God to answer their requests, they too must answer the needs of others. The last phrase, which underscores the possibility of God hearing the curse of the poor in their prayers, suggests as much. The promised blessing of God rests in

---

[15] Translations are my own unless otherwise noted.
[16] See Wright and Camp, 'Who Has Been Tested?', pp. 162–4; Skehan and Di Lella, *Wisdom of Ben Sira*, pp. 10–12, 451–2. See also Harrington, 'Wisdom of the Scribe', pp. 184–5.
[17] *BDAG*, p. 218.

the command to be open-handed towards the needy. The biblical tradition states that a failure to do so incurs guilt (cf. Deut 24:12–15).

Unlike the biblical prophets, Ben Sira does not offer any social critique for those who may have been the cause of the plight of the poor, nor for those who do not follow his advice. This differs widely from the *Epistle of Enoch*, where the rich are explicitly denounced for 'accumulating gold and silver' (*1 Enoch* 94:7), trusting in their riches (*1 Enoch* 94:8), feasting with large amounts of food while the poor go without (*1 Enoch* 96:4–6), and for oppressing the righteous (*1 Enoch* 96:8). Rather, Ben Sira appeals to the Deuteronomistic tradition that states poor people will always be part of the social fabric (Deut 15:11). Thus the responsibility to care for them is not simply one of social ethics in relation to the Greco-Roman world, but one anchored theologically in the Torah.

> Spend your money (ἀργύριον) for a brother or friend and do not leave it under a stone to rot. Appoint your treasure (θησαυρός) according to the command for that will profit you more than gold (χρυσός). Store up almsgiving in your storehouse (ἐν τοῖς ταμιείοις) and it will save you from every evil.
>
> (Sirach 29:10–13)

The term ἀργύριον refers specifically to silver money or coins that one would use in everyday exchange.[18] The implication is that accumulated money has no long lasting value. According to Ben Sira, wealth is a feature of the present age and should be used to help others. This text offers a look at Ben Sira's theological aims. Storing up almsgiving in one's storehouse meets with favour in the eyes of God (Sir 17:20–3) and atones for sin (Sir 3:30). The idea that one should appoint their goods to friends and relatives denotes some degree of negotiating wealth to their own benefit. While Ben Sira's rhetoric may well be sincere, the idea of 'storing up almsgiving' seems somewhat oxymoronic. Moreover, while he exhorts his students to give 'according to the command' he also offers some personal benefits for doing so. The background for this command is probably Deut 15:7–11, in which verse 10 states, 'Give liberally and be ungrudging when you do so, for on this account the Lord your God will bless you in all your work and in all that you undertake.' Thus, the references, 'it will profit you more than gold' and 'it will save you from every evil' have a this-worldly perspective. What is in mind here is the promise of material blessing for obedience, which giving to the poor reflects. If one is faithful in that regard, God will continue to bless

---

[18] *BDAG*, p. 128.

them (cf. Tob 14:10–11). Ben Sira evokes a similar injunction elsewhere (Sir 14:16–17) and states that after death there is no wealth to enjoy.

> Do not exchange a friend for money (διάφορος) or a true brother
> for the gold of Ophir.   (Sirach 7:18–19)

Here friendship is elevated above wealth in the sense that the desire for riches could jeopardize one's relationship. Care is to be taken in relationships especially regarding money. While the text does not categorically denounce wealth it implies that this is an area where friendships can be lost. The Greek translation uses διάφορος to refer to money. The term carries the sense of something distinctly excellent, which is in parallelism to the gold of Ophir. It is used elsewhere to refer to excellent gifts (2 Macc 1:35), revenue, and funds (2 Macc 3:61; 4:28), as well as gain or profit (Sir 27:1; 31:15; 42:5). The gold of Ophir was known for its purity (Isa 13:12) and the imagery here heightens the importance of friendship over wealth.[19]

This admonition demonstrates further that Ben Sira's concern is with how his students live relationally with regard to wealth. Although his underlying concern is faithfulness to Torah, he does not offer in this text any theological background for his exhortation. The warning is not that one would choose wealth over a friend, but that one might actually forsake a friend for the sake of profit. Moreover, these passages stress the importance of using money to help others rather than accumulating it for one's self.

> A person may become rich through a miser's life, and this is
> his allotted reward: when he says, 'I have found rest, now I will
> feast on my possessions!' he does not know how long it will be
> till he leaves them to others and dies.   (Sirach 11:18–19)[20]

The use of imputed speech alerts us to a wrong perspective on wealth: 'I have found rest, now I will feast.' Considering all of the exhortations for the wealthy to care for the poor,[21] this person has only their selfish desires in mind. Ben Sira makes it clear elsewhere that one who deprives himself cannot possibly be generous towards others (Sir 14:5).

This injustice is corrected in the man's death, and it is implied that this is something that comes upon him unexpectedly while he is hoarding

---

[19] See also Sir 30:14–17.

[20] Translation taken from Skehan and Di Lella, *Wisdom of Ben Sira*, p. 236.

[21] Sir 4:1–6; 11:21–2; 14:3–4; 18:30–19:1; 29:8–13; 34:25–7; 41:1–3.

money (cf. Luke 12:16–21). There is no indication of the theological implications of his actions in the afterlife. Ben Sira's focus is on what happens in the present age. And while this does not provide any explicit social critique, there is an implicit theological hint that he is not in accord with the Deuteronomistic injunction to care for others (Deut 15:17–18). In addition, the concern over accumulating wealth in great quantity in and of itself seems also to be in the background (Deut 17:17).

The rich and poor

During the analysis of Ben Sira, two groups emerge that are distinct from the addressees: the rich and the poor. I have attempted to divide the material into two sections, the first dealing with the use of the labels 'rich' and 'poor', and the second, texts in which societal boundaries are explicitly evoked, though there is some degree of overlap.

Rich and poor as labels

Contend not with the powerful (δυνάστης), lest you fall into his hands. Quarrel not with the rich, lest he oppose you with many resources; for gold (χρυσός) has unsettled many, and has destroyed the hearts of kings. (Sirach 8:1–2)

The terms 'the rich' (ἀνθρώπου πλουσίου) and 'the powerful' (ἀνθρώπου δυνάστου) are placed in synonymous parallelism and reflect the same kind of person. Since the writer assumes his own students have money (Sir 4:1–6; 5:1; 11:17; 18:30–3; 29:8–13), these labels may be used in a technical sense to refer to powerful oppressors. At the very least they reflect a higher social class than his readers. The term δυνάστης denotes one who holds power or great influence and this text highlights Ben Sira's perception of the political expediency of dealing with the rich in a proper fashion.[22] He highlights two aspects of the wealthy that are important to note: (1) they are able to destroy their enemies by means of their economic power, and (2) gold or wealth are seen as a possible negative influence on those who possess them. Viewed alongside those who are also economically successful, those who are excessively rich are portrayed as inherently dangerous (cf. Sir 28:10).

---

[22] *LSJ*, p. 452.

> The rich, the honoured (ἔνδοξος), and the poor; their glory is the fear of the Lord. It is not just to dishonour the person who is wise but poor, and it is not proper to give glory to a man who is a sinner.   (Sirach 10:22–4; cf. 10:3–31)

The Hebrew MSS A and B differ from the Greek translation in this passage.[23] MS A reads: 'the sojourner, the proud, the foreigner and the poor, their glory is the fear of the Lord' (וזד נכדי ורש תפארתם י[רא]ה אלהים גר). MS B reads: 'the sojourner, the stranger, the foreigner and the poor' (גר זר נכרי ורש). The reading in MS B is more likely to be original since the difference in וזד and זר is probably the result of a scribal error.[24] In the Hebrew text the four groups of marginalized people originally stood in contrast to the prince, judge, and ruler of verse 24. This implies that all persons, whether marginalized or powerful, find their glory in the fear of the Lord. The grandson, however, only includes three categories, two of which are foreign to the idea expressed in the Hebrew text. The addition of 'the rich' (πλούσιος) and 'the honoured' (ἔνδοξος) alongside 'the poor' demonstrates the grandson's awareness of distinct social categories with which he expected his audience to be familiar. In addition, since Ben Sira speaks of the rich and poor as categories distinct from his readers, the second group, the honoured, could be a reference to the retainer class of scribe/sage that includes him and his students.[25]

More importantly, this text implies that the rich are honoured above the poor based solely on their economic status. This is developed more fully in Sir 13:21–3. There he explains that the rich are helped by many when they stumble though the poor are left to fall. Even when the rich man speaks foolishness he is justified by those around him. On the contrary, when the poor speaks wisdom his words go unheeded. This stems from an overall perception by the wicked that poverty is an abhorrent evil. This concurs with a theology of retribution in which the circumstances of the poor are a result of covenant infidelity. Ben Sira seeks to correct this wrong perspective by defending justly acquired wealth, on the one hand, and correcting wrong attitudes about the poor, on the other.

> Wealth is good where there is no sin; but poverty is evil by the standards of the ungodly (ἀσεβής).   (Sirach 13:24)

---

[23] See Beentjes, *Book of Ben Sira in Hebrew*, pp. 35, 137.

[24] The category of 'proud' ויד does not fit the other three marginalized groups as does 'sojourner' וזד. It is possible that the *resh* could have been mistaken as a *dalet*.

[25] For a discussion of the use of the term scribe/sage, see Horsley and Tiller, 'Sociology of the Second Temple', in Davies and Halligan, *Second Temple Studies III*, pp. 74–107 (esp. 80). See also Wright, *Praise Israel for Wisdom*, pp. 82–9.

This text indicates that Ben Sira does not object to wealth if it is acquired justly. However, it also reveals the writer's awareness of attitudes about the poor held by those who are affluent. These people are referred to as ungodly, which further points to already circulating traditions in which the wealthy, who despise or oppress the poor, are viewed as sinners. This is not the same as the categorical denunciation of the rich that we find in the *Epistle of Enoch*, but emphasizes the need to be discerning. However, its use in this context indicates an association already widely in use.

Societal boundaries between rich and poor

> Whoever touches pitch becomes dirty; and the one who associates with the proud becomes like him. Do not take up a weight too heavy for you or associate with one stronger or wealthier. How can a clay pot associate with the iron kettle? The pot strikes against it and is smashed. The rich does wrong and adds to the insult; the poor is wronged and needs to apologise. If you are profitable he will use you, but if you are in need he will abandon you. (Sirach 13:1–4)

Ben Sira recognizes the importance of keeping within one's social stratum and this passage points out the inevitability of being affected when this boundary is crossed. The effect that higher classes have on the lower manifests itself in the form of oppression. The writer's first reference to the wealthy (Sir 13:2) is qualified in relation to the economic status of his students. Yet, when providing analogies in verses 3–4, the writer reverts to the categorical labels rich and poor. Again, Ben Sira does not offer a categorical denunciation of wealth nor does he provide any social critique. At the same time, he assumes his readers are aware of these social categories.

> What does a wolf share in common with a lamb, or a sinner (ἁμαρτωλός) with the godly (εὐσεβής)? What peace is between a hyena and a dog or between the rich and the poor? Wild asses in the wilderness are the prey of lions; likewise the poor are prey for the rich. Humility is an abomination to the proud; likewise the poor are an abomination to the rich. (Sirach 13:17–20)

This passage makes explicit, by use of synonymous parallelism, that the wicked are categorized with sinners and the poor with the godly.[26]

---

[26] Skehan and Di Lella, *Wisdom of Ben Sira*, p. 254.

The rich are also placed in parallelism with the proud, who oppress
the poor and despise their humble lifestyle. Yet Ben Sira does not offer a
denunciation of the rich. Elsewhere he notes the positive aspects of having
wealth (Sir 11:17, 22; 40:25–6). Indeed, he understands that his readers
can expect to have wealth and considers them to be responsible to care for
the poor (Sir 4:1–6; 11:17, 22; 40:18; 51:27–8). However, this use of the
label 'the rich', and its subsequent association with the term 'sinners' and
wicked behaviour indicates the presence of traditions already circulating
that used the labels rich and poor to identify the wicked and the faithful,
respectively.[27]

Wealth as peril

> Do not rely (ἐπέχω) on your wealth or say, 'I am self-sufficient
> (αὐτάρκη μοί ἐστιν).'   (Sirach 5:1)

In yet another occurrence of imputed speech, Ben Sira warns against
presumption with regard to affluence, which points to a concern over
attitudes of self-sufficiency. The term ἐπέχω typically has the sense 'to
hold fast to'[28] and is a translation of the Hebrew שׁען 'to lean on'.[29] In the
Greek text the emphasis is on trusting in wealth more than the individual
who possesses it, which appears to be the opposite in the Hebrew. The
former uses the third-person singular verb with the dative pronominal
μοί ἐστιν 'it is to me', indicating a decided trust in wealth. The Hebrew
states, 'there is power in my hand' (לאל ידי יׁש), which could point to the
strength of the individual, though in light of his wealth (cf. Prov 3:27).
Moreover, the term הילך could be translated either 'your strength' or 'your
wealth', though the latter is more likely since כוחך 'your strength' is in
synonymous parallelism in the next line. In either case, the text clearly
denounces trusting in wealth.

> Rely not upon unjust (ἄδικος) wealth; it will be no help in the
> day of trouble.   (Sirach 5:8)

This text has in common with the previous passage the concern over
trusting in possessions, yet here the emphasis is on unjust wealth. The
term ἄδικος is a translation of the Hebrew שׁקר 'to lie', thus it is wealth

---

[27] Wright and Camp maintain that Ben Sira does not view riches or poverty as signs
of piety or impiety. While this is true, he does show contact with traditions that use the
language of rich and poor to make these distinctions. See Wright and Camp, 'Who Has
Been Tested?', 172. The text in question is not discussed in their article.

[28] *BDAG*, p. 362.   [29] *NIDOTTE*, vol. IV, pp. 202–3; *HALOT*, vol. II, p. 1612.

gained through fraud.[30] The day of trouble does not refer to eschatological judgement, but calamity in the present age, since the Greek text reads ἐπαγωγῆς, a term used frequently in Sirach with this meaning.[31] Ben Sira's categories of just and unjust wealth differ from the *Epistle of Enoch* in that both feature in the present age. In the *Epistle*, just wealth is only obtained in the eschaton by the faithful who have endured and refused to be associated with rich sinners. There is no expectation by Ben Sira that the righteous will receive any reward after death or in the coming age. Rather, his emphasis is on the practical consequences of obtaining wealth and providing for the needs of others.

> Remember the season of famine in the time of plenty, poverty, and want in the day of wealth.   (Sirach 18:25)

The admonition to remember in relation to wealth is echoed in Deut 8:18, yet it is a charge to remember God. Skehan and Di Lella assert that the language here is reminiscent of the covenant curses that would result in hunger and poverty in the case of unfaithfulness.[32] This passage further attests that Second Temple writers thought about wealth through the lens of a Deuteronomistic theology.

> Do not follow your desires but restrain your passions (ὄρεξις). If you supply your soul with the pleasure of its desires it will make you the laughing stock of your enemies. Do not revel in much luxurious living (τρυφή) or you might encounter need. Do not become impoverished by feasting on borrowed money when there is nothing in your purse. The one who does this will not become rich; the one who despises the small things, by the small things he will be destroyed.   (Sirach 18:30–19:1)

The term ὄρεξις denotes strong sexual desire, which is to be avoided by means of self-control.[33] This language is a standard *topos* in the biblical wisdom literature (Prov 20:1; 21:17; 23:20–1; 31:3–5). One who overindulges himself with wine and women ends up with nothing in the end. Although Ben Sira acknowledges elsewhere that wealth and poverty come from the Lord (Sir 11:14, 17), here he seems to indicate that what God has given, an irresponsible person can lose. Moreover, this

---

[30] *NIDOTTE*, vol. IV, pp. 247–8.

[31] Sir 2:2; 3:28; 10:13; 25:14; 38:19; 40:9. See also LXX Deut 32:36; Isa 10:4; 14:17. Cf. Whybray, *Book of Proverbs*, p. 67.

[32] Skehan and Di Lella, *Wisdom of Ben Sira*, p. 291.

[33] *BDAG*, pp. 721–2. The Hebrew text of 18:30 is not extant.

indicates that even the faithful can act in this way and only incur present consequences.

On this subject Ben Sira differs widely from the Enochic tradition. While the former is more concerned with the consequences of personal actions in this age, the latter employs descriptions of lustful desires and luxurious living to categorically vilify the rich who gain wealth by unjust means and focuses on their eschatological judgement.[34] MS C states 'do not rejoice in momentary pleasures that cause double poverty' (אל תׁשמח שׁמץ תענוג אׁשר פי ׁשנים ריׁשו), a condition that can only occur during one's life. Moreover, rather than encountering need as reflected in the Greek text, the Hebrew text says what little the unfaithful person has will be 'stripped away' (יתערער). This harmonizes with the Deuteronomistic tradition where covenant faithfulness results in material blessing and unfaithfulness results in loss of wealth. The passage holds out the possibility that with care and wisdom one can acquire and maintain wealth (cf. Sir 40:25–6). In light of the many warnings given regarding the responsible use of riches with poverty as the consequence of irresponsibility, Ben Sira uses the threat of poverty heuristically to discourage irresponsible use of wealth.[35]

> A merchant (ἔμπορος) can hardly remain without fault or a peddler (κάπηλος) free from sin. Many have sinned for the sake of money[36] (διάφορος) and the one who seeks to be rich (πληθύνω) will turn away his eyes. Like a peg driven firmly between fitted stones, so also sin will be wedged between buying and selling. Unless one holds fast to the fear of the Lord with sudden swiftness one's house will be thrown down.
>
> (Sirach 26:29–27:3)

Buying and selling were frequently viewed in a negative light in both the Hebrew Bible as well as Second Temple texts.[37] Ben Sira's teaching can be directly related to the Deuteronomistic tradition since the latter explicitly states that correct measurements ensure extended life and prosperity in the land (Deut 25:15). The use of the term 'house' relates to בית in Deut 25:14, 'You must not have in your house different measurements' (cf. Prov 3:33; 12:7; 14:11). The term ἔμπορος refers to a ship

---

[34] *1 Enoch* 93:9–10; 97:8–9; 98:2–3; 102:9–10; 108:6–7.
[35] Pleins, 'Poverty in the Social World', p. 72.   [36] *LSJ*, p. 419; *TDNT*, vol. IX, p. 63.
[37] Lev 19:35–7; Deut 25:13–16; Prov 11:1; 20:23; Amos 8:4–6; Hos 12:7; CD 13:11–16; 1QS 5:14–20; 4Q266 9 iii 1–4.

merchant while κάπηλος denotes a peddler.[38] The word used for the rich denotes one's desire to multiply (πληθύνω) one's goods or possessions. In particular, 'excellent and valuable' (διάφορος) possessions are in mind.[39] The combination of these terms demonstrates that the greedy merchant is not seeking the common necessities of life, but possessions and items of luxury that bring prestige and power. Ben Sira holds out little hope for honesty in buying and selling. The parallelism 'for the sake of profit' and 'one who seeks to be rich' emphasizes the problem: lust for money blinds the eyes of the merchant who soon forgets the fear of God (cf. Deut 8:16–18).

> Sleeplessness over wealth wastes away one's flesh and anxiety drives away sleep... The rich person toils to amass a fortune, and when he rests he fills himself with his luxuries (τρυφή). The poor person toils to make a meagre living, and if ever he rests he becomes needy. One who loves gold will not be justified; one who pursues money (διάφορος) will be led astray by it. Many have come to ruin because of gold... It is a stumbling block to those who are avid for it and every fool will be taken captive by it. Blessed is the rich person who is found blameless and who does not go after gold. Who is he that we may praise him?... Who has been tested by it and been found perfect? (Sirach 31:1–11)

Here sleeplessness refers to worry over money, either the ability to gain more, or fear of losing what one has. Skehan and Di Lella contend that the lack of sleep is caused by a bad conscience.[40] Implicitly this echoes the concern that one might trust in their wealth (Sir 5:1–2). The writer's portrayal of how the rich 'toil' (κοπιάω), 'love' (ἀγαπάω), and 'pursue' (διώκω) luxurious and exquisite items (τρυφή) and how they are subsequently 'taken captive' (ἁλίσκομαι) by them reveals a perception that the rich are completely devoted to their wealth.

The grandson's translation technique comes through in this passage when we consider the Hebrew text. The Greek emphasizes one who loves (ἀγαπάω) gold, while the Hebrew (MS B 3v:8) emphasizes the pursuit (רדף) of gold. While only a slight nuance, the grandson reveals ideas from his period that begin to associate the accumulation of wealth with terms of endearment. In addition, he translates 'one who loves a bribe' (ואוהב מחיר) with 'the one who pursues money' (ὁ διώκων διάφορα).

[38] *BDAG*, p. 325 (cf. Ezek 27:12–36; Rev 18:3, 11, 15, 23); p. 508, respectively.
[39] *BDAG*, p. 240.   [40] Skehan and Di Lella, *Wisdom of Ben Sira*, p. 382.

The former refers more specifically to unjust practices while the latter refers to the pursuit of wealth more generally. The Hebrew text represents more traditional language, while the Greek could be more reflective of Ben Sira's direct cultural influence and unwillingness to critique social injustices.[41]

The restless pursuit of wealth is also portrayed in the biblical tradition where riches sprout wings and fly away when one tries to pursue them:

> Do not wear yourself out to get rich; be wise enough to desist. When your eyes light upon it, it is gone; for suddenly it takes wings to itself, flying like an eagle toward heaven.
>
> (Prov 23:4–5)

Qoheleth also serves as a background:

> The sleep of the labourer is sweet, whether he eats a little or much; but the wealth of the rich will not allow him to sleep.
>
> (Qoh 5:11)

In the biblical tradition the warnings against the pursuit of wealth are more subdued. In both of these passages the danger rests within the pursuit and accumulation of wealth and there is no explicit critique of the rich and poor. In the text of Ben Sira there is a clearer contrast between the circumstances of the rich and poor as well as a more explicit concern that the rich may not be found blameless and may also eventually come to ruin. While Ben Sira is not categorical in his denunciation of affluence or the rich, taken together with the biblical tradition, these passages demonstrate the developing and widely circulating ideas within the sapiential traditions material in the Second Temple period of the dangers of wealth and the absolute devotion required by those who pursue riches.

Wealth as the blessing of God

> Do not be amazed by the works of a sinner, but trust in the Lord and remain in your labour, for it is easy as the Lord sees it, suddenly, in an instant to make the poor man rich. God's blessing is the lot of the just and quickly God causes his blessing to flourish. (Sirach 11:21–2)

This text provides an example of Ben Sira's awareness of the issue of theodicy. Envy directed towards the wicked who prosper finds its

---

[41] Deut 27:25; Ecc 7:7; Prov 28:20; Isa 1:23.

background in the biblical tradition (Pss 37:1; 49:5–6; 73:3; Prov 3:31; 24:1, 19) and is discouraged (Pss 49:5–6; 73:3–19). The association of the rich with sinners reveals a wider tradition that is taken up in a more radical fashion in the *Epistle of Enoch*.[42] Ben Sira envisions a resolution in the present age in which the poor are 'suddenly' made rich. This is a sharp contrast to the *Epistle*, in which the wealthy are destroyed 'suddenly' in an eschatological reversal.[43] Moreover, both the righteous and heaven rejoice over the destruction of rich sinners in the *Epistle*, an idea that is absent in Ben Sira. These two traditions also differ remarkably in that the *Epistle* postpones the Deuteronomistic blessing for the faithful while Ben Sira maintains a theology of retribution in the present age. This is also attested in the following verse:

> Good and evil, life and death, poverty and wealth, are from the Lord.[44] The Lord's gift (δόσις) remains with the godly (εὐσεβής); his favour (εὐδοκία) brings lasting success.
>
> (Sirach 11:14, 17)

Asensio contends that the equivalencies in this passage are: good/life/ wealth and evil/death/poverty.[45] However, if they are to be taken as equivalents at all the more natural grouping would be: good/life/poverty and evil/death/wealth. This corresponds to other passages in which he attributes early death and demise to wrong attitudes and practices regarding wealth (Sir 18:30–19:1; 31:1–11). The more likely scenario is that he is providing three sets of contrasting circumstances that always exist in the present age. In the midst of these circumstances, Ben Sira's theology of retribution remains intact by asserting the material blessing of God for the just, while maintaining here, and in other passages, the fleeting riches of the wicked (Sir 5:8; 11:18–19; 18:30–19:3). More importantly, this language does not include any eschatological emphasis but relates only to the present.[46] The same is evident in the following passages:

---

[42] *1 Enoch* 94:6–10; 95:4–7; 96:4–8; 97:7–10; 98:2–3; 11–16; 99:1–2; 99:11–13; 100:4–9; 102:9–11.

[43] *1 Enoch* 94:1, 6–7; 95:6; 96:1, 6; 97:10; 99:9.

[44] MS A includes vv. 15–16, which are not extant in MS B or any other of the Hebrew MSS.

[45] Asensio, 'Poverty and Wealth', p. 165. If one is to take these as equivalent it should be as follows: good/life/poverty and evil/death/wealth. This corresponds also to other passages where Ben Sira attributes early death and demise to wrong attitudes and practices regarding wealth (Sir 18:30–19:1; 31:1–11).

[46] Skehan and Di Lella, *Wisdom of Ben Sira*, pp. 83–7. See also Di Lella, 'Conservative and Progressive Theology', pp. 143–6.

> Do not deprive yourself of present good things, and do not let
> your portion of good desires pass you by. Will you not leave what
> you acquired by hard work and labour to others to be divided
> by lot? Give, and take, and indulge yourself, *for in Hades there
> are no luxuries to seek*. All flesh grows old like a garment; and
> the eternal decree is, 'You will die!'   (Sirach 14:14–17)

The italicized text indicates that Ben Sira holds no expectation for any
rewards in the afterlife. Wealth is to be enjoyed, shared, and left behind.
There are no eschatological references to wealth and there is no vision
of a reversal of fortunes for the poor.

The Hebrew text reads שׁאול, which is translated in the Greek as ᾅδης.
It likewise states that there are no joys to seek in the netherworld but
further declares 'all is silent.' This understanding of the afterlife is also
present in Qoheleth, 'there is no work, thought, knowledge or wisdom
in Sheol' (Qoh 9:10). Thus, wealth is utterly useless anywhere but in the
present age. This reflects a sharp contrast with the Enochic tradition in
which all hope for material blessing for the faithful is only envisioned in
the coming age (*1 Enoch* 91:12–13).

> O death, how bitter is the thought of you to the one at peace
> among possessions (ἐν τοῖς ὑπάρχουσιν), who has nothing to
> worry about and is prosperous in everything and still is vigorous
> enough to enjoy food! O death how welcome is your sentence
> to one who is needy (ἐπιδέομαι) and failing in strength, worn
> down by age and anxious about everything.   (Sirach 41:1–3)

This passage also attests the lack of hope for material rewards after death.
Prosperity and security with one's position in life along with youth and
vitality will certainly cause death to be unwelcome. Yet the needy, the
aged, and those who are worrisome, see death as a welcome release from
the troubles of the present life. This is not because of some hope in
the afterlife but merely a release from their present circumstances. The
absence of any hope outside of the present life for any enjoyment is what
causes the prosperous to abhor death.

> [R]ich men supplied with resources, living peacefully in their
> homes – all these in their generations were extolled . . . But these
> were merciful men whose righteous deeds are not forgotten;
> after their offspring a good inheritance remains with their grand-
> children. Their offspring will continue forever, and their glory
> will not be wiped away.   (Sirach 44:6–7; 10–15)

This text demonstrates Ben Sira's positive outlook on wealth gained justly and maintained through a faithful lifestyle. This portrayal of the faithful life is the goal for Ben Sira's readers. Four key concepts are highlighted: (1) righteous deeds are remembered after death, (2) wealth and prosperity are passed on to their descendants, (3) the family line is perpetuated, and (4) one's reputation (name) lives on after death. Again we see that wealth is a feature only of the present age, though it can be used to perpetuate one's name after death by helping others in need in this life.

Summary of Wisdom of Ben Sira

Ben Sira offers a realistic, though complex look at life in relation to wealth and poverty. Though he speaks from a neutral perspective, he identifies two distinct social categories, the rich and the poor. Yet even within these categories distinctions are made. The analysis of the passages in Ben Sira that relate to poverty and wealth allow us to make the following conclusions. (1) Wealth in Ben Sira is not rejected but is viewed in light of Deuteronomistic theology. He clearly promotes a life of wealth as one preferable to poverty and expects the faithful to have material blessing (Sir 11:17; 14:16–17; 40:18, 25–26; 44:6–7). Though some may presently experience periods of relative deprivation, he holds out the expectation of the material blessing for the faithful. (2) Wealth is seen as a feature only of the present age. There is no expectation for material rewards in the afterlife nor is there any eschatological focus. (3) Although the faithful can expect the blessing of God, Ben Sira provides a distinct category of rich people that are explicitly described as wicked (Sir 8:1–2; 13:1–4, 24; 26:29–27:3; 31:1–11) and are referred to as 'the ungodly' and 'sinners' (Sir 10:22–3; 11:21–2; 13:17–20). This underscores Ben Sira's awareness of traditions that were circulating that associated riches with wickedness. It also indicates that he is aware of the disparate conditions of his day even among the community of the faithful.

This perception, taken together with his unwillingness to provide an explicit social critique for these circumstances, leads to a modified version of traditional Jewish wisdom that maintains a theology of retribution while simultaneously acknowledging the issue of theodicy. Unlike the *Epistle*, Ben Sira allows for the possibility that both the godly and ungodly can have wealth. And while the righteous may experience poverty the hope is maintained that God will reverse this situation in the present age, though no concrete resolution is provided.

3.2   *Mûsār lᵉMēvîn* (4QInstruction)

This document, known also as Sapiential Work A, *Instruction*, and 4QInstruction, is found in eight manuscripts from Qumran; one from cave 1, 1Q26, and seven from cave 4, 4Q415–4Q418, 4Q418a, 4Q418c and 4Q423.[47] Thus, the designation 4QInstruction is not fitting since it limits the document to the cave 4 material.[48] Two additional instruction-like manuscripts are also extant, 4Q419 and 4Q424, but do not add anything to the discussion of wealth and poverty in the present study. MS 4Q416 is the earliest as it is written in a late Hasmonean/early Herodian hand.[49] MSS 4Q415, 4Q417, 4Q418, and 4Q418a, c, are all early Herodian while 4Q423 is middle to late formal Herodian and is most likely the latest of the manuscripts with the exception of possibly 1QS.[50] Thus, the dates of these manuscripts vary from the middle of the first century BCE to very early first century CE. The cave 4 material does not provide any evidence of a developing tradition in *Mûsār lᵉMēvîn* such as we find in the Damascus Document (D) and Community Rule (S) traditions. A date for the document itself is difficult to determine, although Strugnell and Harrington, on the basis of tradition–historical considerations, place it between Proverbs and Sirach, noting it is a 'venerable missing link in the development of secular or common Israelite wisdom'.[51] Collins, however, states that it may be better understood as 'a missing link between the older Hebrew wisdom and the Hellenistic Wisdom of Solomon'.[52] Prior to the discoveries at Qumran, this document was unknown.

I have included *Mûsār lᵉMēvîn* among the non-sectarian Hebrew documents since it is generally not considered a production of the Qumran community.[53] While it may be sectarian in the sense that it

---

[47] See Tigchelaar, *To Increase Learning*. See also Elgvin, 'Sapiential Work A', pp. 559–80, who argues for seven manuscripts. So also Strugnell, et al., *Qumran Cave 4 XXXIV*, p. 1. In earlier studies Harrington noted only six manuscripts: *Wisdom Texts*, p. 40; 'Jewish Approaches to Wisdom', p. 123. Tigchelaar's study reflects the most recent and thorough examination of the evidence. Consequently, *Mûsār lᵉMēvîn* is attested in the same number of manuscripts as such pivotal texts as 4QMMT (6), *War Scroll* (8), and the *Hodayot* (7), and almost as many as *Damascus Document* (10). While this indicates the importance of *Mûsār lᵉMēvîn* to the Qumran community, it is not possible to know the reasons for its importance.

[48] *Mûsār lᵉMēvîn* is the Hebrew title of the document assigned by Strugnell, et al., the editors of *Qumran Cave 4 XXXIV*.

[49] *Ibid.*, p. 76.

[50] *Ibid.*, pp. 42, 146–7, 217, 476, 501, 506–7.   [51] *Ibid.*, p. 36.

[52] Collins, 'Mysteries of God', p. 304.

[53] See Tigchelaar, *To Increase Learning*, pp. 247–8; and 'The Addressees of 4QInstruction', pp. 74–5. Tigchelaar asserts the document 'is not sectarian, but of a more

derives from another Jewish sect and was merely collected and copied at Qumran, its inclusion here as non-sectarian is only in relation to the Qumran corpus. The document lacks any explicit reference to Torah (תרוה) but equates a 'body of teaching' with pre-existent wisdom, which was recorded before and reflected in the creation of the world (4Q417 1 i:13; 2 i:14–18).[54] Through study and contemplation one can obtain 'the mystery that is to be' (רז נהיה),[55] a term that occurs thirty-five times in the extant manuscripts.[56] This moves beyond traditional Jewish wisdom since it includes the revelation of divine knowledge to an elect group, yet lacks any mediatorial component or heavenly journey. At the same time, it contains a similar 'pedagogical ethos' of traditional sapiential material by emphasizing the acquisition of wisdom through study and contemplation.[57] Within the text, the fleshly spirit (רוח בשר) represents that group of humanity that once had access to the רז נהיה but because of their unwillingness to pursue it, it was taken away from them. The spiritual people (עם רוח) who now have access to this wisdom are encouraged to contemplate the רז נהיה and attain salvation by obtaining wisdom, which results in right ethical behaviour.

general nature'; Harrington, 'Wisdom at Qumran', pp. 137–52 notes the lack of any distinct sectarian terminology. See also Strugnell, 'Sapiential Work 4Q415 ff.', pp. 595–608; Strugnell, et al., *Qumran Cave 4 XXXIV*, pp. 22–30; Lange, *Weisheit und Prädestination*, p. 130 and 'Wisdom and Predestination', 341 n. 2. Lange argues its provenance is Palestinian Judaism. See Lange, 'In Diskussion mit dem Tempel', p. 157. So also, Frey, 'Flesh and Spirit', p. 400; Elgvin, 'The Evidence of 4QInstruction', p. 246. Collins also detects the similarities with sectarian texts but stops short of associating it with the Qumran community: *Seers, Sibyls and Sages*, p. 376. See also Puech, 'Apports des textes apocalyptiques', p. 165. Goff maintains the document is from a sectarian milieu, though not a product of Qumran: *Worldly and Heavenly Wisdom*, p. 227. Jeffries suggests it is a product of the Qumran community but in the context of the 'camps' of the *Damascus Document*: *Wisdom at Qumran*, p. 323. More recently Rey comes to the similar conclusion that the document is related to the Essenes, but not Qumran: *4QInstruction*, pp. 333–6. For a detailed discussion of the problems of placing *Mûsār lᵉ Mēvîn* in the Qumran sectarian corpus, see Wold, *Women, Men and Angels*, pp. 8–20. The present study agrees that the document is sectarian, though not related to the Qumran community.

[54] Lange, 'Wisdom and Predestination', pp. 342–3 equates this written wisdom with Torah. Elgvin argues that this is a written work distinct from the Torah, possibly the *Two Spirits Treatise* or the Book of Mysteries (Harrington, *Wisdom Texts*, p. 49). Collins, however, notes that it may simply be 'the subject matter to which each of these writings refers': 'Wisdom Reconsidered', p. 274.

[55] This phrase has been translated (1) 'the mystery to come', in Barthélemy and Milik, *Qumran Cave 1*, pp. 102–4 and Cryer and Thompson, *Qumran*, pp. 131–9; (2) 'the mystery of existence', in Eisenmann and Wise, *Dead Sea Scrolls Uncovered*, p. 252; and (3) 'the secret of the way things are', in Wise, et al., *Dead Sea Scrolls*, p. 381. Here I am following Collins, 'Wisdom Reconsidered', pp. 272–4.

[56] Harrington, 'The *raz nihyeh*', p. 550.

[57] Goff, 'Pedagogical Ethos of 4QInstruction', pp. 66–7.

The רז נהיה encompasses the entirety of time from creation to the final judgement. Thus the mevin is able to contemplate the natural world and written wisdom in order to learn the secrets of the last days in which the righteous will be blessed and the wicked will be judged. Yet, this salvation, or elect status, is portrayed in the sense that the mevin is promised salvation because of his elect status, but is admonished to obtain the רז נהיה so that this salvation might be consummated in the coming age. Thus the work reflects an inaugurated eschatology wherein 'all ethical behaviour is eschatological insofar as it represents the recovery of a state of fidelity to patterns with creation'.[58] In particular, it will be important to note how wealth is to be negotiated among the faithful (eschatological) community and whether or not it poses any threat to their salvation.

Wealth and wisdom

If the purse (כיס) containing your treasures (צפן) [you have] entrus[ted to your creditor, On account of your friends, you have giv]en away all your life with it. Hasten and give what is his, And take back [your] purse[, and in your speech (do not) act feeble-]spirited. For no amount of wealth (הון) exchange your holy spirit, for there is no price equal in value [to it].

(4Q416 2 ii:4b–7a)[59]

This passage deals with the common *topos* in sapiential literature of making pledges for others.[60] The biblical background is Prov 6:1–5, in which standing surety for a neighbour is discouraged. Ben Sira offers a more progressive approach by stating that a good person will provide surety, though it should be done with caution and within one's means (Sir 8:13; 29:14–20).[61] What is unique to *Mûsār leMēvîn* is the concern that standing surety in some way places the mevin in spiritual peril.

The term כיס refers to a money purse and taken together with צפן 'hidden things' indicates one's personal wealth. Standing surety for a friend is paralleled with exchanging one's holy spirit for wealth. The Hiphil form of מור has the meaning 'to exchange'.[62] In the Hebrew Bible it refers to things that are not to be sold or exchanged because they are holy

---

[58] Macaskill, *Revealed Wisdom*, p. 113.

[59] All translations in this section follow Strugnell, et al., *Qumran Cave 4 XXXIV*, except for minor adjustments into regular English and unless otherwise noted.

[60] Prov 6:1–5; 11:15; 17:18; 20:16; 22:26; 27:13; Sir 8:12–13; 1–7; 14–20.

[61] Harrington, 'Early Jewish Approaches', pp. 29–30.   [62] *HALOT*, vol. I, p. 560.

to the Lord (Lev 27:33; Ezek 48:14). In particular it is used in relation to חרם *herem* law (Lev 27:28–9).

The term מור is also associated with wicked Israel exchanging the glory of God for idols (Ps 106:20; Jer 2:11) and people changing their glory into shame (Hos 4:7). Elsewhere in *Mûsār lᵉMēvîn* restoration to glory is depicted in terms of an inaugurated eschatology wherein the mevin has been seated alongside angelic beings who are also seeking the wisdom of the רז נהיה (4Q416 2 iii:9–14):

> And if [] He restore to you your glory (כבד) walk *in it*
> and by the רז נהיה seek its origins/birth-times
> and then you will know its inheritance (נחל)...
> (11) for out of poverty he lifted your head
> and with the angels (נדיבים) he has seated you.[63]

The restoration to glory in the 'already' sense is equated with the mevin's elect status, which is viewed in the 'not yet' sense in connection with his 'inheritance', which reflects 'a heavenly form of wealth'.[64] In addition, the elect in *Mûsār lᵉMēvîn* who have access to the רז נהיה are referred to as the 'spiritual people' רוח עם (4Q417 1 i:16). Since the glory and inheritance become known by contemplation on the רז נהיה, what may be in mind here is a concern that economic issues such as loans, debts, or standing surety for a neighbour will be a distraction from obtaining wisdom and ultimately achieving salvation. By employing the term מור in connection with wealth, the writer would evoke ideas relating to both a proper dedication to God as well as the idea that wealth poses a risk to idolatry or is idolatry itself.

The mixture of both traditional sapiential and apocalyptic concerns over wealth are evident. On the one hand, in line with the biblical wisdom tradition, surety for a neighbour is discouraged. On the other hand, like the earlier Enochic traditions, the economic realm is one inherently dangerous. Although *Mûsār lᵉMēvîn* does not reject wealth or the rich categorically, it certainly sees it as an outside corrupting influence. This text also suggests that the recipients themselves may not have all experienced material poverty since the mevin apparently has enough money to stand surety for another. What is at stake is entering into a financial

---

[63] Translation follows Wold, 'Metaphorical Poverty', p. 147, in which he has altered Harrington's 'splendour' כבר and 'allotment' נחל (Strugnell, et al., *Qumran Cave 4 XXXIV*, p. 113). See here also his discussion of the term נדיבים as angels rather than nobles. See also Goff, *Worldly and Heavenly Wisdom*, pp. 209–10.

[64] Wold, 'Metaphorical Poverty', p. 147.

transaction that poses the threat of spiritual danger. The passage that follows provides additional clarity.

> [Do not se]ll your soul (נפש) for wealth (הון). It is good for you to become a servant in the spirit (רוח) and to serve your oppressors freely. But for [no] price [s]ell your glory (כבד) or pledge your inheritance (נחלה), lest it dispossess also your body.
>
> (4Q416 2 ii:17–18)

Here the mevin is admonished not to sell his soul for wealth. The term נפש refers to the inner person, the perceptions and desires of the human being.[65] The Deuteronomistic command to love God with all one's soul (נפש) (Deut 6:5; 10:12, 22; 11:13) may be in mind since elsewhere in *Mûsār lᵉMēvîn* it refers to keeping God's commands in one's heart (4Q417 2 i:9). It also relates to losing inner peace over money owed to another (4Q417 2 i:22) indicating that the desire for wealth is viewed as both a hindrance to attaining wisdom in the present age and devotion to God (cf. *ALD* 13:10–15).

Murphy takes this language literally as selling one's self into servitude and understands inheritance language as a reference to land or movable property since she envisions an agricultural society.[66] However, this reading leaves the question of selling one's glory unanswered. Like the previous passage, glory and inheritance are synonymous for the elect status of the mevin and reflect the not yet component of the document's inaugurated eschatology.[67] Goff maintains this is an admonition against unwise economic situations such as loans or standing surety.[68] However, the preposition ב, which should be taken here as 'for' wealth (cf. Ps 44:13) points to a general warning against pursuing wealth *rather than* the רז נהיה. There is nothing in the immediate context that indicates loans or other financial transactions are in mind, though this cannot be ruled out altogether. Rather, the lines that follow speak specifically against revelling in luxury and overindulgence.

Becoming a servant in spirit may refer to taking on a marginalized status in order to avoid the compulsion to seek after wealth since this has eschatological consequences. Similar language occurs elsewhere relating to improper contact with wealth (4Q416 2 iii:4; 4Q418 103 ii:9). In what may be a reference to the Deuteronomistic blessings and curses, one fragment mentions the body being eaten by wild animals (4Q418 127:3

---

[65] *NIDOTTE*, vol. III, p. 133; *HALOT* vol. I, p. 713.

[66] Murphy, *Wealth in the Dead Sea Scrolls*, p. 186.

[67] Goff, *Worldly and Heavenly Wisdom*, p. 164.   [68] *Ibid.*

cf. Deut 32:24). Though it is very fragmented, this text, along with other eschatological references of judgement, shows that the expectation of material blessing may have been reshaped to the degree that the future inheritance is that reward and thus has been postponed. While this idea is ambiguous, what is evident is that wealth is a hindrance to the acquisition of the רז נהיה and that a life of servitude is to be preferred. The physical destruction of those who seek after wealth in the present age is already attested in the Enochic tradition (*1 Enoch* 94:7–9; 97:8–10). Ben Sira also speaks of the person who pursues wealth and luxury as experiencing ruin (Sir 8:2; 11:18–19; 19:1–2). Though these traditions treat these ideas in different ways, they reflect a wider tradition that views affluence as an inherent danger to faithfulness.

> Remember that you are poor . . . [If a deposit/loan] has been deposited with you do not lay your hand on it lest your hand be scorched [And] your body be burned by its fire . . . Moreover, from any man whom you have not known take no wealth (הון) lest he/it increase your poverty (רוש). And if he put the responsibility of it (i.e., of the debt) on your head, Until death take charge of it, But do not let your spirit (רוח) be corrupted by it.
>
> (4Q416 2 iii:2–7)

The reminder that the recipients are poor is one of many in this document (4Q415 6:2; 4Q416 2 ii:20; 2 iii:2, 8, 12, 19). While previous scholars have considered the possibility of the metaphorical use of poverty in *Mûsār lᵉMēvîn*,[69] it has been argued most convincingly in a recent study by Benjamin Wold.[70] Aitken considered whether poverty is metaphorical, suggesting that there was a growing interest in the role of poverty among the faithful as a condition that would be reversed in God's deliverance.[71] Thus he recognized the eschatological aspect of the theme. Murphy and Goff both take the language of poverty as a description of the social circumstances of the recipients.[72] The former acknowledges the figurative use of economic terms in the document, though she does not allow the possibility that poverty is employed in this way.[73] Goff considers various uses for the language of wealth: (1) metaphorically as a spiritual

[69] Harrington, 'Early Jewish Approaches', p. 29; Aitken, 'Apocalyptic', pp. 184–5.

[70] Wold, 'Metaphorical Poverty', pp. 140–53.

[71] Aitken, 'Apocalyptic', pp. 184–5. Cf. *Tg.* Hab. 3:2; *Tg.* Mic. 7:14.

[72] Murphy, *Wealth in the Dead Sea Scrolls*, pp. 171–4; Goff, *Worldly and Heavenly Wisdom*, p. 129; See also Wright, in Collins, et al., *Sapiential Perspectives*, pp. 122–3.

[73] Murphy does acknowledge one instance of metaphorical poverty in 4Q416 1:5–6: *Wealth in the Dead Sea Scrolls*, p. 168.

inheritance, and (2) literally in reference to loans and debt, yet does not allow the same for poverty. Tigchelaar argues that the phrase 'you are poor' is conditional, 'if you are poor'.[74] However, as Wold states, 'poverty is a pervasive theme throughout *Mûsār lᵉMēvîn*, not just in the phrase 'you are poor', and does not appear to be merely a possibility'.[75] He argues that poverty is understood as the weakness of the human condition in obtaining wisdom of the רז נהיה.

The spiritual people עם רוח are able to obtain the רז נהיה, though their human state limits them, a condition that is described as poverty or want.[76] Angels, on the other hand, are portrayed as role models for those pursuing the רז נהיה because they do not grow weary or weak in their pursuit.[77] This may be due to the fact that they are spirit beings and not both flesh and spirit. In either case, a metaphorical reading of poverty in some instances of *Mûsār lᵉMēvîn* provides a better explanation for the problem of wealth increasing one's poverty.

Abegg translates פקד as something 'valuable', though its meaning is disputed.[78] In the first phrase, 'lest he/it increase your poverty', it is difficult to determine whether the person giving the money increases the mevin's poverty or whether it is the money itself. However, in the second phrase, 'but do not let your spirit be corrupted by it', בו refers back to הון rather than the one giving the money.[79] Thus receiving wealth increases poverty because it distracts humans from seeking the רז נהיה.

The expectation of the present age

> [B]ut if you are in poverty (חסר), for what you need borrow without having wealth, for [His] treasure house (אצר) lacks (חסר) nothing . . . [*According to*] His command will everything come into being; And that which he gives you for food eat it, and do not [sc. *eat*] any more Le[st *by your gluttony* you shorten] your life. If you borrow the wealth of men in your poverty, [you will have] no [quietness] day or night, and no rest for your soul [until] you restore to your creditor [what you owe].   (4Q417 2 i:19–22)

74 Tigchelaar, 'Addressees of 4QInstruction', pp. 62–75.
75 Wold, 'Metaphorical Poverty', p. 144.
76 *Ibid.*, p. 153; See also Tigchelaar, 'Spiritual People', pp. 103–18.
77 Stuckenbruck, 'Limits of Early Jewish Monotheism', p. 65.
78 *HALOT*, vol. II, p. 955.
79 Strugnell, et al., *Qumran Cave 4 XXXIV*, pp. 115–16.

This text represents an instance where poverty is used in both literal and metaphorical senses. The second half of the text mentions loans and the necessity of repayment. The lack of sleep day and night may indicate the burden that the impediment places on the borrower. The phrase 'day and night' should be contrasted with the admonition to meditate on the רז נהיה day and night (4Q417 1 i:6; cf. Josh 1:8; Ps 1:2) indicating again that wealth, whether in the case of a loan or a gift, is a distraction from devotion to God.[80]

The first half of the passage reflects a metaphorical reference to gaining wisdom. The one who has need is not to borrow wealth but to draw on God's storehouse of hidden wisdom. Elsewhere the wisdom of the רז נהיה is also alluded to as a storehouse (אוצר) (4Q418 81+81a:9). A similar tradition is attested in *ALD* 13:12–14 in which wisdom resides in 'treasure houses' (אוצרות) and those seeking after wisdom will not lack (חסר). While direct dependence between these traditions cannot be established, it may denote conversation with a wider tradition that viewed speculative wisdom as something kept in God's storehouse and those who had access to this knowledge were not in need or lacking.

The contrast is meant to demonstrate the superiority of wisdom over material wealth. On the one hand, the רז נהיה that resides in God's storehouse lacks nothing. On the other hand, seeking help from humans in the form of material wealth only increases one's inability to successfully obtain the רז נהיה, which is to be pursued day and night, because they are preoccupied with repayment of their debts.

> For what is more insignificant than a poor man? So do not rejoice when you should mourn, lest you have trouble in life. [Gaze upon the mystery] that is to be and comprehend the birth-times of salvation and know who is to inherit glory (כבד) and trouble (עמל). Has not [rejoicing been appointed for the contrite of spirit] and for those who mourn eternal joy?
>
> (4Q417 2 i:10–12a)[81]

By contemplating the רז נהיה the faithful can learn that those who are contrite and mourn are the ones who inherit eternal glory. Glory and inheritance are equivalent to the mevin's elect status and reflect a form of

---

[80] Though the reading in the latter reference is a reconstruction. See discussion *ibid.*, p. 157.

[81] This text finds a parallel in 4Q418 77:2–4:[] mystery that is to come and grasp the nature of [m]an and gaze on the prosperi[ty] [and the punishment of] his [ac]tivity; then you will discern the judgement on mankind and the weighing [].

future heavenly wealth. Thus, poverty is the antithesis of this inheritance, which elsewhere he has been admonished not to exchange for material wealth.[82] What is clear from the present passage is that the expectation of the righteous in the present age is one of humility, mourning, and seeking wisdom in contrast to the pursuit of wealth, while the language of inheritance and blessing is yet future.

> [L]ike a spring of living water that contains go[odn]ess [. . . from] your merchandise (מסחורכה) do not mingle (ת[רוב]) . . . lest it become a case of forbidden mixtures like the mule, and you will become like a garment of wool and flax mingled; or your work might be like one who ploughs with an ox yoked to a donkey; or your produce might be [to you] like one who sows improper mixtures, of which the seed and the full yield and the produce of [the vineyard] should be holy . . . your money () with your body and [even] your life, all will perish together, and in your life you will not find it.   (4Q418 103 ii:6–9)

The background for the instruction regarding proper mixtures is found in Lev 19:19 and Deut 22:9. Murphy and Goff both view this passage in relation to farmers who are instructed on how to properly plant and harvest their crops according to the biblical tradition.[83] However, neither offers sufficient answers for why the injunction includes wealth or why the final line speaks in terms of one perishing along with their possessions. On the latter point, it is not clear whether Murphy agrees with Strugnell and Harrington's assertion that this may refer to Egyptian burial practices or whether it is meant to be taken proverbially as 'you can't take it with you'.[84] Neither suggestion is completely satisfactory. Goff thinks it refers to the temporal nature of wealth in view of the eternal inheritance.[85] While this idea is expressed elsewhere in the document, the possibility that this could reflect some sense of sectarian practice of separation has not been seriously considered. While it is possible that the addressees may have included farmers and landowners, it is problematic to reconstruct a socio-historical setting from such a fragmented text. Moreover, Murphy's and Goff's position that poverty is to be taken literally overall is problematic if the addressees are actually landowners.

[82] Goff, *Worldly and Heavenly Wisdom*, pp. 150, 164.

[83] *Ibid.*, 147–8; Murphy, *Wealth in the Dead Sea Scrolls*, pp. 204–6.

[84] Murphy, *Wealth in the Dead Sea Scrolls*, p. 205.

[85] Goff, *Worldly and Heavenly Wisdom*, p. 150.

The only imperative in the passage warns against mixing merchandise (סחר), and the use of simile ('*like*' כ) indicates that the biblical models are not to be taken literally but only serve as examples. Thus, the writer is developing the biblical tradition to include an injunction on commercial trade. The term for merchandise (סחר) occurs twenty-eight times in the Hebrew Bible and in every instance it refers to merchants, their merchandise, or the act of trading.[86] Thus, it frequently occurs as a technical term for commercial activity.[87] With this in mind, since the document can be situated within a sectarian milieu,[88] and given its popularity within the Qumran community and the separatist economic system they developed, a similar sectarian concern over economic activity between the faithful and outsiders may be expressed here. This same apprehension over commercial activity is also levelled in Ben Sira in which he finds little possibility of buying and selling without incurring guilt (Sir 27:2). Other passages allude to the possible results that such a withdrawal from the wider economic system may have produced:

> And if you lack food in your poverty, then your surpluses [bring
> in together].   (4Q417 2 i:17)

This text may attest a very early indication of communal goods in the case of some who may have been lacking in food. Poverty here can also be taken metaphorically to refer to the elect status of the spiritual people and their pursuit of wisdom. In that case, the question becomes, what would cause a lack of food? If it is possible to understand this as a concern over economic activity with outsiders, the fleshly people, then these conditions would derive from an economic withdrawal from the larger system. Elsewhere, the mevin is warned against selling his soul for wealth and pledging his inheritance (4Q416 2 ii:17–18). In the same context he is encouraged to serve his oppressors freely. Withdrawal from the economic system would certainly cause some degree of oppression.

Even if the language is taken literally to refer to farmers, the issue of mingling merchandise in trade must still be dealt with since the biblical tradition offers no such injunction. Whether we can say the document encourages economic withdrawal must be considered as a separate issue. However, what we can know is that it reflects a sectarian mindset, though

---

[86] Gen 37:28; Isa 23:2–3, 8; 47:15; Jer 14:18; Ezek 27:36; 38:16; 1 Kgs 10:28; 2 Chr 1:16; 9:14. Prov 3:14; 31:14, 18; Isa 23:18; 45:14. Gen 23:16; 34:10, 21; 42:34; Ezek 27:12, 16, 18, 21.

[87] *HALOT*, vol. I, p. 750; *NIDOTTE*, vol. III, pp. 242–3.

[88] Goff, *Worldly and Heavenly Wisdom*, p. 227.

not that of the *Yaḥad*, and that it demonstrates a concern that wealth and certain commercial transactions become a distraction from the reception of the wisdom of the רז נהיה and ultimately obedience to God.

3.3   *Two Spirits Treatise* (1QS 3:13–4:26)

This document is attested in the Qumran sectarian manuscript of the *Community Rule* (1QS 3:13–4:26).[89] It is included here under the heading of non-sectarian Hebrew documents because it is not regarded as a production of the Qumran community.[90] It is also attested in 4Q255, which is comprised of four fragments, which may have contained a shorter, alternative version.[91] MS 4Q257 consists of two small fragments that also contain variants.[92] 4Q255 is dated between 125 and 100 BCE. while 4Q257 is dated between 100 and 75 BCE.[93]

TST contains both cosmic and ethical dualism, the former being reflected in the Prince of Light and the Angel of Darkness, which correspond to the spirit of truth and the spirit of wickedness, respectively. The latter relates to the degree to which humans demonstrate the operations of these spirits in their deeds. Compassion, humility, purity, and truth characterize those who share in the lot of the righteous, while greed, wickedness, lying, and pride are the marks of the wicked. Interestingly, the work demonstrates that the sons of light also seem to be characterized at times by the same deeds as the children of darkness. According to TST, God created humanity and placed within them the spirit of truth and the spirit of wickedness (1QS 3:17–18). Each person has a predetermined share of these spirits, one or the other being dominant. Furthermore, humanity is under the authority of two cosmic forces: the Prince of Light, who has governance and authority over all righteous people (1QS 3:20) and the Angel of Darkness, who rules over the wicked. However, in the present age, God has allowed the authority of the Angel of Darkness to extend over the righteous as well (1QS 3:21–3). Consequently,

---

[89]   1QS is treated individually in section 4.2, below.

[90]   See Lange, *Weisheit und Prädestination*, pp. 121–6, who argues convincingly that this is a non-Qumran document. See also Metso, *Textual Development*, p. 113; Frey, 'Patterns of Dualistic Thought', pp. 275–335.

[91]   Metso, *Textual Development*, p. 91. For discussions concerning the redaction and/or development of TST, see Licht, 'Analysis', pp. 88–9; Puech, *La croyance des Esséniens*, pp. 430–2. Both Licht and Puech argue for literary unity. See also Peter von der Osten-Sacken, *Gott und Belial*, pp. 17–18; Duhaime, 'L'instruction sur les deux esprits', pp. 572–94, who discuss the development of the text. The present study takes the final form of the text as preserved in 1QS as a literary unit.

[92]   See Tigchelaar, 'These are the Names', pp. 531–47.   [93]   *Ibid.*, p. 546.

their iniquity and sinful actions are attributed to his prompting. This explanation for the sinful actions of the faithful resolves a serious theological problem among the Qumran sect, the difficulty of visibly distinguishing the righteous from the wicked. The incorporation of this tradition into the *Community Rule* reveals their concern over the visible character of the faithful over against their opponents.[94] For this reason the community looks forward to the eschatological visitation when God will purify his people and they will become 'unambiguously perfect participants of the covenant for which they are chosen'.[95]

While TST maintains that the division of the righteous and wicked will not be fully realized until the end of the age, there is still some indication that they can be distinguished in a visible manner. The spirit that predominates within a person becomes evident in their overall lifestyle (1QS 4:26). What is important for the present study is the eschatological hope for the righteous that includes a reference to future blessing.

> Through a gracious visitation all who walk in this spirit will know healing, bountiful peace, long life, and multiple progeny, followed by eternal blessings and perpetual joy through life everlasting. They will receive a crown of glory with a robe of honour, resplendent forever and ever. (1QS 4:6–8)[96]

TST and *Mûsār lᵉMēvîn* share a similar expectation of an eschatological blessing for the faithful.[97] On the one hand, TST is like *Mûsār lᵉMēvîn* in that this is the realization of the mevin's elect status in which he receives glory and eternal joy. On the other hand, it reflects a more traditional understanding of the promise of material blessing in the Deuteronomistic tradition. Here the righteous are promised healing, length of days, and multiple progeny, all language found in the Deuteronomistic blessings (Deut 28:4, 27, 35; 30:16, 20; 32:39). Thus, this passage is important for the present study in that it attests a wider circulation of a postponement of reward into a future age (cf. *1 Enoch* 91:12). Its inclusion in the sectarian *Community Rule* is important for understanding the basis for how the Qumran community negotiates wealth among its members.

---

[94] See Stuckenbruck, 'Wisdom and Holiness', p. 59.

[95] Frey, 'Patterns of Dualistic Thought', p. 294.

[96] Translation follows *DSSR*, vol. IV, p. 273.

[97] See Lange, 'Wisdom and Predestination', pp. 347–8. He contends that these traditions were written within the same milieu. For a detailed discussion of this thesis, see Lange, *Weisheit und Prädestination*, pp. 121–70 (esp. 128–9). See also Goff, *Worldly and Heavenly Wisdom*, pp. 119–20.

4

DEAD SEA SCROLLS: SECTARIAN HEBREW DOCUMENTS

4.1 *Damascus Document* (DD)

DD[1] is found in two medieval manuscripts known as CD-A and CD-B, which were found in the Cairo Genizah towards the end of the nineteenth century.[2] Manuscript CD-A is the fullest version, while CD-B offers pages 19–20, the former (19) having some overlap with CD-A 7–8, and the latter (20) having no equivalent in CD-A.[3] It is also attested in ten manuscripts from the caves of Qumran (4Q266–73; 5Q12; 6Q15).[4] Six of the manuscripts (4Q267–4Q270, 4Q272, 4Q273) are written in Herodian script, which dates them paleographically somewhere between the late first century BCE (30–1) and early first century CE (1–30).[5] 4Q271 is dated to the mid to late first century BCE (50–30). 4Q266 is the oldest and the longest manuscript from cave 4 and is written in a Hasmonean semi-cursive hand dating it paleographically to around the first half of the first century BCE (100–50).[6] This manuscript provides the beginning and the end of the genizah texts, which are attested in 4Q266 1–2 and 4Q266 11, respectively. 5Q12 is dated from the mid to late first century BCE, while 6Q15 is early to mid first century CE. Thus, the Qumran materials demonstrate a tradition that covers almost 200 years.[7]

---

[1] When referring to the *Damascus Document* as a tradition, the abbreviation DD is used. The initials CD refer only to the *Cairo Genizah* manuscripts. CD is cited primarily with a list of parallels from the cave 4 manuscripts. Where there are reconstructions, they are noted.

[2] These genizah manuscripts were originally referred to as *Fragments of a Zadokite Work*, in Schechter, *Documents of Jewish Sectarians*.

[3] Milik, *Ten Years of Discovery*, pp. 38–9, 152.

[4] 5Q12 and 6Q15 were published in Baillet, Milik, and de Vaux, *Les 'Petites Grottes' de Qumrân*, vol. I, pp. 128–31, 181.

[5] See Table 1 in Murphy, *Wealth in the Dead Sea Scrolls*, p. 28.

[6] Baumgarten, *Damascus Document*, vol. XVIII, p. 26. See also Milik, *Ten Years of Discovery*, pp. 38–9.

[7] Murphy, *Wealth in the Dead Sea Scrolls*, p. 27.

The document is generally divided into two sections: (1) admonitions, and (2) regulations. The pages containing the admonitions are 1–8, 19–20 and the regulations are found in pages 15–16 and 9–14, respectively.[8] The admonitions provide the framework for the present circumstances of the Damascus community by giving a historical recounting of the past, locating where the wicked went astray, and establishing how and why the faithful community was chosen as the elect (3:11–15). The disobedient are referred to as 'those who follow their own wilful heart' (שרירות לבם ויתורו אחרי). This, of course, is set in contrast to those in the camps, to whom God has revealed hidden things; these follow 'the desire of His will' (וחפצי רצונו).[9] The dualistic world view that shapes the admonitions sets the stage for the regulations in which the innocent and the guilty are clearly demarcated. Murphy has rightly noted that texts dealing with wealth are included in almost every generic category of the document. Moreover, within these categories, wealth issues are present at every redactional stage demonstrating 'a consistent interest in the disposition of wealth across time'.[10] This decided concern over wealth is one means by which the community formed its identity and created boundaries with outsiders.

Economic identity

[W]hen that happens of which it is written by Zechariah the prophet, Awake, O sword, upon my shepherd and upon the man (who is) close to me, – God says – strike the shepherd so the sheep will be scattered, and I will turn my hand to the little ones (צערים). Those who guard it (the precept) are the poor of the sheep (עניי הצאן). They will escape at the time of the visitation. But those who remain will be handed over to the sword when the Messiah of Aaron and Israel comes.   (CD-B 19:7–11)[11]

The Damascus community's self-identification as 'the little ones' highlights the degree to which its identity was grounded in economic terms. The imagery of scattering sheep is a citation from Zech 13:7, which contextually refers to God dispersing his people in order to purify for himself a remnant. The phrase 'the poor of the sheep' (עניי הצאן) is taken from Zech 11:7–11 in which a faithful remnant is also in view. The LXX

---

[8] Milik, *Ten Years of Discovery*, pp. 38–9, 151–2 n. 3.   [9] CD 3:15–16.

[10] Murphy, *Wealth in the Dead Sea Scrolls*, p. 32.

[11] All translations of *Damascus Document* are taken from *DSSHAG*.

renders the latter phrase εἰς τὴν Χαναανῖτιν. This is a result of a misreading of the Hebrew לכן עניי הצאן as לכנעניי הצאן,[12] which is translated 'sheep merchant'.[13] Thus, the NRSV reads, 'on behalf of the sheep merchants, I became shepherd of the flock'. Given the context of affliction through slavery (Zech 11:4–5), and the misreading of the LXX, the preferred reading is 'I became shepherd of the poor of the sheep'.[14]

Murphy contends that their identity as 'the poor' may have developed as a result of some form of economic oppression from outsiders. However, there is no indication within the document or from a reconstruction of the historical setting that can substantiate this argument. Each member of the community was responsible to give two days' wages to the common fund each month. This, it is argued, was the community's version of the Temple tax whereby it served as a social alternative to the responsibilities of the Temple that were presently being neglected.[15] Part of the community's function was to care for the poor and needy (עני ואביון) (CD 6:21; 14:14). More importantly, this indicates that members worked, earned money, and were held stringently accountable for reporting their income (CD 14:20). The ability to give two days' wages each month is evidence that they were not destitute. Other passages suggest that at least some of the members owned slaves and livestock (CD 12:8–10; 4Q267 9 iii:4; 4Q271 5 ii:2–4), which further indicates that some may have even been landowners. The communal assets of the Damascus covenanters would have collectively represented a large amount of wealth, relative to the number of members. In view of these apparent assets of the community members, taken together with the extensive critiques of the Temple cult, which they viewed as greedy and corrupt (CD 4:12–19; 6:14–17), the self-designation of 'the poor' functions as an identity marker rather than a description of their economic circumstances. The Damascus community took a voluntary position of marginalization in order to gain a voice in the dominant religious discourse as the faithful remnant of God.

> [T]o separate themselves from the sons of the pit and to refrain from the wicked wealth (which is) impure due to oath(s) and dedication(s) (חרם), and to (being) the wealth of the sanctuary,

---

[12] *HALOT*, vol. I, p. 856.

[13] Hos 12:7; Prov 31:24; Job 40:30; Ezek 17:4; Zeph 1:11. See Meyers and Meyers, *Zechariah 9–14*, pp. 261–2; Smith, *Micah – Malachi*, p. 268.

[14] So NET, NIV, NLT, TNIV. See Foster, 'Shepherds, Sticks, and Social Destabilization', pp. 735–53.

[15] Davies, *Damascus Covenant*, pp. 136–40; See also Murphy, *Wealth in the Dead Sea Scrolls*, pp. 76–9, who contends that the community views itself as an alternative to the Temple.

(for) they (the sons of the pit) steal from the poor of his people, preying upon widows and murdering orphans.

(CD 6:14b–17a)

The wealth of the opponents is made impure by means of a breach of חרם law, which is a critique of the leadership of the Jerusalem temple cult.[16] There are two kinds of חרם attested in the Hebrew Bible, voluntary and mandatory. The former refers to offerings and tithes for the priesthood and is initiated by man (Lev 27:28; Num 18:14; Ezek 44:29). These items dedicated to God cannot be placed back into common use. In the case that dedicated חרם is used, the person and the object both become mandatory חרם, which is initiated by God and represents things set apart for destruction (Lev 27:29; Deut 7:26; 13:17; Josh 6:18; 7:13).[17] In the context of wealth, it is likely that the Damascus community viewed the Temple leadership's handling of devoted wealth as a violation of חרם law.[18]

The threefold reference to the poor, widows, and orphans in this text alludes to Isaiah 10:2. It also recalls language from the Deuteronomistic tradition in which a curse is promised for those who neglect widows and orphans (Deut 27:19). This may be further evidence that the Temple leadership was using money devoted for the care of the poor for personal or otherwise questionable purposes (2 Macc 3:9–12). More importantly, the text exhibits heightened language that exploits the consequences of these actions in terms of robbery, murder, and preying on widows (cf. Mark 12:40; Luke 20:47). We cannot know the degree to which all of the claims made against the opponents could be maintained. What we can know is that the Damascus community found the handling of wealth by the Jerusalem Temple leadership objectionable. By emphasizing their own covenant fidelity and acting as a surrogate for properly carrying out the responsibilities of the Temple (CD 6:21; 14:14), they underscore the degree to which the greed of their opponents has become a hindrance to proper devotion to God. As a response, they harshly calumniate their opponents and distinguish themselves in terms that denote their rejection of affluence in spite of their own economic wellbeing.

---

[16] Murphy asserts that this phrase is to be read in light of the Aramaic economic term מנקרה based on certain Idumean Ostraca from the fourth century BCE that refer to 'pits' that are communal storage places for grain, *Wealth in the Dead Sea Scrolls*, pp. 76–7, 373–9. Baumgarten, on the other hand, transcribes 'iniquity' [העו]ל (*Damascus Document*, vol. XVIII, p. 41). The only occurrence in the Hebrew Bible that resembles the phrase בני השחת is in Isaiah 1:4 in reference to 'children who act corruptly' (בנים משחיתים).

[17] For a discussion of mandatory and voluntary חרם in the Hebrew Bible, see Park, *Finding Herem?*, pp. 49–52.

[18] Murphy, *Wealth in the Dead Sea Scrolls*, pp. 76–7; Park, *Finding Herem?*, p. 79.

> When his (the dissenter's) works become apparent, according to
> the interpretation of the Torah, in which walk the men of perfect
> holiness, let no man share (יאות) with him in wealth (הון) or in
> labour.   (CD 20:6–7)

This passage reflects a later interpolation into the document at a time when
the community was either experiencing some degree of apostasy or had a
fear of subversiveness.[19] The injunction against agreeing with dissenters
in wealth refers to the position the community took in relation to economic
activity with one another and demonstrates the degree to which wealth
was a primary boundary marker between the community and outsiders.
Members were not allowed to buy and sell among themselves but could
only trade by means of barter.[20] Once dissenters are marked as outsiders
they can no longer share in communal property and lose their place in
the economic life of the community.

Wealth as peril

The language of wealth in DD also functions to warn the members against
competing affections that lead one astray from complete loyalty both to
the community and to God. This is accomplished in the admonitions by
portraying the present age as a time of wickedness in which wealth is a
trap set by Belial.

> But during all those years, Belial will run unbridled amidst
> Israel, as God spoke through the hand of the prophet Isaiah,
> son of Amoz, saying, 'Fear and a pit and a snare are upon you
> O inhabitant(s) of the land.' This refers to the three nets of
> Belial, of which Levi, the son of Jacob, said that he (Belial)
> entrapped Israel with them, making them seem as if they were
> three types of righteousness. The first is unchastity, the second
> wealth (הון),[21] and the third, a defilement of the sanctuary. He
> who escapes from this is caught by that and he who is saved by
> that is caught by this.   (CD 4:12b–19a)

[19] Davies, *Damascus Covenant*, pp. 181–6.   [20] CD 13:14–15.

[21] Charlesworth's translation reads 'arrogance' החין. Murphy agrees with this reading
arguing that the second net is explained in CD 5:11–16, *Wealth in the Dead Sea Scrolls*,
pp. 38–40. Murphy's proposal is not without warrant since the manuscript does read החין.
Some caution should be expressed, however, in her suggestion that 'waws and yods in CD
are clearly distinguished'. There are instances where *yods* are not distinguishable from
waws. In addition, the term חין 'arrogance' is not attested elsewhere in CD or any other
manuscripts from Qumran. הון, however, is used extensively in CD and always refers to
material wealth.

This pesher of Isa 24:17 highlights the inevitable fate of the wicked in escaping the precarious traps of Belial, which have the appearance of righteousness. The first and third nets are explicated in the text that follows, though there is no mention of the second.[22] The absence of any explanation for the trap of wealth reveals an already shared sense of understanding among the community that (1) the opponents were identified primarily by their avarice, and that (2) affluence was not a feature of the present age for the faithful. The wealth of the opponents would have reflected a visible sign of God's favour in terms of the Deuteronomistic tradition and thus the pesher serves to demonstrate that, while it may appear that they are the recipients of covenant blessing, it is in reality demonic (cf. *1 Enoch* 96:4). This perspective on the present age as an extended time when God allows wickedness to reign and distinguishes more clearly between the wicked and the faithful agrees with the cosmology and eschatology of the early Enochic traditions.[23]

As we have seen in previous passages, the *Damascus Document* does not denigrate wealth per se, but rejects the pursuit of wealth that comes at the expense of faithfulness to God, as demonstrated by the corrupt leadership of the Jerusalem Temple. It regards faithfulness to God as a priority over the individual pursuit of affluence. In effect, while the community itself possesses wealth, it plays down its importance and favours an existence of relative deprivation among its members. This reflects the community's understanding of the future eschatological age when wealth will be available to the faithful, but greed and status based on individual wealth will not be present. Thus, it does not reject a Deuteronomistic theology of wealth, but in light of a perceived perversion by others, recognizes its postponement, and seeks to express in the present age what will be realized in the eschaton.

> [The o]ne who [li]es about money (ממון) knowingly shall be [*separat*]*ed from the purity* [for one year] [and shall be pu]nished for six days.   (CD 14:20)[24]

Murphy rightly notes that the punishment for lying about wealth stands at the beginning of the penal codes of both the D and S traditions,

---

[22] Collins, *Seers, Sibyls and Sages*, p. 240.

[23] A similar perspective can be detected in the Aramaic Targums in which there is a developing sense that the present age has been extended and the wicked are distinguished by their failure to worship God (*Tg.* Hab. 3:2; *Tg.* Mic. 7:12–16).

[24] This passage is reconstructed from CD 14, 4Q266 (italics) and 1QS (bracket-underlined). For a discussion of the textual reconstruction, see Murphy, *Wealth in the Dead Sea Scrolls*, p. 53.

indicating it was either the most frequent point of contention within the community or reflected the 'most concrete symbol of behavioural fidelity'.[25] She further contends that the lack of any similar prohibition in the penal codes of Greco-Roman associations points to a background in Jewish traditions that give priority to economic ethics and establish the acquisition of wisdom as the basis for eschatological judgement.[26] Thus, the community behind DD, in that sense, does not emphasize the future reward of covenant blessing so much as it seeks to establish itself as a community that embodies life in anticipation of the eschatological age. This expression includes the equal distribution of assets among the faithful and categorically rejects the individual accumulation of wealth. This is seen more clearly in their internal economic practices:

> None of those who have entered the covenant of God shall buy from or sel[l] to the Sons of Dawn; rather, (let them give) from hand to hand.[[27]] Let no man do anything involving buying and selling without informing the Examiner of the camp.
>
> (CD 13:14–15)

This injunction establishes a system of barter and most likely arises out of concern for unscrupulous business practices. Traditions were already circulating that provide little hope that honesty can be maintained in economic transactions (Sir 27:2) and this regulation would prevent one member from profiting from another. Moreover, such painstaking processes to prevent the elevation of one member over another in terms of economic status demonstrates that it is within the economic realm that the community thought that the ideal expression of faithfulness to God could be compromised.

This is also evident in the need for the Examiner of the camps to supervise economic transactions with outsiders. Throughout the admonitions the community is warned about the wicked wealth of outsiders and the defiled wealth of the Temple. If they are to take seriously the condemnation of their opponents, the Overseer must evaluate economic transactions to make sure defiled wealth does not enter the community. Moreover, it prevents members from being tempted to make unscrupulous deals with outsiders and in effect become like them. This exclusiveness provides the community with a sense of power and validation of their piety and

[25] *Ibid.*   [26] *Ibid.*, i.e. *Epistle of Enoch.*

[27] See *DSSHAG*, vol. II, p. 55, n. 203. Rabin provides the following translation: 'And let no man of all the members of the covenant of God trade with the children of the pit, except for cash' (Rabin, *Zadokite Documents*, p. 66). However, see Baumgarten, 'The Sons of Dawn', 81–5, who argues convincingly for the rendering adopted above.

functions further to denigrate their enemies who claim their economic success is a visible sign of covenant fidelity even though they lack obedience and commitment to God.

Other passages in the regulations seem to indicate that some in the community behind the *Damascus Document* were engaged in the practice of acquiring wealth and unjust gain (הון ובצע). Five times in DD wealth (הון) and profit (בצע) are mentioned together, twice in the admonitions, one in an earlier recension (8:7), one later (19:19), and three times in the regulations. The term הון is primarily a sapiential term for wealth or possessions.[28] In the Hebrew Bible it occurs twenty-seven times, nineteen of these in Proverbs. Otherwise, it occurs in the description of the wealth gained by Tyre's merchant trade in Ezek 27.[29] The root of the term בצע means to cut or sever and in the economic sense can have the meaning 'to make one's cut' or profit.[30] It frequently occurs in the context of unjust gain (Ps 119:36; Prov 15:27; 28:16; Jer 6:13; Hab 2:9). However, its use within DD raises the question of whether it is used in that sense. The following are the passages in which the terms occur:

> Let no man desecrate the Sabbath for the sake of wealth and profit on the Sabbath.   (CD 11:15)

> Let no one stretch forth his hand to shed the blood of a man from the gentiles for the sake of wealth or profit. Also, let him not carry off any of their wealth so they will not blaspheme, except by the counsel of (the) association of Israel.   (CD 12:6–8)

> And on the Sabbath day a man shall not talk disgraceful and empty talk. He shall not demand payment from his neighbour for anything.[31] He shall not make judgments concerning wealth and gain. He shall not talk about the work and the task to be done the next morning.   (CD 10:17–19)[32]

---

[28] *HALOT*, vol. I, p. 242; *NIDOTTE*, vol. I, p. 1020.

[29] It occurs once in Deut 1:41 in the Hiphil, meaning 'to be easy'. It is questionable whether it occurs in Hab 2:5, where the MT has יין, 'wine'. This variant is discussed in detail below in the section on *Pesher Habakkuk*.

[30] *HALOT*, vol. I, p. 147–8; *NIDOTTE*, vol. I, p. 694.

[31] Cf. Schiffman, *Halakhah at Qumran*, p. 87. Schechter reads, 'None shall demand any debt of his neighbour'. Murphy posits, 'He should not hold anything against his neighbour'.

[32] These texts most likely reflect the meaning of Isaiah 58:9, which contrasts honouring the Sabbath and pursuing one's own interests. See Schiffman, *Halakhah at Qumran*, pp. 87–90; *DSSHAG*, 47 n. 162. Here, these pursuits are particularly economic, suggesting that the community thought the desire to earn profit or engage in business on the Sabbath indicated personal interest in attaining wealth was a competing influence that detracted from worshipping God.

The Sabbath regulations, taken at face value, assume that during the week members were engaged in the business of wealth and profit.[33] Given the concerns over the activities of outsiders, this assessment raises the question of the real differences between the community and its opponents. In addition, one wonders why there is a regulation against the violent attack of Gentiles in order to take their wealth and possessions. That these regulations provide no explicit punishment or fine suggests they may serve a different rhetorical function altogether. Newsom's comment on the polemical function of sectarian texts is especially helpful in this regard:

> A sectarian text would be one that calls upon its readers to understand themselves as set apart within the larger religious community of Israel and as preserving the true values of Israel against the failures of the larger community. A text may do so in a variety of ways. *There may be overtly polemical rhetoric of an 'us vs. them' sort.*[34]

In light of this observation, the regulations, while they serve as a guide for how the community *should* live, also function as a polemic against the outsiders who are seen as already committing these offences.[35] If the outsiders are viewed as those who have an excessive interest in gaining wealth even to the abuse of the Sabbath and oppressing and stealing from Gentiles, then these regulations are boundary markers, in the form of regulations, which further distinguish the community from its wicked opponents.

4.2   *Community Rule* (1QS)

This document is attested in the manuscript 1QS, one of the original finds of the Qumran material, and is largely intact. It is also attested in manuscripts from caves 4 and 5.[36] 1QS represents the latest stage in the development of the *Community Rule*. Three of the 4Q manuscripts, 4Q256, 4Q258, and 4Q259, while later than 1QS, may reflect an earlier version of the document. A number of hypotheses have been put forward concerning the development of the *Community Rule*; taking into account the different recensions reflected in the manuscripts one can posit several

---

[33] Schiffman, *Halakhah at Qumran*, p. 90.

[34] Newsom, '"Sectually Explicit" Literature', pp. 178–9 (italics added).

[35] See, however, Hempel, *Laws of the Damascus Document*, p. 188, who does not recognize the regulations as entirely a sectarian creation.

[36] 4Q255–64; 5Q11, 5Q13.

stages of redaction.[37] The extant text of 1QS is sufficient for the purposes of the present study and has a palaeographic date around the beginning of the first century BCE.[38] Mention will be made where the 4Q material shows a variant reading that is critical to selected texts. These variants will demonstrate that the issue of wealth exists in every redactional stage and 'in every generic category of material in the document'.[39] Thus, like the Damascus community, the *Yaḥad* shows an interest in wealth over an extended period of time. There are fifteen passages in the *Community Rule* that speak directly to the issue of wealth and are categorized accordingly in light of patterns that emerge from the material: (1) The Duty of Sharing Wealth, (2) Shared Wealth as Boundary, (3) Wealth as Peril to Devotion, and (4) Wealth and the Penal Code.

The duty of sharing wealth

The first passage that deals with wealth in the *Community Rule* does so immediately following the opening instructions (1QS 1:1–10) for the leader of the community:

[37] A number of composite parts of 1QS have been identified: 1–4 (1QS 1:1–15, introduction, 1:16–3:12, covenant ceremony, 3:13–4:26, the *Two Spirits Treatise*); 5–7 (5:1–6:23, organizational rules of the community, 6:24–7:25, penal code); 8–10:8 (8:1–9:11, early rules or 'Manifesto'); 9:12–26a (duties of the *Maskil*), 9:26b–10:8 (a liturgical calendar); 10:9–11:22 (closing hymn of praise). See Knibb, *EDSS*, vol. II, pp. 793–4. These sections were studied individually before the discovery and publication of the cave 4 manuscripts 4Q255–64, providing numerous theories as to the development of 1QS. See Leaney, *Rule of Qumran*, p. 115; Murphy-O'Conner, 'La Genèse littéraire', 529; Milik, 'Milkî-sedeq et Milkî-resa', 135. Two more recent studies, however, take into account all of the cave 4 and 5 material. Alexander proposes that the text of 1QS should have priority taking into account the paleographic dating of it and the 4QS material. Thus, he maintains that 4Q256, 4Q258, and 4Q259, because they are later manuscripts, have intentionally edited material to fit the present needs of the community which clarified ambiguities and inconsistencies, 1QS then representing the older form of the document. See Alexander, 'Redaction History', pp. 452–3. Metso, on the other hand, acknowledges the composite character of 1QS taking into account the textual content of all of the cave 4 and 5 data. While Alexander's thesis relies too strongly on paleographic dating, Metso engages the content of the texts to show that, although later, 4Q256, 4Q258, and 4Q259 represent an earlier, and often times shorter, form of the text. She argues that 4Q256 and 4Q258 represent one stream of tradition while 4Q259 represents another, both of these formed from an earlier version. See Metso, *The Serekh Texts*, p. 17. The earlier version then did not include 1QS 1–4, which contains the *Two Spirits Treatise*, or 10–11, the final hymn of praise. She thus concludes that there exists no 'single, legitimate and up-to-date version of the *Community Rule*' (Metso, *Textual Development*, pp. 152–3). A more recent work argues that the different manuscript traditions reflect various versions of rule texts produced by different communities that were eventually placed together in 1QS. See Schofield, *From Qumran to the Yaḥad*, pp. 162–73. We can generally deduce, however, the unity of 1QS as a final version of the document for our purposes.

[38] Alexander and Vermès, *Qumran Cave 4*, p. 9.

[39] Murphy, *Wealth in the Dead Sea Scrolls*, p. 161.

> All those who freely offer themselves to his truth are to bring all
> of their knowledge, strength, and wealth (הון) into the community
> of God in order to purify their knowledge according to the
> statutes of God, and regulate their strength according to his
> perfect ways and all their wealth according to his righteous
> counsel.
>
> (1QS 1:11–13)[40]

The tripartite formula of Deut 6:5, the central command for faithful Jews
to love God with all their heart, soul, and strength, can be detected in this
passage.[41] In the opening lines of the document the *Maskil* is instructed
to teach the community to 'love God with all their heart and with all
their soul . . . just as he commanded through Moses and all his servants
the prophets' (1QS 1:2–3). Newsom notes that if a member of the *Yaḥad*
were asked why they joined the community, this passage may have served
as their answer, even though it does not sound particularly sectarian.[42]
Only upon a close examination of the *Yaḥad's* actual economic practice
does the community's desire to distinguish itself from other Jewish sects
become evident; and this, by reshaping that Deuteronomistic pledge into
something more concrete and visible. A similar reshaping of the biblical
tradition is attested in the Aramaic Targums in which the term 'strength'
(מאד) is rendered 'money' or 'possessions' (ממון) (*Tg.* Deut. 6:5), suggesting that an association between wealth and faithfulness to God was more
widespread.[43] These traditions, however, do not reshape the passage as
radically as the *Yaḥad*. While membership in the community is voluntary,
the abandonment of wealth is not. Taken together with physical separation, complete abandonment of material possessions becomes a visible
expression of what it means to completely devote one's self to God in the
same way commanded in the *Shema*.

---

[40] All translations of 1QS are taken from *DSSR*, pp. 1.2–7, 20–41.

[41] See Black, *Scrolls and Christian Origins*, pp. 36, 123; Leaney, *Rule of Qumran*, pp. 122–3; Murphy, *Wealth in the Dead Sea Scrolls*, pp. 117–25.

[42] Newsom, *Self as Symbolic Space*, p. 91.

[43] This interpretation is also widely attested in the Rabbinic tradition; *b. Ber.* 61b; *b. Pes.* 25a; *b. Yoma* 82a; *b. Sanh.* 74a. These state: 'If it says "with all your soul" why should it also say "with all your might", and if it says "with all your might" why should it also say "with all your soul"? Should there be a man who loves his life more than his money, for him it says: "with all your soul", and should there be a man who loves his money more than his life, for him it says: "with all your might"'. See Grossfield, *Targum Onqelos to Deuteronomy*, pp. 34–5. See also Clarke, *Targum Pseudo-Jonathan*, p. 26; McNamara, *Targum Neofiti 1*, p. 50. 1QS also uses the terms הון and ממון interchangeably.

Shared wealth as boundary

The relationship between the S and D traditions is highly debated. Some argue that D reflects a proto-Qumran community that preceded the community behind S.[44] Others maintain that the latter represents the earliest communal ideas that were later taken up in the *Damascus Document*.[45] Still others question whether a community can be located behind these traditions at all. The present thesis understands S to be the later of the two. One key element that differs between D and S is how wealth becomes a more concrete boundary marker. Most noticeably is the absence of any overt critique of the unjust practices of outsiders in obtaining wealth that we find in D. Thus, S does not find it necessary to establish the impurity of outside wealth as much as D and reflects a greater degree of shared understanding and thus a more developed sect. Rather, the focus turns within the community itself, though there is still some concern with how wealth is to be negotiated with those outside the community. There are three distinct groups in relation to the *Yaḥad* between whom wealth becomes a clear boundary: (1) new initiates, (2) outsiders who do not voluntarily join, and (3) apostates.

Boundary from initiates

After entering into the community, initiates pledged their resources as a mandatory act of obedience. However, it was not mixed with that of the community until they passed an examination by the *Yaḥad* leadership. 1QS 6:13–23 contains the initiation process for those who volunteer to join. First, the leader of the community examines the initiate to determine by his understanding and deeds whether he is fit for instruction:

> If anyone of Israel volunteers for enrolment in the Council of the Yaḥad, the man appointed as leader of the general membership shall examine him regarding his understanding and works.
>
> (1QS 6:13b–14)

If accepted, he offers repentance (1QS 6:15) and is given the basic instruction of the *Yaḥad*. Then he stands before the general membership and is

---

[44] Davies, *Damascus Covenant*, pp. 173–204; Hempel, *Laws of the Damascus Document*, pp. 101, 150; Metso, 'Constitutional Rules', pp. 208–9; Schofield, *From Qumran to the Yaḥad*, pp. 274–8.

[45] Milik, *Ten Years of Discovery*, pp. 83–93; Stegemann, *Library of Qumran*, pp. 116–18; Regev, *Sectarianism in Qumran*, pp. 187–96.

interrogated as to his affairs at which time they decide whether he should be allowed to enter the community (1QS 6:16b).

> [H]e must stand before the general membership and the whole chapter shall interrogate him about his particulars. According to the decision of the Council of the general membership, he shall either proceed or depart.   (1QS 6:15b–16a)

If he is accepted, certain limitations are placed on the initiate until a full year and a subsequent examination have passed. These restrictions mark the foundational boundaries of identity for the *Yaḥad*: (1) he cannot participate in the purity meals, and (2) his property is not yet mixed with the *Yaḥad*.

After one year, if approved to continue, he is given the secret teaching of the *Yaḥad*. In addition, he is allowed to eat but cannot touch the pure drink of the community, and his wealth comes under the authority of the Overseer, but is not yet distributed among the community (6:18–21a). After passing a second year, the initiate is examined, and if he passes is allowed to proceed to full membership at which time his wealth is mixed with the community. This long procedure indicates that the *Yaḥad* has developed an alternative society where knowledge is preeminent over wealth. Moreover, the fact that the final stage of acceptance into the *Yaḥad* is marked by mixture of possessions further suggests that it is within the economic realm that unfaithfulness and, more importantly, impurity resides.

> [T]hen he shall be initiated further into the secret teaching of the Yaḥad. They shall also take steps to incorporate his property, putting it under the authority of the Overseer together with that of the general membership.   (1QS 6:19–20a)

What is important to note here is not the structure of the initiation process, but the role wealth plays in the community. In the initial phase of commitment, the surrender of wealth to the *Yaḥad* is fundamental in declaring one's obedience to God. The initiation phase highlights the need for the community to guard its purity and thus does not allow the newcomer's assets to be included until he is proven. At this stage, shared wealth becomes a boundary within the *Yaḥad* that separates those who are full members and those who are not. Thus, the renouncement of possessions becomes an indicator of one's commitment to God, while the acquisition of knowledge takes precedence as to one's fitness to serve God. Affluence has no place in the *Yaḥad*.

Boundary from outsiders

> He (anyone who refuses to enter the Yaḥad) is not to be reckoned
> with the upright. His knowledge, strength and wealth are not to
> enter the society of the Yaḥad.   (1QS 1:1a–2b)

The *Community Rule* is clear that outsiders are unclean and cannot be
engaged by members of the *Yaḥad*. The inclusion of the tripartite formula
used to describe the *Yaḥad* members is used here in the opposite sense to
distinguish the outsiders. However, it is not necessary to assume that the
document reflects a particular community that separated itself from the
outside world in the desert. On the contrary, much like the camps in DD,
there is some indication that members may have also lived in localized
groups within the larger population of Palestine (1QS 5–7).[46] This does
not preclude the possibility that an internal group, who followed a more
stringent set of rules (1QS 8–9), did eventually separate itself in the
desert.[47] At the same time, these different sections may reflect various
developments in the life of the sect. What is important to note is that
regardless of which circumstances are envisioned, wealth remains one
of the primary boundaries between the *Yaḥad* and outsiders. This is also
attested in the following:

> [T]he holy men who walk blamelessly. Their wealth is not to
> be admixed with that of rebellious men, who have failed to
> cleanse their path by separating from perversity and walking
> blamelessly.   (1QS 9:8b–9a)

Entrance into the community is described in terms of the two ways teaching. On the one hand, those who volunteer for truth have cleansed their
path (דרך) and walk (הלך) blamelessly, language that can be directly
associated with the *Two Spirits Treatise* (1QS 3:20–1; 4:2, 6, 12, 24).
On the other hand, those who have refused to enter are continuing in
the path of wickedness. As pointed out above, the inability to visibly
distinguish between the two on occasion because of the sin of the community members (1QS 3:22–3) becomes more visibly distinct in the concrete boundary of wealth. As stated above, this text may reflect a more
stringent group within the *Yaḥad* that physically separated in the desert.
If so, then this reflects a consistent tradition whereby those who view

---

[46] Collins, 'Forms of the Community in the Dead Sea Scrolls', pp. 97–111.
[47] Berg, 'An Elite Group', pp. 161–77.

themselves as the faithful in contrast to others find concrete expression
in the incompatibility of sharing wealth.

> And none is to be united with him (the man of iniquity) in his
> work or his wealth lest he cause him to become guilty of sin.
>
> (1QS 5:14b–15a)

The *Yaḥad* was forbidden to engage economically with outsiders and
this may indicate further that the members worked among the general
population and would have been able to do so. More importantly, however,
is the language of Lev 22:16, 'lest he cause him to become guilty of sin'.
In this portion of the Holiness Code, strict guidelines are provided to
keep lay people from eating the sacred donations (Lev 22:10–16), which
only the priest and those within his household were permitted to eat.
Thus, in the *Community Rule*, the biblical tradition is reshaped so that
wealth functions as or is considered to be sacred donations from which
only the pure members can partake. This reflects the same idea found in
the *Epistle of Enoch*, in which participation with sinners brings the same
guilt and punishment (*1 Enoch* 97:4). Here, it is specifically invoked
in relation to wealth indicating that guilt could result from improper
economic relationships.

> None belonging to the Yaḥad is to discuss with such men matters
> of Law or legal judgment, nor to eat or drink what is theirs, nor
> yet to take anything from them unless purchased (מחר).
>
> (1QS 5:15b–17a)

Unlike DD, there is no allowance for buying and selling with outsiders.
Community Rule views all outsiders as inherently evil and demonstrates
extreme concerns over impurity (1QS 4:5; 5:14, 20). Accordingly, the
two primary community boundaries are evident in this passage: food
and drink, and wealth. Some allowance is made, however, for receiving goods, though they must be purchased. This could suggest that the
previous passage (1QS 5:14–15a) may reflect more of a long-term business relationship. The present passage may evoke the biblical example of
Abraham's unwillingness (Gen 14:21–4; cf. 23:6–16) to take possessions
from others for fear that his wealth may be attributed to them. However,
the transaction itself more likely serves a redemptive purpose to guard the
member from defilement. Murphy notes it was a 'necessary buffer that
shielded the sectarian from defilement in a more sinful economy'.[48] This

---

[48] Murphy, *Wealth in the Dead Sea Scrolls*, p. 58.

provision for only one-directional exchange between the member and the outsider highlights the boundary between the two.

Boundary from apostates

Wealth is also viewed in terms of apostates, though in more extreme form. Whereas admixture of property was to be avoided with initiates, and incurred sin from outsiders, sharing wealth with apostates resulted in termination from the group.

> Any man who has been in the congregation of the Yaḥad who has fulfilled ten years and returns to the spirit of acting treacherously so that he goes out from the congregation of the Yaḥad to walk in the stubbornness of his own heart shall not ever be able to return to the congregation of the Yaḥad again. And any man of the Yaḥad who shares with him in his pure food or in his wealth which [] the Many, his judgment will be the same, he will be sent a[way].   (1QS 7:22–5)

The degree of severity over engagement with apostates is indicative of the community's understanding that entrance into the *Yaḥad* meant entrance into a covenant of faithfulness to God (1QS 3:11–12). Turning away from the *Yaḥad* ultimately expressed unfaithfulness to God and interaction, either through the pure meals or wealth, also resulted in a breach of covenant faithfulness.

Wealth as a distraction from devotion

Like the passages analysed in the previous sections, *Community Rule* also demonstrates a concern that the desire to accumulate wealth is a distraction from complete devotion to God.

> He (the Instructor) shall leave them (Men of the Pit) their wealth and trouble like a slave does his master – presently humble before his oppressor, but a zealot for God's law whose time will come: even the Day of Vengeance.
> (1QS 9:22b–23a) [par. 4Q256 18:5–6; 4Q258 8:6–7]

This passage occurs at the end of what has been considered the 'core' material of the *Community Rule* and refers to the original founding of

the *Yaḥad*, what Murphy-O'Conner referred to as the 'Manifesto'.[49] This
has been refuted more recently by Metso, though the text is still very
early.[50] The language is idealized and may be seen as a general rejection
of affluence as a distraction from devotion to God, which is the primary
point of the text.[51] The language of slavery and oppression reflects the
burden that wealth places on the Men of the Pit, a similar idea as that found
in *Mûsār lᵉMēvîn*. Murphy has attempted to locate this sobriquet (Men
of the Pit) historically with commercial agents who traded commodities
such as grain, wine, and oil.[52] While this thesis is attractive, it is difficult
to reconstruct the historical background from terminology in sectarian
texts, which at times can be very idealized. If this does reflect commercial
agents of some kind, then it highlights the community's concern over
those engaged in business for economic gain. The term שחת is used in
the Hebrew Bible to refer to wicked behaviour in general (Deut 31:29;
32:5), while the term בני שחת refers to wicked people (Isa 1:4). Here
it may allude specifically to outsiders who are viewed as those who
pursue wealth rather than knowledge. In either case, the text represents
a rejection of economic participation for individual gain and material
possessions.[53]

The use of language depicting a future Day of Vengeance implies a
reversal of fortunes in the age to come. The *Maskil* sees the present
age as one in which he must be devoted entirely to God's law while
those who pursue riches continue to be in bondage. In addition, the
parallel in 4Q256 18:6, which most likely reflects an earlier version
of the *Rule*, uses the terms 'wealth' (הון) and 'unjust gain' (בצע) rather
than 'wealth' and 'trouble' (עמל), and may betray contact with antecedent
traditions that envisioned a postponement of the Deuteronomistic scheme
and emphasized the unjust wealth of the present age (cf. *1 Enoch* 91:12).

> My zeal shall not be tarnished by a spirit of wickedness, neither
> shall I lust (אוה) for riches (הון) gained through violence (חמס).
> (1QS 10:18–19) [par. 4Q260 4:6–7]

Taken from the closing *Hymn of Praise*, this passage reflects how
the document turns more negative towards wealth. Here the zeal for
righteousness is shown to be incompatible with a spirit of wickedness,

[49] Murphy-O'Conner, 'La Genèse littéraire', p. 529. See also Leaney, *Rule of Qumran*,
p. 211; Knibb, *Qumran Community*, p. 129. See also Charlesworth, 'Morphological and
Philological Observations'.
[50] Metso, *Textual Development*, pp. 117–19, 124.   [51] Metso, *Serekh Texts*, p. 36.
[52] Murphy, *Wealth in the Dead Sea Scrolls*, p. 373.
[53] Knibb, *Qumran Community*, p. 143.

which is mentioned alongside a desire for wealth. The verb (אוה) is used in the Deuteronomistic command in relation to 'coveting' one's neighbour's wife or possessions (Deut 5:21). The parallelism in the passage contrasts the *Maskil*'s righteous zeal for God with a wicked desire for wealth. However, the spirit of wickedness can be seen as coherent with riches gained through violence and corresponds to the *Two Spirits Treatise* in which this spirit is characterized by greed, pride, and fraud. No discernable parallel for the phrase 'lust for riches' can be found in the Hebrew Bible, although the prophetic tradition offers what appears to be the beginning of this idea. Ezek 33:31 states, 'they come to you as my people and they hear what you say but they will not do it; for with lustful talk in their mouths they act; their heart is set on their unjust gain'.[54]

The sectarian communities demonstrate a tendency to ground their identity in the prophetic tradition. The phrase 'lust for riches' appears to be a further development towards a sharper critique against wealth. The first person speech in the *Hymn of Praise* functions as much to indict the opponents of the *Yaḥad* as it does to represent the piety of the *Maskil* (cf. Luke 18:11–12). The text explicitly demonstrates the idea that wealth was viewed as a distraction from complete devotion to God.

Legal matters concerning wealth

Several passages of the *Community Rule* demonstrate the seriousness of the *Yaḥad's* proscription of affluence and the need to develop a separate economic system in which all property was held communally. Since the previous passages have already demonstrated the high priority placed on wealth as one of the primary boundaries in the identity of the community and the danger it posed to complete devotion to God, here it is only necessary to discuss one focal text.

> These are the rules by which cases are to be decided at a community inquiry. If there be found among them a man who has lied about money (הון),[55] and done so knowingly, they shall bar him from the pure meals of the general membership for one year; further, his ration of bread is to be reduced by one-fourth.
> (1QS 6:24–5) [par. 4Q261 3:3]

The fact that this rule is the first in the list of communal regulations demonstrates the importance placed on wealth within the community. This is best stated by Murphy:

---

54 Cf. Jer 22:17; Qoh 6:2; *1 Enoch* 102:9.
55 In the parallel ממון is used in place of הון.

> The fact that lying about wealth is the first case introduced for discussion indicates its significance either as the most commonly contested point of law or *as the most concrete symbol of covenant fidelity to the community.*[56]

The punitive consequences for misrepresenting one's possessions are a reduction in food rations and removal from the communal meals. This may relate to members who worked outside and earned income and did not properly report their earnings. In doing so, they would demonstrate: (1) a desire for affluence, and (2) a trust in accumulated wealth. Lying about other matters only brought a penalty of six months' reduction of rations and no separation from the pure meals (1QS 7:4–5). Since sharing in communal meals and being allowed to mix one's wealth with the community are the primary identity markers within the community and boundary markers from outsiders, the ban from communal meals is significant. It demonstrates that the dedication of one's wealth to the community wholeheartedly was not only the most concrete symbol of fidelity, but also served as a visible manifestation of that faithfulness. The breach of this commitment resulted in the visible separation from the other more faithful members in what may have been the most intimate time of communal fellowship. This separation reinforced the community's rejection of affluence by reflecting on the member a visible loss of status.

4.3   *War Scroll* (1QM)

Among the first seven scrolls discovered in cave 1 is one describing the final eschatological war in which the forces of good achieve victory over the forces of evil. Also referred to as the *War of the Sons of Light against the Sons of Darkness*, this document is unique in that no other text from the Second Temple period presently known parallels the material in the *War Scroll*.[57] This document is found in 1QM, while related material, which may attest recensions and various traditions, can be found in the cave 4 fragments 4Q491–7.[58] In addition, two other fragments also contain common material that lie behind what is found in 1QM, 4Q285, and 11Q14.

---

[56] Murphy, *Wealth in the Dead Sea Scrolls*, p. 53 (italics added).

[57] Schultz, *Conquering the World*, p. 10.

[58] For a detailed discussion of the cave 4 manuscripts and their relationship to 1QM, see *DSSHAG*, vol. II, pp. 81–3. See also Schultz, *Conquering the World*, pp. 17–30; Strugnell, et al., *Qumran Cave 4 XXXIV*, p. 439.

The earliest manuscript is 4Q493, dated to the first half of the first century BCE, while 4Q496, 4Q497, and 4Q471 are dated around 50 BCE, all four of which are earlier than 1QM.[59] MSS 4Q492, 4Q495, and 4Q285 are all contemporary with 1QM,[60] 4Q491, 4Q494, and 11Q14 all being later.[61] Dating the *War Scroll* as a single document is difficult, although the literary dependence on Dan 11:40–12:3 provides a *terminus a quo* of 160 BCE for particular sections.[62] Dating based on historical reconstruction is tenuous at best, although the Kittim have been recognized by many as the Romans, whose occupation of the eastern Mediterranean can be dated in the mid first century BCE.[63] However, it is probably better to rely on the literary and palaeographic evidence. For the present study it will suffice to date 1QM somewhere between the late first century BCE and early first century CE.[64] There is one text that deals explicitly with the issue of wealth:

> Fill your land with glory and your inheritance with blessing; a multitude of cattle in your fields, [silver] (כסף) and gold (זהב) and precious stones (חפצ אבנ) in your palaces. Zion rejoice greatly! Shine forth in jubilation, Jerusalem. Be glad all you cities of Judah! Open [your] gate[s] continually, that through them may be brought the wealth (הון) of the nations. Their kings shall serve you; all your oppressors shall bow down before you.
>
> (1QM 12:12–14)[65]

This text evokes the Deuteronomistic promise of blessing for the faithful (Deut 8:12–16; 28:8), yet it places it explicitly in an eschatological context. In addition, there is a shift in language that goes beyond the Deuteronomistic tradition to include the wealth of the nations as part of that reward. MSS 4Q285 8:4–12 and 11Q14 ii:7–14a also reflect a tradition of reversal, though they lack the more extensive wealth imagery of silver, gold, precious stones, and the wealth of the nations. The former attests in a small fragment (4Q285 10:3) the phrase 'forsake wealth and unjust gain' (עוזב הון ובצע).[66] If this reflects an altogether different

---

[59] Schultz, *Conquering the World*, p. 31.

[60] *DSSHAG*, vol. II, p. 81; Strugnell, et al., *Qumran Cave 4 XXXIV*, p. 232.

[61] Schultz, *Conquering the World*, p. 33.

[62] *DSSHAG*, vol. II, p. 84.   [63] *EDSS*, p. 967.

[64] *Ibid.* See also Yadin, *Scroll of the War*, p. 243; Cross, 'Development of Jewish Scripts', p. 138; *DSSHAG*, vol. II, p. 84.

[65] Translation from *DSSHAG*, vol. II, p. 121.

[66] See this reconstruction in *DSSR*, vol. I, pp. 246–7.

composition that is closely related to 1QM,[67] the inclusion of this phrase may suggest that some streams of this tradition took a more negative view of wealth in the present age and did not include material possessions in the future reward.

Schultz has argued that an original version of the *War Scroll* containing columns 1–9 circulated that was based on the tradition of the war between the king of the north and the king of the south found in Daniel 11, a reference to the Seleucid and Ptolemaic wars.[68] However, as the Romans became a real political adversary in the latter part of the first century BCE, which is reflected in *Pesher Habakkuk* (references to the Kittim), there was a need to reshape and expand the tradition since there seemed to be no end to Roman domination.[69] Consequently, the addition of columns 11–19 reflects a more universal and miraculous account of the final war based on Ezek 39 and developed the reversal of fortunes in which the faithful obtain the wealth of all the nations.[70] It is not possible to state whether the plundering by Roman armies was the catalyst for such an addition, though passages from *Pesher Habakkuk* and the *Sibylline Oracles* point in that direction.[71] What we can know is that the community saw the present age as a time of suffering, identified themselves as the 'poor' (1QM 14:7; CD 14:7), and postponed the Deuteronomistic promise of blessing to a time in the future.

4.4   *Pesher Habakkuk* (1QpHab)

This document is contained in the scroll 1QpHab, which is one of the first of seven scrolls found in the Qumran caves. There are no other extant manuscripts for 1QpHab. It is written in a Herodian script and marked by its use of the Tetragrammaton, which is written in palaeo-Hebrew script.[72] This palaeographic evidence allows a date in the second half of the first century BCE.[73] MS 1QpHab demonstrates a decided concern for wealth and makes reference to such more than any of the exegetical texts from Qumran.[74] There exist textual variants between 1QpHab and the Masoretic Text of *Habakkuk*, one of which is important for the present study and is discussed in more detail below.

---

[67] Schultz, *Conquering the World*, p. 392.   [68] *Ibid.*, p. 401.

[69] 1QpHab 2:12, 14, 16; 3:4, 9; 4:5, 10; 6:1, 10; 9:7.

[70] Schultz, *Conquering the World*, p. 402.

[71] 1QpHab 6:1; *Sib. Or.* 3:175–90; 635–43. These documents are treated in detail below.

[72] Trever, *Scrolls from Qumran Cave I*, pp. 150–63.

[73] *EDSS*, p. 647. See also *DSSHAG*, vol. VI, p. 157.

[74] Murphy, *Wealth in the Dead Sea Scrolls*, p. 235.

Wealth and the Kittim

> 'Therefore he sacrifices to his net . . . for by them his lot in life
> is enriched and his food is abundant.' This refers to the Kittim,
> and they added to their wealth (הון) by all their plunder (שלל)
> like the fish of the sea . . . 'For by them his lot in life is enriched
> and his food is abundant', means that they impose their yoke
> and their taxes: this is 'their food,' on all the peoples yearly,
> thus ruining many lands.   (1QpHab 5:12a–6:8a)[75]

This text clearly demonstrates the perception of economic oppression by
the Roman armies.[76] Here the nets and dragnets are interpreted as the
weapons by which the Kittim secured their wealth through taxes obtained
by oppression. This does not reflect a categorical denunciation of riches
but is concerned more with the means by which they are obtained. Moreover, the language of worship underscores the community's perspective
that the pursuit of wealth was a rival form of devotion.

Wealth and the wicked priest

> And indeed, riches (הון) betray the arrogant (יהיר) man and he
> will not last; he who has made his throat wide as Hades, and who,
> like Death, is never satisfied. All the Gentiles will flock to him,
> and all the peoples will gather to him. Look, all of them take up
> a taunt against him, and invent sayings about him, saying, 'Woe,
> He who grew large on what is not his, how long will he burden
> himself down with debts?' *vacat*. This refers to the Wicked
> Priest who had a reputation for reliability at the beginning of
> his term of service; but when he became ruler over Israel, he
> became exalted in his heart and forsook God and betrayed the
> commandments for the sake of riches (הון). He amassed by force
> the riches of the lawless who had rebelled against God seizing
> the riches of the peoples, thus adding to the guilt of his crimes,
> and he committed abhorrent deeds in every defiling impurity.
>   (1QpHab 8:3–13a)

This passage includes a pesher on Hab 2:5, though there is a variant in the
reading between the MT and 1QpHab. The former reads 'Indeed, wine
(היין) is treacherous', while 1QpHab reads 'riches' (הון). Translators are

---

[75] All translations follow *DSSR*, vol. II, pp. 78–93.

[76] For a discussion of the identity of the Kittim as the Romans, see Brooke, 'The Kittim',
pp. 135–59. See also *ABD*, vol. IV, p. 93; *EDSS*, pp. 469–71.

mixed on how to interpret the biblical tradition, though it is clear that the Qumran commentator has reshaped the text to read wealth (הון).[77] This passage is very similar in its critique of the leadership of the Jerusalem Temple cult as we find in CD 4:12–5:11. It includes both a reference to wealth and a concern over ritual defilement, two of Belial's traps mentioned in CD 4:17–18. However, here the crimes are attributed to a particular person, the Wicked Priest. While it is outside the scope of the present study to identify this (these) person(s), we can know that he is labelled as wicked in direct correlation to his pursuit of affluence.[78] This desire for riches is placed in contrast to following the commandments of God, suggesting the two are mutually exclusive.

The emphasis on the pursuit of wealth by the Wicked Priest is also associated with other apostate Jews.[79] These people probably reflect other corrupt leaders of the Jerusalem Temple who are referred to more generally in CD. The calumniation of wealth in these passages is different from that of the Kittim. Here the critique is levelled on theological grounds of covenant faithfulness to God. This is seen in the description of the Wicked Priest in which his extravagant lifestyle is compared to having an uncircumcised heart (1QpHab 11:12–13). Thus, affluence and faithfulness to God are set in stark contrast.

Correction of injustices

'Yes, you yourself have plundered many nations, now the rest of the peoples will plunder you.' [This refers to] the priest who rebelled [and violated] the commandments of [God . . . they mis]treated him . . . his afflictions with the punishments due to such wickedness, perpetrating upon him the horrors of painful diseases, acts of retaliation against his mortal body. But the verse that says, 'Yes, you yourself have plundered many nations, now

---

[77]   The MT of Hab 2:5 reads, 'Indeed wine (היין) betrays the arrogant man'. It is possible that this is a scribal error in which a *yod* was mistaken for a *waw*. However, since there are two *yods*, which would be much more difficult to mistake, and in light of the present context that deals with the economic crimes of the Wicked Priest, this is more likely a deliberate change in wording on the part of the interpreter. See Brownlee, *Pesher of Habakkuk*, p. 132 and 'Revelation of Habakkuk', pp. 323–4.

[78]   For discussions concerning the identity of this figure, see Brownlee, 'The Wicked Priest, the Man of Lies and the Righteous Teacher', pp. 1–37; van der Woude, 'Wicked Priest or Wicked Priests?', pp. 349–59; Lim, 'The Wicked Priests', pp. 415–25; Martínez, 'Judas Macabeo Sacerdote Impío', pp. 169–81; Eshel, *Hasmonean State*, pp. 29–61; Collins, *Seers, Sybils and Sages*, pp. 242–8.

[79]   Brownlee, *Pesher of Habakkuk*, p. 132.

the rest of the peoples will plunder you', refers to the later priests of Jerusalem, who will gather ill-gotten riches (הון ובצע) from the plunder of the peoples, but in the Last Days their riches and plunder alike will be handed over to the army of the Kittim, for they are 'the rest of the peoples'. (1QpHab 8:13b–9:7)

This passage reveals the punitive consequences in the present time that the author seeks to portray to his audience for obtaining wealth unjustly. The background can be found in Jer 30:16, 'those who plundered you will be plundered and those who pillaged you I will give over to be pillaged'. Note also Ezek 39:10, 'and they will spoil those who spoiled them and they will plunder those who plundered them'. In the prophetic tradition this speaks of the armies that plundered Israel. Yet here the writer attributes this judgement to the Wicked Priest while referring to the Kittim as the administrator of this judgement, the reverse scenario of that seen in the prophetic tradition. This follows the biblical model in which the wickedness among those who consider themselves to be the people of God are punished by foreign oppressors. It also fits the model of the curses of the Deuteronomistic tradition. Because those in positions of leadership in the Jerusalem Temple are living extravagant lifestyles, God is bringing against them foreign powers that will bring about a correction of injustices as portrayed in the prophetic tradition (cf. 1QpHab 12:2–10).

Wealth in *Pesher Habakkuk* is viewed negatively in relation to the Kittim and the wicked leadership of the Jerusalem Temple cult. Both are guilty of obtaining wealth by unjust means, though the latter are categorized as unfaithful purely on the grounds of their desire for affluence. The Kittim rob wealth from people because of their wicked nature. The corrupt leaders of the Jerusalem Temple do so because they have abandoned God for the sake of riches. This critique does not include the eschatological reversal of fortunes seen in the *War Scroll*. Rather, what is envisioned here is a correction of what the writer saw as a temporary injustice that would soon be remedied by God.

4.5   *Hodayot* (1QHa)

While there are hymns of thanksgiving present in other Qumran documents, such as the Hodayot-like texts,[80] this section is interested in the two manuscripts found in cave 1, 1QH^a and 1QH^b, and the six manuscripts

---

[80]   4Q433, 4Q433a, and 4Q440. See Schuller, 'Hodayot', pp. 233–54.

found in cave 4, 4QH[a–f], the latter of which do not yield any significant variants for the present study. A palaeographic date can be assigned to 4QH[b] around the early to middle first century BCE, while 4QH[a, c–f] can be located from the middle to late first century BCE.[81] 1QH[a] and 1QH[b] can also be dated somewhere from the late first century BCE to the mid first century CE. The dating of 4QH[b] allows us to say that the hymns themselves date back to the latter part of the second century BCE.[82] These eight manuscripts represent the material to be examined under the rubric *Hodayot*.

There are two types of hymns that can be distinguished in this collection, 'Hymns of the Teacher' and 'Hymns of the Community'.[83] However, Newsom has correctly noted that this distinction does not affect the rhetorical function of the hymns within the sect in serving as a vital part of establishing the identity of the community.[84] Her insights are particularly helpful in understanding how the hymns of the Teacher serve not only to reveal his personal experiences but also as the formative example of behaviour set for the community members. The community hymns, though cast in first person language, help to form within the community members certain distinctives that set the *Yaḥad* apart from the dominant discourse of Second Temple Judaism.[85] This is especially important for the present study in terms of wealth language since the hymns reflect not only the disposition of the *Yaḥad*, but also serves as a mirror for opposing views of wealth among communities that considered themselves faithful.

> I will not exchange (מור) your truth for wealth (הון), nor any of your judgments for a bribe.   (1QH[a] 6:31)[86]

In this hymn the Teacher states his unwillingness to compromise the truth of the *Yaḥad* and indicates he cannot be bribed into doing so. In the biblical tradition the term מור refers to wicked Israel 'exchanging' the glory of God for idols (Ps 106:20; Jer 2:11). In addition, it also denotes people changing their glory into shame (Hos 4:7). This latter sense is most likely in mind since a similar idea is evoked in the censure against the Wicked Priest who exchanged his honour for shame by abandoning the commandments of God for riches (1QpHab 8:8–11; 11:12–13). This passage reflects the

---

[81] *Ibid.*, pp. 74–5.   [82] *EDSS*, p. 367.

[83] Schuller, 'Hodayot', p. 74; See also Kuhn, *Enderwartung und gegenwärtiges Heil*, pp. 16–33. The Hymns of the Teacher occur in cols 10–17 while the community hymns are in cols 1–9 and 18–26.

[84] Newsom, *Self as Symbolic Space*, pp. 196–8.   [85] *Ibid.*, p. 194.

[86] All translations taken from and numbered according to Stegemann and Schuller, *Incorporation*.

Yaḥad's view of the inherent danger of wealth in the present age. The 'I' in the hymn further functions to emphasize what may be perceived as crimes already committed by past dissenters (Wicked Priest), for which the writer does not need to offer an explanation (cf. Luke 18:11–12).

> I know that no wealth compares with your truth . . . and your holiness.   (1QH^a 7:22–3)

Here we see another contrast between wealth and truth. The community seeks after the knowledge of the truth while the wicked pursue wealth (1QH^a 7:31–2). Truth (אמן) in the *Hodayot* is a key concept that separates the faithful from the wicked. God and his judgements are truth (1QH^a 7:38; 9:32; 12:41; 14:12, 15) and his children, the chosen, are also considered truth (1QH^a 6:13, 26) and are referred to as the council of truth (1QH^a 5:19; 6:32). He has revealed to the faithful knowledge and truth (1QH^a 6:36; 13:11, 28; 15:19, 29, 41), while he has given the wicked a spirit of derision (1QH^a 10:12). The paths of truth are contrasted with the works of the wicked (1QH^a 5:20) and those who reject the covenant are said to hate truth (1QH^a 7:31). In light of the many references to truth and those who reject it and who conversely love riches, we can see that truth and knowledge are associated with the faithful, while wealth is associated with the wicked. What is important to note here is both a direct critique of the wealthy and a concern over the accumulation of wealth on the part of the faithful. In other words, a love for and pursuit after wealth is the visible distinction between the wicked and the faithful.

> You have redeemed the soul of the oppressed (אביון), to whom they planned to put an end, pouring out his blood because he served you . . . But you my God, have helped the soul of the destitute and poor (רוש) against one stronger than he.
>   (1QH^a 10:32–4) [par. 4Q428 3; 4Q432 3–4]

In this passage the Teacher is categorized as oppressed, destitute, and poor. Whether this reflects an actual experience is not as important as the function it serves within the community. Here he is able to proclaim the deliverance of God in the time of trouble and persecution, which, in turn, serves as the example for the community members. Like the Psalms in the Hebrew Bible, God is shown to help the oppressed. However, Newsom has noted a distinctive element in the formulation of thanksgiving in the Psalms that is absent in the *Hodayot*; the cry for help or complaint.[87] The *Hodayot* simply thanks God for deliverance without recording any past

---

[87] Newsom, *Self as Symbolic Space*, pp. 207–8.

cry for help or complaint that God heard and answered.[88] In addition, unlike the biblical tradition, neither the hymns of the Teacher nor the *Yaḥad* asks to be delivered from their present state. Rather, they see the present age as a time when God, through difficult circumstances, purifies the hearts of the faithful (1QH[a] 4:29–36) and keeps them aware of his deliverance in the coming age (1QH[a] 6:13–16).[89]

In that sense, the hymn betrays the voluntary nature of the marginalized position being evoked. This further suggests that the community understood the present age as one in which the faithful should not expect material blessing or comfortable circumstances and concretely assumed that kind of lifestyle. This marginal status is the basis of their identity and to have their circumstances changed would result in losing it. This does not mean that the community did not expect God to intervene on behalf of the *Yaḥad*. Rather, it simply indicates that until that time the faithful are to be characterized by their marginal status.

> You have not put my support upon unjust gain (בצע) or wealth (הון) [acquired by violence] . . . The strength of the mighty (rests) upon an abundance of luxuries [and they delight in] an abundance of corn, wine, and oil. They pride themselves on property and acquisitions . . . the soul of your servant abhors wealth and unjust gain and does not   in the abundance of luxuries. For my heart rejoices in your covenant and your truth delights my soul.   (1QH[a] 18:22–25a; 29b–31a) [par. 4Q428 11]

This passage offers the most explicit rejection of wealth in the *Hodayot* in the statement, 'the soul of your servant abhors wealth and unjust gain'. We know from other sectarian texts that the members of the community worked, earned money, pooled their resources collectively, and developed their own economic system. Thus, what the text refers to here is not the necessity of wealth but the pursuit of and desire for affluence. This is antithetical to the *Yaḥad's* communal economic system in which knowledge and obedience to Torah and the rules of the community were the indicators of honour and status (1QH[a] 18:29–30). In that sense, the desire to obtain wealth is seen as a distraction from faithfulness. This passage also highlights the difference from the biblical psalms in that there is no cry for deliverance. Rather, the member is happy about his marginal status and thankful that he is not like the outsiders whose strength and happiness are found in the accumulation of wealth.

---

[88] Pss 12:5; 34:6; 70:5; 72:12; 74:21; 86:1.
[89] Murphy, *Wealth in the Dead Sea Scrolls*, pp. 244–5.

The *Hodayot* offers a window into the importance of verbal praise and community discourse within the *Yaḥad*. Through the reading and hearing of these hymns in worship, the community members' identity as the poor, afflicted, righteous remnant would be reinforced.[90] The persistent denunciation of wealth over against the desire to seek truth in obedience to God would also formulate within the members of the *Yaḥad* a distinction from rival communities in which they saw the characteristics of the things that they themselves denounce. Thus, the renouncement of wealth in exchange for truth and obedience becomes a mark of faithfulness. Consequently, those who pursue wealth are marked as outside the purview of the faithful community.

4.6   Summary of Hebrew traditions

The sectarian texts from Qumran demonstrate different areas of emphasis across the various documents. The D tradition portrays the present age as a time of testing when God in his mystery allows Belial to go unrestrained and uses wealth as a demonic trap. It provides a sharp critique of wealth against its opponents in similar fashion to the *Epistle of Enoch*, the unjust and violent actions of the opponents being elaborated in the descriptions of their riches. Consequently, the community distinguishes itself by means of the label 'the poor ones' and develops a quasi-independent economic system in which members of the community bartered with one another and all buying and selling with outsiders was done under the scrutiny of the Overseer. As a likely response to what the *Damascus Document* views as a perversion of the Deuteronomistic theology of wealth, the community behind the text sought to reflect the visible expression in the present of life in the yet future eschatological age.

The S tradition lacks the harsh critique of wealth against outsiders as that found in D. Rather, it focuses on the acquisition of knowledge and total commitment to God in concrete terms of renunciation of personal possessions. The same can be said of the *Hodayot*, though these hymns include a harsher critique of affluence. The desire for wealth stands in contrast to the acquisition of knowledge, similar to *Aramaic Levi Document*, *Mûsār leMēvîn*, and Ben Sira.

There are at least two descriptions given as a remedy for the present circumstances of the wicked rich and the righteous poor. On the one

---

[90] For an analogy of this, see Newson, *Self as Symbolic Space*, p. 203, and Holland, et al., *Identity and Agency*, p. 66.

hand, *Pesher Habakkuk* maintains that a correction of injustices will take place in the life of the Wicked priest who forsook God for the sake of wealth and aligned himself with other unfaithful Jews who pursue wealth. In this document wealth is only viewed as a feature of the present age. This corresponds to the sapiential traditions of Ben Sira and the biblical tradition where unjust wealth does not last. On the other hand, the *War Scroll* provides a complete reversal of fortunes in the final eschatological battle where the wicked are destroyed and the righteous receive the material blessings promised in the Deuteronomistic tradition. This is a more developed understanding of the eighth week in the AOW.

These various perspectives on wealth across different documents demonstrate the willingness of the Qumran community to take on board whatever traditions were available to them in order to strengthen the particular issues they were facing. Thus, a coherent view of wealth is difficult to establish. However, in light of the analysis above, two conclusions can be made based on elements that pervade the sectarian documents: (1) the individual accumulation of wealth is viewed negatively and is inconsistent with faithfulness to God, and (2) the material blessing of the Deuteronomistic tradition is not undermined per se, but has been postponed to a future age.

5

OTHER JEWISH LITERATURE

Included in this discussion of Second Temple texts are documents that were not found at the Qumran site but contain apocalyptic ideas concerning wealth. These documents are largely attested in Greek, though some of the Enochic traditions are extant only in Ethiopic.

5.1   Wisdom of Solomon

The blend of philosophical rhetoric, traditional Jewish wisdom, and apocalyptic eschatology found in Wisdom of Solomon, also referred to as the Book of Wisdom, has caused many to consider it a pastiche of numerous sources and authors, portions of which were originally written in Hebrew.[1] However, it is now generally accepted as a unified document composed in Greek and can be dated sometime between 30 BCE and 70 CE.[2] It also demonstrates contact with Aramaic and Hebrew apocalyptic traditions attested only in documents such as *1 Enoch* and other literature among the Dead Sea Scrolls. For example, the writer believes in the immortality of the soul, which can be sharply contrasted with traditional sapiential literature from the Hebrew Bible and Ben Sira (Sir 17:30), yet also differs from Platonic immortality since only the righteous souls live forever. To this author, the gift of immortality is a reward for right behaviour (Wis 2:22–4; 5:15–16) and is not simply related to the soul's own nature.[3]

The writer also shows contact with traditions that envision an eschatological war in which God intervenes on the part of the righteous during his visitation (Wis 5:17–23). In the passages that precede this final battle

---

[1] Speiser, 'Hebrew Origin', pp. 455–82. See also von Focke, *Die entstehung der Weisheit Salomos*; Horbury, 'Christian Use and Jewish Origins', p. 183.

[2] Collins, *Jewish Wisdom*, pp. 179–80; Horbury, 'Christian Use and Jewish Origins', pp. 182–3; Grabbe, *Wisdom of Solomon*, pp. 24–5, 87–90; Winston, *Wisdom of Solomon*, pp. 3, 23.

[3] Puech, 'Book of Wisdom', p. 128.

the righteous are said to shine forth (Wis 3:7) like sparks, rule over people and nations (Wis 3:8), obtain rest (Wis 4:7), are placed among the angels (Wis 5:5), and receive a crown of glory (Wis 5:16). The idea of the righteous shining or being resplendent is attested in both Dan 12:3 and *1 Enoch* 104:2. That the righteous will rule nations and people is found in the eschatological battle of the *War Scroll* (1QM 12:14) in which the oppressors bow down and kiss the feet of the righteous (cf. 1QH^a 11:20–37; 14:32–9). The promise of rest may correspond to the assurance of peace in *1 Enoch* 105:2, which is contrasted throughout the *Epistle* with the announcement of judgement to the wicked, 'you will have no peace' (*1 Enoch* 98:11; 101:3; 103:8; cf. also *1 Enoch* 5:4–5) and 'you will have no rest' (*1 Enoch* 99:14).[4] More importantly, being placed among the angels is attested only in *1 Enoch* 104:5 and in the DSS (1QH^a 9:21–2; 19:10–11; 4Q416 2 iii:9–14). Finally, the crown of glory is mentioned in TST (1QS 4:7) as well as the *Hodayot* (1QH^a 17:25). These points of contact do not suggest any direct literary dependence but demonstrate that various streams of these traditions were circulating in Alexandria at the time of the composition of Wisdom of Solomon and that the Aramaic and Hebrew apocalyptic traditions were having an impact on Greek writers.[5]

Like Ben Sira, it is accepted into the canon of Scripture in the Catholic Church and appears among the books of the NT as early as 200 CE in the Muratorian Canon.[6] Wisdom is generally divided into three parts: (1) the book of eschatology (1:1–6:11), (2) the book of wisdom (6:12–9:18), and (3) the book of history (chaps. 10–19).[7] The former two contain passages that mention wealth. They are discussed according to these divisions in the order that they occur.

The book of eschatology

'Come, therefore, let us enjoy the good things (τῶν ὄντων ἀγαθῶν) that exist and make use of the creation to the full as in youth. Let us take our fill of costly (πολυτελής) wine and perfumes and let no flower of spring pass us by. Let us crown ourselves with rosebuds before they wither. Let none of

---

[4] See Stuckenbruck, *1 Enoch 91–108*, p. 421, who suggests the two phrases 'no rest' and 'no peace' are parallel and stand as pronouncements of judgement.

[5] Collins, 'Reinterpretation of Apocalyptic Traditions in the Wisdom of Solomon', p. 154.

[6] *Ibid.*

[7] Winston, 'A Century of Research', pp. 1–18; Nickelsburg, *Jewish Literature*, p. 205.

us fail to share in our arrogance; everywhere let us leave signs of enjoyment because this is our portion and this is our lot. Let us oppress the righteous poor (πένητα δίκαιον) man; let us not spare the widow or regard the grey hairs of the aged. But let our might (ἰσχὺς) be our law of right for what is weak proves itself to be useless.'   (Wisdom 2:6–11)[8]

This text includes the rhetorical device of imputed speech to identify the misunderstanding of the ungodly (Wis 1:16) as they explain their perspective on life and the afterlife. In Wis 2:1–5 they contend that life is short, death is certain, everything happens by chance, and there is no eternal existence. They conclude that there are no consequences for their actions and that they should live life to its fullest (cf. Ps 10:1–4; *1 Enoch* 104:7). This attitude towards life is attested in a Greek inscription found in the tomb of Jason from the time of Alexander Janneus, stating, εὐφραίνεσθε οἱ ζῶντες τὸ δε... λοιπόν πιεῖν ἅμα φαγεῖν 'rejoice you who are living . . . drinking and eating'.[9] This same idea is echoed in Ben Sira and Qoheleth, both of whom encourage their readers to eat, drink, and enjoy the good things of life since there is no expectation of wealth in the afterlife (Sir 14:16–17; Qoh 2:24; 3:13; 5:18; 8:15; cf. Isa 22:13). Yet, in the eschatological book, Wisdom portrays those who take this attitude as rich, wicked oppressors of God's people, a move that goes beyond the biblical tradition. In addition, the righteous are characterized as poor (πένης), a term used nowhere else in the entirety of Wisdom. More importantly, the notion that life and rewards extend beyond the present life is especially important to the writer's admonition to reform his readers' ethical behaviour. The imputed speech of the rich serves to contrast what they say now with what they will say in the final judgement.

When the unrighteous see them they will be shaken with dreadful fear and they will be amazed at the unexpected salvation of the righteous. They will speak to one another in repentance and in anguish of spirit they will groan and say . . . 'What has our arrogance profited us? And what good has our boasted wealth brought us?'   (Wisdom 5:2–3, 8)

The inclusion of a judgement scene in which the wicked admit their guilt is only foretold in the earlier Enochic traditions (*1 Enoch* 100:6; cf. 96:4). The acknowledgement of their wealth and arrogance, taken together

---

[8] Translations based on NRSV.
[9] Winston, *Wisdom of Solomon*, p. 118.

with the description of the righteous as poor (Wis 2:10) underscores the irreversible consequences of aligning oneself with those who live an extravagant lifestyle in the present age.

The eschatological section of Wisdom betrays contact with the Enochic tradition on several fronts. (1) Those who despise wisdom also have evil children through forbidden and adulterous relationships in what seems to be a veiled reference to the *Book of the Watchers* (Wis 3:12–13, 16 cf. Wis 14:6–13).[10] (2) They enjoy possessions (τῶν ὄντων ἀγαθῶν),[11] (Wis 2:6–9; cf. *1 Enoch* 97:8–9; 98:2–3), feast and drink very expensive (πολυτελής) wine[12] (Wis 2:9; cf. *1 Enoch* 96:5, 8), and oppress the righteous (Wis 2:10–20; *1 Enoch* 95:7; 96:5, 8; 97:8–9; 98:2–3; 100:2). (3) The righteous are explicitly contrasted with the ungodly rich and (4) the wicked reveal a similar world view as the rich in the *Epistle of Enoch*:

> Whenever you die, the sinners speak of you like this: 'As we die, so the righteous die. What benefit did their deeds bring them? See? They die in grief and darkness just like us. What advantage is theirs? We are exactly the same from this point. And how will they arise? Just what will they look upon for eternity? Look, they have really died. From now on they will never again see the light.'   (*1 Enoch* 102: 6–8)

In the judgement, the wicked suddenly become aware that they were wrong and make specific reference to the uselessness of their riches (cf. *1 Enoch* 100:6). This coincides with the biblical tradition, which indicates unjust wealth will not last and is of no use in the day of trouble (Prov 11:4; Sir 5:8; 40:13). Unlike the biblical tradition, however, Wisdom includes a reversal of fortunes where the righteous poor receive a reward for faithfulness (Wis 5:15–16). In the present, the testing of the righteous is compared to refined gold (Wis 3:1–6) and the author views the age as a time of wickedness when humankind can be corrupted by the evil desires of the world (Wis 4:11–12). The unrighteous are enjoying wealth and prosperity while the faithful undergo hardship and death, which ushers in a new level of existence while they await the final judgement. Consequently, the ungodly live in spiritual death with no hope in the afterlife.

---

[10] Note especially that the writer highlights the arrogance of the wicked. In Wis 14:6 he mentions the arrogant giants from the *Book of the Watchers*. The writer, in some way, is aligning the opponents with the descendants of the fallen angels; not so much as actual descendants, but in line with wicked oppressors that are foreshadowed in the Watchers myth.

[11] *BDAG*, p. 3.   [12] *Ibid.*, p. 850.

The book of eschatology reveals several similarities with apocalyptic literature from the Second Temple period, and serves to conform ethical behaviour. More importantly, it does so in the context of how the faithful are to view wealth in the present age using typical apocalyptic categories of rich and poor as wicked and faithful, respectively. In doing so, it also exposes an expectation that the Deuteronomistic promise of blessing has been postponed.

The book of wisdom

> I called on God and the spirit of wisdom came to me. I preferred her to sceptres and thrones and I accounted riches (πλοῦτον) as nothing in comparison to her. Neither did I liken to her any priceless gem (λίθον ἀτίμητον) because all gold (χρυσὸς) is but a little sand in her sight and silver (ἄργυρος) will be accounted as clay before her. I loved her more than health and beauty and I chose to have her rather than light because her radiance never ceases. All good things (τὰ ἀγαθὰ) came to me along with her and in her hands uncounted wealth (ἀναρίθμητος πλοῦτος). I rejoiced in them all because wisdom leads them; but I did not know that she was their mother. I learned without guile and I impart without grudging; I do not hide her wealth (πλοῦτον) for it is an unfailing treasure (θησαυρός) for mortals; those who get it obtain friendship with God commended for the gifts that come from instruction. (Wisdom 7:7b–14)

This text is formative for the wisdom section of the book and finds its own background in 1 Kgs 3:5–15 and 2 Chr 1:7–12. Here Solomon is granted by God an unlimited request in which he asks for wisdom. Because he valued wisdom above riches and wealth, God granted those to him as well (cf. Wis 8:5, 11–18; 10:9–11). Using this same motif, the writer not only demonstrates wisdom's value over wealth, but also agrees with the biblical tradition in its expectation that the acquisition of wisdom also brings with it material blessing (cf. Philo, *Praem.* 104).[13] This further suggests that traditions like Ben Sira and Wisdom do not have a systematic understanding of wealth but see the disparity in the world around them and try to provide an explanation based on inherited traditions. In doing so, Wisdom incorporates apocalyptic traditions in the eschatological section in order to defend the piety of the righteous

---

[13] Winston, *Wisdom of Solomon*, pp. 167–71; Bullard and Hatton, *Handbook on the Wisdom of Solomon*, pp. 110–11; Lambronac'i, *Commentary on Wisdom of Solomon*, pp. 173–4; Engel, *Das Buch der Weisheit*, p. 129.

poor, while maintaining the expectation of wealth for the faithful in the wisdom section.

This is also seen in the blending of literal and metaphorical uses of wealth language in the present passage. In conjunction with 'all good things', Wisdom has in her hands uncounted wealth (ἀναρίθμητος πλοῦτος). Since Wisdom is personified we can assume that the wealth mentioned here is also metaphorical.[14] This is made clearer by the statement, 'I do not hide her wealth' (τὸν πλοῦτον αὐτῆς οὐκ ἀποκρύπτομαι), which is epexegetical to 'I distribute abundantly' (ἀφθόνως τε μεταδίδωμι). That is, by imparting instruction Pseudo-Solomon does not hold back the riches of wisdom from other people because it is an unfailing treasure. It is likely that uncounted wealth (ἀναρίθμητος πλοῦτος) and unfailing treasure (ἀνεκλιπὴς θησαυρός) are different expressions for the same idea and that neither refers to material wealth.

> But they considered our existence an idle game and life a festival held for profit (ἐπικερδής) for they say, 'it is necessary to make a profit (πορίζω) however one can, even by unjust (κακοῦ) means'.   (Wisdom 15:12)

As the author calumniates the makers of idols, he does so in the context of their desire for economic gain. He points out their awareness that they are sinning (cf. *1 Enoch* 96:4), which further highlights the degree to which sinners pursue wealth. This also highlights their belief that there are no consequences for their actions and that their deeds will go unpunished (*1 Enoch* 104:7). As a result, their destruction will take place suddenly (Wis 14:14; cf. *1 Enoch* 94:1, 6–7; 96:1; 98:6; 99:9). In addition, the writer of Wisdom indicates that the idol makers are oppressors of God's people, an idea not explicit in the biblical tradition but present in the *Epistle*. This connection indicates that characterizations of the wicked rich in the *Epistle* have become paradigmatic for how those who pursue wealth were portrayed in later traditions.

5.2   *The Similitudes (1 Enoch 37–71)*

The *Similitudes* or *Book of Parables* is a later addition to the Enochic tradition that consists of three parables (*1 Enoch* 38:1–44:1; 45:1–57:3; 58:1–69:29) revealed to Enoch concerning the fate of the wicked and the righteous. Although the book immediately follows the BOW and precedes

---

[14] Cf. *ALD* 13:10, 12, 13. Cf. 4Q417 2 i:19; 4Q418 81+81 a:9–10.

the AB, it is the last major addition to be added and is dated between the first century BCE and the late first century CE.[15] Its absence among the DSS has been the cause of attributing a late date to the document. It is not extant in any Greek or Aramaic manuscripts but is only attested in the Ethiopic tradition.

> 'And this Son of Man whom you have seen will rouse the kings and mighty up from their soft beds and the powerful from their thrones! He will loosen the reins of the powerful and break the teeth of the sinners. All their deeds exhibit iniquity (indeed, are iniquity itself), and their power rests upon their wealth. Their faith is in the gods which they have fashioned with their own hands and they deny the name of the Lord of Spirits. They persecute the houses of his congregation and the faithful who depend upon the name of the Lord of Spirits.'
>
> (*1 Enoch* 46:4, 7–8)[16]

At this stage in the development of the Enochic tradition, the enemies of the faithful have been firmly established as rich, powerful oppressors (*1 Enoch* 94:6–9; 95:7; 96:5–8; 97:7–10; 99:11–16; 102:9), allowing the writer(s) of the *Similitudes* to refer to them simply as the kings and the mighty. The chiastic structure of verse 4 demonstrates they are parallel with the sinners.

> *He will rouse the kings and mighty up from their soft beds*
> *And the powerful from their thrones*
> *He will loosen the reins of the powerful*
> *[He will] break the teeth of sinners*

In this passage the sinners are portrayed as those who blaspheme God, deny his name, worship false gods, and persecute the faithful (cf. Wis 15:10–14). They live an opulent lifestyle owing to their power and possessions and their strength is rooted in their wealth. Prior to the present text, the kings and the mighty have been referred to as sinners, the wicked, and those who possess the earth (*1 Enoch* 38:1–5). Some have argued that they represent either 'the later Hasmonean princes and their Sadducean supporters',[17] or Gentile kings and rulers,[18] to which

---

[15] Nickelsburg, *1 Enoch 1*, p. 7; Olson, *Enoch*, pp. 11–12.

[16] All translations in this section follow Olson, *Enoch*.

[17] Charles, *Book of Enoch*, p. 67.

[18] Suter, *Tradition and Composition*, p. 30; Nickelsburg, *Jewish Literature*, p. 250.

is attributed the charge of idol worship. Yet this dichotomy is unnecessary. The reference to kings may have Gentiles in mind, though the reference to the mighty and the powerful could also, indirectly, point to the leadership of the Jerusalem Temple cult who could be seen as guilty of the same crimes as the wicked kings by association. Those who have corruptly procured the priestly offices are guilty of involvement with the wicked Gentile kings, while those who enjoy the economic success through these relationships are guilty by way of participation (*1 Enoch* 97:4). More important to the present study, this passage further attests that the description of the sinners in the *Epistle* has become formulaic for later traditions in distinguishing the people of God from the wicked in terms of wealth.

> And it will come to pass in those days that no one will be saved by gold or by silver and no one will be able to escape. There will be no iron for war nor will anyone put on a breastplate. Bronze will be useless. Tin will also be useless and count for nothing. And lead? No one will want it.   (*1 Enoch* 52:7–8)

In the earliest Enochic traditions metallurgy is viewed negatively since gold and silver are used to amass wealth and power, to make idols, and for adornment and licentious activity (*1 Enoch* 8:1–2; 97:8–9; 98:2; 99:6).[19] This is an indirect reference to those who trust in gold, silver, and idols. Elsewhere, the mountains representing each of these metals become 'impotent' and melt at the appearance of the Chosen One (cf. 1:6). The phrase 'in those days' envisions a time in the future when the wickedness set in motion by Asael, which birthed the era of oppression and violence, will be resolved (54:6; 65:6–8). Here a correction of injustices is in view, in which evil will be eradicated and righteousness restored (*1 Enoch* 53:2). While the deeds of the wicked rich are emphasized in the *Epistle*, here the root of their wickedness, the secrets of metallurgy, and subsequent judgement are in focus.

> And they will praise and glorify the Lord of Spirits saying, 'Blessed is the Lord of Spirits and the Lord of Kings and the Lord of the Mighty and the Lord of the Rich and the Lord of Glory and the Lord of Wisdom.' Then they will say to themselves, 'Our souls are glutted with ill-gotten gains, but they will not prevent our descent into the pit of Sheol.'   (*1 Enoch* 63:2, 10)

---

[19] Olson, *Enoch*, p. 34.

This passage demonstrates a similar judgement scene to the one depicted in Wisdom 5:1–15, in which the wicked acknowledge the futility of their affluence in the Day of Judgement. The ungodly are consumed by their wickedness and have no eternal existence. In contrast to the judgement of the wicked, the *Similitudes* hold out the promise of a complete reversal of fortunes for the faithful, which includes the material blessing of the Deuteronomistic tradition:

> But the wisdom of the Lord of Spirits has revealed him to the holy and the righteous for he has preserved the inheritance of the righteous because they have hated and despised this world of iniquity and hated all its works and ways.
>
> (*1 Enoch* 48:7; cf. 45:4; 62:14–16)

Here, the righteous can expect a reward in the age to come as a direct result of their rejection of the present world order of power and greed. They are contrasted with the kings of the earth and the powerful who possessed the land during the present age. While previous Enochic traditions harshly denounced rich sinners and warned the faithful to refrain from becoming their companions (*1 Enoch* 104:6; cf. 97:4), here we have a more explicit rejection of wealth in the phrase, 'they hated and despised this world' (*1 Enoch* 48:7). The inheritance of the faithful is envisioned elsewhere as a transformed earth where the righteous are blessed:

> On that Day . . . I will transform the earth and make it a blessing, and I will settle my chosen ones there; but those who commit sin and wickedness will not set foot upon it. (*1 Enoch* 45:4–6)

This language of settling and blessing coincides with the Deuteronomistic promise of material blessing (Deut 17:14; 19:1; 26:1). Like the *Epistle of Enoch*, the *Similitudes* envision a complete reversal of fortunes at which time the righteous will be given time to carry out judgement against the kings and the mighty (*1 Enoch* 38:5; 48:9; 95:7; 96:1; 98:12). Thus it is evident that the *Similitudes* include the postponement of the Deuteronomistic promise of blessing and mark the faithful as those who reject wealth in the present age.

5.3   *Eschatological Admonition (1 Enoch* 108)

This final appendix to *1 Enoch* is only extant in the Ethiopic tradition with no known attestation in Aramaic or Greek manuscripts. In addition, it is not found among the Dead Sea Scrolls. This document introduces new ideas into the Enochic tradition and most likely represents the ideas and concerns of a community that viewed itself as a later expression of the Enochic communities reflected in the earlier texts.[20] The different concerns of this writer and community have been incorporated into the Enochic tradition probably due to its sustained discussion regarding the suffering of the righteous and issues concerning wealth and poverty. However, we will see in this tradition that suffering and a lifestyle of poverty are a decided position rather than the result of oppression. It is most likely among the latest additions to the Enochic tradition and has been dated sometime in the first century CE.[21]

> Those who love God have loved neither gold nor silver nor any of the good things which are in the world; rather they have given over their bodies to torture. From the time they came into being, these have not craved earthly food but have instead counted themselves as a breath that passes away, and this they have preserved. And the Lord has tested them much, but their spirits have been found pure so that they might praise his name. I have recounted all their blessings in the books. He has assigned them their reward for they proved to be those who loved heaven more than their life in the world.   (*1 Enoch* 108:8–10)

In contrast to the prophetic tone of the *Epistle*, which addresses the rich sinners in the second person and focuses on their sinful activity, here the writer focuses more on the description of the faithful in relation to wealth.[22] Not only this, but the crimes of the opponents do not overtly include economic references. They are categorized as 'sinners' and 'those who do evil', yet there is no mention of their economic power so frequently portrayed in the *Epistle*. Instead, they are guilty of wrongly interpreting the prophets. Although the earlier Enochic traditions take a prophetic stance, this document refers to the prophets in the biblical tradition as a distinct body of revelation. Moreover, the writer also emphasizes obedience to Torah as a distinguishing mark of the community (*1 Enoch* 108:1). These features indicate that the concerns being addressed here are quite distinct from the earlier communities.

The faithful, on the other hand, are described in economic terms as 'those who have loved neither gold or silver nor any of the good things

---

[20] Stuckenbruck, *1 Enoch 91–108*, p. 693.

[21] Nickelsburg, *1 Enoch 1*, p. 554; Stuckenbruck, *1 Enoch 91–108*, pp. 693–4.

[22] *1 Enoch* 94:6–10; 95:4–7; 96:4–8; 97:3–10; 98:2–99:2; 99:11–16; 100:7–9; 101:4–102:3, 9; 103:5–8; 104:7–9.

which are in the world'. This language denotes a decided position of marginalization in which loving God and loving silver and gold are mutually exclusive (cf. Luke 16:13). The mention of blessings being recorded in the books corresponds to the books that record the deeds of sinners. This indicates there is an expectation of future reward that does not take place in the present age but only comes as a result of perseverance in testing. Proving one's self faithful, it is presupposed, manifests itself in a categorical rejection of wealth or any other pleasures in the present age. The faithful are aware of the temporal nature of this age and look forward to a future reward in heaven.

The absence of any second person address of opponents or critique of oppression may indicate that this community was not experiencing any programmatic persecution but attached itself to the Enochic tradition in order to establish its identity as the oppressed. The antithesis constructed between loving God or wealth, heaven or the world, and the promise of reward in the future indicates that the mark of the faithful here is a categorical rejection of riches.[23]

5.4 *Sibylline Oracles*

The *Sibylline Oracles* are a literary phenomenon that is found in both Greco-Roman and Jewish traditions. While the former represents the more likely origin of such material, the latter used this idiom as a means to communicate the truth of the monotheistic beliefs of Judaism in a thoroughly Hellenistic society.[24] Moreover, by adapting the rhetorical convention of the *Oracula Sibyllina*, the Jews were able to exploit the history they possessed that pre-dated the Hellenistic traditions.[25] They share characteristics of the prophetic tradition in that they often predict calamities that will take place concerning people and nations and have been described as the 'Apocalyptic of Hellenistic Diaspora Judaism'.[26] The third book in particular demonstrates similarities with the Enochic tradition.[27] The attribution of a genealogical connection with Noah is a prominent feature in the Enochic tradition and provides the pseudonymous writer with a starting point for his revelation that precedes the

---

[23] Stuckenbruck, *1 Enoch 91–108*, pp. 721–2.

[24] Collins, *Sibylline Oracles of Egyptian Judaism*, p. 19; Bate, *Sibylline Oracles*, pp. 19–20.

[25] Parke, *Sibyls and Sibylline Prophecy*, p. 8.

[26] Schneemelcher, *New Testament Apocrypha II*, p. 560.

[27] Schürer, *History of the Jewish People*, p. 638.

Jewish–Gentile distinction. Though the Sibyl is closely related to mantic wisdom in that she receives her revelation through ecstatic events,
she serves an intermediary role between God and mankind and takes on
a somewhat similar superhuman position to one who is closely related
to God.[28] Both traditions also demonstrate a 'compatibility of pagan
prophecy with a Jewish hero'.[29] In addition, both provide a universal
perspective in their messages. Most importantly, they portray the wicked
in economic terms as wealthy oppressors and affirm a negative outlook
on wealth in general.

Their particular value to the present study is that they offer insight
into the prevalent beliefs and attitudes towards the socio-political milieu
and life in general under Roman rule and they demonstrate the degree
to which apocalyptic views of wealth circulated in Diaspora Judaism.[30]
Scholarship is generally agreed that the traditions in Book 3 represent
a strand of Alexandrian Judaism probably from Leontopolis.[31] This is
based on the writer's favourable disposition and persistent references to
the Ptolemies and the Hellenistic flavour of the work in general. However,
it has more recently been argued that Roman Asia Minor may have been
the place of origin given the detailed topographical information revealed
by the writer and the overall emphasis on the region.[32] In addition, the
writer claims to be the famous Erythaean Sibyl from Asia. If this is the
case, the use of these oracles is widespread and provides insight into the
views related to wealth in the Diaspora. Overall, the place of origin does
not affect our interpretation of the wealth passages, although these various
provenances would support a view for a more widespread circulation of
these views.

Book 3

Book 3 is a composite work that consists of a number of shorter oracles.[33]
Three stages have been identified in the development of the book: (1) the
main corpus – verses 97–349 and 489–829; (2) first addition of oracles

---

[28] Cf. 'Enoch walked with God' (Gen 5:22, 24). See also Lightfoot, *Sibylline Oracles*,
pp. 72–3.

[29] *Ibid.*, p. 77.   [30] Collins, 'Sibylline Oracles', 322.

[31] Bartlett, *Jews in the Hellenistic World*, vol. II, p. 37. Collins, *Apocalyptic Imagination*,
pp. 124–5.

[32] Buitenwerf, *Book III*, pp. 130–3.

[33] Geffcken, *Komposition und Entstehungszeit*, pp. 1–17. See also Bate, *Sibylline Oracles*, pp. 21–3; Nilsson, *Geschichte des griechischen Religions*, vol. II, p. 112; Collins,
Sibylline Oracles of Egyptian Judaism, p. 21.

against different nations – verses 350–488; and (3) a second addition – verses 1–96.[34] The last can be further subdivided into two sections: 1–45 and 46–96.[35] The first two texts presented below come from this stage, one from the former and one the latter. The date of verses 1–45 is unknown. It is certainly Jewish and has an ethical stance, emphasizing monotheism and denouncing idolatry. Collins notes close parallels between this text and Philo, as well as the Jewish Orphic fragments, which are dated in the second century BCE,[36] yet no firm date can be assigned to this section. Collins dates verses 75–92 shortly after 31 BCE, based on the figure of Cleopatra as the widow in contrast to being the luxurious queen in 350–80. However, the passage may simply reflect circumstances from the period and is *ex eventu* prophecy. More recently, Buitenwerf has argued that 3.1–96 was originally part of a second book of the earliest collection of Sibylline Oracles, the remainder of which has not survived, and should be studied apart from 3.97–829.[37] In addition, the entirety of the third book has only been preserved through Christian transmission and may contain later interpolations.[38] Since the dating of this section is uncertain, I will only examine passages from Book 3.97–829.

The remainder of our texts can be dated somewhere between the late second and early first centuries BCE. As these are discussed, relevant dating and other introductory comments will be given. For now, it is safe to assume that all of the texts dealt with in this section can be dated no later than the late first century CE, reflecting prevalent attitudes and ideas about wealth and poverty within the Second Temple period from a different stream of tradition from what we find in Palestinian Judaism and the Qumran communities.

Oracles against Rome and the nations

It (the Roman kingdom) will rule over much land and will shake many and will thereafter cause fear to all kings. It will sack much gold and silver from many cities. But there will again be gold on the wondrous earth and then silver also and ornament. They will also oppress mortals. But those men will have a great fall when they launch on a course of unjust haughtiness. Immediately

---

[34] Collins, *Sibylline Oracles of Egyptian Judaism*, p. 28.

[35] vv. 63–74 are also considered later than the rest of the material in 1–96 but are not important to the present study.

[36] Collins, 'Sibylline Oracles', 360.

[37] Buitenwerf, *Book III*, p. 91. See also Lightfoot, *Sibylline Oracles*, p. 443.

[38] Buitenwerf, *Book III*, p. 125.

compulsion to impiety will come upon these men... It will cut up everything and fill everything with evils with disgraced love of gain (φιλοχρημοσύνη), ill-gotten wealth (κακοκερδέι πλούτῳ), in many places, but especially Macedonia.

(*Sibylline Oracles* 3:175–90)[39]

This passage is part of the larger oracle (3.162–95), which provides a historical account of kingdoms beginning with the reign of Solomon. It reflects the view that Rome's present conquests are the result of their avarice (φιλοχρημοσύνη). The reference to sacking much silver and gold may be attested in 1 Macc 8:1–3, in which the Romans secured the silver and gold mines of Spain.[40] This description of the Romans as greedy for money is also attested among the DSS (1QpHab 3:1–5; 6:1–8; 9:6–7), though the Sibyl takes a purely socio-political stance. This is a critique of the conquests of the Roman armies and the growing kingdom. The expectation that 'there will again be gold on the wondrous earth and then silver also and ornament' underscores the writer's expectation of a correction of these injustices when the Romans no longer rule. It should be noted, however, that the third book of oracles does not contain any cosmological or eschatological interests but is focused solely on the present and the earthly realm. There is an eschatological sense but not one that includes a final judgement of the wicked. All corrections of injustice take place in the present age on the earth. This highlights the political emphasis of the writer and the anti-propagandistic nature of the text (cf. *Sib. Or.* 3:350–3).

King will lay hold of king and take away territory. Peoples will ravage peoples and potentates, tribes. All leaders will flee to another land. The land will have a change of men and foreign rule will ravage all Greece and drain off the rich land of its wealth (πλοῦτος), and men will come face to face in strife among themselves because of gold and silver. Love of gain (φιλοχρημοσύνη) will be shepherd of evils for cities.

(*Sibylline Oracles* 3:635–43)

This text is part of the original corpus of the third book of oracles and is dated in the middle of the second century BCE.[41] The language of the passage indicates eschatological disasters, which were common *topoi* in apocalyptic literature (2 Esd 6:24; 9:3; 13:30–1; 2 Bar 70:3; 1 Enoch

---

[39] Translations follow Collins, 'Sibylline Oracles', pp. 362–80.   [40] *Ibid.*, p. 186.

[41] Collins, *Sibylline Oracles of Egyptian Judaism*, p. 33.

99:4). The text reveals an expectation that the last days will be marked by a love of money (φιλοχρημοσύνη) among humankind, which results in great wickedness. This coincides with the AOW, in which the seventh week is a time of great wickedness where the rich oppress the righteous (*1 Enoch* 93:9–10; 91:11).

Praise of the Jews

> But they care for righteousness and virtue and not love of money (φιλοχρημοσύνη), which begets innumerable evils for mortal men, war and limitless famine... nor does neighbour move the boundaries of neighbour nor does a very rich man (πολύ πλουτῶν) grieve a lesser man nor oppress widows in any respect... Always a prosperous man among the people gives a share of the harvest to those who have nothing but are poor (πενίχρομαι).   (*Sibylline Oracles* 3:234–45)

This passage occurs within the fourth section of the book and describes the history of the Jews as a people and God's dealing with them through exile and restoration. In describing their behaviour a sharp contrast is given between loving righteousness and virtue and loving money (φιλοχρημοσύνη). This same term occurs elsewhere in describing the avarice of the Romans (3:189; 624). This coincides with the Enochic tradition where those who love riches are contrasted with the righteous (*1 Enoch* 93:9–10; 95:7; 96:4; 99:16; 102:9–10; 108:8–15). However, here we do not have a categorical rejection of wealth as in the *Epistle* since some Jews are portrayed as being very rich (πολύ πλουτῶν τις ἀνήρ). This is because the present text reflects a time of faithfulness before the Babylonian exile. When the Jews turn away from God and are taken into captivity, the lines that follow indicate 'you will see innocent children and wives in slavery to hostile men. All means of livelihood and wealth will perish' (3:270–1). Thus, the retributive justice of the Deuteronomistic tradition is evident in this passage. A concern for covenant blessing is also evident in other comments about the faithfulness of the Jews: (1) just measurements (*Sib. Or.* 3:237; cf. Lev 19:35; Deut 25:15), (2) not moving a neighbour's boundary (*Sib. Or.* 3:240; cf. Deut 19:14; 27:17), and (3) providing a share of the harvest to the poor (*Sib. Or.* 3:241–5; cf. Lev 19:9–10; 23:22; Deut 24:19). All of these descriptions have socio-economic implications that contrast the faithful Jews with the activity of the wicked Romans in traditional language.

The present text functions to encourage faithfulness to God in light of his previous dealings with the Jews. Obedience and faithfulness brought God's peace and blessing while disobedience resulted in exile. The political aspect of the passage comes through in other texts where the Greeks are encouraged to be faithful to God. It also serves as a promise that God will pour out justice on Rome for its wicked practices just as he did on Babylon and Assyria. In light of the present situation, it looks forward to a future time of restoration and blessing for the Jews and judgement for the present wickedness of the Romans.

Future reversal

[F]or peace will come upon the land of the good. Prophets of the great God will take away the sword for they themselves are the judges of men and righteous kings. There will also be just wealth (πλοῦτος δίκαιος) among men for this is the judgment and dominion of the great God. Rejoice, maiden, and be glad, for to you the one who created heaven and earth has given the joy of the age. (*Sibylline Oracles* 3:780–6)

This text occurs in the last exhortation to righteous behaviour and the realization of the eschatological kingdom of God (3:762–808).[42] This kingdom is the realization of God's heavenly rule in political form on the earth. Its description is unusual in the portrayal of prophets as judges (cf. 1 Macc 14:41–3), yet what is portrayed here is the rule of the Jewish people over other nations in God's kingdom (Dan 7:18, 22, 27; Wis 3:8; *1 Enoch* 91:12–13; 1QM 12:14–15). More importantly, specific mention is made of πλοῦτος δίκαιος 'just wealth'. This same idea is present in the AOW when in the eighth week the faithful gain riches righteously (*1 Enoch* 91:12–13; cf. *Sib. Or.* 5:414–17).[43] There are differences in the traditions since the present passage occurs after the final judgement while the Enochic tradition places the judgement after the kingdom.[44] This indicates that traditions regarding the future material blessing of the

---

[42] Buitenwerf, *Book III*, p. 288; Collins, 'Sibylline Oracles', pp. 379–80.

[43] Olson, *Enoch*, p. 223. The fifth book is comprised of four central oracles: pp. 52–110, 111–78, 179–285, and 286–434, with 1–51 and 435–531 added later as an introduction and conclusion respectively. See Collins, *Sibylline Oracles of Egyptian Judaism*, p. 74. These later additions can be dated sometime after the revolt of 115 CE but before the Bar Kokhba revolt of 132 CE since vv. 46–9 portray Hadrian in a positive way. See Lanchester, 'Sibylline Oracles', p. 373.

[44] Olson, *Enoch*, p. 222.

faithful in terms of righteous wealth were widely circulating in different forms during the second century BCE.

The third Sibylline Oracle depicts the present wickedness and avarice of the Romans in their expanding kingdom. Its focus is primarily political and seeks to encourage the Greeks to follow the God of Israel and be faithful in light of his future intervention into history and the coming of his kingdom on earth. This kingdom, of course, is viewed in entirely earthly terms and lacks the cosmological concerns of the Jewish apocalypses. However, the reversal of fortunes for those who are faithful in this age, whether Jew or Greek, will result in the distribution of righteous wealth after the wicked Romans and their cohorts are destroyed. It lacks a categorical rejection of affluence such as we find in the *Epistle of Enoch* but certainly calumniates the oppression of others and wealth gained by unjust means. It also depicts the eschatological age prior to the coming of God's kingdom as a time when men will have an excessive desire to accumulate wealth.

5.5   Preliminary conclusions

In the Introduction to Part II, two fundamental considerations were proposed to keep in mind while examining the Second Temple texts: (1) that the basic premise of material blessing promised in the Deuteronomistic tradition may be an effective way of thinking theologically about wealth since all Jews, regardless of to which group or sect they were aligned, would understand this underlying theological concept and (2) whether these traditions interpret this theological premise in different ways.

In the case of the former, all of the documents examined in Part II demonstrate awareness of a theology of retribution by using language related to the Deuteronomistic tradition – most importantly the blessings and curses – when speaking about wealth or the rich. This justifies the methodology of thinking theologically rather than historically about wealth. In relation to the latter, I stated at the outset that a thorough analysis of the texts was necessary before we could know whether these documents reflect different, and sometimes opposing, perspectives on wealth in relation to the faithful community. These distinguishing features did in fact become evident during the course of the investigation and allow us at this point to make the following conclusions:

(1)   Two streams of tradition are evident in the Second Temple period relating to the expectation of material blessing as reflected in the

Deuteronomistic tradition. Of the sixteen documents examined, Ben Sira provides the clearest expression that affluence is the expected lot of the faithful in the present age. At the same time, it demonstrates a decided concern over the degree to which one can remain faithful in the course of buying and selling, this concern being unrelated to any critique of the economic system overall. There is no expectation of a future blessing for the faithful nor any hope for the enjoyment of wealth after death. Wisdom of Solomon attests both an underlying expectation of wealth in relation to wisdom while contrasting the righteous and wicked in terms of material wealth. In contrast, the Enochic tradition explicitly demonstrates a postponement of the Deuteronomistic promise of material blessing and is widely circulated in the Second Temple period, though it is attested in a variety of expressions.[45] These documents reject affluence as a feature of the present age for the faithful community.

(2)   Beginning with the BOW, and developed further in later apocalyptic texts, a view of the present age emerges in which evil as an organized, external force in the cosmos is active through the agency of fallen angels and the spirits of the bastard offspring. BOW (esp. *1 Enoch* 6–16) reflects the earliest attestation of the immortality of the spirits of humankind and distinguishing fates for the wicked and the faithful in the afterlife. *Damascus Document* attests a version of this tradition in which Belial is an active force in the world that seeks to lead Israel astray by means of appealing to their desire for affluence (CD 4:14–19). Accordingly, the Damascus community rejects affluence and develops a system for negotiating wealth among its members and outsiders. Other traditions also view wealth as a hindrance to gaining wisdom and to proper devotion to God.[46] The present evil age is viewed as a time of testing for the faithful until God intervenes and vindicates the righteous.[47]

(3)   A tradition emerges that associates the righteous with the poor and the wicked with the rich. This is most extensively

---

[45] *1 Enoch* 11:1; 45:4–6; 48:7; 91:13; 108:10, 12; 1QS 4:6–8; 4Q416 2 i:10–12; iii:9–14; 4Q417 2 i:10–12; *Sib. Or.* 3:780–86; Wis 5:15–16.

[46] *ALD* 13:10–12; 1QS 10:18–19; 1QHa 6:31; 7:22–3; 1QpHab 8:9–13; 4Q416 2 ii:4–7; ii:17–18; iii:2–7; 4Q417 2 i:21–2.

[47] *1 Enoch* 54:6; 56:4; CD 4:12–18; 1QM 16:11, 15; 17:1; 11Q19 54:12; 4Q177 9:2; 10 11:10; Wis 1:16; 3:5–6.

developed in the *Epistle of Enoch* in which the affluent are categorically characterized as sinners, although a view of the faithful as poor is only implicit (*1 Enoch* 96:5). This tradition becomes paradigmatic for later apocalyptic writers who make the same distinction (CD 19:9; Sir 8:2; 10:22–4; Wis 2:10) and further state that the godly reject material wealth altogether (*1 Enoch* 48:7; 108:10–12; 1QS 10:18–19; 1QH^a 6:31; 18:22–31; 4Q260 4:6–7). Consequently, the idea develops that the poor will inherit salvation while the rich are destined for destruction (*1 Enoch* 104:6; 108:10; CD 19:9–13; 4Q417 2 i:10–12; Wis 5:2–8). The righteous are admonished not to become attached to the affluent but to persevere. The labels 'rich' and 'poor' do not always refer to actual economic circumstances, which is attested in the Qumran sectarian documents in which community members worked, earned money, and owned slaves and livestock. And while earlier apocalyptic traditions may have taken shape within a setting of persecution, later traditions that indicate a marginal status is the visible distinguishing feature of the faithful community do so based on a voluntary position of marginality.

(4)   Among the Second Temple writers, the use of imputed speech becomes a common feature to denote the misperceptions of rich sinners. This device occurs across a variety of texts that evince opposing perspectives on wealth, though in most cases it emphasizes attitudes directly related to misunderstandings about accumulated riches.

The Second Temple period supplies a wide variety of texts that deal with the issue of wealth, though some have opposing expectations. This allows us to consider the degree to which this was a widely disputed topic among groups that considered themselves to be the people of God. The extent to which traditions preserved in the *Epistle of Enoch*, as well as other Enochic texts, were influencing later Greek writers into the first century CE who developed these traditions further, indicates it is reasonable to ask whether the same may be true of the Apocalypse. Moreover, the more concrete expressions of a categorical rejection of material wealth in direct relation to the faithful that were developing in the late first century CE make this an even more attractive possibility. To this end, we turn our attention to the Johannine Apocalypse to consider whether it is possible to say that these traditions have shaped our author's perspective on wealth for the faithful Christian community.

PART III

Wealth, poverty, and the faithful community in the Apocalypse of John

Introduction

Two distinct streams of tradition emerged from the analysis of Second Temple texts in Part II in relation to expectations for the promise of material blessing in the Deuteronomistic tradition. On the one hand, wealth is seen as the sign of God's favour and the expectation for the righteous. These traditions do not foresee any reward for the faithful in the afterlife but view wealth as a feature of the present age only. On the other hand, the apocalyptic texts demonstrate a developed cosmology that includes the postponement of any expectation for reward to the eschaton and portrays the righteous in the present age as the faithful poor, while associating affluence with the wicked.

These traditions emerged from faith communities that sought to justify their own piety in light of the obvious economic disparity that existed between themselves and what they deemed the corrupt leadership of the Jerusalem temple cult and other wealthy oppressors in the Greco-Roman world. If the Deuteronomistic promise of blessing was based on covenant obedience, how could the faithful poor defend their piety while they suffered and the wicked flourished? This was all the more important within Judaism when the corrupt religious leaders gained wealth and power through their positions of influence and cultural assimilation and attributed their wealth to the favour of God. In light of this economic disparity, apocalyptic communities attached themselves to the prophetic tradition in which the wicked from Israel's past were viewed as corrupt oppressors while the marginalized poor were viewed as the faithful. They advance this idea further by developing a cosmology that seeks to answer the problem of evil in the world in which the faithful suffer while the wicked flourish. This world view includes an interim period, which represents the present age in which God tests the faithful and allows sinners to prosper, and pushes the expectation of God's blessing into the future when there will be a complete reversal of fortunes. As demonstrated in the later apocalyptic traditions, these ideas develop further in the first century CE to the degree that the faithful are portrayed as those who reject affluence in the present age while the rich are categorically associated with the wicked.

These findings make it reasonable to consider whether John's calumniation of wealth in the Apocalypse is shaped in part by traditions that were already widely circulating rather than being an ad hoc response to the Roman Empire and imperial cults. Therefore, the present chapter will consider whether the author's theological world view demonstrates any familiarity with the apocalyptic paradigm that emerges from the Second Temple period. To the extent that these traditions can be detected in the Apocalypse, it may become possible to say that John was already predisposed to reject the pursuit of affluence by the righteous and is offering a more comprehensive theological perspective. We shall ask whether for John material blessing for the people of God is something to be realized at all in the present age. Related to this, we shall consider the degree to which the author's cosmology relates to certain expectations of wealth in the future and whether riches or affluence in the present constitute a threat to faithfulness or loyalty to God.

Following the methodology advanced in Part I, selected passages concerned with wealth will be discussed in their order of appearance in the Apocalypse. Since the first reference to the rich and poor occurs in the seven messages, the investigation will begin there, examining the references to wealth and poverty in Rev 2:9 and 3:17.[1] This will be followed by an analysis of John's throne-room vision and the breaking of the seven seals in Rev 4–6, since wealth is mentioned in relation to the Lamb (Rev 5:12) and the third horseman holds in his hands the economic image of balancing scales (Rev 6:5). Next, the reference to the mark of the beast in relation to 'buying and selling' will be considered (Rev 13:16–18). Finally, the climax of John's critique of wealth

---

[1] The message to Philadelphia (Rev 3:8) will be treated along with Smyrna (Rev 2:9), since they are the only two churches that are not admonished to repent and both are portrayed as marginalized communities.

in the destruction of Babylon will be discussed (Rev 18). A brief summary will follow in which our findings will be considered together to determine whether we can speak of a theology of wealth in the Apocalypse as a whole.

6

THE LANGUAGE OF WEALTH AND POVERTY IN THE SEVEN MESSAGES: REV 2–3

6.1   The Seven Messages

The peculiar character of the Book of Revelation is reflected in its combination of the apocalyptic idiom, its understanding of its message as prophecy, and its address to seven faith communities by means of a circular epistle.[1] While it is not within the scope of this thesis to resolve the rhetorical force of this combination, certain aspects of it are important. On the one hand, a remarkable linguistic unity throughout the work allows us to approach the text in its final form as it was probably presented to the original readers/hearers.[2] On the other hand, the distinguishable textual units of Revelation expose its composite nature and conception over time. Early source-critical scholars were zealous to find countless redactional units, though many of their conclusions were drawn from a reconstruction of historical events thought to underlie the text.[3] Throughout

---

[1] Charles, *Revelation*, vol. I, pp. 37–47 argued that the seven messages were originally independent letters sent to the churches, which were later edited to fit into the Apocalypse as a whole. Other scholars who view the messages as letters include Mounce, *Revelation*, pp. 83–130; Osborne, *Revelation*, pp. 104–6; Ramsay, *Letters*, pp. 38–9. Kirby, 'Rhetorical Situations', p. 200 sees a close similarity with the Hellenistic epistolary form. Aune recognizes similarities with letters to Persian kings and royal edicts but acknowledges there is 'not a single characteristic feature of the early Christian epistolary tradition': *Revelation 1–5*, p. 125. Fiorenza, *Vision*, p. 53 does not regard them as real letters to individual churches but as a rhetorical device to provide a schematized picture of the church in Asia Minor overall. At the same time she highlights the epistolary nature of the Apocalypse as a whole and contends that John is following the Pauline epistolary tradition. See Fiorenza, 'Apokalypsis and Propheteia', p. 125. For a similar argument, see also Beale, *Revelation*, p. 133 and Karrer, *Johannesoffenbarung als Brief*, pp. 159–65.

[2] See Thompson, *Apocalypse and Empire*, pp. 37–52. See also Mounce, *Revelation*, pp. 45–7; Beasley-Murray, *Revelation*, pp. 29–32; Roloff, *Revelation*, pp. 15–17; Beckwith, *Apocalypse*, pp. 216–39; Lohmeyer, *Offenbarung*, pp. 185–289; Boxall, *Revelation*, 17.

[3] For classic examples of source-critical approaches to the Apocalypse, see Bousset, *Offenbarung*, pp. 283–4, 324–30, 346–58, 410–15 (esp. 414–15); Charles, *Revelation*, vol. II, pp. 144–54; Whealen, 'New Patches on an Old Garment', pp. 54–9. The present study follows closely Aune's proposal that there were two editions of the Apocalypse, though with some minor variations. He argues that the first edition consisted of 1:7–12a

the study there will be opportunities to interact critically with these attempts, though the identification of some such units can be regarded as certain. For example, there is wide scholarly agreement that the seven messages were formulated independently of the apocalypse proper (Rev 4–22) that was written earlier, albeit by the same hand.[4] Additionally, the messages (Rev 2–3) display a certain coherence and comprehensiveness that discourage us from viewing them as discrete pieces of communication. Although the text of the Apocalypse has been subjected to a plethora of source-critical theories only a few have detected significant interpolations or revisions there.[5]

Aune has argued that the seven messages follow the form of royal and imperial edicts,[6] while in content they demonstrate the characteristics of parenetic salvation–judgement oracles that were employed by early Christian prophets.[7] He argues that the τάδε λέγει formula was used in rescripts and letters of Persian kings and 'corresponds to the simple λέγει' in edicts of Roman emperors and magistrates.[8] Aune presses the discussion in the direction of imperial edicts in an effort to establish John's strategy of portraying Christ as the true king over against the Roman emperor.[9] While it is possible to detect some similarities in form between the seven messages and royal edicts, there are significant reasons why they should be viewed in their Jewish context in both form and function as prophetic messages. (1) John refers to the Apocalypse explicitly as prophecy (προφητεία) and the tripartite formula of 1:19, 'write what you have seen, what is, and what is to take place after these things (ἃ μέλλει γενέσθαι)', may indicate that the writer is following a traditional prophetic

---

and 4:1–22:5 and the second edition included 1:1–6; 1:12b–3:22 and an epilogue 22:6–21. I see 1:7–8 as part of the first edition, with 1:1–3 and 1:9–3:22 added at a later date with the epilogue 22:6–21. My conclusions are not affected by this arrangement since the primary issue is that the seven messages were added to the Apocalypse proper (4–22:5) at a later time, though probably by the same writer; contra Kraft, *Offenbarung*, pp. 49–50. For a summary of the various source-critical theories, see Fiorenza, *Justice and Judgment*, pp. 160–4; Osborne, *Revelation*, pp. 27–30; Aune, *Revelation 1–5*, pp. xc–cxxxiv (esp. pp. cxx–cxxxiv).

[4] Aune, *Revelation 1–5*, p. cxxxii; Kraft, *Offenbarung*, p. 17; Prigent, *Apocalypse*, p. 149; Roloff, *Revelation*, pp. 41–2; Ramsay, *Letters*, pp. 38–9.

[5] See, however, Charles, *Revelation*, vol. I, pp. lvii–lix; Spitta, *Offenbarung*, pp. 236–313.

[6] Aune, 'Form and Function', 182–204; also Aune, *Revelation 1–5*, pp. 126–9.

[7] Aune, *Prophecy in Early Christianity*, p. 326.

[8] Aune, *Revelation 1–5*, p. 127.

[9] See discussion below concerning John's vision of Christ in the throne-room vision for the difficulties in Aune's position: foremost, an *a priori* assumption that John's primary concern is with the Roman Empire and the emperor.

formula.[10] (2) The phrase τάδε λέγει κύριος occurs 324 times in the LXX, over 250 of which are preserved in the prophetic messenger formula that translates the phrase כה אמר יהוה 'thus says Yahweh',[11] and over half of which occur in the prophetic tradition.[12] (3) The author utilizes a significant number of prophetic speech forms as well as extensive language and imagery from the prophetic tradition (Rev 1:7–8, 17–20; 2–3; 13:9–10; 14:8, 13; 16:15; 18:3, 9–19; 21–24; 21:3–8; 22:7, 12–14. 18–20).[13] (4) While the messages demonstrate some elements of imperial edicts, it has been noted, taken as a whole, that they do not conform to any known literary form.[14] (5) A more problematic detail is the degree of indirect mediation within the seven messages, which does not feature in royal edicts. Imperial edicts were written from the emperor or magistrate himself directly to the region or people to whom they were addressed. The Apocalypse, however, displays several layers of mediation. On the one hand, the Revelation is given to Jesus by God and is made known by sending an angel to John. On the other hand, John acts as mediator to the churches in giving them the message and does so by writing messages from Christ to the angel of each of the churches.[15]

---

[10] See van Unnik, 'A Formula Describing Prophecy', pp. 85–94; Aune, *Revelation 1–5*, pp. 105, 112–14. The statement cited above (1:19) has frequently been viewed as an outline for the content of the Apocalypse. Thus, the introductory vision (1:9–20) is what John has seen, the seven messages (2–3) contain what is, and the Apocalypse proper (4–22) contains what is to take place after. So Bousset, *Offenbarung*, p. 198; Lohse, *Offenbarung*, p. 22; Charles, *Revelation*, vol. I, p. 33; Boring, *Revelation*, p. 84; Prigent, *Apocalypse*, p. 145. However, this view is not sustainable in light of the many references throughout the apocalyptic section (4–22) that refer to events past, present, and future. It is more likely that this phrase refers to the entire vision of John in the whole of the Apocalypse. So Caird, *Revelation*, p. 26; Aune, *Revelation 1–5*, p. 105; Fiorenza, *Justice and Judgment*, p. 58; Boxall, *Revelation*, p. 44; Roloff, *Revelation*, p. 38; Smalley, *Revelation*, p. 57.

[11] Aune, *Revelation 1–5*, p. 121. Cf. also *3 Bar* 1:3; 4:15; 15:4; 16:1; *T. Job* 4:3; 7:9; *T. Abr.* 8:5; *Asc. Isa.* 3:4; *Life of Adam and Eve*, 22:2.

[12] Beale, *Revelation*, p. 229.

[13] See Müller, *Prophetie und Predigt*, pp. 47–107; Aune, *Prophecy in Early Christianity*, pp. 274–88. Aune's earlier work examines the Apocalypse in light of its Jewish context.

[14] Karrer, *Johannesoffenbarung als Brief*, pp. 159–60; Aune, *Revelation 1–5*, p. 125; Hartmann, 'Form and Message', p. 142.

[15] The angelic recipients of the seven messages are viewed in two broad categories: (1) supernatural angelic beings and (2) human messengers. The latter is further divided into two possibilities: (1) leaders or bishops in the churches and (2) local Christian prophets. However, this approach is compromised by the fact that the term ἄγγελος never refers to human beings in the entirety of the Apocalypse. See Charles, *Revelation*, vol. I, p. 34; Bousset, *Offenbarung*, pp. 200–1. Others have suggested that they refer to visionary counterparts to local Christian prophets. See Fiorenza, *Justice and Judgment*, pp. 145–6. However, they are most likely a literary device that the author uses (1) to indicate to the churches that there is a cosmological link between the churches and heaven and (2) to remove himself from the discussion one step in order to send a sharp rebuke to the churches

Taken together with the prophet-to-prophet confrontation between John and Jezebel and the author's concern over 'those who say they are Jews but are not', the seven messages are best seen in their Jewish context. However, this does not mean that the readers/hearers would not have heard echoes of imperial edicts when the messages were read. What it does mean is that the writer is more likely to be following the τάδε λέγει formula as it was used in the OT prophetic tradition, and, in that sense, they should be viewed as prophetic messages.

The stylistic pattern that persists throughout each message and the use of seven churches indicates the author's strategy was to streamline the messages into a single literary form that would coincide with the apocalyptic visions (4–22).[16] As such, they function to provide a 'schematized picture' of the state of the church as a whole in Asia Minor.[17] In addition, the circular nature of the letter implies that the messages directed to each individual church were relevant for all. So we can expect that the conditions described (i.e., of being poor or rich) also had a more comprehensive referent since these communities in Asia Minor would have represented a variety of socio-economic classes.[18] While Royalty is correct to exercise caution in attributing the problems raised in the messages to the actual socio-historical circumstances of the churches, the relation between these concerns and the socio-historical realities should not be ignored. In the same way, the prophetic rivalry between John and the prophetess Jezebel is not a literary construction, however heightened it may be, but may well reflect a genuine dispute between these two Christian prophets.[19] And while John is intent on establishing his authority over that of Jezebel, this is not his chief aim.

---

indirectly. For a more detailed discussion of the possibilities, see Aune, *Revelation 1–5*, pp. 108–12; Stuckenbruck, *Angel Veneration*, pp. 234–40; Müller, *Offenbarung*, pp. 87–9.

[16] Each message very generally includes: (1) command to write (2) prophetic messenger formula (3) 'I know' section (present situation) (4) accusation (5) call to repent (6) warning (7) admonition, and (8) promise. Of course, the messages to Smyrna and Philadelphia do not include (4) or (5). Cf. also the author's use of seven stars, lampstands, churches, spirits, torches, seals, eyes, horns, trumpets, angels, thunders, heads, diadems, plagues, bowls, mountains.

[17] Fiorenza, *Vision*, p. 53. So also Beale, *Revelation*, p. 226. It is reasonable to assume that there were a number of house churches in each of the regions mentioned in the seven messages. See Royalty, *Streets of Heaven*, p. 70.

[18] Luke 19:2–8; Acts 4:34–5:2; 16:14; Rom 16:1–15, 23;1 Cor 16:2, 19, Philem 1–11. See Meeks, *First Urban Christians*, pp. 51–73; Malherbe, *Social Aspects*, pp. 29–59; Theissen, *Social Setting*, pp. 69–110.

[19] John's dispute with a rival 'prophetess' also validates the thesis that the τάδε λέγει formula functions in the seven messages to highlight the prophetic authority of John's communication.

His use of pejorative labels to denounce opponents and draw vivid boundaries between insiders and outsiders demonstrates a remarkable sectarian character.[20] This further suggests that this is as much a theological or interpretive dispute as it is a conflict over authority.[21] To be sure, the two are closely linked together since the issue of prophetic authenticity is what validates one interpretation over another.[22] The question then becomes, what is the dispute that John is addressing?

Royalty surmises that the messages focus on two overriding issues: (1) endurance through suffering and (2) the church's reception of false teachers, the former resulting from the rejection of the latter.[23] Yet, when we consider the formulaic pattern of the seven messages, two distinct interruptions in this uniformity stand out. First, the call to repentance is absent in only two messages. The church at Smyrna is experiencing poverty (πτωχεία) while Philadelphia has few resources (μικρὰν δύναμιν). Second, only the message to Laodicea includes the rhetorical device of imputed speech in which members of the church boast in their accumulated wealth, something only found elsewhere in the Apocalypse in John's harsh critique of riches in Rev 18. The presence of these two instances, taken together with the praise of poverty and the calumniation of affluence, indicates that the interpretive dispute at hand in some way revolves around the degree to which John's readers/hearers can accumulate wealth, on the one hand, and remain faithful to God, on the other.

While five churches are called to repent, all seven are admonished to 'conquer'. This indicates that (1) John considers a number of his readers/hearers are presently involved in or hold to teaching that is in conflict with his understanding of faithfulness. That the author has affixed an introductory text which reflects such a diverse set of circumstances to a single apocalypse, taken together with the stylistic pattern and literary unity of the messages, suggests that (2) the comprehensive solution to each of these circumstances finds its resolution in 'conquering'.[24]

---

[20] See M. Collins, *The Use of Sobriquets in the Qumran Dead Sea Scrolls*, pp. 196–207; Malina and Neyrey, 'Conflict in Luke-Acts', pp. 97–122; Barclay, 'Deviance and Apostasy', pp. 121–5; Pietersen, 'Despicable Deviants', pp. 343–52; and 'False Teaching, Lying Tongues and Deceitful Lips', in Campbell, et al., *New Directions*, pp. 166–81. See discussion below.

[21] Baumgarten, *Flourishing of Jewish Sects*, pp. 55–8, 77–80; Bengtsson, 'Three Sobriquets', in Charlesworth, *Hebrew Bible*, pp. 241–73; deSilva, 'The Revelation to John', pp. 375–95; Yarbro Collins, 'Insiders and Outsiders', pp. 187–218.

[22] Cf. 2 Cor 11:12–15; Titus 1:11, 13; 3:11; 2 Pet 2:1; 1 John 4:1; Rev 2:2.

[23] Royalty, *Streets of Heaven*, p. 152.

[24] The author has intricately woven the content of the Apocalypse into the messages in order to provide the churches with a more localized reality of his apocalyptic visions. For

Sitz im leben: an ecclesial situation

As noted in Part I, scholars are divided on the degree to which the *Sitz im Leben* of the Apocalypse is dominated by a crisis of persecution. Although it is questionable to assume any programmatic or widespread persecution through the imperial cults and trade guilds, John knows of at least one person who has died (Rev 2:13) and indicates that the possibility of death is an increasing reality for the faithful (Rev 2:9; 6:11; 11:7–10; 14:13; 17:6; 18:24; 19:2). Moreover, he states that he too is a sharer (συγκοινωνός) in the persecution, kingdom, and patient endurance (ὑπομονή) of Jesus (Rev 1:9). Caution should be exerted, however, in assuming that John's suffering refers to a so-called exile or banishment to the isle of Patmos enforced by the Roman Empire. It is not entirely clear why John was on the island, although he indicates it is 'because of (διά) the word of God and the testimony of Jesus'.[25] Given the sectarian nature of the text, John's Patmos stay may have been entirely voluntary in order to separate visibly from his opponents.[26] What we can know about the statement is the author's presupposition that sharing in the kingdom of Jesus includes suffering and endurance.

example, the importance of repentance, which is called for in the messages to Ephesus, Pergamum, Thyatira, Sardis, and Laodicea, is demonstrated in those who do not repent and suffer God's judgement (Rev 9:20–1; 16:9–11). Language involving conquering (Rev 5:5; 6:2; 11:7; 12:11; 13:7; 15:2; 17:14; 21:7), nakedness and shame (Rev 16:15), the tree of life (Rev 2:7; 22:14, 19), the second death (Rev 2:11; 20:6, 14; 21:8), Jezebel's adultery (Rev 2:22; 14:8; 17:2; 18:3: 19:2), Satan (Rev 2:9, 13, 24; 3:9; 12:9), and the New Jerusalem (Rev 3:12; 21:2) comes into play in the apocalyptic section (Rev 4–22) that ties the visions to the churches. In addition, admonitions to the churches are repeated throughout the Apocalypse (Rev 4–22): Let the one who has an ear hear (Rev 13:9); Behold I am coming like a thief (Rev 16:15). See Thompson, *Apocalypse and Empire*, pp. 179–80.

[25] The early church fathers believed that John had been banished to Patmos by the Roman Empire (Jerome, *Hom. Matth.* 7.51, 16.6; Clement, *Quis div.*, 42; Eusebius, *Hist. eccl.* 3.18). However, the phrase 'on account of the word of God and testimony of Jesus' (διά + accusative) can indicate either purpose or result (BDF § 222). Thus it is possible to suggest that John could have gone to the island for the purpose of proclaiming the word and testimony of God and Jesus. However, John frequently uses the construction διά + accusative to denote result (2:3; 4:11; 6:9; 7:15; 12:11; 13:14; 18:10), and one instance in particular describes the death of Christians as a result of their testimony (20:4). On this, see Boxall, *Revelation*, p. 39; Aune, *Revelation 1–5*, pp. 80–2. Ancient writers mention the island but never as a place of banishment: Pliny, *Nat.* 4.69–70; Tacitus, *Ann.*, 4.30; Thucydides 3.33. For a list of islands that are explicitly referred to as places of exile, see Saffrey, 'Relire L'Apocalypse à Patmos', p. 398. It is possible to suggest, in light of the conflict portrayed with the prophetess Jezebel, that John fled to the isle of Patmos for the purpose of physically separating from the opponents he envisions in the church. A similar situation is reflected among the community that settled at Qumran (1QpHab 2:1–3; 5:10–11; 7:4–5; 9:9–10 (esp. 11:4–6); cf. CD 20:14). Given the sectarian nature of John's language and message, this cannot be entirely ruled out.

[26] See Perry, 'Critiquing the Excess of Empire', p. 494.

The language of persecution and social injustices permeates the Apocalypse and thus it would be wrong to disregard the *ethos* of hostility and conflict the author creates. At the same time, John can only name one martyr apart from Jesus while all other explicit references to such persecution appear in his visionary world.[27] In addition, the seven messages show that only a minority of believers are experiencing persecution, which makes it possible to detect a disconnect between the author's expectations of hostility for the faithful and what is being taught and practised in the churches. For this reason, the present section will draw attention to this disparity and how it coincides with what faithfulness means for the author in relation to wealth.

We have noted that the most immediate crisis in the Book of Revelation is not a Neronic or Domitianic persecution but occurs as a prophetic rivalry between John and at least three rival teachers: Jezebel, Balaam, and the Nicolaitans.[28] Yet it should be noted that this conflict is portrayed only from the author's perspective. John reveals that he has confronted Jezebel and asked her to repent (Rev 2:21). Her unwillingness to do so suggests she and her adherents do not perceive the situation the same way as John; indeed, the reception of her teaching by so many in the church indicates that John may have held a minority opinion. This may provide additional evidence that John's stay at Patmos was occasioned by internal conflict that resulted in his attempt to separate himself physically from his opponents (cf. CD 7:13–15; 1QM 1:3; 1QpHab 11:6; 4Q242 1 3:4). That is, John draws on the language of exile and suffering (συγκοινωνός ἐν τῇ θλίψει) in anticipation of the radical call to separate that he imposes throughout the Apocalypse (Rev 13:16–17; 18:4).

When referring to his opponents John takes the approach of name-calling or labelling in order to associate them with the wicked enemies of

[27] deSilva, *Seeing Things John's Way*, p. 53 maintains that the author portrays martyrdom only in the past and the future. To some degree this is correct, though the distinction should be between the single incident of Antipas and the author's assumption that more widespread faithfulness among the church would lead to a greater degree of martyrdom. Thus, Antipas reflects not only the author's idea of faithfulness but also his perception that this kind of faithfulness is lacking.

[28] Aune, *Revelation 1–5*, p. 203 asserts that Jezebel was an influential woman in this Christian community. Others note the connection between Lydia, the seller of purple from Thyatira (Acts 16:14–15) and the prophetess mentioned by John. See Boxall, '"Jezebel" of Thyatira', pp. 147–51; Thompson, *Apocalypse and Empire*, p. 124. Royalty, *Streets of Heaven*, pp. 27–38 contends that the conflict is over authority. Duff, *Who Rides the Beast?*, pp. 31–60, rightly places the dispute within the economic realm and even notes John's anti-commerce rhetoric. However, he limits the possibility of John's critique to a response to idolatry in the imperial cults. His thesis is a good balance between Kraybill and Royalty, though it is still limited by its dependence on historical setting.

God's people in the sacred traditions of the Hebrew Bible.[29] This practice, which is not unique to John, is also attested, for example, among the
sectarian documents from Qumran. Here the labels Builders of the Wall,
Boundary Shifters, and the Man of the Lie each reformulate prophetic
language to associate opponents of the community with notorious evil-
doers from Israel's past.[30] Labelling of deviant behaviour can take place
within any kind of social group and normally arises from internal political conflict.[31] However, within the context of ancient Jewish groups this
phenomenon typically occurs within the context of sectarian disputes.[32]
In any given society one may belong to several social groups and break
the rules of one simply by obeying those of another.[33] Thus the behaviour
labelled as deviant may or may not be so in society at large but only in
relation to a particular community or the one doing the labelling.[34] It is a
response to behaviour the labeller considers deviant but may or may not
be considered as such by everyone (or anyone) else.

Labels are applied in this way not merely to describe the iniquitous
deeds of the indicted actors but to serve as an attempt to discredit their
entire character.[35] Thus, by utilizing nicknames such as Jezebel and Balaam, John's prophetic speech effectively places his opponents outside
the purview of the faithful community.[36] Royalty's assertion that a dispute over authority is the central issue in the Apocalypse does not go far
enough. Rather, to John it is a matter of whether one adheres to teaching that he maintains is incompatible with faithfulness. The practice of
deviance occurs within a group when certain members express the degree
of diversity that can be tolerated in response to the actions or views of
other members that the former believe threatens the community's distinctive shape or unique identity.[37] John's use of labels then indicates that
he has an already formulated understanding of the basis of the identity
of the church on the one hand, and the particular shape that it should
take on the other. Given the two perspectives on wealth that develop in

[29] Bengtsson, 'Three Sobriquets', in Charlesworth, *Hebrew Bible*, pp. 241–73. See also
Johns, 'Dead Sea Scrolls and the Apocalypse', pp. 271–4; Goranson, 'Essene Polemic',
pp. 455–6.

[30] M. Collins, *The Use of Sobriquets in the Qumran Dead Sea Scrolls*, pp. 182–93.

[31] Becker, *Outsiders*, p. 7.

[32] Baumgarten, *Flourishing of Jewish Sects*, pp. 18–19.

[33] Becker, *Outsiders*, p. 8.

[34] This is referred to as the 'interactionist theory of deviance'. See Becker, *Outsiders*,
p. 181.

[35] *Ibid.*, pp. 33–4; Schur, *Politics of Deviance*, pp. 12–14.

[36] Yarbro Collins, *Crisis and Catharsis*, p. 170.

[37] Erikson, *Wayward Puritans*, p. 11.

the Second Temple period, this encourages us to consider whether John and Jezebel, respectively, hold such opposing views. An examination of John's characterization of the rival teachers and their teaching may help to shed additional light on the nature of the dispute.

Unlike Jezebel, to whom he refers specifically, the writer only makes reference to the teaching and works of the Nicolaitans and Balaam.[38] These, one could argue, do not represent actual persons so much as they describe the kind of teaching being promoted. Charles emphasized the etymological significance of these two sobriquets. The former, he argued, is constructed from νικᾷ 'he conquers' and λαός 'the people.' Similarly, the latter is derived from בלה / בלע 'he destroys' and עם 'the people'.[39] Given the plural suffix (-τῶν) of the former and the writer's consistent use of the participial form of νικάω in the seven messages, it is better rendered 'the conquering people'.

Aune and Räisänen have both rejected this proposal, stating that the term was associated with a real person who bore the name Nicolaus, yet the reconstruction of any historical connection between these churches and this figure is tenuous.[40] They note that Nicolaus is a name of honour similar to Alexander, while Balaam is a pejorative label, so there can be no connection between the two. Yet, this argument is only valid if the label can be associated with such a name or person. In any case, every name used in the seven messages is pejorative, something which poses a problem for considering any positive connection with a historical Nicolaus, at least in John's mind. Räisänen discounts the possibility of any etymological significance casually, considering Charles's thesis dubious.[41] This, he states, is because νικᾶν and בלה have nothing to do

---

[38] See Duff, *Who Rides the Beast?*, p. 149 n. 15. See also deSilva, *Seeing Things John's Way*, p. 59 n. 105.

[39] Charles, *Revelation*, vol. I, p. 52. So also Lohmeyer, *Offenbarung*, p. 26; Farrer, *Revelation*, p. 74; Kirby, 'Rhetorical Situations', p. 207 n. 41; Boring, *Revelation*, p. 93; *ABD*, vol. IV, p. 1107.

[40] Aune, *Revelation 1–5*, p. 149; Räisänen, 'The Nicolaitans', p. 1608. The latter, based on patristic evidence, argues that the Nicolaitans attached themselves to the name of Nicolaus of Antioch. See Irenaeus, *Haer.*, 1.26.3; Clement of Alexandria, *Strom.* 2.20; 3.4. Cf. Tertullian, *Marc.* 1.29; *Praescr.* 33 who distinguishes Gnostic Nicolaitans of his own day from those in the Apocalypse. Yet, this patristic evidence is wide ranging in its views of who the first century Nicolaitans were and is not helpful in establishing them as a Gnostic sect. So 'Nicolaitans', *ABD*, vol. 4, p. 1107, contra Fiorenza, *Justice and Judgement*, pp. 114–32. Moreover, it is not clear that these authors are actually referring to a particular group in the Apocalypse as much as they are associating the character of contemporary groups with the biblical example. See also Barrett, 'Gnosis and the Apocalypse', pp. 125–37. There is general agreement that we cannot know historically who this group represents.

[41] Räisänen, 'The Nicolaitans', p. 1608.

with one another. While this may be true, Räisänen still does not address the etymological link between the root (νικ-) and the persistent use of the term 'to conquer' (νικάω) throughout the Apocalypse (Rev 2:7, 11, 17, 26; 3:5, 12, 21; 5:5; 6:2; 11:7; 12:11; 13:7; 15:2; 17:14; 21:7). Moreover, the text clearly equates the teaching of the Nicolaitans and Balaam (Rev 2:14–15) suggesting an etymological link may not be as dubious as Räisänen supposes.[42]

This kind of wordplay is not uncommon, especially in relation to the name Balaam (Philo, *Cher.* 32; *b. Sanh.* 105a). Traditions were already circulating that connected the name with ideas of buying and selling and greed.[43] It should also be noted that all of the names used in the seven messages are fictive sobriquets that attempt to marginalize John's opponents. Thus, even if the designation Nicolaitans was related in some way to a person named Nicolaus, this does not preclude John's ability or willingness to put a negative spin on the group's own self-designation in relation to his persistent reference to conquering in each of the seven messages.[44]

Two ways of conquering are represented throughout the Apocalypse. (1) The evil cosmic forces of the present age make war against the faithful to conquer and kill them (Rev 6:2; 11:7; 13:7). (2) The faithful are admonished to conquer and are given specific promises for doing so (Rev 2:7, 11, 17, 26; 3:5, 12, 21; 21:7). The realization of these promises are depicted in scenes where the faithful have conquered the Dragon and the beast (Rev 12:11; 15:2), while, paradoxically, they have been conquered. In each of these situations, the death of the faithful is in view. Thus, their conquering is bound up with that of the faithful Lamb who also conquered through death (Rev 3:21; 5:5–6).[45] Given the writer's systematic admonition in each of the seven messages to conquer, it is plausible to think that the teaching proposed by the Nicolaitans commended a way of conquering economically that is in complete opposition to John's. The notion that riches (πλοῦτος) helped to overcome (νικάω) the difficulties of life was present in the ancient world, though these terms, occurring together, most frequently indicate wealth gained through the victory of

---

[42] Aune, *Revelation 1–5*, p. 188; Boxall, *Revelation*, p. 59.

[43] Philo, *Mos.* 1:294–9; Josephus, *Ant.* 4:126–30. See also *m. 'Abot* 5:19–22; *Tg.* Num 24:14; *Midr. Rab.* Num 20:23. Cf. Jude 11; 2 Pet 2:15.

[44] See Barr, *Tales of the End*, p. 56.

[45] Räisänen identifies the connections between John's concerns over commercial activity, the mark of the beast, the rejection of the economic system and the subsequent suffering that would result, yet, in the entirety of his very fine article, conquering is never discussed.

battle.[46] In Jewish apocalyptic texts, the idea of wealth acquired through oppression is placed within the context of the suffering righteous and is developed most extensively in the early Enochic tradition.[47] If, however, conquering is very much John's language, this may reflect more the author's characterization of the opponents rather than what they openly said. And, in anticipation of his concerns over participation (συγκοιν-ωνός) in Babylon's sins (Rev 18:4), it indicates that those who pursue wealth are likewise guilty of the oppression of the faithful in the Apocalypse (cf. *1 Enoch* 97:4). Thus, the sobriquets Balaam and the Nicolaitans do not represent actual historical groups or persons with whom John is in conflict as much as they are negative labels that malign a certain kind of teaching that is identical to that of Jezebel.

The content of the false teaching opposed by John consists of: (1) eating meat sacrificed to idols (εἰδωλόθυτος), and (2) the practice of fornication (πορνεύω). The former is a term used to describe meat that has been sacrificed on a pagan altar, part of which was eaten by the priest while the remainder was sold in the marketplace.[48] This could have been a point of contention for John since it may have been impossible to distinguish sacrificed meat in the marketplace and thus his readers/hearers would most likely have all been guilty of idolatry.[49] Yet it is interesting that one of the churches that is compromising in this way is directly associated with the only faithful witness, suggesting the area of concern for John is not directly related to eating sacrificial meat. Paul deals with this same issue in the Corinthian correspondence and indicates that these idols did not represent real gods since there was only one true God (1 Cor 8:4). Thus Jezebel may have been in agreement with Paul, yet John disagrees sharply, if this is what he has in mind.[50]

It would have also been difficult for John's affluent recipients, or those who aspired to become rich, to avoid sacral meals in the *collegia* and other pagan celebrations and festivals in which social and economic

---

[46] Euripides, *Ion*, 629–30; Philo, *Deus*, 147; Josephus, *J. W.* 3.24.55–6; Xenophon, *Hell.*, 2.4.17.2–5; Diodorus, *Bib. Hist.*, 10.34.12.1–5. Cf. 1QpHab 5:12–6:8; *Sib. Or.* 3:175–90.

[47] *1 Enoch* 8:2; 9:1, 9–10; 94:6–10; 95:4–7; 96:4–8; 97:3–10; 98:2–99:2; 99:11–16; 100:7–9; 101:4–102:3, 9; 103:5–8; 104:7–9.

[48] *BDAG*, p. 280. Some scholars have argued that it is a technical term that refers specifically to eating meat in the presence of an idol or in the temple precincts. See Witherington, 'Not so Idol Thoughts', 237–54. However, there is no substantive evidence for this view. See also Fee, *Corinthians*, pp. 357–63. This definition is too narrow since the term can also refer to sacrificial meat sold in the marketplace. See Willis, *Idol Meat in Corinth*, pp. 37–45; Cheung, *Idol Food in Corinth*, p. 320.

[49] Fotopoulos, *Food Offered to Idols*, p. 8.

[50] Fiorenza, *Justice and Judgment*, pp. 107, 116–18; and *Vision*, pp. 56–7; Boxall, *Revelation*, p. 64.

networks were so closely linked. Furthermore, all meals, both private and public, would have involved formal cultic customs to some degree since the cults permeated every aspect of society.[51] Thus, potentially all of John's recipients would have regularly participated in meals that involved some degree of cultic activity. It seems, then, that what John objects to is participation in public festivals and meals for the express purpose of gaining wealth and acquiring or maintaining positions of power and influence.[52] In that sense, eating sacrificial meat is a secondary issue to the accumulation of wealth, which may be the reason why there is no further mention of εἰδωλόθυτος in the entirety of the Apocalypse.[53] It should be noted, however, that the word never occurs by itself but in both instances is qualified within a phrase 'to eat meat sacrificed to idols and to commit fornication' (φαγεῖν εἰδωλόθυτα καὶ πορνεῦσαι). The persistent use of πορνεία here and throughout the text may shed additional light on John's concerns.

The term πορνεία and its cognates occur nineteen times in the Apocalypse (Rev 2:14, 20, 21; 9:21; 14:8; 17:1–2, 4–5, 15–16; 18:3, 9; 19:2 [×2]; 21:8; 22:15). Three occur in the seven messages and ten in the visions of the whore and Babylon (Rev 17–18). Scholars are generally agreed that the term in chapters 17–18 refers to the economic activity of the kings of the earth and the merchants who have grown rich from the luxurious lifestyle of Babylon (Rev 18:3).[54] The imagery of the whore drinking her immoral wine from a golden cup and the name on her forehead all pick up on economic language the author has adopted in previous passages (Rev 13:16–17; 14:8–10).[55] Taken together with John's concern regarding the economic status of his readers/hearers, the occurrences in the seven messages may also have economic overtones. By means of the words πορνεία and πλανάω the author connects Jezebel with the Dragon (Rev 12:9), the beasts (Rev 13:14), the whore (Rev 17:2, 4), and Babylon (Rev 14:8; 18:3, 9). And given the economic language in these texts we may argue that John intends to portray the teaching of Jezebel in terms that undermine her view of wealth in relation to the faithful community.

[51] Meggitt, 'Meat Consumption', pp. 137–41.

[52] Duff, *Who Rides the Beast?*, p. 55; deSilva, *Seeing Things John's Way*, pp. 60–1.

[53] The term εἴδωλον occurs in 9:20 and sinners are referred to as idolaters in 21:8; 22:15, though in this context they are associated with several names, i.e. murderers, cowards, liars, etc.

[54] Aune, *Revelation 17–22*, p. 988; Kraybill, *Imperial Cult and Commerce*, p. 54; Yarbro Collins, *Crisis and Catharsis*, p. 121.

[55] Aune, *Revelation 17–22*, p. 988; Beale, *Revelation*, pp. 895–7; Boxall, *Revelation*, p. 256; Royalty, *Streets of Heaven*, pp. 208–9.

It is important to note as well that when she is confronted she is only summoned to repent of her fornication (πορνεία) and there is no mention of εἰδωλόθυτος. This indicates (1) that the term πορνεία is a 'metaphorical reiteration' of εἰδωλόθυτος,[56] or (2) that the author's primary concern is with economic participation as reflected in later passages, or (3) that he regards εἰδωλόθυτος as generally referring to the means by which Jezebel is teaching the readers/hearers to utilize the networks available through pagan festivals, the *collegia*, and the broader culture itself to gain affluence.[57] Given the prominence of (2) within the remainder of the document, and the likelihood that this would aid in gaining economic advantage, it is likely that (2) and (3) are both at work. Yet this does not mean that John's overall concern is with participation in trade guilds and imperial cults themselves. Rather, he is focused on challenging affluence among the faithful, in which participation in the social world is simply a means to that end (cf. 1 Tim 6:6–10). An analysis of the selected texts that deal with wealth and poverty explicitly will help to support this thesis.

The message to Smyrna

'I know your affliction (θλῖψιν) and your poverty (πτωχείαν),
even though you are rich (πλούσιος).'   (Rev 2:9)

Apart from the obvious lack of any call for repentance in the message to Smyrna, the most distinguishing feature of the passage above is that the author acknowledges their suffering and poverty while simultaneously describing them as rich. More importantly, this parenthetical statement interrupts the flow of the sentence and conspicuously assumes a shared understanding on the part of the readers/hearers. The poverty (πτωχεία) mentioned here has been understood to refer either to the confiscation of the goods of the community or to the result of their unwillingness to compromise by participating in the pagan economic system.[58] In either case, the contrast the author provides in the statement, 'but you are rich', taken together with the language of affliction (θλῖψις), indicates that some form of literal poverty is in view.[59] Boxall notes that this is a real 'apocalyptic unveiling' in that what the world sees as poverty is actually

---

[56] Duff, *Who Rides the Beast?*, pp. 56–7; deSilva, *Seeing Things John's Way*, p. 60 n. 106.

[57] Price, *Rituals and Power*, p. 100; Kraybill, *Imperial Cult and Commerce*, pp. 132–9.

[58] Charles, *Revelation*, vol. I, p. 56; Caird, *Revelation*, p. 35; Blount, *Revelation*, p. 55; Boxall, *Revelation*, p. 53. Duff, *Who Rides the Beast?*, p. 44 suggests that the majority of the church in Smyrna came from the lower economic strata, though this is not likely.

[59] Royalty, *Streets of Heaven*, pp. 153–4.

true wealth.[60] When compared with the only other church that lacks a call for repentance, the idea that this refers to some form of social or economic marginalization becomes clearer.

In the comparable message to Philadelphia, Christ says, 'you have little power' (μικρὰν ἔχεις δύναμιν), which may allude to a marginalized status with the meaning they have few resources.[61] The term δύναμις is used elsewhere in the Apocalypse to refer to the power accorded to God and the Lamb (Rev 1:16; 4:11; 5:12; 7:12; 11:17; 12:10; 15:8; 19:1), and the power of the Dragon, his beasts, and the kings of the earth (Rev 13:2; 17:13). Two occurrences of δύναμις are used in direct relation to wealth: (1) in 5:12, the Lamb is worthy to receive power and wealth; (2) in 18:3, the merchants have grown rich by the power of Babylon's luxury (στρῆνος) (cf. Rev 18:7, 9). It is reasonable to assume that for John the power of God is not something the Philadelphians lack since they are not called to repent. Thus their lack of power must in some way reflect a position of marginalized status either socially or economically. The absence of the need to repent in the messages to Philadelphia and Smyrna, taken together with the similarities in circumstances, makes it plausible to conclude that John portrays faithfulness in terms of an expectation of social and economic marginalization.

Scholars frequently contend that the poverty and lack of power attributed to these churches come from their refusal to compromise in the pagan culture vis-à-vis festivals, trade guilds, and withdrawal from certain economic activity.[62] While such a withdrawal would result in persecution, the author's ideological strategy precludes us from reconstructing precise historical circumstances behind these particular communities.[63] That is to say, while we cannot know whether this reflects actual circumstances that the readers/hearers are experiencing, we can know that the author considers a marginalized status to be consistent with faithfulness. But in what way does this bear upon the state of being rich?

Nothing in the immediate context or in the Apocalypse as a whole indicates that John is referring to spiritual riches or spiritual gifts.[64] The

---

[60] Boxall, *Revelation*, p. 53.

[61] See *BDAG*, p. 263. Cf. *1 Enoch* 103:9–11. See also Xenophon. *Anab.*, 7.7.36; Deut 8:17.

[62] Bousset, *Offenbarung*, pp. 242–3; Charles, *Revelation*, vol. I, p. 56; Fiorenza, *Vision*, p. 56; Aune, *Revelation 1–5*, p. 161; Kraybill, *Imperial Cult and Commerce*, p. 29.

[63] Royalty, *Streets of Heaven*, pp. 153–4.

[64] Kraft, *Offenbarung*, p. 60; Lohse, *Offenbarung*, p. 26; Osborne, *Revelation*, p. 130; Roloff, *Revelation*, p. 48; Mounce, *Revelation*, p. 92; Prigent, *Apocalypse*, p. 166; Beale, *Revelation*, p. 239; Boxall, *Revelation*, p. 53; Smalley, *Revelation*, p. 65; Müller, *Offenbarung*, p. 106.

author's tendency to weave prominent themes throughout the Apocalypse is evident and the absence of any such language here or elsewhere that refers to such is problematic for that view. Royalty asserts that the Smyrneans are rich in deeds though there is nothing in the immediate context to support this position. Elsewhere the author refers to the works (ἔργα) of the other churches and the term occurs frequently throughout the Apocalypse.[65] Surprisingly, it does not occur in this passage. Royalty also indicates that it is the Smyrnean suffering and not poverty that is the basis for being called rich. However, given that the terms rich and poor are juxtaposed only here and in the message to Laodicea, it seems that the author is offering a different perspective on what it means to be rich or poor from what his readers/hearers presently understand.[66] Thus, being 'truly rich' cannot simply refer to participation in struggles with the Jewish synagogue.[67] The suffering John has in mind is much larger than that. The slander (βλασφημία) of the pseudo-Jews (Rev 2:9; 3:9) and the devil (διάβολος) (Rev 2:10), who is about to cast them into prison, are directly associated in John's visions with the cosmological figures of Satan, the beasts, and Babylon (Rev 12:9, 12; 13:1, 5–6; 16:9, 11, 21; 17:3; 20:2, 10).

Death is a prominent theme in Rev 2:9–10 and is anticipated for those who remain faithful, which seems to undermine Royalty's assertion that the author is in conversation with Stoic ideas of wealth. Greco-Roman philosophical traditions were not as interested in the afterlife as much as they emphasized virtues through which one could acquire happiness in the present life. John is certainly not interested in such happiness since he lays stress on faithfulness to the point of death.[68] It is not clear how true riches in this sense would be of any value to the suffering poor since their death may be imminent. The eschatological promises for conquering through death indicate that something else entirely is at work. John is not simply trying to advance an ideological agenda or establish his own authority as much as he is attempting to change the behaviour of his readers/hearers. And the lack of any call for repentance in this message indicates that suffering and poverty are the ideals John seeks for the remainder of the churches. The question then becomes, how can John, in

---

[65] Rev 2:2, 5–6, 19, 23, 26; 3:1–2, 8, 15; 9:20; 14:13; 15:3; 16:11; 18:6; 19:8; 20:12.

[66] The terms are used together in *merismus* (where antithetical terms function to express the whole) to highlight the totality of humankind (cf. 6:15; 13:16).

[67] Royalty, *Streets of Heaven*, p. 163.

[68] They are to be faithful ἄχρι θανάτου. The preposition ἄχρι denotes 'acts or conditions that prevail up to a certain point' indicating 'until death': *BDAG*, p. 160.

such an unambiguous way, ascribe riches to those who are persecuted, poor, and on the brink of death?

The examination of Second Temple traditions in Part II shows that ideas were already widely circulating that envisioned a reversal of fortunes for the faithful who suffered at the hands of rich oppressors in the present age (*1 Enoch* 11:1; 45:4–6; 48:7; 91:12–13; 108:8–15; 1QM 12:12–14; *Sib. Or.* 3:780–6).[69] These traditions also evince a perception of the latter days as being marked by a love for wealth and affluence and increasing wickedness on the earth[70] (*Sib.Or.* 3:175–90; 635–43). Correspondingly, faithfulness is exhibited in a rejection of material wealth and a refusal to associate with the rich and powerful (*1 Enoch* 104:6). This is especially evident in the following passage:

> Those who love God have loved neither gold nor silver nor any of the good things which are in the world; rather they have given over their bodies to torture. From the time they came into being, these have not craved earthly food but have instead counted themselves as a breath that passes away, and this they have preserved. And the Lord has tested them much, but their spirits have been found pure so that they might praise his name. I have recounted all their blessings in the books. He has assigned them their reward for they proved to be those who loved heaven more than their life in the world.
>
> (*1 Enoch* 108:8–15; cf. 2 Macc 6:18–20; 7:1–42)

This text presupposes the portrayal of the wicked and the righteous in terms of wealth reflected in the *Epistle*. The sharp contrast between loving God and heaven more than the material wealth of the world suggests 'a principled enjoinder to reject worldly goods because they compromise devotion and faithful obedience to God'.[71] This conspicuous withdrawal from participation in the broader economic system would certainly lead to social marginalization and persecution. The Qumran sectarian texts

---

[69] Aune, *Revelation 1–5*, p. 161; contra Royalty, *Streets of Heaven*, p. 160, who connects the Smyrneans wealth with the image of Christ in the opening vision and does not make any connection with the linguistic parallels in chapters 20–1. He states, 'Christ does not promise the Smyrneans wealth after death (although the crown of life suggests a future reward) but claims they are rich *now*' (italics original).

[70] Dan 12:4; Matt 24:7–12; Mark 13:19; Luke 21:23; 2 Tim 3:1–4; 1QM 1:11–12; *Sib.Or.* 3:175–90; 635–43; 2 Esd 5:2, 10; 13:30–1; *1 Enoch* 91:5–7; 93:9–11; 99:3–5; 100:1–4; 106:19–107:1.

[71] Stuckenbruck, *1 Enoch 91–108*, p. 722.

also demonstrate a similar motif in which faithfulness to God is set in contrast to the desire for affluence in the present age.[72]

John refers to the present suffering of the poor as testing (Rev 2:10) and maintains that the deeds of humankind are recorded in books (Rev 20:12).[73] Thus, Royalty's connection between wealth and deeds is not altogether wrong since the Apocalypse is clear that humankind will be rewarded or judged according to their works (Rev 2:23; 20:12). However, the promise of reward for the faithful is related directly to conquering, which in the literary world of the Apocalypse is only achieved through death (Rev 3:21; 5:5; 11:7; 12:11; 13:7; 15:2). The marginalized faithful are promised entrance into the New Jerusalem (Rev 3:12) and a complete eschatological reversal of fortunes in which the opponents will bow down before their feet (Rev 3:9; cf. Isa 45:14; 1QM 12:14–15).[74] John can say that those who are currently poor and persecuted are in fact rich since their present state attests the faithfulness required for their inheritance. This depiction of faithfulness in terms of poverty and persecution becomes more obvious in the message to Laodicea, which bears a different emphasis.

The message to Laodicea

'For you say, "I am rich (πλούσιός εἰμι), I have prospered (πεπλούτηκα), and I need nothing." You do not realize that you are wretched, pitiable, poor (πτωχὸς), blind, and naked.'

(Rev 3:17)

In this passage John deals with the same issue addressed in Rev 2:9, though from a different vantage point – that is, the rich are truly poor. Like the previous text, commentators frequently argue that the writer is speaking metaphorically of the Laodiceans' boast in their spiritual wealth in relation to their pride in salvation and their spiritual complacency.[75]

---

[72] CD 4:19; 1QS 10:18–19; 1QpHab 8:10–11; 1QHa 6:31; 7:22–3; 18:22–5, 29–31; 4Q417 2 i:10–12; 4Q416 2 ii:6–7, 17–18.

[73] Cf. 1QS 8:7; 1QM 16:11, 15; 17:1; 1QHa 10:15–16; 23:28; Dan 7:10; *1 Enoch* 81:1–2; 93:2; 103:2; 106:19; 108:3, 7.

[74] In the Isaiah text the reversal is realized in the restoration of Israel back to the land, whereas the Qumran text is more eschatologically focused as is the passage in Revelation.

[75] Bousset, *Offenbarung*, pp. 231–2 argues that their wealth is to be taken figuratively since it is the church community at Laodicea that is being addressed and not the wealthy city itself. His early dating indicates that the city would not have yet recovered from the earthquake in 60 CE. Thus, their claim is to intellectual wealth; so also Prigent, *Apocalypse*, p. 216. The following see this as a claim of being rich in spiritual gifts: Kraft, *Offenbarung*, p. 85; Müller, *Offenbarung*, p. 136; Boring, *Revelation*, pp. 94–7; Roloff, *Revelation*,

Others take a similar approach but contend that this attitude grows out of their excessive wealth.[76] Their affluence is typically associated with the economic success of the city of Laodicea through its banking industry and wool manufacturing.[77] Yet, Ephesus, Pergamum, and Smyrna, being *neokoros* cities, were most likely just as wealthy and powerful as Laodicea. Taken together with the comprehensive nature of the seven messages and the implication that many of John's readers/hearers may be in agreement with Jezebel, the message has a broader embrace than a situation at Laodicea. An analysis of the particular speech form the author utilizes when making his accusation, however, may provide a better understanding of the author's strategy, since it provides a rhetorical link to chapter 18 where rich Babylon makes a similar claim of self-sufficiency:

> 'I rule as a queen, I am no widow and I will never see grief.'
> (Rev 18:7b)

This particular form of imputed speech occurs only in Rev 3:17 and 18:7, which are both critical of the rich. Certain features indicate that the author is drawing an ideological connection between the rich in the church and Babylon. (1) Both passages denote an attitude of self-sufficiency. The rich in the church boast of their wealth while Babylon brags of her sovereignty and inability to be destroyed. She, too, is portrayed as rich and living a luxurious lifestyle. (2) Both texts occur within the context of a prophetic speech form. Within the seven messages the Laodicean correspondence reflects a parenetic salvation–judgement oracle[78] while the critique of Babylon includes prophetic announcements of judgement (Rev 18:2–3; 6, 8, 10, 16, 19)[79] and a judgement oracle (Rev 18:21–4).[80] While both

---

pp. 64–5. Fiorenza, *Vision*, p. 130; *Justice and Judgment*, p. 119 relates this in some way to their boasting in assurance of salvation. Aune, *Revelation 1–5*, p. 259 is not clear on whether he understands this to mean literal or figurative wealth. The following take this as a reference to literal wealth: Swete, *Apocalypse*, p. 61; Charles, *Revelation*, vol. I, p. 96; Caird, *Revelation*, p. 57; Lohse, *Offenbarung*, p. 34; Mounce, *Revelation*, p. 126; Yarbro Collins, *Apocalypse*, p. 30; Royalty, *Streets of Heaven*, pp. 166–8; Beale, *Revelation*, pp. 304–5; Smalley, *Revelation to John*, p. 98; Boxall, *Revelation*, p. 77.

[76] Charles, *Revelation*, vol. I, p. 96; Müller, *Offenbarung*, p. 136; Caird, *Revelation*, pp. 56–7; Beale, *Revelation*, pp. 304–5; Osborne, *Revelation*, p. 206; Boxall, *Revelation*, p. 77, highlight John's concern over assimilation into the socio-economic culture.

[77] Hemer, *Letters*, pp. 178–208. It is also suggested that their refusal to accept financial assistance following the earthquake of 60 CE testifies to their great wealth.

[78] Aune, *Prophecy in Early Christianity*, pp. 276–9. See, however, Müller, *Prophetie und Predigt*, pp. 57–76, 93–107 who contends that the messages function as sermons of repentance.

[79] See Yarbro Collins, 'Revelation 18', pp. 192–7.

[80] Aune, *Prophecy in Early Christianity*, pp. 284–5.

are guilty of basically the same offence, only John's recipients who are enjoying affluence are given the opportunity to repent. This distinguishing feature reflects the author's overall rhetorical strategy, which is illumined by a brief discussion of the speech form itself and its use in antecedent Jewish tradition.

Imputed speech is found throughout the biblical tradition[81] and many commentators suggest that the present text is alluding to Hos 12:9 (LXX) 'Ah, I am rich, I have gained wealth for myself; in all of my gain no offence has been found in me that would be sin.'[82] Likewise, Zech 11:5 states, 'Blessed be the Lord for I have become rich.' Yet in both of these passages the emphasis is on wealth gained by unjust means. The prophet Hosea is criticizing merchants who use a false balance (ζυγός; Hos 12:7 [LXX]) and oppress the poor, whereas Zechariah speaks of those who participate in the slave trade and then attribute their wealth to God. John's use of the balancing scales in the vision of the third rider (Rev 6:5–6) attests a similar concern to Hosea, while his inclusion of slaves (σωμάτων) and human souls (ψυχὰς ἀνθρώπων) in the merchants' luxurious cargo list (Rev 18:13) finds agreement with Zechariah. Thus, the author's use of the prophetic tradition is evident, though these texts do not denote an attitude of self-sufficiency such as we find in Revelation. Rather, the device serves to highlight the misunderstanding that God is the source of their wealth. John's emphasis on affluence and self-sufficiency would attest a reshaping of the biblical tradition. Thus it may be helpful to consider how more recent interpretive traditions also utilize this device.[83]

In the Second Temple period, speech is frequently placed in the mouth of those portrayed as rich sinners who are opposed to God and his people.[84] One paragraph in particular attests a very close similarity to the present passage:

> We have grown very wealthy and have amassed possessions, and we have acquired everything that we desire. Now let us do whatever we wish for we have hoarded silver in our treasure storerooms and lots of good things in our houses.
>
> (*1 Enoch* 97:8–9)[85]

---

[81] Pss 10:13; 35:25; Prov 24:12; Isa 29:15; 47:8; Jer 2:23; 13:22; 21:13; 42:13–14; Ezek 18:19; Amos 7:16; Luke 12:19; Jas 4:13; Rev 18:7.

[82] Kraft, *Offenbarung*, p. 85; Charles, *Revelation*, vol. I, p. 96; Beale, *Revelation*, p. 304; Beasley-Murray, *Revelation*, p. 105. Charles, *Book of Enoch*, p. xcvii.

[83] See the discussion above, pp. 50 ff.

[84] Wis 2:1–20; 5:4–13; *1 Enoch* 102:6–8; 104:7. Cf. Sir 5:1; 11:17–19.

[85] Olson's translation.

Like the prophetic tradition, the Enochic text maintains the idea that the rich have gained their wealth by unjust means, yet the emphasis has become their self-sufficient attitude in their accumulation of wealth. In the immediate context of this quote the writer states explicitly that the rich have incurred guilt by participating with sinners (*1 Enoch* 97:3–5), an idea also advanced in the call for the faithful to 'Come out' of Babylon (Rev 18:4). This does not imply any direct dependence or genealogical link between the two texts but simply indicates that these authors shared a similar world view in which the rich incur guilt through their participation in an economic system that ultimately results in oppression of the righteous (cf. *1 Enoch* 104:6). Thus, the device functions within the Apocalypse (1) to emphasize the inability to distinguish the rich in the church from the wicked eschatological opponents of God and his people as portrayed in Babylon, (2) to indicate that at some point the consequences of arrogance and self-sufficiency in wealth and power become irreversible and lead to judgement, and, (3) effectively, to place the rich outside the purview of the faithful community in the same way as the sobriquets Jezebel and Balaam.

Within the matrix of John's world view wealth makes it difficult to distinguish the faithful from the larger social landscape that accommodates those who assimilate into the culture. John's polarizing language in the seven messages draws firm, clear boundaries between the faithful and the wicked. This is most likely the basis for John's complaint that the rich are lukewarm. If they were either cold or hot one could detect whether they were insiders or outsiders; that is, if they were either poor and persecuted or rich sinners one could know how to categorize them. As it is, their confession, on the one hand, and their affluence, on the other, blur the boundary between their supposed commitment to God and their wealth, which makes them virtually indistinguishable from the outside evil world. This differs from traditions like Ben Sira in which the author's world view allows for wealth among both the faithful and sinners.[86] While the righteous can expect to receive wealth through wisdom and the blessing of God, they are expected to care for the poor who are without. The wicked rich are not encouraged or expected to do this but reflect a group who are to be approached with care (Sir 8:2; 13:4, 19). John, however, expects the faithful to be poor and distinguishes them more sharply using wealth to create that distance. The faithful must be visibly distinguishable from the broader socio-economic world.

---

[86] Sir 8:2; 11:18–19; 11:21; 27:1; 31:8; 44:6.

It is also possible to detect the language of the Deuteronomistic curses in John's censure of the rich. Nakedness is conventional language, associated with both idolatrous behaviour (Ezek 16:36–7) and judgement from God (Isa 20:4; 47:3; Ezek 23:29; Hos 2:3; Nahum 3:5), and is one of the curses for covenant disobedience (Deut 28:48).[87]

Blindness also reflects covenant infidelity (Deut 28:28–9).[88] In the prophetic tradition it is realized in Israel's disobedience and refers both to the people (Isa 6:9–10) and to their false prophets and seers (Isa 29:9–10). This blindness is a metaphor for Israel's inability to understand or comprehend the plan of God, a reversal of which is promised in Proto-Isaiah (32:1–3). In the Second Temple period, blindness is increasingly related to wealth and the wicked lifestyle of the rich. Wisdom of Solomon highlights the unsound reasoning of the rich by stating, 'they were led astray, for their wickedness blinded them' (Wis 2:21). Ben Sira relates blindness to the effect of favours and gifts that blind the wise (Sir 20:29; cf. 11Q19 51:13–14). Among the Dead Sea Scrolls, *Damascus Document* associates blindness with a lack of spiritual understanding or insight (CD 1:9; 2:14; 16:2). In the *Two Spirits Treatise* it is listed as one of the operations of the spirit of falsehood (1QS 4:11). *Pesher Hosea A* relates it to the spiritual blindness of those who were deceived by the Man of Lies (4Q166 2:5–6), whose crimes are stated in *Pesher Habakkuk* as 'rejecting the law of God for the sake of riches' (1QpHab 8:8–12). In the *Animal Apocalypse*, blindness reflects periods of rebellion in Israel's history. Two opposing groups are described: the sheep who go blind and those who are able to see, which clearly delineates between the righteous and the wicked.[89] The *Epistle of Enoch* likewise links blindness to rebellious Israel and with the activities of the wicked rich (*1 Enoch* 93:8; 99:8).

There is significant language in ancient Jewish tradition to attribute poverty, blindness, and nakedness to conditions denoting a breach of covenant fidelity. Yet, it is the minority faithful in the church who are actually experiencing what appear to be the curses for disobedience. For this very reason, John highlights the temporary paradox in circumstances by attributing the language of infidelity to the rich and their need to repent. This is a perspective on wealth not found in the Hebrew Bible and grows distinctively out of Jewish apocalyptic thought from the Second

---

[87] Müller, *Offenbarung*, p. 137 is correct in attributing the language of nakedness to Jewish tradition but only connects it with Ex 20:26 and *Jub.* 3:31. Cf. 4Q166 2:12.

[88] See Berger, 'Kollyrium', pp. 174–95; Jackson, 'Eye Medicine', pp. 2228–51; Hemer, *Letters*, pp. 196–9.

[89] *1 Enoch* 89:32, 41, 44, 54; 90:6–7, 9, 26, 31–6.

Temple period. In particular, the author(s) of the *Epistle of Enoch* takes a similar approach to the rich by pointing out the paradox of what appears to be a collapse in the promise of blessing for the faithful in the present age (*1 Enoch* 102:4–103:15). The concern over the present appearance of the rich and their eschatological fate is also evident:

> Woe to you sinners for your riches give you the appearance of righteousness but your hearts convict you of being sinners, and this fact will serve as a witness against you – a testament to your evil deeds!   (*1 Enoch* 96:4)

As demonstrated in Part II, this perspective arises out of a pre-understanding that the promise of material blessing has been postponed to the coming age, while the faithful are tested through marginalization in the present.[90] This correlates with John's admonition to the rich that they buy (ἀγοράζω)[91] from Christ gold refined by fire so that they might become rich (Rev 3:18).[92] This is also traditional language from the Hebrew Bible that alludes to God testing his people.[93] Thus, John is encouraging the rich in the church to reject riches in the present age and to receive the reproof and discipline of God (Rev 3:19), which reflects an 'alternative, otherwordly' economic system.[94] This demonstrates the writer's presumption that faithfulness in the present age is evidenced by poverty and a life of suffering while affluence denotes unfaithfulness.

---

[90] Wis 3:5–6; *1 Enoch* 102:5–104:6; 108:8–15; 1QS 4:20; 1QHa 10:15–16, 32–4; 15:12; 23:28; 1QM 14:8–15; 4Q177 9:2; 4Q381 46a+b:5; 4Q414 2 ii 4:1; 4Q434 1 i:7; 11Q19 54:12.

[91] See, *BDAG*, p. 14. Here it refers to the means by which the faithful become eschatologically rich (cf. Rev 2:9).

[92] The use of the subjunctive (πλουτήσῃς), taken together with the fact that indicative forms of πλουτέω occur only in the seven messages and in relation to the rich who are judged in chapter 18, highlights the author's emphasis that the affluent need to repent from their current perspective on wealth in order to be deemed faithful. The language of white robes indicates purity and faithfulness (Rev 3:4–5; 4:4; 7:9; 19:14; cf. 7:12; 22:14). Washed robes have a close association with the martyrs in heaven (Rev 6:11; 7:13–14). While this may or may not suggest taking a position of martyrdom, at the very least it implies a radical obedience to the Lamb that might include death (cf. Rev 2:9–10). The anointing (ἐγχρίω) of eyes is frequently associated with a medical school in Laodicea that purportedly produced an eye-salve. See Ramsay, *Letters*, pp. 413–30; Hemer, *Letters*, pp. 198–200. However, the Rabbinic tradition associates Torah with 'eye-salve' (*Midr*. Ps 19:15) in that it enlightens the eyes granting life and healing to the reader (*Midr. Rab.* Lev 12:3; *Midr. Rab.* Deut 8:4). John may be in conversation with similar traditions in his admonition to the Laodiceans to enlighten their eyes through faithfulness to God in relation to his own apocalyptic visions.

[93] Prov 17:3; 27:21; Job 23:10; Isa 48:10; Jer 9:7; Dan 11:35; Zech 13:9; Mal 3:2–3; 1 Pet 1:6–9. Cf. *1 Enoch* 54:6; 56:4; CD 4:12–18; 1QM 16:11, 15; 17:1; 11Q19 54:12; 4Q177 9:2; 10 11:10; Wis 1:16; 3:5–6.

[94] Goranson, 'Essene Polemic', 459.

In light of the Second Temple traditions discussed it would be wrong to interpret the paradox presented in the seven messages in terms of spiritual wealth and poverty. The reason John rejects the teaching of Jezebel is not so much because it is associated with assimilation into the culture through trade networks that are permeated by imperial cults, but that she promotes these means as an end to accumulating wealth. In order to discern the degree to which perspectives on wealth consistently agree with this apocalyptic world view, it is necessary to analyse the remaining selected wealth passages.

7

THE PRESENT ESCHATOLOGICAL AGE:
REV 4–6

Immediately following the seven messages, John is taken into heaven, where his apocalyptic visions begin.[1] The vision of the slain Lamb in the throne-room report is vital for understanding the entirety of the Book of Revelation.[2] In relation to the present study, imagery of precious stones and jewels and references to riches in relation to the Lamb are of special concern. In addition, the vision of the four horsemen also provides wealth imagery, especially in relation to the balancing scales carried by the third rider.

7.1 The inauguration of the eschatological age

The throne-room vision: Rev 4:1–11

The vision of the throne-room and the Lamb (Rev 4–5) begins with the phrase, 'I looked and behold, a door was open in heaven' (θύρα ἠνεῳγμένη). In the seven messages Christ indicates that he has opened a door (θύραν ἠνεῳγμένην) for those who are marginalized (Rev 3:8). A door is also present in the message to Laodicea, though it is closed (Rev 3:20). Viewed in light of the contrast between the faithful poor and the rich, the door imagery may have functioned to allude further to the hindrance wealth posed in obtaining access to the throne-room of God.[3] This does not mean that they are unable to discern John's heavenly visions. Rather, their inability to see things clearly is the reason for John's visions, which presses them to answer Christ's knock at the door by rejecting wealth and embrace a life of faithfulness and thereby gain access and be counted faithful.

---

[1] See Aune, *Revelation 1–5*, p. cxxiv.

[2] Fiorenza, *Vision*, p. 58; Boring, *Revelation*, p. 109; Caird, *Revelation*, pp. 74–5; Achtemeier, 'Rev 5:1–14', pp. 284–5; Johns, *Lamb Christology*, pp. 159–60.

[3] Boxall, *Revelation*, p. 82.

The vision of the open door is followed by a heavenly ascent, a common *topos* in both Greco-Roman and Jewish antecedent traditions.[4] Himmelfarb rightly notes that the development of heavenly journeys to the divine throne-room in ancient Jewish tradition begins with the ascension of Enoch (*1 Enoch* 14).[5] This initial development takes place within a vision but includes the ascension of the seer (cf. *ALD* 4; *T. Levi* 2–8).[6] John is 'in the spirit', a phrase which denotes a trance-like state that involves an ascent apart from the body.[7] Other traditions that take up the heavenly ascent motif include multilayered heavens, much like what is found in the later Enochic traditions and the Hekhalot literature.[8] The BOW and Revelation, however, only know of a three-tiered cosmos consisting of underworld, earth, and heaven (*1 Enoch* 10:12–13; 14:5; 15:10; Rev 4:1–2; 12:7–12; 20:2–3). Since other texts closely associated with early Christian texts also attest a three-tiered universe,[9] we can conclude that these, as well as John, were in conversation with a stream of tradition such as that reflected in *1 Enoch* 14.

The throne-room vision of Rev 4:1–11 is germane to our discussion for two reasons: (1) the description of the throne of God contains wealth language and imagery, and (2) the author's eclectic method sets a precedent for how he utilizes antecedent traditions throughout the visionary part of the Apocalypse. John has included in his throne-room vision language from Ezek 1, Isa 6, Dan 7 and *1 Enoch* 14:8–25.[10] This pastiche of traditions has been reshaped to fit his own purposes and one should be cautious in considering that the author is

---

[4] Bousset, 'Die Himmelsreise der Seele', p. 143 dismisses the idea of an ascent of the soul in Revelation. Similarly, Himmelfarb, *Ascent to Heaven*, p. 34 also plays down the ascent in Revelation. For a discussion of ascent traditions in the Hellenistic world, see Segal, 'Heavenly Ascent', pp. 1333–94. See also Dean-Otting, *Heavenly Journeys*. For a discussion of the relationship between Merkavah Mysticism and Hekhalot texts with early Jewish ascent traditions, including Rev 4, see Gruenwald, *Apocalypticism and Merkavah*, pp. 29–72. See also Gooder, *Only the Third Heaven?*, pp. 83–103.

[5] Himmelfarb, *Ascent to Heaven*, p. 9.

[6] Aune, *Revelation 1–5*, p. 277 notes the difference between a throne-room *report* and a *description*.

[7] Bousset, *Offenbarung*, p. 192; Charles, *Revelation*, vol. I, p. 22; Kraft, *Offenbarung*, p. 95; Roloff, *Revelation*, p. 32; Boxall, *Revelation*, p. 39.

[8] See Gruenwald's discussion of Hekhalot texts, *Apocalypticism and Merkavah*, pp. 98–123. See also 2 *Enoch* 18–22; *3 Bar.*; *T. Levi* 2–8; *Apoc. Abr.* 9–19; *Ques. Ezra* 19–21; *Asc. Isa.* 6–9; cf. 1 Cor 12:1–10.

[9] *T. Abr.* 8:1–12; 2 Esd 4:7–12; *2 Bar.* 1:11; 3:29; 6:55. See Rowland, *Open Heaven*, p. 81; Minear, 'Cosmology of the Apocalypse', pp. 23–37.

[10] Rowland, *Open Heaven*, pp. 218–26; Hurtado, 'Revelation 4–5', 106; Royalty, *Streets of Heaven*, pp. 47–58.

interpreting these texts or elevating the significance of one tradition over another.[11]

In John's vision, there are four living creatures like those in Ezek 1:4–18, though each creature has only one of the four faces of Ezekiel's vision. In addition, the creatures are described in terms of the seraphim of Isaiah 6 in that they have six wings rather than four and they sing praises to God.[12] They worship God day and night, a phrase that occurs in *1 Enoch* 14:23 but is absent in the prophetic tradition.[13] The absence of wheels is also evident, though the creatures themselves are full of eyes (cf. Ezek 1:18). Collins has noted that the plural form of thrones in Dan 7 may have influenced the twenty-four thrones on which the elders are seated.[14] However, the description of the throne in terms of jewels and precious stones is a feature found only in Ezekiel.

Royalty has argued that the vision of *1 Enoch* 18:6–8 may have also influenced the wealth imagery of Rev 4. In the Enochic text the seer is taken on an other-worldly journey (*1 Enoch* 17:1–5) where he sees three mountains. The mountain at the centre reaches to the heavens 'like the throne of God' and the summit of the throne is sapphire (σάπφειρος). The other mountains are also described in terms of precious stones, jewels, and pearls.[15] Royalty concludes that the throne-room vision in Rev 4 includes a 'higher concentration of wealth motifs than any other Second Temple throne vision'.[16] He also states, 'God, in the Apocalypse, dwells in a wealthier heaven than any Old Testament text describes'.[17] However, a brief analysis of Ezekiel's throne-room vision reveals that this assessment may be overstated.

---

[11] For example, Beale suggests that Dan 7 is the dominant framework for John's throne-room vision. See Beale, *Use of Daniel*. The possibility exists that the author may have in mind a dominant tradition. However, a consideration of such may be better viewed in light of the author's theological world view rather than the use of vocabulary or clusters of allusions.

[12] Fekkes, *Isaiah and Prophetic Traditions*, p. 144.

[13] Nickelsburg, *1 Enoch 1*, p. 266.

[14] Collins, *Daniel*, p. 301; Beale, *Use of Daniel*, p. 191. Contra Montgomery, *Book of Daniel*, p. 296.

[15] Royalty contends that John is following the ancient practice of displaying the wealth and strength of a king. Here he cites Newsom, 'Development of 1 Enoch 6–19', p. 324. This does not take into account, however, the use of simile in the Apocalypse in which the description is said to be 'like' emeralds, jewels, and precious stones. Thus the author is not indicating that the throne is made of jewels nor does he attribute positive or negative connotations to such a description, though the imagery is excessive. See Holtz, *Offenbarung*, p. 56.

[16] Royalty, *Streets of Heaven*, p. 79.   [17] *Ibid.*, p. 58.

John's throne vision consists of the terms jasper (ἴασπις), carnelian (σάρδιον), emerald (σμαράγδινος), gold (χρυσός), and crystal (κρύσταλλος), while the Greek version of Ezekiel's vision includes bronze (χαλκός), beryl (θαρσις), sapphire (σάπφειρος), crystal (κρύσταλλος), and amber/gold alloy (ἤλεκτρον). The last can mean either a bright stone the colour of fire, which should be rendered gleaming amber, or a bright metallic substance yellow in colour such as brass or gold, which is reflected in LXX traditions.[18] It most likely refers to some kind of gold alloy.[19] Thus, a synoptic comparison of the description shows that Ezekiel has the same number of terms that refer to jewels and precious stones.

John's use of wealth motifs in the throne-room vision is not overly conspicuous but is a result of the author's conflation of prophetic traditions.[20] John's conversation with traditions found in the Enochic tradition, however, is evident in the open door imagery, the day and night language, and the heavenly ascent. This last motif, taken together with the extensive language and imagery from the prophetic tradition, makes it possible to locate the author within the framework of the biblical prophets, though within a trajectory of prophetic literature from the Second Temple period. The ascent motif further functions to strengthen the author's message in the midst of his prophetic rivalry with Jezebel. John's perspective on wealth is so radically different from that proposed by the rival teachers that he enters into the throne-room of God and expands the readers' understanding of the universe by offering a view of the cosmos from the very place where God resides.[21] This does not mean the throne-room is without wealth language. On the contrary, in the vision of the Lamb we have an explicit use of the term 'riches' (πλοῦτος).[22]

7.2   Worthy is the Lamb to receive wealth

> Worthy is the Lamb that was slaughtered to receive power and
> wealth (πλοῦτος) and wisdom and might and honour and glory
> and blessing!   (Rev 5:12)

---

[18] *NIDOTTE*, vol. II, p. 316; Herodotus, *Hist.*, 3.115; Homer, *Od.* 15.460; *LSJ*, p. 768; Hesiod, *[Scut.]*, 142; Homer, *Epigr.* 15.10.

[19] Muraoka, *Lexicon of the Septuagint*, p. 319; Lust, et al., *Lexicon of the Septuagint*, p. 266.

[20] John is also influenced by socio-historical factors in his throne-room vision. See Aune, 'Influence of Roman Imperial Court', pp. 2–26; Stevenson, 'Conceptual Background', pp. 257–72.

[21] Kraft, *Offenbarung*, p. 94; Holtz, *Offenbarung*, p. 55. See also Thompson, *Apocalypse and Empire*, p. 31.

[22] Royalty does not include this text in his study.

The hymnic praise to the Lamb (Rev 5:12) differs from the one directed to God (Rev 4:11) in that a reference to wealth is absent in the latter. The Lamb's worthiness to receive riches indicates that the author does not reject wealth per se, but is making the important distinction that wealth is merited through conquering, that is, through suffering and death (Rev 3:21; 5:9, 12).[23] Jesus likewise promised the conquerors in the seven messages that they too will have a seat on his throne (Rev 3:21), which implies that wealth will be a natural consequence for those who follow him.[24] One could argue that not wealth but the Lamb himself is the inheritance of the faithful. However, the promises to the poor in the seven messages, also coincide with language used to describe the inheritance of the gold-and-jewel-laden new Jerusalem (Rev 3:12; 21:7). Interestingly, the open door motif and the language of conquering in relation to Christ, indicate that both heaven and the new Jerusalem are reserved only for the faithful. Moreover, these promises are given only to those who reject wealth in the present age and experience the suffering that followers of the Lamb can expect. Thus, the wealth imagery in the throne-room and new Jerusalem draws attention to the spatial aspect of the future blessing of the faithful poor; that is, it reinforces the apocalyptic language of reversal. That blessing, while cast in terms of material wealth, is ultimately accessed through fellowship with God and the Lamb in the eschatological age for those who persevere.[25] Yet, this raises the question of the role Christ plays with regard to those who reject a life of poverty and choose a life of affluence. Does the slaughtered Lamb in the Apocalypse have a salvific effect in the sense that all of the addressees are viewed as faithful? Can the rich continue in this lifestyle and yet expect the same eschatological bliss promised to the faithful poor? A brief examination of John's portrayal of the Lamb in the throne-room may shed light on what is at stake for the rich who are admonished to reject wealth.

---

[23] Charles, *Revelation*, p. 140; Caird, *Revelation*, p. 71; Aune, *Revelation 1–5*, p. 349; Holtz, *Christologie*, p. 45.

[24] The distinction between the rich in the Laodicean message and Babylon and the riches ascribed to Christ is not one of just and unjust wealth since the author does not utilize the traditional language that accompanies such a view. See CD 6:11–18; 8:4–9; 10:18–19; 11:15; 1QS 10:18–19; 1QHa 18:25; *1 Enoch* 97:8–10; Sir 5:8; *Sib. Or.* 3:188–190. Rather, it underscores the spatial distinction between wealth on the earth, which belongs to the wicked, and wealth in heaven and the new Jerusalem that belongs to Christ and the faithful. It is in this sense that the faithful poor are rich.

[25] The postponement of blessing to the eschaton is reinforced by the speech of the martyrs: 'How long will it be before you judge and avenge our blood' (Rev 6:10), which indicates they have not yet been rewarded.

John's vision of Christ as the slaughtered Lamb differs significantly from Christ's appearance in the introductory vision at Patmos.[26] In addition, the many attributions of Christ in the seven messages lack any reference to a lamb.[27] In the beginning chapters (Rev 1–3) of the Apocalypse, Christ is revealed as an angelomorphic, juridical figure, even to John on Patmos. However, in the dramatic opening scene of Rev 5 in which no one is found worthy to open the seven-sealed scroll, the author includes a visual shift in the exclamation, 'Look (ἰδού), the Lion of the tribe of Judah has conquered', and the subsequent 'vision' (εἶδον) of the slaughtered Lamb. Stuckenbruck contends that the Lamb imagery in the throne-room may have been influenced by the writer's reticence to place a man-like figure who receives worship alongside the throne of God.[28] Thus, the image of a Lamb served as a rhetorical choice more conducive to a monotheistic framework. Loren Johns provides an extensive analysis of the background of lamb imagery and concludes that John's aims are socio-political and the lamb imagery functions to persuade the hearing/reading audience to practise a non-violent resistance to the idolatry of the Roman imperial system.[29] Thus, the faithful community should follow the example of Christ in peaceful resistance through witness and possibly martyrdom.[30] Beale maintains that the church can overcome because the Lamb has already overcome the evil forces that threaten the churches.[31] While this is true, both he and Johns emphasize the encouraging or persuasive aspect of John's message but do not identify what is at stake for those who do not repent. John does not speak in terms of mere possibilities. His message is equally clear that those who do not conform to his idea of faithfulness cannot understand their relationship

---

[26] Rowland, *Open Heaven*, pp. 222, 420 sees chapter 4 as entirely Jewish and representative of the era before the advent of Christ and the vision of the Lamb in light of it. Thus, he sees two distinct visions: the throne-room, which is entirely Jewish, and the vision of the Lamb, which is entirely Christian. Hurtado corrects this misunderstanding and identifies the Christian elements in the throne-room report in chapter 4. He maintains that chapters 4–5 reflect two closely related scenes contained in one unified vision. See Hurtado, 'Revelation 4–5', p. 110. John uses the term ὁράω in the introduction to the vision in chapter 4 and does not use it again until 5:1. It then occurs four times in the vision of the Lamb alone. Although in 5:1 it is frequently translated 'Then I saw,' the temporal conjunction ὅτε does not occur until 6:1 where a new scene begins. Chapters 4 and 5 are separated by a καί, which can be taken as 'then', but not in the sense that a new vision has begun. Rather, it denotes a sense that the seer continues to look at the throne-room and the more he looks the more he sees; that is, the clearer things become.

[27] Rev 1:5, 8; 2:1, 8, 12, 18; 3:1, 7, 14.   [28] Stuckenbruck, *Angel Veneration*, p. 263.

[29] Johns, *Lamb Christology*, pp. 202–5.

[30] So also Bauckham, *Theology of Revelation*, p. 92.   [31] Beale, *Revelation*, p. 350.

to Christ in the same way as the conquering faithful. John's shift from lion to lamb imagery highlights what is at stake.

Bauckham and Fekkes emphasize the contrast between this imagery and conclude that the image of a slaughtered lamb beside a figure of military conqueror functioned to replace the messianic warrior expectation with the idea of conquest through sacrificial death.[32] While his reappropriation of received traditions does reflect a new idea (a slaughtered warrior Lamb), the writer's conflation of various traditions in the throne-room vision implies that he may have employed this dual image to allow for more than one connection. This is indicative of the way John exploits antecedent traditions and is why caution should be exercised when attempting to ascertain one single association as the background for his language and imagery.

Hoffmann has thus focused not on a contrast in images but on a twofold role of Christ as Destroyer and Lamb.[33] On the one hand, similarities between the introductory Patmos vision (Rev 1:14–16), the Son of Man figure (Rev 14:14–20), and the rider on the white horse in chapter 19 (Rev 19:11–21) function to portray Christ in angelomorphic terms as the Destroyer of those who oppose God and his people (Rev 1:14–16; 19:11–21). On the other hand, he is the paschal lamb from the Exodus tradition who saves God's people in the time of judgement.[34] This distinction can also be detected in the seven messages, in which he makes war with the sword of his mouth (Rev 2:16; 19:15, 21), rewards the wicked according to their works (κατὰ τὰ ἔργα) (Rev 2:23; 18:6), catches the wicked by surprise (Rev 3:3; 16:15; 18:9–20), and kills the children of Jezebel (Rev 2:23; cf. 12:17; 21:7). At the same time he comforts the faithful by telling them not to be afraid and assures them that they will not be harmed by the second death (Rev 2:11; 20:6, 14; 21:8). He also promises to give them white robes (Rev 3:5, 18; 7:13–14) and golden crowns (Rev 2:10; 3:11), that he will wipe every tear from their eyes (Rev 7:14; 21:4) and will make

---

[32] Bauckham, *Climax of Prophecy*, p. 215; Fekkes, *Isaiah and Prophetic Traditions*, pp. 156–8.

[33] Hoffmann, *Destroyer and the Lamb*, pp. 117–34. He asserts that the background of Christ as a lamb was based on the Passover, an idea that was already circulating in the early Christian communities. Cf. 1 Cor 5:7; 1 Peter 1:19. So also Holtz, *Christologie*, pp. 44–7; Aune, *Revelation 1–5*, p. 353; Bauckham, *God Crucified*, pp. 61–2; Roloff, *Revelation*, pp. 78–9; so also Fiorenza, *Justice and Judgment*, pp. 95–6, though she suggests the kingly messianic features predominate. Contra Johns, *Lamb Christology*, p. 133. For discussions on the use of lamb and ram imagery in ancient Jewish and Greco-Roman traditions, see Aune, *Revelation 1–5*, pp. 367–73; Fiorenza, *Justice and Judgment*, pp. 95–6; Johns, *Lamb Christology*, pp. 130–3; Laws, *Light of the Lamb*, pp. 27–8.

[34] Hoffmann, *Destroyer and the Lamb*, pp. 249–51.

their enemies bow before their feet in acknowledgement that God loves them (Rev 3:9). The need to demonstrate God's love for the faithful in this language of reversal indicates that the lifestyle John imposes would give the appearance of covenant infidelity to those thinking through a Deuteronomistic theology of wealth.

John combines the imagery of the messianic conqueror with the paschal lamb to highlight the dual function Christ serves in relation to the faithful and their opponents. This sets up a twofold perspective of the present role of Christ that will become more evident to the readers/hearers as John's visions unfold. The salvific role of Christ as paschal lamb does not imply that the faithful will be spared from conflict, persecution, or death. On the contrary, the language of death and martyrdom indicates that it is to be expected (Rev 2:10; 11:7; 12:11; 13:10, 15; 14:13; 21:4). Jesus' followers can expect to live and die without fear of the second death for it is through death in the present age that they will ultimately conquer (Rev 3:21; 12:11; 15:2). Thus, the Lamb becomes the lens through which faithfulness is revealed to the righteous poor on the one hand, and judgement to those who are aligned with John's opponents on the other.

Johns notes that the Lamb represents how God works in history and that Christ is the window through whom God is revealed.[35] The Lamb is also the window through whom God's will for his people is revealed. If Christ conquered through suffering and death (Rev 3:21; 5:6), it is reasonable for John to assume that the same fate will befall the followers of the Lamb. Moreover, he is the window through whom the judgement of wicked humankind is revealed. John's imagery of Christ in angelomorphic terms in the introductory Patmos vision, the Son of Man figure, and the rider on the white horse show a familiarity with traditions of the Son of Man as a juridical figure who holds to account the wicked and powerful sinners (*1 Enoch* 46:1–8; 69:26–9).[36] The consequences for refusing to repent in the seven messages (Rev 2:16, 22; 3:3) that are later realized in the judgements on the earth dwellers (Rev 9:18–20; 16:5, 9, 11; 19:15, 21) forces on the readers/hearers aligned with Jezebel an expectation of judgement from Christ as Destroyer. And even though his image of the slaughtered Lamb is taken from the Exodus tradition and denotes God's protection for his people, it also coincides with the Second Temple traditions that expect suffering, poverty, and death for the righteous in the present age (cf. Rev 1:9; 2:10, 13). This makes it possible to say that the

---

[35] Johns, *Lamb Christology*, p. 163.

[36] Collins, 'Son of Man in First-Century Judaism', pp. 462–4; Hoffman, *Destroyer and the Lamb*, p. 41; Müller, *Messias und Menschensohn*, p. 196.

author's expectation for the faithful community does not include wealth in the present eschatological age but is one of growing hostility. This idea is further demonstrated in the breaking of the seven seals.

7.3   Breaking the seven seals

After the dramatic scene introducing the seven-sealed scroll finds resolution in the appearance of the slaughtered Lamb, Christ begins to break the seals and set in motion the events of the eschatological age.[37] The first four seals release onto the scene four horsemen riding various coloured horses. They are correlated with the four living creatures, each of which says 'Come' when a seal is broken. Given the economic overtones of the balancing scales, the third rider is of particular importance to the present study. In order to appreciate the context in which the third rider appears, a brief synopsis of the overall vision is warranted.

The four horsemen

John's imagery of horses is drawn from the prophetic tradition. Twice in Zechariah the writer mentions these animals. (1) In Zech 1:8–11 the prophet sees a man riding a red horse with other red, white, and dappled grey horses behind him. (2) Zech 6:1–8 mentions four chariots being pulled by four different coloured horses: red, black, white, and dappled grey.

The use of colours in these texts does not carry any significance other than distinguishing the direction that the chariots take.[38] There is also no emphasis placed on the rider in Zech 1, and no riders are mentioned in Zech 6. The idea of horses, and implicitly riders, presenting themselves before God gives the indication that these are some form of angelic beings that serve to patrol the earth for God and carry out his plans. As such, the visions function to establish both the omniscience and omnipotence of God in the world through these divine agents.[39]

---

[37] The seven-sealed scroll is the eschatological plan of God in which the destiny of humankind is revealed. Charles, *Revelation*, vol. I, p. 138; Yarbro Collins, *Combat Myth*, p. 24; Boxall, *Revelation*, p. 95. For a discussion of the various views of the form, content, and function of the scroll, see Aune, *Revelation 1–5*, pp. 338–46. The imagery of heavenly records in books or scrolls in which the events of the last days are sealed is a common *topos* in Jewish literature. Ezek 2:8–3:3; Dan 10:14, 21; 12:4, 9; *1 Enoch* 81:1–3; 90:20–1; 93:2; 103:1–4; 106:19–107:1; 108:7.

[38] Meyers and Meyers, *Zechariah 1–8*, pp. 320–1; Smith, *Micah–Malachi*, pp. 213–14.

[39] Meyers and Meyers, *Zechariah*, p. 318.

John's vision of the horsemen also draws on language from the Deuteronomistic and prophetic traditions.[40] God's anger against the Israelites in the desert took the form of hunger, consumption, pestilence, and wild beasts (Deut 32:23–4; cf. Lev 26:22–6), language also used by the prophet Ezekiel (Ezek 14:21). John, however, has reshaped the imagery and language into an entirely new vision so that the riders represent four angelic beings that go out into the world and carry out the plan of God in the eschatological age.

Fiorenza argues that these riders reflect the oppressive power of the Roman Empire.[41] Their association with persons and events from the first century, and specifically with Rome, are commonplace among early commentators.[42] A similar approach is taken with regard to the beasts, the whore, and Babylon in subsequent visions, though this historical-critical method does not respect the author's intentional ambiguity or the theological significance of the visionary experience apart from the socio-historical setting. Along these lines Rowland rightly states:

> The importance for us is that the visionary experience, while *conditioned* by life under Roman dominion, *is not determined by it*. It is the Beast and Babylon, not Rome and Caesar, which are the vehicles of John's message. As such they have a wider appeal than a narrowly focused political analysis rooted in particular historical events.[43]

Likewise, the vision of the riders portrays conditions that coincide with the author's expectations for the eschatological age. At the same time, the readers/hearers would be expected to interpret the visions based on their experience in their own social world. If a minority of the recipients are experiencing a degree of persecution as depicted in the seven messages, then Fiorenza is correct that some of John's readers/hearers may have been able to associate the imagery with oppressive conditions. However, the disparity in circumstances among the churches suggests that some would have found it difficult to see themselves in a universe that reflected such conflict. Thus, John's vision is not a critique of the oppressive actions of the Roman Empire but a description of conditions

---

[40] Court, *Myth and History*, pp. 49–54 argues that the plague sequences in the seven seals are dependent upon the material in the Little Apocalypse of Mark 13.

[41] Fiorenza, *Vision*, p. 63.

[42] Bousset, *Offenbarung*, pp. 263–9; Charles, *Revelation*, vol. I, pp. 153–61.

[43] Rowland, *Revelation*, p. 24 (italics added).

he thinks are integral to the present age.[44] Thus, the vision encourages the readers/hearers to place themselves within the imagery in a way that questions the easy lifestyle of the rich and explains the persecution and suffering of the faithful.

The first rider is portrayed in white and goes out conquering and to conquer (νικῶν καὶ ἵνα νικήσῃ). He mimics very generally the image of Christ in chapter 19, though the only exact similarity between them is the white horse.[45] The first rider wears a crown (στέφανος) while Christ wears many diadems (διαδήματα). His white horse and gold crown reflect his deceptive nature in having the appearance of righteousness. The language of conquering associates him with the seven messages (Rev 2:7, 11, 17, 26, 28; 3:5, 12, 21), the Lamb (Rev 5:5), the beast (Rev 13:7), and the Dragon (Rev 12:11), though the ambiguity in the imagery would not allow the readers to draw any connection with the latter two at this stage of the reading/hearing. However, this rider conquers in a militaristic fashion in contrast to the Lamb just seen in the throne-room vision, who conquered through death. An association with Christ is awkward since he is the one opening the seals. In some way this rider reflects a kind of antichrist figure who makes war on the saints and conquers them (cf. Rev 11:7; 13:7) and should be viewed in contrast to the conquering Lamb of 5:6 and finally the vision of Christ in chapter 19.[46]

The second and fourth riders also represent malevolent creatures that are released onto the earth in the eschatological age. The second rider takes peace from the earth and the fourth is Death who brings with him

[44] Yarbro Collins, *Crisis and Catharsis*, p. 170. Cf. Fiorenza, *Vision*, pp. 64–5.

[45] Various interpretations of the first rider have been proposed: (1) Christ: Irenaeus, *Haer.* 4.21.3; Lenski, *Revelation*, 222–3; Hengstenberg, *Revelation*, vol. I, pp. 251–2; Hendricksen, *More than Conquerors*, pp. 113–17; Bachmann, 'Der erste apokalyptische Reiter', pp. 240–75; Considine, 'Rider on the White Horse', pp. 406–22; (2) the victory of the gospel: Zahn, *Offenbarung*, vol. II, p. 592; Ladd, *Revelation*, p. 99; Weiss, *Offenbarung*, p. 59; (3) war or military conquest: Charles, *Revelation*, vol. I, p. 163; Roloff, *Revelation*, pp. 80–1; Beckwith, *Revelation*, pp. 517–19; Mounce, *Revelation*, p. 154; Aune, *Revelation 1–5*, p. 395. Within the literary world of the Apocalypse, the first rider is like the Dragon (Rev 12:1–10) and deceptive beast (Rev 13:14), who have great power (Rev 13:4) and deceive the inhabitants of the world and make war against the saints. Beale, *Revelation*, p. 377 sees this figure as a satanic force, though Müller, *Offenbarung*, p. 164 is correct that at this point in the reading the readers/hearers would not recognize him as such. He asserts that the imagery of an antichrist figure here is too vague and thus sees the first rider as a warrior. Fiorenza, *Vision*, p. 63 sees him as a precursor of 'the victorious parousia Christ' in chapter 19.

[46] Boxall, *Revelation*, p. 107; Cowley, *Apocalypse*, p. 229; Rissi, 'Rider on the White Horse', pp. 407–18; also Rissi, *Zeit und Geschichte*, pp. 89–94; Smalley, *Revelation*, p. 150. See also Kerkeslager, 'Prophecy and the Rider on the White Horse', pp. 116–21 who suggests it may reflect false prophecy and a parody of the true prophetic word.

Hades. The breaking of the seven seals and the subsequent release of these riders reflect an eschatological age that is filled with difficulty, deception, and conflict. Those within the faithful community that are enjoying affluence and self-sufficiency would find it difficult to see the world as John portrays it. From his heavenly perspective, he sees forces at work in the universe that seek to deceive the faithful who will acquiesce, and make war with those who will not. The image of the third rider indicates that one of these forces is in some way connected to the economic system.

7.4   The third rider

> When he opened the third seal, I heard the third living creature call out, 'Come!' I looked, and there was a black horse! Its rider held a pair of scales (ζυγός) in his hand, and I heard what seemed to be a voice in the midst of the four living creatures saying, 'A quart of wheat for a day's pay, and three quarts of barley for a day's pay, but do not damage the olive oil and the wine!'   (Rev 6:5–6)

Two distinguishing features of the third rider indicate that the author may be drawing special attention to this horseman: (1) this rider alone lacks the divine passive (ἐδόθη), and (2) after he appears a voice is heard from among the four living creatures.

John's tendency towards aesthetic organization of imagery thus far in the Apocalypse makes these differences stand out. Each of the seven messages follows a somewhat regimented formula. There are four living creatures, each with six wings, each with eyes all around. There are twenty-four elders each sitting on a throne, each with a golden crown and they all worship at the same time saying the same thing. There are seven churches, the Lamb has seven horns and seven eyes, there is a scroll with seven seals and there are four horsemen, each of which corresponds to one of the living creatures and follows a similarly symmetrical pattern. This break in uniformity draws attention to particular aspects of this vision. A similar strategy was evident in the seven messages in which John highlighted the circumstances he values for the faithful community in the absence of repentance in the messages to Smyrna and Philadelphia.

The most widely held view on the third rider is that it refers to famine.[47] Scholars frequently attribute this to the black colour of the horse yet

---

[47] Bousset, *Offenbarung*, p. 267; Lohmeyer, *Offenbarung*, p. 61; Kraft, *Offenbarung*, p. 117; Charles, *Revelation*, vol. I, p. 166; Caird, *Revelation*, p. 81; Roloff, *Revelation*, p. 87; Mounce, *Revelation*, p. 144; Beale, *Revelation*, pp. 380–1; Boxall, *Revelation*, p. 110; Smalley, *Revelation*, p. 153.

provide no evidence for this conclusion. Commentators also note that the fourfold language from Ezek 14:21, sword, famine, pestilence, and beasts, refers back to all four horsemen (Rev 6:8), thus aligning famine with the third rider.[48] However, it is not possible to draw a one-to-one correlation between these four plagues and the preceding riders.[49] Rather, the fourfold language of sword, famine, pestilence, and wild beasts is traditional language used to describe the judgement of God (Deut 32:23–4; Ezek 5:16–17; 14:21; Jer 14:12; 29:17–18; *Pss. Sol.* 13:2–3).[50] Thus, the authority given 'to them' (ἐδόθη αὐτοῖς) refers to its closest antecedents, Death and Hades, and the means by which they perform their eschatological function.[51]

The colour black (μέλας) occurs only five times in the LXX, referring to black hair (Lev 13:37; Cant 5:11), a black person (Cant 1:5–6), and the black horses of Zechariah. In the NT the word is limited to describing hair (Matt 5:36), ink (2 Cor 3:3; 2 John 12; 3 John 13), and two occurrences in Revelation. The first refers to the black horse of the third rider while the second refers to the sun turning as black as sackcloth (σάκκος). In other Jewish traditions black is usually attributed to the impurity of sin (*Apoc. Ezek.* 2:1; *3 Bar* 13:1), or mourning one's death (*Jos. Asen.* 10:9–11; *Life of Adam and Eve* 35:4–36:3). In the *Animal Apocalypse* the corrupt line of Cain is related to a black bull calf and the wicked giant offspring from the forbidden union of angels and women are referred to as large black cattle.[52] Greco-Roman traditions also relate black to evil and the underworld.[53]

While the colours of the horses in Zechariah seem somewhat arbitrary, John has cast his vision in a way that is significant. I have already suggested that the ambiguity of the white horse reflects deception by having

---

[48] Lohmeyer, *Offenbarung*, p. 62; Farrer, *Revelation*, p. 100; Beale, *Revelation*, p. 383.

[49] Aune, *Revelation 6–16*, p. 402.

[50] Cf. also the tripartite formula in Jer 14:12; 21:9; 24:10; 27:8, 13; 29:17–18; 32:24, 36; 38:2; 42:17, 22; 44:13; Ezek 6:11; 12:16; 4Q171 1 2ii:1; 4Q504 1 2Riii:8.

[51] Some suggest the phrase 'they were given authority over a fourth of the earth, to kill with sword, famine, and pestilence, and by the wild animals of the earth' is a comprehensive statement referring back to all four riders. This is problematic for the following reasons. (1) The preposition μετά is used 'with the genitive of person in company with whom something takes place': *BDAG*, p. 636. Since there are two riders in the last seal, the phrase 'with him' μετ' αὐτοῦ requires the plural pronoun αὐτοῖς to clarify that authority has been given to both riders. (2) In every other instance ἐδόθη refers only to the horseman to which it is attached. (3) If the third rider reflects only a limited famine, it does not make sense that the famine mentioned in the fourth rider is capable of killing a large number of people. (4) The description of the means of death does not correspond directly to the other horsemen and seems to be an elaboration of the means given to personified Death and Hades.

[52] *1 Enoch* 85:3; 86:2; 89:9.

[53] Homer, *Il.* 2.834; *Od.* 12.92; Euripides, *Frag.* 533.1; Sophocles, *Oed.*, 29, 1278; Hesiod, *Op.*, 155.

the appearance of righteousness. The red horse has a direct connection with the rider in Zechariah since they both speak of peace on the earth. The colour green (χλωρός) of the fourth rider coincides with Greco-Roman traditions that denote extreme sickness and death.[54] Thus, there is some correlation between the colours of the horses and the function of the riders. In light of both Jewish and Greco-Roman traditions that relate the colour black to evil,[55] this is most likely the writer's intent here. I have not found any instances in which black is directly related to famine. Rather, this rider represents some form of evil.

The balancing scales

There are two prominent views concerning the scales in the hand of the third rider:[56] (1) in connection with the black horse, the scales refer to famine, and (2) they have an economic referent.[57] By far, the first is the most widely accepted view and is based on references to measuring grains during times of famine in two OT texts: Lev 26:26; Ezek 4:16. However, this view is problematic for the following reasons. (1) In these OT passages the term ζυγός or its Hebrew equivalents מאזנים or פלס do not occur. (2) Aune rightly notes that the emphasis in verse 6 is the *cost* of grain and not its *weight*.[58] This suggests that a correlation to measuring grain in times of famine is incongruent. (3) The term ζυγός is never used in relation to famine in the Hebrew Bible but only refers to commerce, in particular to being honest in economic transactions.[59] (4) Having shown already that the famine mentioned in connection with the fourth rider is not associated with the third, one

[54] Hippocrates, *Progn* 2; Homer, *Il.*, 7.479; *Od.*, 11.43.

[55] *BDAG*, p. 626. *TDNT*, vol. IV, pp. 549–51.

[56] A third view argues for astrological connections. See Boll, *Offenbarung Johannis*, pp. 84–7. However, if John has employed this imagery he has done so with no astrological ideas in mind (Müller, *Offenbarung*, p. 166) since the voice that follows clearly associates the scales with grain and barley. See Bousset, *Offenbarung*, p. 267; contra Aune, *Revelation 6–16*, p. 396.

[57] Vanni, 'Il terzo "sigillo" dell'Apocalisse (Rev 6:5–6)', pp. 691–719 contends the scales reflect the economic injustice of the Roman Empire. See also Ellul, *Apocalypse*, pp. 149–50.

[58] Aune, *Revelation 6–16*, p. 396.

[59] Isa 46:6; Jer 32:10; Ezek 45:9–10; Hos 12:8–9; Amos 8:4–6; Mic 6:11; Lev 19:35–36; Prov 11:1; 16:11; 20:10, 23; Ezek 45:9–10; Sir 42:1–4; Philo, *Hypoth.*, 7.8. See also *1 Enoch* 99:12. The reading *la-masfarta* ('measures of') is based on most Eth. 1 and some Eth. 2 manuscripts (Olson, *Enoch*, pp. 240–1). However, EMML 2080 reads *la-masarata*, 'woe to you who lay the foundation of sin and deceit'. So Stuckenbruck, *1 Enoch 91–108*, pp. 413, 419, and Nickelsburg, *1 Enoch 1*, 495.

wonders why famine would be mentioned in relation to two consecutive riders.

The term ζυγός also refers to a yoke, relating to animals, slaves, and the oppressive burden of other nations.[60] In Greco-Roman literature, it is almost always employed in this way.[61] In the third *Sibylline Oracle* the yoke is mentioned in relation to one's wealth since it draws the attention of stronger nations who come and plunder their riches, highlighting the temporary nature of their wealth and the ultimate grief it brings.[62] Other passages refer to cosmic scales where humans are weighed either in reference to their significance in the universe or against their earthly deeds.[63] Apocalyptic traditions relate the imagery of scales to that of judgement.[64]

From a tradition-historical perspective the most viable options are: (1) a weighing or measuring device used in day-to-day business practices, (2) the yoke of an ox or horse, (3) the burden of oppression, or (4) a reference to judgement. We can rule out altogether the possibility of (2) and the inclusion of the great white throne judgement in chapter 20 makes (4) an unlikely choice since there is no equivalent language. The suggestion that the writer is opposing the oppressive Roman Empire makes (3) an attractive choice, though the Lamb's statement concerning the prices of wheat and barley almost certainly points to some kind of economic referent. It is also possible, in light of the critique of wealth in chapter 18, that (1) and (4) are included, evoking both the evil nature of the economic system and its impending doom.[65] What we can know is that the term is not used in either Jewish or Greco-Roman sources in relation to famine. However, an evil economic system seems to be an integral part of the author's expectations of the last days and coincides with other traditions that anticipate an increase in avarice and escalating conflict in the eschatological age.[66]

---

[60] Gen 27:40; Num 19:2; Deut 21:3; 2 Chron 10:4, 9–14; Psa 2:3; Isa 5:18; 9:4; 10:27; 14:25; 47:6; Jer 5:5; 27:8; 28:14; 30:8; Ezek 34:27; Zeph 3:9; 1 Macc 8:18, 31; 13:41; *3 Macc* 4:9; Sir 28:19–20; 33:27; 40:1; 51:26. Cf. *Sib. Or.* 3:391, 448, 508, 537; 4:87, 104; 8:126, 326; 11:67, 76, 217; 13:94; 14:308; *Jub.* 26:34; *Pss. Sol.* 7:9; 17:30.

[61] Euripides, *Frag.*, 475.1; *Med.*, 242; *Andr.*, 301; *Hel.*, 392; Sophocles, *Frag.* 591.6; Homer, *Il.*, 10.293; 13.706; 16.470; 19.406; 23.294; *Od.*, 3.846; 15.184; Herodotus, *Hist.* 4.5.10; 8.20.6; Hesiod, *Op.*, 815.

[62] *Sib. Or.* 3:391, 448, 508, 537, 567.

[63] Ps 62:9; Job 6:2; 31:6; 39:10; Isa 40:12, 15; Dan 5:27. Cf. *2 Enoch* 49:2; *2 Esd* 3:34; 4:36; *Pss. Sol.* 5:4.

[64] Dan 5:27; *1 Enoch* 41:1; *2 Enoch* 49:2; *T. Abr* 12:8–18; 13:9–10.

[65] Ellul, *Apocalypse*, pp. 149–50.

[66] Dan 12:4; Matt 24:7–12; Mark 13:19; Luke 21:23, *1 Enoch* 54:6; 56:4; 91:6; 99:3–5; 100:1–3; 106:19–107:1; CD 4:12–18; 1QM i 11–12; 16:11, 15; 17:1; 11Q19 54:12;

7.5   A voice from the midst of the throne

'A quart of wheat for a day's pay, and three quarts of barley for
a day's pay, but do not damage the olive oil and the wine!'

(Rev 6:6)

Commentators have identified the speaker in this phrase as the voice of
Christ.[67] Osborne argues the voice is that of the four living creatures.[68]
However, the close correspondence of these creatures to the breaking of
the first four seals indicates that the writer is distinguishing the Lamb's
voice from the four living creatures that say, 'Come.' Aune asserts the
readers/hearers would assume this is the voice of God.[69] However, the
author is careful to indicate the voice comes from the midst (μέσος) of
the throne, the same term used to describe the location of the Lamb (Rev
5:6–7). If this is the case, then the only time speech is attributed to the
Lamb is in relation to the rider who holds sway over the powerful, corrupt
economic system of the eschatological age.[70]

The phrase itself bears a resemblance to Elisha's statement, 'a measure
of choice meal shall be sold for a shekel, and two measures of barley
for a shekel', though this reflects the exact opposite scenario to what we
have in Revelation (cf. 2 Kgs 6:25; 7:1). While this does indicate that
people spoke in terms of a day's pay when referring to extreme grain
prices, it does not resolve the problem presented by our text. Aune has
conservatively determined that the prices reflected in this statement are
five to eight times the normal price for grain in the Roman Empire.[71]
At the same time the prohibition against harming the wine and the oil
suggests it is only a limited famine.[72] Boxall explains that the Lamb
'ameliorates its effect', though one wonders how this is helpful since
these items would have been unaffordable in light of the grain prices
and would only benefit the rich.[73] If it is a limited famine, why are the
prices for the grain so exorbitant? In addition, why does the third rider
represent a limited famine when in the very next seal the fourth rider kills

---

4Q177 9:2; 10 11:10; Wis 1:16; 3:5–6; 2 Esd 5:1–13; 6:20–24; 9:3–4; 13:30–31; *Sib. Or.*
3:175–90; 635–43; *2 Bar.* 70:2–8; *Jub.* 23:16–21.

[67] Bousset, *Offenbarung*, p. 267; Charles, *Revelation*, vol. I, p. 166; Roloff, *Revelation*,
p. 87; Beale, *Revelation*, p. 381; Boxall, *Revelation*, p. 110.

[68] Osborne, *Revelation*, p. 280.

[69] Aune, *Revelation 6–16*, p. 397. Lohmeyer, *Offenbarung*, p. 61, maintains the identity
is purposefully hidden.

[70] The angelomorphic Christ speaks in the introductory vision and the seven messages.

[71] Aune, *Revelation 6–16*, p. 397. See also Beale, *Revelation*, p. 381.

[72] Kraft, *Offenbarung*, p. 117.   [73] Boxall, *Revelation*, p. 110.

one-fourth of the population of the earth with complete famine? Thus the limited famine view does not compel.

If wine and oil were luxury items, this would reflect economic injustice since the prices for the rich are not affected, though it has been pointed out that oil and wine were not luxury items and were generally available during times of plenty.[74] However, their availability is not an indication of whether they represented necessities. Psalm 104:15 refers to 'wine to gladden the heart, oil to make the face shine, and bread to strengthen the heart'. This sentiment is echoed in Prov 21:17, where oil and wine are mentioned in synonymous parallelism with pleasure. It is obvious that a person who is paying exorbitant prices for basic food items would not be able to purchase wine and oil for these purposes. Thus, in this kind of oppressed market they would in fact be considered a luxury. This is strengthened by their inclusion in the list of luxury items in the cargo list in chapter 18.

Others have argued that the statement reflects the conditions of war produced by the first rider.[75] Thus the prices would indicate inflationary conditions that would directly affect the poor but not the rich. The difficulty of this view in connection with the Lamb has drawn questions as to its coherence with modern expectations. For example, Mounce states, 'it would be difficult to understand why the Lamb would issue an order favouring the rich and aggravating the plight of the poor'.[76] The question here, however, is not whether the Lamb is issuing an order but whether John is providing a description of the economic system that the third rider represents, on the one hand, while raising the question of whether his readers have aligned themselves with this system, on the other.

We should regard the statement as containing typical, exaggerated apocalyptic language for rhetorical effect.[77] Thus, it would be a phrase couched in irony and sarcasm proclaiming the nature of the unjust economic system that manipulates prices that ultimately bring hardship on the poor.[78] Yarbro Collins has pointed out at least two instances of bread riots during the reigns of Domitian and Trajan where the poor citizens

[74] Lohse, *Offenbarung*, p. 47; Caird, *Revelation*, p. 81; Moffat, 'Hurt Not the Oil and the Wine', pp. 362–3. See also Aune, *Revelation 6–16*, p. 398; Beale, *Revelation*, p. 381. Some commentators argue that this refers to a vine edict of Domitian. See Bousset, *Offenbarung*, p. 135; Roloff, *Revelation*, p. 87; Hemer, *Letters*, p. 158. However, this presses the imagery too far towards a historical link. So Charles, *Revelation*, vol. I, p. 168; Beckwith, *Apocalypse*, p. 522; Aune, *Revelation 6–16*, p. 400.

[75] Kraft, *Offenbarung*, p. 117.   [76] Mounce, *Revelation*, p. 144.

[77] Maier, *Apocalypse Recalled*, p. 177.

[78] Vanni, 'Il terzo "sigillo" dell'Apocalisse (Rev 6:5–6)', p. 711; Maier, *Apocalypse Recalled*, pp. 177–8.

accused the rich of hoarding grain in order to get more money for their product.[79] This underscores a level of suspicion among the poor masses towards those who controlled the prices of grain (Dio Chrysostom, *Orat.* 46.10–11). One might argue, then, that John has left the divine passive out of this seal since the wicked economic system is not something he has commanded, but is indicative of the nature of the system itself, which is demonically empowered.[80]

However, it is likely that both of these are at work. John certainly understands that the Lamb is sovereign over all creation. Thus, while these forces may be wicked, they have their authority to reign in the present age directly from the Lamb. This coincides with traditions already circulating that envisioned an organized evil force that deceives humankind by means of wealth (CD 4:14–19). By attributing the speech to Christ, John lifts up the dual role of Destroyer and Lamb and emphasizes Christ's awareness of the corruption in the economic system. This would encourage his readers/hearers to consider whether they can be aligned with such activity. At the same time, the vision of the horsemen serves a dual function: (1) it highlights the hostility and conflict envisioned in the eschatological age bringing into question the circumstances of the rich, and (2) since Christ is ultimately responsible for these catastrophes, the vision functions to portray the present age as a time of testing (Rev 3:18).

This coincides with the seven messages. John values the poor status of Smyrna and Philadelphia and condemns the wealth of the Laodiceans. His admonition to the Laodicean rich to accept a marginalized state (Rev 3:18) anticipates the author's negative portrayal of the economic system in the third rider. In this same passage (Rev 3:17–19) Christ says he disciplines and reproves those whom he loves. The portrayal of Christ as one who has conquered through death and the subsequent inauguration of the eschatological age in terms that indicate tumultuous circumstances underscores John's theological understanding of the last days as a time when conditions will grow worse for the righteous while they get better for the wicked.[81] More importantly, the author takes care to emphasize that this expected conflict finds expression in the realm of the economy.

---

[79] Yarbro Collins, *Crisis and Catharsis*, pp. 94–7.

[80] However, see section 8.6, below in reference to the active use of δίδωμι in relation to the Dragon and the first beast.

[81] 1QM i 11–12; 2 Esd 5:1–13; 6:20–4; 9:3–4; 13:30–1; *2 Bar.* 70:2–8; *1 Enoch* 91:6; 99:3–5; 100:1–3; *Jub.* 23:16–21.

8

BUYING AND SELLING IN SATAN'S WORLD: REV 12–13, 18

8.1   The mark of the beast

> Also it causes all, both small and great, both rich and poor, both free and slave, to be marked on the right hand or the forehead, so that no one can buy or sell (ἀγοράσαι ἢ πωλῆσαι) who does not have the mark, that is, the name of the beast or the number of its name.
> (Rev 13:16–17)

While the present section will focus on the passage cited above, the entirety of Rev 12:18–13:18 provides relevant contextual links to the seven messages: (1) by means of the phrase, 'If anyone has an ear, let him hear' (Εἴ τις ἔχει οὖς ἀκουσάτω) (2:7, 11, 17, 29; 3:6, 13, 22; 13:9), and (2) the writer's persistent anxiety over economic issues, which is evidenced in his reference to 'buying and selling' (ἀγοράσαι ἢ πωλῆσαι). In addition, the material finds correlation with the throne-room vision and the third horseman in the following ways. (1) The beast from the sea is given a throne (θρόνος) and authority (ἐξουσία) (Rev 13:2), and both beasts are described in terms that parody the Lamb (Rev 13:2–3, 11). (2) The phrase 'to buy or sell' relates directly to the economic imagery of balancing scales carried by the third rider.

In order to discern the function of the phrase 'to buy or sell', this section will provide some degree of context by discussing the function of the Combat Myth and other antecedent traditions in Revelation 12 since it is strategically connected with what follows in chapter 13.[1] A brief analysis of the traditions related to the two beasts will be analysed in terms of the significance of how they, together with the Combat Myth, expose the world view of the author and the traditions that have shaped his cosmology. First, however, a consideration of the passage cited above is warranted in light of its immediate concern with worship in order to

---

[1]   Bousset, *Offenbarung*, p. 357.

discern what relationship John is suggesting exists between buying and selling on the one hand and worship on the other.

The expression 'buying and selling' is firmly connected to the mark of the beast and cannot be discussed apart from it. However, it is not within the scope of this book to identify the referent behind the mark or to determine its calculation.[2] Rather, we will consider its function within the literary world of the Apocalypse and its meaning in relation to the author's perspective on economic participation.

The mark (χάραγμα) of the beast and the seal (σφραγίς) of God delineate between the wicked and the faithful and thus the author is deliberate in distinguishing the terms. At the most basic level, the mark is a means of *identification* from a cosmological perspective that denotes loyalty and worship to the beast, while the seal of God indicates the same towards the Lamb.[3] The writer indicates no one is excluded from receiving the mark; both small and great, rich and poor (τοὺς πλουσίους καὶ τοὺς πτωχούς), free and slave (Rev 13:16). The use of *merismus* in conjunction with 'all' (πάντες) is used in these pairings to express totality.[4] Royalty has pointed out that the inclusion of both rich and poor in this text demonstrates that God does not show any partiality to the poor but emphasizes the universality of the judgements being poured out on the earth (Rev 6:15; 13:16; 19:18).[5] While this is true to some degree, this statement needs qualification. As already pointed out, Christ does favour the economic situation of the faithful poor in the seven messages over the rich and those related to the false teachers. Thus, John has identified two distinct groups within the seven messages to whom the terms rich and poor have been applied (Rev 2:9; 3:17). At the same time, even those who are not called to repentance are admonished to conquer, an activity that is inherently bound up in rejecting the economic mark of the beast (Rev 15:1–4). Thus, it is likely that the writer includes this phrase because

---

[2] The mark of the beast has been variously interpreted as representing Jewish phylacteries (*TDNT* vol. IV, pp. 635–7; Charles, *Revelation*, vol. I, pp. 362–3), imperial images or stamps on Roman coinage or commercial documents (Bousset, *Offenbarung* (1896), p. 428; Kraft, *Offenbarung*, pp. 182–3; Witherington, *Revelation*, p. 184; Kraybill, *Imperial Cult and Commerce*, pp. 138–41), and the branding of slaves (Mounce, *Revelation*, p. 258; Ford, *Revelation*, p. 225). For discussions related to the use of gematria in the ancient world, see Beale, *Revelation*, pp. 718–28; Aune, *Revelation 6–16*, pp. 769–73; Bauckham, *Climax of Prophecy*, pp. 384–452; Driver, 'The Number of the Beast', pp. 75–81.

[3] Note the connection between worship and receiving the mark of the beast in Rev 14:9, 11; 15:2; 16:2; 19:20; 20:4. The 144,000 who have God's seal are contrasted with the former group immediately after the passage in question (Rev 14:1).

[4] Aune, *Revelation 6–16*, p. 765; See also Honeyman, 'Merismus in Biblical Hebrew', pp. 11–18.

[5] Royalty, *Streets of Heaven*, p. 182.

he thinks that many in the churches are already involved at this level of economic involvement, but leaves open the possibility that the faithful minority are also in danger of being tempted.

John is emphasizing the way God distinguishes the faithful from the wicked from a heavenly perspective and in this text the phrase 'to buy or sell' becomes significant for making that distinction. It does, however, refer to a particular activity. When describing the inner workings of a thriving πόλις, Plato refers to those who were responsible for merchandizing the goods of others.[6] When the two terms occur together as a phrase it generally denotes the activity of trading in the marketplace to earn a living or acquire one's means of subsistence.[7] The terms do not occur together in the Hebrew Bible although they are found in other Jewish traditions. Ben Sira demonstrates a negative attitude towards the engagement of business stating that 'sin is firmly wedged between "buying and selling"' (Sir 27:2).[8] The precarious nature of honesty in trade is a common *topos* in biblical sapiential literature.[9] The phrase also occurs in the *Damascus Document* in which the community precludes members from buying and selling (ולממכר למקח) without the consent of the Overseer (CD 13:14–15; 4Q266 9 iii:1). In addition, they are prevented from buying and selling to one another but must only use a barter system (CD 13:14–15). Though economic activity is allowed, there are some distinct restrictions (CD 12:8–11). This suggests that the community was allowed to engage in trade to the degree it could sustain itself and provide for the needs of the camps. However, individual affluence ran counter to the ideology of the Damascus covenanters who referred to themselves as 'the poor ones' (CD 19:9).

The phrase also occurs in the early Christian tradition. In Matthew's Gospel it refers to trading in general (Matt 25:9) as well as to the merchandizing of the wicked that took place within the Temple (Matt 21:12; Mark 11:15). Luke in particular uses the terms together when speaking of the activities of humankind leading up to the Flood and those of the last days (Luke 17:28). Though part of a collection of everyday activities in which people are engaged, they function to emphasize the inability of

---

[6] Plato, *Resp.* 2.371–2. Cf. Strabo, *Geogr.* 15.3.19; Plato, *Leg.* 6.917–18.

[7] Thucydides, 7.39.2.6; Homer, *Il.*, 1.490; Aristophanes, *Ach.*, 625; Xenophon, *Anab.*, 1.5.5.8; Plato, *Leg.*, 849.D.1; 1 Macc 12:35–13:49.

[8] Ben Sira's grandson uses the terms πράσεως καὶ ἀγορασμοῦ in his translation, which indicates the idiom was also known in different forms. However, the same meaning is implied.

[9] Prov 11:1; 16:11; 20:10, 23; Sir 5:8; 42:4–5.

sinners to discern the impending judgement of God. This text finds a parallel in Matthew's version of the Olivet Discourse (Matt 24:38), though it lacks the phrase buying and selling. Luke's expansion of Matthew's account may indicate that this was part of a tradition already circulating in the Second Temple period that was not part of the hypothetical Q source.[10] While it is outside the scope of this thesis to engage this issue in detail, Luke's addition may suggest that the phrase was becoming part of a list that described activity that so consumes humankind in the last days that they will be unable to prepare for the coming judgement.

John has most likely over-contextualized the phrase 'to buy or sell' in a way that associates this activity directly with the accumulation of wealth that he so adamantly opposes (Rev 2:9; 3:17). He leaves the image of the mark of the beast ambiguous with regard to time so that it is not possible to determine whether this is something he indicates has already occurred, is happening, or will take place in the future. Those in the churches who are engaged in economic trade do not have the luxury of pretending they have time to continue in their activity until the event takes place. John's contrastive language clearly aligns the wicked with Satan (Rev 13:16–17) and the faithful with the Lamb (Rev 15:2; 20:4). He places the phrase within the context of worship and categorically rejects any and all economic participation. It is difficult to say whether the author would allow for trade necessary to sustain the faithful community. However, John does not allow for any exceptions since this would undermine his overall rhetorical strategy. Like the over-contextualization of the phrase, 'to buy or sell', John too heightens his rhetoric to indicate to his readers/hearers that his position, if adopted, will most likely lead to harsh persecution and even death (Rev 2:10; 12:11; 13:7). Yet in light of his portrayal of the slaughtered Lamb and his language of conquering, the faithful are cast in a far better light than what the possible consequences might bring. They will not be harmed by the second death, they will wear white robes and receive golden crowns, they will be with Jesus and rejoice over the destruction of the wicked, and they will inherit the gold and jewel-laden new Jerusalem. At the same time, the remainder of humankind who receive the mark of the beast will be destroyed and cast into the lake of fire (Rev 19:21; 20:15; 21:8).

In light of his censure of the rich as being lukewarm and the emphasis here on the visible distinction between the faithful and the wicked, the author's radical rejection of economic activity becomes a tangible means

---

[10] Bock, *Luke 9:51–24:53*, vol. II, p. 1433; Fitzmyer, *Luke (X–XXIV)*, pp. 1165, 1171. Cf. Marshall, *Gospel of Luke*, p. 662; Manson, *Sayings of Jesus*, p. 143.

by which the faithful are to be distinguished from the wicked on the earth. Buying and selling within the system promoted by Satan and his beasts is antithetical to faithfulness. This censure of economic participation reflects a radical sectarian ideology and imposes on the Christian community a difficult decision. Thus it becomes necessary to examine the way in which John brings his readers/hearers to the point of what is at stake in the position he is imposing.

8.2   The function of myth and tradition in Rev 12–13

In the seven messages John shows a preference for poverty and a rejection of wealth among the faithful. In doing so he maintains that persecution and possibly death are consistent with faithfulness. This is buttressed in his portrayal of Christ as the slaughtered Lamb in the throne-room vision and the expected conflict that stems from the inauguration of the eschatological age. Yet, in the throne-room vision no explicit contrast is drawn between the faithful and the wicked. There is an indication of a righteous remnant in the sealing of the 144,000, though the wicked are not yet identified. Consequently, neither of these visions reflects an antagonism between these groups. Hostility becomes more evident in chapter 11 when the text refers to the violent deaths of the two witnesses who are killed and the subsequent party in the streets by the inhabitants of the earth (Rev 11:7–10). This antipathy, however, comes directly from the beast who rises from the bottomless pit (Rev 11:7), the first mention of a demonic, antagonistic beast.[11] This struggle illustrates for the readers the likely outcome for the faithful who remain loyal to God on the earth. In chapter 12, the author turns the readers'/hearers' attention to the war in heaven and provides the basis for a more explicit expectation of conflict and difficulty for the faithful in the present age.

Since the turn of the twentieth century scholars have considered the degree to which John is in conversation with mythical traditions in relation to the downfall of Satan in Rev 12.[12] The source-critical approach these studies take provides analyses of the many versions of the Combat Myths that circulated in ancient Greek and early Jewish traditions. Examinations in comparison to John's use of ancient myth quickly reveal that,

[11] The term is also used in Rev 6:8, though it is plural and refers to wild animals of the earth. Rhetorically, however, it does serve to ready the hearers for the ideas presented in chapter 13.

[12] Bousset, *Antichrist Legend*; Ernst, *Eschatologischen Gegenspieler*, p. 137; Yarbro Collins, *Combat Myth*, pp. 61–156; Forsyth, *Old Enemy*, pp. 248–57; Auffarth and Stuckenbruck, *Fall of the Angels*, 119–47; Busch, *Der gefallene Drache*.

like his conflation of conventional language and imagery in the throne-room vision, here too he has conflated several traditions to formulate the vision of Satan's expulsion from heaven.[13] Yarbro Collins argues that two traditions have been conflated to fit the pattern of the Python–Leto–Apollo myth.[14] However, certain inconsistencies suggest that the author may not have been following such a strict pattern since several features have been reformulated.[15] At the same time her proposal is correct that the writer was in conversation with traditions reflected in the various Combat Myths as well as the story of the fallen angels in the BOW.[16] Since previous studies have established the extent to which the Combat Myth, or variations thereof, was widespread in ancient Near Eastern, Greek, and Jewish traditions, and have identified a number of sources, a discussion along these lines is not warranted.[17] Rather, we will focus on *how* these traditions have been conflated to fit John's rhetorical aims. Hence the question: what kind of world view does John's version of the Combat Myth betray and what overall function does it serve in establishing what is at stake in exhibiting absolute, unequivocal loyalty to the Lamb within the economic realm?

In order to place some limits on the discussion, two points of emphasis seem to arise in the author's use of this material: (1) the irreversible shift of Satan's place on earth, and (2) the primary object of his anger during his temporary reign.

The fall of Satan

As a result of the defeat of Satan and his angels in the heavenly battle, John can say there was no longer any place for them in heaven (Rev 12:8), and in the verse that follows they are cast down to the earth.[18] Here a

---

[13] Contra Aune, 'Apocalypse Renewed', 58. Cf. Thompson, *Apocalypse and Empire*, p. 38.

[14] Yarbro Collins, *Combat Myth*, pp. 142–3; Fontenrose, *Python*, pp. 262–73; Saffrey, 'Relire L'Apocalypse à Patmos', pp. 385–417.

[15] i.e. Dragon not defeated (within mythical framework), time of woman's birth, no death of the champion (child).

[16] Auffarth and Stuckenbruck, *Fall of the Angels*, pp. 119–20; Yarbro Collins, *Combat Myth*, pp. 129–30; Forsyth, *Old Enemy*, pp. 248–57; Aune, *Revelation 6–16*, pp. 664–7.

[17] Yarbro Collins, *Combat Myth*, pp. 57–100; Busch, *Der gefallen Drache*, pp. 45–85; Aune, *Revelation 6–16*, pp. 670–6. For traditions related to the fall of Satan, see *Jub.* 4:15, 22; 10:8; *Life of Adam and Eve* 12–17; *2 Enoch* 7:3–4; 29:4–6; 31:3–4; *T. Reub* 5:1–6; *T. Naph* 3:5.

[18] The imagery of the Dragon sweeping one-third of the stars to the ground refers to the angels who followed Satan's rebellion (Rev 12:4). Beale, in *Use of Daniel*, argues that John is dependent upon Dan 8:10 and that the stars represent the persecuted saints since

sharp spatial distinction is made no fewer than three times, indicating the realm that they now occupy (εἰς τὴν γῆν) (Rev 12:4, 9, 13; cf. 12:12) and is the basis for the author's call for heaven to rejoice while simultaneously pronouncing 'woe' to those who inhabit the earth. This marks a significant shift from the Combat Myth, the Fall of the Watchers, and stories that tell of the fall of Satan in that the present text lacks any form of immediate resolution that is evident in these antecedent traditions. In the Combat Myth the dragon is defeated by the champion and order is restored in the universe. While it is true that Satan is ultimately bound in the final judgement scene (Rev 20:2, 7, 10), in comparison with the Combat Myth this feature has been curtailed. The myth of the Watchers finds partial resolution in the destruction of the bastard offspring (*1 Enoch* 10:9–10; 12:6; 14:6) and the binding of the fallen angels (*1 Enoch* 10:4–13). Yet, the evil spirits of the offspring continue to roam the earth oppressing humankind (*1 Enoch* 15:8–16:2). Even here, however, the expectation of conflict is vague and generalized. In the Apocalypse, John portrays the world in such a way that Satan's downfall inaugurates an irretrievable and categorical conflict.

In addition, traditions that speak of the fall of Satan locate this event in primordial time.[19] While it is not easy to discern John's use of time in the Apocalypse, it is clear that the defeat of the Dragon and his angels is closely connected to the ascension and enthronement of Christ (Rev 12:5, 10) and the subsequent inauguration of the eschatological age.[20] Jewish traditions also viewed Satan as one who has access to both the throne-room of God and the earth (Job 1:6–7; Zech 3:1; *1 Enoch* 40:7). John, however, indicates that a definitive moment has occurred which limited his activity to the earthly realm (cf. *1 Enoch* 14:5). Furthermore, the Dragon is aware that the eschatological age has been inaugurated and he has only a limited time (Rev 12:12). The imagery of the Dragon being flung down to the earth and the knowledge of his impending doom is that of a wild animal cornered before it is killed, lashing out in a last attempt to inflict as much damage as possible. Thus, his anger is directed squarely

the faithful are reflected in star imagery in the *Similitudes*. *1 Enoch* 43:1–3 does refer to the faithful in these terms, though Olson, *Enoch*, p. 84 rightly points out that fallen stars typically refer to the wicked (*1 Enoch* 86:1; 88:1–3; 90:24; Jude 13; *T. Sol.* 20:16; *Apoc. El.* 4:11; cf. Luke 10:18). Fallen stars are associated with rebellion against God both in nature and in reference to angels in the Enochic tradition; *1 Enoch* 18:11–16; 21:1–7; 43:2–44:1. This imagery is also associated with burning mountains and angels, a similar motif found in the Book of Revelation. Cf. *1 Enoch* 18:13; 88:1; 90:24; Rev 8:8, 10; 9:1; 10:1.

19 *2 Enoch* 18:3–5; 29:4–6; *Life of Adam and Eve* 12–16.

20 Maier, *Apocalypse Recalled*, pp. 156–9. Rev 12:10 speaks of the authority of the Messiah and the inauguration of God's kingdom.

in the present age at the people of God against whom he goes out to make war.[21] This text gives the impression that John has written off the present age on earth entirely and that there is no hope for anyone who remains. It also implies that those who remain faithful can expect harsh persecution, though they can also look forward to a better place in the cosmos if they die. This calls into question the circumstances being enjoyed by John's affluent readers and hearers and those who are assimilating into the culture and enjoying the benefits of economic participation.

Yarbro Collins emphasizes the political nature of the dragon imagery, and states, 'in the first century CE, a Jew reading about a δράκων μέγας πυρρὸς would place that image in a political context'.[22] Yet John goes out of his way to identify the Dragon in non-political terms such as the ancient serpent, the Devil, Satan, and the deceiver of the whole world (Rev 12:9). And while Yarbro Collins thinks the Dragon would evoke ideas of a 'long line of national enemies and foreign powers', John's image is larger than that.[23] The political aspect of John's communication should not be overstated since he is concerned with presenting the universe in such a way that it changes the behaviour of the faithful community, not the Empire. Nevertheless, the readers/hearers are called to evaluate all aspects of their participation in the Roman Empire, which embodies John's imagery in the present time and space. This is realized more locally in chapter 13, which presents a more concrete, localized understanding of the consequences of Satan's fall in relation to the world in which the audience presently lived.

Satan's beasts

In chapter 13 John expands his vision of the fall of Satan (Rev 12:1–17) and connects the vision of the two beasts (Rev 13:1–18) with the phrase, 'he stood on the sand of the sea' (Rev 12:18).[24] The Leviathan–Behemoth myth serves as a framework for this vision and was a widely known convention that appears in both the Hebrew Scriptures and traditions contemporary to the Apocalypse.[25] This continued development

---

[21] Yarbro Collins, *Combat Myth*, p. 144 notes that the inclusion of the pursuit of the Dragon and her seed functions to heighten the conflict as an introduction to chapter 13.

[22] *Ibid.*, 119.   [23] *Ibid.*   [24] Aune, *Revelation 6–16*, p. 732.

[25] Whitney, *Two Strange Beasts*, pp. 5–26. In the Hebrew Scriptures, this is found in its most developed form in the book of Job (Job 40:15–41:34). Traditions related to Leviathan and Behemoth are found separately and different forms refer to them by various names. Gunkel, *Schöpfung und Chaos*, pp. 30–61, 69–81, 612–69 notes that these creatures are known by a number of different names in the Hebrew Bible: Rahab, Sea Dragon, Serpent,

of antecedent traditions creates an increasingly disconcerting *ethos* that suggests all the opponents of God are banding together in the eschatological age under the authority of Satan in an effort to direct worship away from God.

The seven heads and ten horns of the beast from the sea emphasize its connection to the Dragon (Rev 12:3). The imagery is also taken over from the vision of the four beasts in Dan 7, though the characteristics of a leopard, lion, and bear are combined to form a new creature (Dan 7:1–8). In Dan 7 the beasts are associated with four earthly kingdoms, the fourth being a political power that has not yet arrived. Rabbinic sources interpreted the fourth beast of Daniel as Rome.[26] Thus, many commentators have associated the beast from the sea with the Roman Empire.[27] Yet, the author's intentional depiction of the Dragon in non-political language discourages an overemphasis on political connections that may limit or skew our understanding. The author's reformulation of these traditions also suggests this is not his primary aim. For example, (1) the Daniel tradition, which employs the divine passive (ἐδόθη), has the kingdoms of the earth receiving their authority from God (Dan 7:4–7). John, however, has inserted active verbs that directly ascribe the source of the beast's authority to Satan (Rev 13:2, 4).[28] The passives that follow should also be attributed to the Dragon. (2) The fourth kingdom of Daniel is portrayed as a dreadful beast with iron teeth that devours, tramples, and breaks the whole world into pieces (Dan 7:23). John's beast is alluring and the inhabitants of the earth are amazed (θαυμάζω) by it and worship it.

Leviathan, and Behemoth. While the account in Job alludes to the idea that Leviathan is a sea creature and Behemoth resides on the land, later traditions (2 Esd 6:49–52; *2 Bar.* 29:3–4; *1 Enoch* 60:7–10) develop this to make it clearer. For example, 2 Esd 6:49–52 states that they were separated on the fifth day of creation, while *2 Bar.* 29:3–4 and *1 Enoch* 60:7–10 place this information in an eschatological context. Cf. Isa 27:1. The former, in particular, is explicit in stating that they will make an appearance in the eschatological age. Leviathan's abode is in the sea, the place of chaos in the earthly realm, and represents the wicked forces of evil that are opposed to God. It was seen as a monster that sums up cosmic evil, one that had been defeated by God, though not completely destroyed. See Gordon, 'Leviathan: Symbol of Evil', 9.

[26] *Midr. Rab.* Gen 44:17; 76:6; *Midr. Rab.* Ex 15:6; *b. Šebu.* 6b; *b. 'Abod. Zar.* 2b; *Pesiq. Rab.* 14.15.

[27] Gunkel, *Schöpfung und Chaos*, p. 336; Bousset, *Offenbarung*, p. 418; Charles, *Revelation*, vol. I, pp. 333, 351; Kraft, *Offenbarung*, p. 175; Caird, *Revelation*, p. 162; Fiorenza, *Vision*, p. 84; Beale, *Revelation*, p. 684; Boxall, *Revelation*, pp. 187–8. While certain aspects of the first beast can be correlated with historical realities of the Roman world, caution should be exercised in attempting to find single, concrete referents for John's imagery.

[28] The absence of the divine passive in the vision of the third horseman could anticipate Satan's endowment of power and authority over the economic system in the vision of the beasts.

Some commentators have associated the beast from the land with the High Priest of the imperial cult that demands worship from faithful Christians.[29] Others have noted the connection between the pressure placed on followers of Christ to participate in local trade guilds and societies that also participated in worship to emperors and local deities.[30] While these associations can be deduced from the socio-historical world, an overemphasis on historical-critical method does not respect the intentional abstraction that does not allow for a single referent. One is able to find equally convincing historical parallels in the modern world as John's readers/hearers would have found possible in the first century. And his intentional ambiguity has allowed countless recreations throughout the last two millennia. By limiting the vision to these historical referents, John would only be providing a more colourful, imaginative portrait of what his readers/hearers already know. On the contrary, the author's use of horrific language of beasts, which would evoke ideas of the frightful imagery of Daniel, framed in the context of worship and amazement, functions to expose the deceptive nature of the economic world system and its demands on those who participate. His aim to is to provide a view of the universe as a whole that portrays the present age as irredeemably evil, something he does not think his readers/hearers presently understand. Thus, beasts, dragons, and whores are not merely socio-rhetorical devices that draw boundaries between the faithful and the enemies of God. Rather, their alliance with Satan and their hostile actions towards the faithful reflect how much the present age is utterly incompatible with loyalty to God.

The two beasts of chapter 13 serve a polarizing function. On the one hand, though grotesque in its features, the first beast has an appeal that causes the inhabitants of the earth to worship it. The question 'Who is like the beast and who is able to make war with it?' is an attribution of deity to the beast by the earth dwellers.[31] Thus, the opponent John has in mind may find expression in the Roman Empire, but his vision is not limited to it, nor does he wish to make it dependent upon it. Rather, he portrays the eschatological opponent as a force of evil that derives from Satan and is reflected in anything that seeks to influence the faithful from

---

[29] Bousset, *Offenbarung*, pp. 365–6; Charles, *Revelation*, vol. I, p. 357; Kraybill, *Imperial Cult and Commerce*, pp. 26–7; Boxall, *Revelation*, p. 194.

[30] Kraybill, *Imperial Cult and Commerce*, pp. 55–6.

[31] Job 41:2–3 (LXX). Cf. Ex 15:11; Pss 34:10; 70:19; 112:5 (LXX); Jer 27:44 (LXX). The phrase καὶ ἐθαυμάσθη ὅλη ἡ γῆ ὀπίσω τοῦ θηρίου could be taken as 'the whole world followed the beast, full of wonder': *BDAG*, pp. 445, 716. See also BDF §196, which translates it: 'they marvelled over the beast and went after him'.

complete devotion to God.[32] It is this opponent, whatever it represents, that John wants his readers/hearers to forsake.

For this reason the beasts are formulated to parody the Lamb in the throne-room vision. The first beast has a head that is wounded as if dead (ἐσφαγμένην),[33] is given a throne, authority over every tribe, people, nation, and language, and it too is worshipped, though it represents all that is opposed to God. The second beast has the appearance of a lamb but speaks like a dragon.[34] This parody signals the importance of the visions in relation to chapters 4–6. On the one hand, the emphasis on worship signals to the readers/hearers the circumstances and criteria that determine one's allegiance. While the Lamb conquered on behalf of God's people, the beast from the sea seeks to conquer and kill the faithful. On the other hand, their deceptive nature is underscored in their similarities to the Lamb; they are able to deceive the faithful into thinking they are righteous. This coincides with the deceptive teaching of Jezebel (Rev 2:20), the lukewarmness of the rich (Rev 3:17), and the first rider of the

---

[32] Beale, *Revelation*, p. 691; Lohmeyer, *Offenbarung*, p. 115; Kraft, *Offenbarung*, p. 180.

[33] Commentators frequently draw attention to John's allusion to the Nero *redivivus* myth. See Bousset, *Antichrist Legend*, pp. 184–5; Aune, *Revelation 6–16*, p. 737; Roloff, *Revelation*, pp. 156–7; Prigent, *Apocalypse*, pp. 405–6; Smalley, *Revelation*, p. 338. In Jewish and Christian texts the figure of Belial will become incarnate in a Roman king (*Sib Or* 3:63–70; *Asc. Isa.* 4:1–14). However, there is sufficient reason to discount the idea that John is alluding *exclusively* to Nero *redivivus* to the degree that the first beast is to be identified with a particular person. See Lohmeyer, *Offenbarung*, p. 147. See also Beale, *Revelation*, pp. 690–1. The traditions found in *Asc. Isa.* and the *Sibylline Oracles* are more explicit in their identification of Nero as 'one who killed his mother' and coming from the *Sebastanoi*. Moreover, the Leviathan myth that was related to Lotan the seven-headed dragon is pictured in Ugaritic artwork as having four of its heads already killed. See Gordon, 'Leviathan: Symbol of Evil', p. 5. John includes motifs related to Nero *redivivus* and other mythic language as a conglomeration of ideas of wickedness that were circulating in that day. In doing so, he reformulates them to portray the ruling powers as the chaotic, demonic forces of the eschatological age that the faithful are to resist. See Yarbro Collins, *Combat Myth*, pp. 176–90. The phrase (ἐσφαγμένην) is used more to emphasize radical obedience to the Lamb in contrast to the Satanic powers of the earth than it is to refer to Nero. However, it would certainly evoke such images in the mind of his readers/hearers.

[34] Aune, *Revelation 6–16*, p. 757 argues that the lamb imagery is problematic since sheep do not have horns. Thus, the ram and dragon contrast stands in parallel to the lion and lamb imagery. However, the Dream Visions of *1 Enoch* attest the interchangeable use of rams and sheep when indicating a leader figure for the flock, i.e. Saul, David, Solomon (cf. *1 Enoch* 89:41–9). Moreover, Judas Maccabeus is portrayed as a sheep on which a large horn grows, indicating his military prowess (*1 Enoch* 90:9–12). John has already shown a propensity to reshape imagery into completely new forms and does not slavishly follow any single antecedent tradition. Thus it is possible he combines the Daniel and Enochic traditions to portray an eschatological foe who takes the form of a leader of God's people and whose speech can be associated with Satan.

white horse (Rev 6:2). These beasts amaze and deceive the world and detract people from worshipping the Lamb.

It is for this reason that the faithful find conflict and hostility in the world. And John has squarely placed this conflict within the economic realm because it is a demonic force that seeks to distract the faithful from worshipping God by alluring them into the false, self-sufficient security of accumulated wealth. Participation in the economic world in order to gain security and strength – that is, to conquer the difficulties of the present age – requires that one be devoted to this system which compromises commitment to God and loyalty to the Lamb. In addition, it promotes a way of conquering that is antithetical to John's portrayal of Christ and his world view that presupposes that only the wicked are rich.

Thus the call to conquer in the seven messages would be evoked once again by the phrase 'If anyone has an ear, let him listen' (Rev 13:9). This is a theologically pregnant statement taken directly from the Jesus tradition. In the gospel narratives Jesus uses this phrase when speaking in parables; those who listen are the faithful who are privy to the secrets of the kingdom of God, while those who do not listen are outsiders (Matt 13:9–13; Mark 4:9–11; Luke 8:8–10). The occurrence of the phrase in the middle of the vision of the two beasts and in the seven messages is significant. It assumes a mixed audience, and John clearly distinguishes the faithful by their refusal to worship the beast and their inclusion in the book of life. On the other side, John associates worship of the beast with economic participation (Rev 13:16–17) and anticipates hostility and even death for non-compliance (Rev 13:10, 15). The phrase does not assume that the entire audience will recognize the deceptive nature of these beasts; this would include those in the seven messages who are being deceived by Jezebel. Thus, John is calling the true faithful to discern his visions, withdraw from the present economic system, and tangibly demonstrate their alignment with and loyalty to the Lamb.

Here John further expands the readers'/hearers' understanding of Christ by portraying him as the Lamb who was slaughtered 'before the foundation of the world' (τοῦ ἀρνίου τοῦ ἐσφαγμένου ἀπὸ καταβολῆς κόσμου).[35] This implies a certain incompatibility between Christ and the

---

[35] The phrase ἀπὸ καταβολῆς κόσμου 'before the foundation of the world' refers either to the time when the names were written in the Book of Life or when the Lamb was slaughtered. A similar phrase occurs in 17:8, which lacks the reference to the Lamb. Reading 17:8 back into 13:8 allows a reading that emphasizes the writing of the names. In light of the cumulative character of the Apocalypse, however, it is best viewed as a developing idea that is to be related first to the vision of the Lamb in chapter 5, which is the only place σφάζω is used with this connection (Rev 5:6, 9, 12). A similar expression of Jesus' death was already

earthly realm in that hostility, conflict, and death were not some tragic, surprising event but were part of the plan of God (cf. Acts 2:23). As such, the followers of the Lamb can also expect the same kind of hostility. John goes on to highlight the incompatibility of the faithful with the present age by using the same phrase in relation to their being written into the book of life (Rev 17:8). It is through this perspective on Christ that John wants his readers/hearers to understand the call for conquering and faithfulness in the seven messages. Worship has become contextualized in the economic world, which John views as a place where loyalty to the Lamb is easily compromised. A Deuteronomistic theology of wealth as a result of faithfulness to God has no place in a world in which the gain of wealth is so much at odds with loyalty and worship to God. Rather, John postpones any expectation of wealth for the people of God into the coming age (Rev 2:9; 3:17; 21:7) and his language encourages a radical obedience in the form of a tangible withdrawal from the economic system.

8.3   The climax of economic critique: Rev 18

The previous discussion demonstrates how John increasingly heightens the expectation of conflict for the faithful in terms of the economic realm of the present age. His praise of poverty and denigration of wealth in the seven messages, taken together with the demonic characterization of the economic system in the vision of the third horseman, the fall of Satan, and the mark of the beast, develops a world view that postpones material blessing for the faithful to the future age. In Rev 18, that critique of wealth in the present world reaches both a climax and a resolution in the judgement of Babylon. The longest sustained critique of affluence takes place in chapter 18 and it is here that John deals with wealth as an issue.

The length of the present passage and the extensive language of wealth throughout make it necessary to divide the discussion into manageable segments. This is most easily done by analysing the various speech forms

---

circulating in the early church. (Cf. 1 Pet 1:20, 'πρὸ καταβολῆς κόσμου'. Here Peter states that Jesus is the paschal Lamb that was destined before the foundation of the world. Peter's comment evokes a similar idea as the statement in Acts 4:28 that Jesus' death was part of the design of God's will.) This implies an incompatibility between Jesus and the evil on earth and, as the Apocalypse develops, the faithful are portrayed as having their names written ἀπὸ καταβολῆς κόσμου (17:8) highlighting in principle their own incompatibility with the present evil age. Given the natural word order of the sentence, it is best understood as 'the Lamb who was slaughtered before the foundation of the world'.

that pervade the chapter. Because the study is concerned primarily with wealth and the faithful community, these speech forms will be discussed in the following order: (1) the 'Summons to Flight' motif in 18:4–5, (2) the prophetic announcement of judgement over Babylon in 18:2–3, 6–8, and (3) the 'woe' oracles of 18:9–20. Since the symbolic action performed by the angel in 18:21–4 refers to the merchants only briefly in verse 24, the material in this pericope will be brought into the discussion at relevant points but will not be discussed independently.

8.4   Wealth and the faithful: Rev 18:4–5

The call for separation to 'my people' provides some insight into the function of the prophetic speech forms used in Rev 18.[36] John employs the prophetic tradition extensively in this chapter, borrowing wealth language and imagery from Isaiah, Ezekiel, and Jeremiah. As elsewhere, John has reshaped and conflated antecedent traditions, particularly imagery and language from the 'Oracles to the Nations', to formulate an entirely new vision for his audience.[37] Since sufficient attention has been given to the author's use of the OT prophets and the texts to which he makes allusion, a discussion along these lines is not warranted.[38] Rather, the primary concern is to see *how* these traditions have been reshaped and what kind of world view concerning John's expectation for the faithful community this exposes.

Come out of her my people

Then I heard another voice from heaven saying, 'Come out of her, my people, so that you do not take part in her sins, and so that you do not share in her plagues.'   (Rev 18:4)

---

[36] Chapter 18 consists of various small units that comprise three prophetic speech forms: (1) a prophetic taunt song (18:1–3); (2) summons to flight (18:4–20); and (3) a symbolic action and interpretation (18:21–4): Aune, *Revelation 17–22*, p. 976. Yarbro Collins, 'Revelation 18', p. 203 understands the chapter as a whole to be a dirge. The individual dirges within the chapter function to create some degree of sympathetic awe, though only for dramatic effect. This *pathos* is cut short with the call for rejoicing (18:20), which serves to show the proper attitude toward Babylon's demise.

[37] Isa 13–23, 47, Ezek 26–7, and Jer 50–1. See Fiorenza, *Justice and Judgment*, pp. 102, 135–6; Yarbro Collins, 'Revelation 18', p. 198; and *Crisis and Catharsis*, p. 48; Thompson, *Apocalypse and Empire*, pp. 50–1.

[38] See Charles, *Revelation*, vol. I, pp. lxviii–lxxxvi; Vanhoye, 'L'Utilisation du livre d'Ézéchiel', pp. 436–76; Ruiz, *Ezekiel in the Apocalypse*, pp. 226–517; Fekkes, *Isaiah and Prophetic Traditions*, pp. 106–278; Beale, *Use of Daniel*, pp. 154–270; and *Use of the Old Testament*, pp. 318–55.

The call for John's audience to 'Come out' occurs just after an indictment on the kings of the earth and the merchants who have become
drunk on the wine of Babylon the whore, committed fornication with
her, and 'have grown rich from the power of her luxury' (Rev 18:3).
This admonition interrupts the prophetic taunt song over Babylon (Rev
18:2–3) and introduces a second prophetic speech form, the summons
to flight.[39] The summons to flight motif in the prophetic tradition (Jer
51:45; cf. Jer 50:8; 51:6; Isa 48:20; 52:11) indicates the need for the
faithful remnant geographically to flee the foreign nation of Babylon.
The failure to return to Jerusalem and remain in the wicked land would
result in experiencing the wrath that God would bring on the Babylonians
vis-à-vis the Persian armies. If Babylon is meant to represent Rome in
chapter 18 then one must ask whether it would be possible for the faithful
to escape the Roman Empire, since it ruled the known world.[40] This, of
course, would not be possible and reveals that John's concerns are much
larger. Moreover, since the readers/hearers lived in Roman Asia Minor,
it certainly would not mean fleeing the city of Rome.[41]

The suggestion by commentators that this reflects a spiritual separation
is unconvincing and is based on the idea that the churches are not being
called to separate from the world but are to bear witness in the world.[42]
Yet, in the literary world of the Apocalypse, 'witness' is only done
effectively through radical obedience that usually results in death (Rev
6:9; 11:3, 7; 12:11; 14:3; 17:6; 20:4) an understanding that seems to

---

[39] The speaking voice comes from heaven and is most likely the voice of Christ. So
Charles, *Revelation*, vol. II, p. 97; Allo, *l'Apocalypse*, p. 290; Aune, *Revelation 17–22*,
p. 990; Osborne, *Revelation*, p. 638; Boxall, *Revelation*, p. 256. Bousset, *Offenbarung*
(1896), p. 482 contends that the voice may be that of God or Christ. Others indicate the
voice is that of an angel. See Lohmeyer, *Offenbarung*, p. 149; Kraft, *Offenbarung*, p. 228;
Roloff, *Revelation*, p. 205; Yarbro Collins, 'Revelation 18', p. 193.

[40] Aune, *Revelation 17–22*, p. 991.

[41] Boxall, *Revelation*, p. 257. While Babylon was frequently used to refer to Rome in
literature contemporary to the Apocalypse (*2 Bar.* 67:7; *Sib. Or.* 5:143, 159; 2 Esd 16:1.
Cf. 3:1–2; 15:46; 1 Pet 5:13), some have argued that Babylon represents Jerusalem. See
Ford, *Revelation*, pp. 285–6, 296–307; Beagley, *Sitz im Leben*, pp. 92–106. Provan, 'Foul
Spirits Fornication and Finance', pp. 81–100 provides a tempered version of this argument
that discourages any historical referent. Rather, it is a true symbol that need not be limited
to an actual historical city or any one single referent. See Humphrey, *The Ladies and the
Cities*, p. 115 n. 97; Lohmeyer, *Offenbarung*, 138–9.

[42] Beale, *Revelation*, p. 898; Witherington, *Revelation*, p. 226; Smalley, *Revelation*,
pp. 446–7. Boring, *Revelation*, p. 189 considers this a call for an 'inner reorientation'.
Boxall, *Revelation*, p. 257 suggests John's community is being admonished to renounce the
idolatrous culture in which they live. So also Roloff, *Revelation*, p. 205. Kraybill, *Imperial
Cult and Commerce*, pp. 29–30 rightly implies that this is a call for radical separation from
the economic system.

be at odds with modern ideas of witness. To be sure, only Antipas and Christ are referred to as faithful witnesses (Rev 1:5; 2:13; 3:14).[43] Thus, the witness John has in mind is not remaining in the world system but a radical separation, by means of a visible withdrawal from the outside world system and ultimately death. The author is able to impose this radical position on his audience because his world view is shaped by traditions that view the present world as irretrievably evil and portray the faithful as those who reject the present age entirely (cf. *1 Enoch* 104:6; 108:8–10).

The separation called for involves the avoidance of what the author envisions as present participation (συγκοινωνέω) in the sins of Babylon, which are inherently tied to the accumulation of wealth (Rev 13:16–17; 17:2; 18:3, 7, 9, 15, 19) and are a distraction from worship of God. The term (συγκοινωνέω) occurs elsewhere only in 1:9 in which John states he is a 'participant' (συγκοινωνέω) in the persecution (θλῖψις) and endurance (ὑπομονή) in Jesus. These two exclusive uses of the term suggest John is alerting his audience to two forms of participation: either suffering, which reflects faithfulness, or the luxurious life of Babylon, which ends in destruction. Effectively, he is encouraging his readers/hearers to abandon their present affluent lifestyle and participate with him in suffering, which he equates with faithfulness, and not the sins of rich Babylon, which aligns them with the wicked (cf. *1 Enoch* 104:6).

In the message to Philadelphia Christ promises the faithful poor that he will keep them from the hour (ὥρα) of testing (πειράζω) that will come upon humankind. At the same time, the poor are about to be tested (πειράζω) by being cast into prison (Rev 2:9–10). Within the context of the Son of Man figure, whose hour (ὥρα) to reap has come (Rev 14:14–15), a *makarism* is provided for those who 'die in the Lord from now on' (Rev 14:13). It also occurs in the destruction of Babylon when her rich lovers cry out that she and her wealth have been destroyed in one hour (μιᾷ ὥρᾳ) (Rev 18:10, 17, 19). Thus, the hour of testing from which the poor have been kept involves the destruction of the wicked in the judgement of Babylon. Taken together with the author's portrayal of the mark of the beast and the refusal of the faithful to participate in chapter 13, the call to 'Come out' (Rev 18:4) serves as the final, decisive time for John's readers/hearers to take sides.[44] This further suggests that

---

[43] The two (ὁ μάρτυς, ὁ πιστός) (ὁ μάρτυς μου, ὁ πιστός μου), of course, are distinguished by the insertion of first person pronouns when referring to Antipas.

[44] Yarbro Collins, 'Revelation 18', p. 202. See also Duff, *Who Rides the Beast?*, pp. 68–70 who surprisingly can state that John's denunciation here in chapter 18 is toned down and that he is careful to attack only commerce but not the accumulation of wealth.

John thinks that many of his readers/hearers, at least those reflected in five of the seven churches, are currently in danger of being caught up in the judgement of God because of their affluent lifestyles that have been fed by the luxury and power of Babylon.

The shift from a geographical summons to flight to one that involves the need to remove oneself from economic involvement marks a radical shift from the biblical prophets. However, traditions were already circulating in the Second Temple period that share this perspective:

> What will you do, O sinners? And where will you flee on that Day of Judgment, when you hear the prayers of the righteous? (And you, who face this accusation: *'You have been the associates of the sinners', you will share their fate.*) In those days the prayers of the righteous will reach unto the Lord, and for you, the days of your judgment will come. (*1 Enoch* 97:3–5)[45]

Several points of contact can be noted between traditions reflected in this text and John's eschatological pre-understanding. (1) At a decisive point in time the prayers of the righteous will be heard and will result in God's intervention in the world that involves the judgement of the wicked (*1 Enoch* 8:4; 9:2, 10; cf. 22:5; 4Q530 1:4).[46] When the Lamb breaks the seventh and final seal there is silence in heaven, at which time the prayers of the saints are presented at the altar and the trumpet and other subsequent judgements begin (Rev 8:1–3). (2) Those who participate with sinners share their eschatological fate. Other Jewish traditions denote participation with sinners causes one to become like them (Prov 13:20; 28:24; Sir 12:14; 37:11–12; *Jub.* 22:16). However, here and in Rev 18:4 the emphasis is on the eschatological consequences of participation with rich sinners in the social injustices carried out on the righteous; that is, these prophetic speech forms function not to emphasize the immediate effects of collusion but provide an irrevocable testimony from which the rich sinners cannot escape.[47] John's radical call to 'Come out' is based on a theological understanding of the way the already inaugurated eschatological age will play out. Thus, this prophetic passage (Rev 18:4)

---

[45] Cf. 4Q416 2 ii:17–18; 4Q418 103 ii:6–9.

[46] Note the development between the BOW and the *Epistle* in that the former attests a cry for mercy by the wicked before final judgement is announced. The latter has no petition for mercy, only the announcement of judgement. Likewise, in the Apocalypse, the wicked never repent but demonstrate the irreversible consequences of their association with wicked Babylon (Rev 9:20–1; 16:9, 11). See Stuckenbruck, *1 Enoch 91–108*, pp. 311–12.

[47] Stuckenbruck, *1 Enoch 91–108*, p. 312.

functions as a formal announcement from heaven to choose sides (cf. *1 Enoch* 94:3; 104:6).

8.5   Wealth and Babylon

Like the summons to flight, the prophetic taunt song functions as a formal announcement, although one of judgement on wicked Babylon. Several key phrases and images are designed to connect the woman in chapter 17 with Babylon. For example, both are portrayed as a woman (Rev 17:1, 7, 9, 15–16; 18: 3, 7, 16) and a city (Rev 17: 5, 18; 18:2, 4, 10, 18, 21), both will be judged (Rev 17:1; 18:20), and burned with fire (Rev 17:16; 18:8). However, the depiction of Babylon as a rich, rapacious whore is a deliberate strategy that elevates John's disdain for the accumulation of wealth. The whore and Babylon both fornicate with the kings of the earth (Rev 17:2; 18:3, 9) and deceive the nations with their immoral wine (Rev 17:2; 18:3). The woman in chapter 17 is decked out in gold, pearls, and purple garments (Rev 17:4), which accentuates her wealth and coincides with the expensive cargo list (Rev 18:12–13), and follows the description of Babylon (Rev 18:16). She drinks from a golden cup that is full of the impurities of her fornication and is drunk from the blood of the saints (Rev 17:6; 18:24).

So spectacular and luxurious is the vision of the whore that the interpreting angel asks John, 'Why are you so amazed?' (θαυμάζω) (Rev 17:6–7). Taken together with the implication that the inhabitants of the earth were amazed by the satanic beast (Rev 13:3; 17:8), this implies that the seer presents even himself in danger of being lured by the greatness of these deceptive forces of evil. John uses the image of a whore not because harlots are repugnant but because they are attractive and lure men into illicit relationships through their beauty and willingness to provide what men crave. For this reason John pictures the whore in such outlandish terms. The beauty and sexually attractive nature of the prostitute is shown as it is seen from heaven: filthy, greedy, and disgusting.

The connection made between economic participation and the whore's wine in the previous passages underscores that the wealth of the world system is wholly evil, impure, and able to deceive the faithful. The mark on her forehead (Rev 17:5) associates her directly with Satan and the beasts and emphasizes her identity with the economic system (Rev 13:16–17). Moreover, the filth of her abominations in her golden cup are reiterated in the fact that she is the mother of whores and the earth's abominations. The title on her forehead does not simply indicate that she is a participant in the economic system but that she embodies that worldly system whereby humankind is able to gain affluence and exert power over others. She is an external, cosmic evil empowered by Satan that deceives the nations of the world *through* the offer of economic wellbeing. She is very rich and has deceived the kings, nations, and merchants into an illicit relationship that brings with it irreversible consequences.

Fallen, fallen is Babylon the great!: Rev 18:2–3

> He called out with a mighty voice, 'Fallen, fallen is Babylon the great! It has become a dwelling place of demons, a haunt of every foul and hateful bird, a haunt of every foul and hateful beast. For all the nations have drunk of the wine of the wrath of her fornication, and the kings of the earth have committed fornication with her, and the merchants of the earth have grown rich from the power of her luxury.'   (Rev 18:2–3)

Three reasons are given for Babylon's demise: (1) the nations have drunk her immoral wine, (2) the kings have committed fornication with her, and (3) the merchants have grown rich by her wealth. The language of wine as a metaphor for economic activity was first introduced in 14:8, in which it occurred in the midst of a command to worship God. Here the nations who drink her wine are linked to those who receive the mark of the beast (Rev 14:10; cf. 13:8, 20:15). It also marks the first occurrence (Rev 14:8) of the wine metaphor in connection with fornication (πορνεία), which becomes more developed in the vision of the whore (Rev 17:2, 4). Here the abominable wine that she drinks from her golden cup is the blood of the saints (Rev 17:2, 6; 18:24); John finds a direct correlation between economic success and the oppression and persecution of the faithful.

In the prophetic tradition Babylon herself is the golden cup (Jer 51:7), evoking ideas of wealth, and is a metaphor for the intoxicating effect of her great riches.[48] Thus, the wine of her immoral passion can be linked directly to the mark of the beast and economic participation. The fornication of the kings of the earth is a reformulation of language taken from Isa 23:17 and Ezek 27:33 in which Tyre's economic agreements with other nations are viewed in terms of prostitution (זנה).[49] The LXX

---

[48] Holladay, *Jeremiah 26–52*, vol. II, p. 422; McKane, *Jeremiah*, vol. II, pp. 1300–1. Cf. Jer 25:15–17, where Jeremiah is the one who dispenses the cup of the wine of God's wrath. See also *Tg. Jer.* 51:7, where a similar idea is expressed.

[49] Ezekiel 27:12–34 contains the only use of the term σύμμικτος in the entirety of the prophetic book. As an adjective, it refers to something mixed or mingled and can have the meaning of promiscuity. See *BDAG*, p. 650. The verbal form (συμμίγνυμι) can have the meaning of being united with someone sexually. See *BDAG*, p. 957; Herodotus, *Hist.* 4.114; Plato, *Symp.*, 207b; *Leg.*, 930d. In Ezek 27:12–34 it is used to refer to the merchandise of Tyre that was traded with other nations. The connection between wealth

renders the phrase, 'she will be a market (ἐμπόριον; cf. Rev 18:3, 11, 15, 23) for all the kingdoms of the world'. Within the narrative world of the text, and in light of the passages already discussed, she is treated as guilty of deception by means of the economic system and the riches it provides.[50]

Two features distinguish the prophetic tradition from John's material: (1) a restoration within the present age is envisioned for Tyre, at which time her profits will be used to provide for the people of God (Is 23:17–18), and (2) the harlotry of Tyre is described in terms of economic activity on a national level (Ezek 27:12–24). In the Oracles to the Nations there is little attention given to the individuals who are involved in this activity. John develops the language of individual affluence most extensively in relation to the merchants (ἔμπορος). While the nations (Rev 2:26; 11:2, 18; 12:5; 14:8; 15:3–4) and the kings of the earth (Rev 1:5; 6:15; 17:2, 18) have already been introduced in the Apocalypse, this third group, which would also include the sailors and seafarers, has gone unmentioned in the text until this point. Given the extended discourse of their lament over the destruction of Babylon in 18:11–19, and their absence in the Apocalypse thus far, their presence here is significant.[51]

Of special importance is their description as those who have grown rich (πλουτέω) by the power of her luxury. The verb πλουτέω denotes the act of becoming rich; that is, of accumulating wealth, and occurs only in the message to Laodicea (Rev 3:17–18) and here in the judgement of Babylon (Rev 18:3, 15, 19).[52] Taken together with the arrogant self-sufficient speech of the rich in the seven messages and wealthy Babylon, the gain of wealth suggests that John has in view those among the seven churches who are following the teaching of Jezebel that allows for affluence among the faithful.

8.6   Excursus: the use of merchant and sailor imagery in Jewish traditions

In *Imperial Cult and Commerce*, Kraybill has pointed out the language of merchant shippers in Rev 18 arguing that John is dealing with Christians who were involved in merchant shipping and considering the problem of

---

accumulated through trade and prostitution is most likely one of the reasons why these traditions were used so extensively here.

[50] *TDNT* vol. I, p. 515 n. 11. Cf. Isa 23:17; Royalty, *Streets of Heaven*, pp. 209–10; Beale, *Revelation*, pp. 895–6.

[51] See section 8.6.   [52] MM, p. 521; *TDNT*, vol. VI, p. 319; *BDAG*, p. 831.

whether they could participate economically in trade guilds that had been thoroughly infiltrated by the imperial cults. Taking Rev 18 as his point of departure, he bases his thesis on the inclusion of the language of merchants, sailors, and shippers in John's critique of the wealth of Babylon. However, an analysis of this language within the Apocalypse in comparison with the larger context of the Hebrew Bible and Second Temple traditions reveals that this approach may reflect an overemphasis on the immediate socio-political and economic setting of the Roman Empire that cannot be substantiated. For example, the terms 'merchant' (ἔμπόρος), 'ship captain' (κυβερνήτης), 'sailor' (ναύτης), and 'seafarers' (ὁ πλέων) occur only here in the entirety of the Apocalypse. While the author has expressed a concern over wealth and economic trade throughout the text, there has been no mention of these social categories elsewhere. Those who have focused on parallels from the Greco-Roman Mediterranean world like Kraybill are overstating the case of its importance and the Hebrew Bible and Second Temple traditions have something to contribute to the discussion.

In the Hebrew Bible the terms for sailors and seafarers are attested in Jonah 1 and Ezek 27.[53] Both Jewish and Greco-Roman sources frequently portray merchants in a negative light.[54] The stigma of involvement in commerce was avoided by the aristocrats by hiring agents to trade on their behalf, and sailors in particular were considered immoral and greedy for gain.[55] In Jonah the ναύτης and ὁ πλέων reflect the characters in the story in which Jonah flees from God, and serve as a foil to Jonah who claims to worship God though hiding and running away (Jonah 1:7–10). Couched in sharp irony, they are ultimately shown to fear God more than Jonah (Jonah 1:14–16). Moreover, the futility of riches is underscored in these Jewish traditions when the merchants and sailors throw their cargo overboard when their lives are in peril (Jonah 1:5; *1 Enoch* 101:5; Acts 27:18–19, 38). In Ezek 27 κυβερνῆταί function to emphasize the horror of the great destruction of Tyre and thus only serve a rhetorical purpose rather than being descriptive of a particular group of people. In other

[53] The only other occurrences of any of these terms are κυβερνήτης: Prov 23:34. Cf. *4 Macc* 7:1; ναύτης: 1 Kgs 9:27.

[54] Cicero, *Off.*, 1.150–1.

[55] Kirschenbaum, *Sons, Slaves, and Freedmen*, pp. 31–88; D'Arms, *Commerce and Social Standing*, pp. 39–40; 103–4; Horace, *Saec.* 3.6.29–32; Philostratus, *Vit. Apoll.* 4.32; Strabo, *Georg.* 8.6.20; Petronius, *Satyricon*, 26–78; 1 Macc 3:41; 2 Macc 8:34; Sir 26:29; 37:11. See MacMullen, *Roman Social Relations*, pp. 100–15; de Ste. Croix, *Class Struggle*, pp. 120–33, 270–5. For a succinct overview of Greco-Roman sources that denigrate commercial trade, see Royalty, *Streets of Heaven*, pp. 102–7.

words, they function to highlight those involved in the economic activity of Tyre whoever that may be.

The language of merchants (ἔμπορος) occurs in Isa 23:8, 18 and Ezek 27:12–38, the texts our author has conflated, though in the Second Temple period the term is used to refer negatively to greedy oppressors (1 Macc 3:41; 2 Macc 8:34; Sir 26:29; 37:11).[56] Merchants and sailors are a common *topos* in Jewish literature when conveying helplessness in the time of God's judgement on the open seas (Jonah 1:1–16; *1 Enoch* 101:4–102:3; Ezek 27:12;38; Acts 27).

Thus, John's use of the language of merchants and shippers here is not so much descriptive as it is stock imagery borrowed from Jewish tradition. There are several literary reasons for John to incorporate this imagery into this text: (1) Ezek 27 already contained significant wealth language; (2) the merchants and seafarers and land and sea correlate to the totality of Satan's dominion (Rev 12:12; 13:1, 11); and (3) the merchant imagery coincides with the author's economic language in the seven messages (Rev 3:18), the commercial imagery of the rider with balancing scales (Rev 6:5), and the concern over economic participation (Rev 13:16–17). The reputation of merchants and shippers as greedy and dishonest fits John's critique of those who are following Jezebel's teaching and accumulating wealth. The stereotypical function of John's language is obvious when we consider that not all merchants were rich. Finley has pointed out that most merchants involved in buying and selling were not wealthy but were normal Roman citizens, a point he contends is true for much of antiquity.[57]

This is not to say that there were not wealthy merchants. Rather, it is to point out the way that John has conceptualized being a merchant with being rich. This underscores how, in the midst of their buying and selling, they have been blinded to God's coming judgement and that in the destruction of Babylon there is now no hope that they will be saved (*1 Enoch* 98:12, 14). Thus the imagery draws attention to the place where John sees that loyalty and obedience to the Lamb can be compromised. Within the greater economic world system, John's readers/hearers could have been regarded as relatively poor. However, the stereotypical characterization of the rich in the form of imputed speech (Rev 3:17) is as much a critique against any temptation they may have had to become rich as it

---

[56] Cf. Nahum 3:16. The only other occurrences of ἔμπορος are Gen 23:16; 37:28; 1 Kgs 10:15, 28; 2 Chr 1:16.

[57] Finley, *Ancient Economy*, pp. 145–6. Contra Rostovtzeff, *Social and Economic History*, pp. 93, 28, 232.

is against their actual wealth; that is, their energy and commitment are directed to the accumulation of wealth rather than worshipping the Lamb. Their desire is to conquer the disparity between the relative deprivation of the people of God and the economic success of the greater Empire. Thus, the language of merchants and sailors is not descriptive of a historical segment of John's audience that were involved in shipping, though we can surmise that some probably were. Rather, it functions to highlight the author's rejection of wealth in the present age in stereotypical imagery on the one hand, and how the visible manifestation of faithfulness should be realized on the other.

The dual proleptic aorist in the phrase 'Fallen, Fallen is Babylon' (ἔπεσεν ἔπεσεν Βαβυλὼν), which mimics the Hebrew prophetic perfect, emphasizes the certainty of Babylon's destruction.[58] As part of the eschatological plan of God inaugurated in the opening of the seven-sealed scroll, the destruction of Babylon is irreversible. This prophetic speech pattern is a common motif in the Oracles Against the Nations (Isa 13–23, Ezek 25–31, Jer 46–51).[59] However, we must exercise caution in overemphasizing the degree to which Babylon serves as the primary aim of John's critique. For example, Hayes rightly notes:

> It is obvious that these speeches [oracles] were not primarily spoken or written to be heard or acted upon by the nations mentioned in the texts. Their function and importance were not dependent on the foreign powers' knowledge of or response to them. The importance of the speeches must not be sought, therefore, in what they 'said' to the enemy but rather in the *function which they performed within the context of Israelite society.*[60]

Thus, the prophetic announcement of judgement on Babylon (Rev 14:8; 18:2) has more to say to the faithful community than it does to Rome.[61] For this reason John has included this announcement of judgement twice in the Apocalypse, the first of which requires some discussion.

---

[58] Fanning, *Verbal Aspect*, pp. 270–4. See also GKC § 106 n.

[59] Hayes, 'Use of Oracles', p. 81. Tucker, *Form Criticism*, pp. 59–68. See also Westermann, *Forms of Prophetic Speech*, pp. 98–128; Aune, *Prophecy in Early Christianity*, p. 92.

[60] Hayes, 'Use of Oracles', p. 81 (emphasis added).

[61] Bauckham, *Climax of Prophecy*, p. 338 asserts that Revelation 18 represents 'one of the most effective pieces of political resistance literature from the period of the early empire'. However, I am arguing that politics are not the primary concern of the author. Rather, the visionary world that John constructs for his readers relates directly to the conflict over rival teachers in the churches and potential theological debates.

The verbal similarities between 14:8 and 18:2–3 indicate the former is redactional and functions to anticipate the judgement of Babylon in our present text.[62]

Rev 14:8	Rev 18:2–3
ἔπεσεν ἔπεσεν Βαβυλὼν ἡ μεγάλη	ἔπεσεν ἔπεσεν Βαβυλὼν ἡ μεγάλη
ἐκ τοῦ οἴνου τοῦ θυμοῦ τῆς	ἐκ τοῦ οἴνου τοῦ θυμοῦ τῆς
πορνείας	πορνείας
αὐτῆς πεπότικεν πάντα τὰ ἔθνη	αὐτῆς πέπωκαν πάντα τὰ ἔθνη

The protasis of the first class conditional sentence that follows (Rev 14:9), 'If anyone worships the beast and receives his mark', indicates that these worshippers will also (καὶ) 'drink the wine of God's wrath unmixed'. This language of reversal not only anticipates judgement for associating with Babylon but also serves more clearly to connect the ideas of economic participation (receiving the mark of the beast) with idolatrous worship and drinking the immoral wine of Babylon (Rev 14:8; 17:4, 6; 18:3). John portrays the faithful 144,000 as 'those who have not defiled themselves with women' (Rev 14:4), an obvious contrast to those who commit adultery with Jezebel (Rev 2:22) and who fornicate with the whore Babylon (Rev 17:2; 18:3).[63] The former teaches freedom to assimilate culturally and participate in the economy while the latter embodies what Jezebel's teaching promotes. John has effectively connected Jezebel with Satan, the beast from the earth, and Babylon through the use of the term πλανάω (Rev 2:20; 12:9; 13:14; 18:23; 19:20).[64] Thus in John's portrayal of the universe, fornication, drinking the wine of Babylon, and worshipping the beast all point to those who have been deceived into devotion to an evil world system empowered by Satan. Likewise, those who are in agreement with Jezebel can only find themselves in alignment with the enemies of God and his people.

At the end of the three angelic announcements, the author includes a *makarism* for 'the dead, who die in the Lord from now on' (Rev 14:13; cf. *1 Enoch* 100:3).[65] This same term is used to refer to those who hear and

---

[62]   Aune, *Revelation 6–16*, p. 832.

[63]   See Olson, "Those Who Have Not Defiled Themselves', p. 501 whose emphasis is on showing that the virgins are an anti-image of those who follow the beast. Of course, this also implies that the beast's worshippers are prefigured in the fallen angels. See also Yarbro Collins, 'Women's History', p. 89. For a discussion of celibacy in antiquity, see Aune, *Revelation 6–16*, pp. 818–22.

[64]   Duff, *Who Rides the Beast?*, pp. 113–25.

[65]   See Aune, *Revelation 6–16*, p. 788 n. 13 d-d for an explanation of the problem with punctuation in this passage. The phrase ἀπ' ἄρτι is translated temporally 'from now on' in most translations (ASV, NASB, NRSV, NIV, NLT). However, it is possible that it could be

obey John's prophetic message (Rev 1:3; 22:7), are invited to the marriage supper of the Lamb (Rev 19:9), participate in the first resurrection (Rev 20:6), and enter into the new Jerusalem (Rev 22:14). Thus, faithfulness here is spoken of in terms of death, which elsewhere is associated with the poor in Smyrna (Rev 2:9–10), those who conquer the Dragon (Rev 12:11), and those who refuse to worship the beast (Rev 13:15–17). In yet another *makarism*, which is parenthetical (Rev 16:15) and most likely a later interpolation, the blessed are those who stay awake and are clothed as opposed to naked and exposed to shame.[66] These two terms only occur elsewhere in Rev 3:18, in which nakedness and shame are equated with being rich. Taken together with the phrase 'Behold I come like a thief', the author is drawing a direct connection between the seven messages (Rev 3:3) and the critique of wealth in chapter 18. Thus, the faithful are those who have not been deceived by the lure of wealth and are aware of the nature of the present age and the eschatological enemy of God that is manifest in the wicked empires of the world. Although John leaves open the possibility that those in the church who presently side with Jezebel, Satan, and Babylon can repent, there is also an implicit sense of urgency; some will be deceived up to a point where the consequences of their participation become irreversible.

The punishment of Babylon: Rev 18:6–7a

Render to her as she herself has rendered, and repay her double for her deeds; mix a double draught for her in the cup she mixed. As she glorified herself and lived luxuriously, so give her a like measure of torment and grief.   (Rev 18:6–7a)

The announcement of judgement over Babylon ends much like it begins, by stating that the merchants were the magnates (μεγιστᾶνες) of the earth (Rev 18:23). The term μεγιστᾶνες refers to court officials or those who hold sway in positions of leadership.[67] The exact phrase μεγιστᾶνες τῆς γῆς is attested in *Pss. Sol.* 2:32 and refers to the leaders of the world, also called sinners, who are associated with the dragon of the land and sea and oppress the righteous (*Pss. Sol.* 2:22–35).[68] Within the Apocalypse

---

read as ἀπαρτί 'truly' or 'certainly' and belongs with the phrase that follows: 'Truly the Spirit says they will rest' (BDF § 12.3).

[66] Charles, *Revelation*, vol. II, p. 49; Aune, *Revelation 6–16*, p. 896.

[67] *BDAG*, p. 625. Cf. Matt 6:21; Rev 6:15.

[68] The phrase οἱ ἔμποροί σου ἦσαν μεγιστᾶνες τῆς γῆς is most frequently considered an allusion to the phrase οἱ ἔμποροι αὐτῆς ἔνδοξοι, ἄρχοντες τῆς γῆς in Isa 23:8 (LXX).

they are the opposite of those who have little power or resources (Rev 3:8). Consequently, the indictment against her is that the blood of the apostles, prophets, and the saints were found in her.[69] For this reason she will be repaid (ἀποδίδωμι) for her crimes. Though this term is not used in the Apocalypse in literal economic terms, its root (δίδωμι) is used in all of the seven messages in the promise for obedience. Thus there is an underlying *economy of deeds* at work in the Apocalypse that is directly associated with the accumulation of wealth on the one hand, and obedience to the Lamb on the other (Rev 22:12; cf. *1 Enoch* 95:6).

More importantly, Rev 18:6 seems to indicate that the righteous take part in the judgement that is being announced. Rev 18:4–6 contains four second-person plural imperatives, and the lack of any identification of a new addressee and the continued use of aorist imperatives, of which 'my people' are the subject in 18:4, shows that the faithful are being addressed.[70] This passage reflects a radical reshaping of the prophetic tradition (Jer 50:29) in which God summons armies against Babylon. Some contend, however, that this refers to angels of retribution who carry out the judgement on Babylon.[71] Others have also pointed out the role of heaven in this judgement elsewhere in the Apocalypse (Rev 6:10; 11:18; 14:10; 19:2). This position is largely taken out of an attempt to rectify the problem of believers taking vengeance on their enemies, an idea in tension with the teaching of Jesus.[72] While Jesus did in fact teach the disciples to love their enemies, a view that persists throughout the NT, John has placed this command within an eschatological context.[73] Thus, he is not suggesting that the recipients rise up against Rome in rebellion and overthrow the idolatrous Empire in an attempt to reform that earthly kingdom. John has already portrayed the earthly realm as one that is irretrievably evil and unable to be redeemed. Rather, he is describing events that are predetermined to take place in the eschaton. John is able to make these claims with no explanation to his audience

So Aune, *Revelation 17–22*, p. 1010; Fekkes, *Isaiah and Prophetic Traditions*, pp. 221–2; Smalley, *Revelation*, p. 464. However, the similar motifs of the dragon, the land, and sea between Revelation and *Psalms of Solomon* and the similarity in the phrase μεγιστᾶνες τῆς γῆς indicates that John was also in conversation with the latter, or perhaps that both were in contact with a shared tradition.

[69] In contrast to the twofold claim that 'nothing will be found' in her any more (Rev 18:21–22).

[70] So Aune, *Revelation 17–22*, p. 994.

[71] So Bousset, *Offenbarung*, p. 420; Zahn, *Offenbarung*, p. 573; Beckwith, *Apocalypse*, p. 714; Caird, *Revelation*, p. 224. Boxall, *Revelation*, pp. 257–8.

[72] Smalley, *Revelation*, p. 448; Matt 5:44–6; Luke 6:27–35.

[73] Rom 12:17–20; 1 Thess 5:15; 1 Pet 3:9.

and fully expects them to understand. Instead, he refers to these events as if they are happening on the one hand, while assuring their certainty on the other. In doing so, he reveals a certain pre-understanding that is shaped by antecedent traditions not found in the Hebrew Bible.

In the AOW, the Enochic author provides a chronological sequence of world history placed within the framework of ten weeks that coincide with John's order of eschatological events: (1) the righteous execute judgement on the wicked for a limited time (*1 Enoch* 91:12; Rev 18:6–7), (2) there is a temporary kingdom on earth (*1 Enoch* 91:13–14; Rev 20:4), (3) a final judgement (*1 Enoch* 91:15; Rev 20:11–12), and (4) a new heaven and earth (*1 Enoch* 91:16; Rev 21:1).[74] A similar sequence is also attested in *1 Enoch* 50:1–51:5. Thus, we can say that traditions were already circulating that envisioned the involvement of the righteous in the judgement of their enemies in an eschatological context (*1 Enoch* 90:19; 91:12; 95:3, 7; 96:1; 98:12; cf. *Jub.* 23:30). Moreover, these apocalyptic traditions portray the enemies of God as rich, powerful sinners. This and other passages already discussed show that the author's concerns over the accumulation of wealth among the faithful may be better placed in conversation with traditions that were already in circulation from the Second Temple period. This proposal may be further strengthened by an examination of the laments of the merchants and sailors.

The 'woe' oracles: Rev 18:9–20

Just as the prophetic announcement of judgement over Babylon (Rev 14:8; 18:2) and the call for the faithful to 'Come out' (Rev 18:4) are conveyed in conventional language and imagery, so too the speeches of her cohorts are conveyed in known forms of discourse taken from the prophetic tradition. However, chapters 17–18 deliberately intensify wealth language and imagery in the description of Babylon and her associates and their subsequent destruction. To do this, the author has reshaped the prophetic tradition and conflated a series of passages (Jer 51:7 [LXX 28:7], Isa 23:15–17, and Ezek 27:12–38).

Rev 18:9–20 contains three dirges that function like prophetic announcements of judgement.[75] These laments are placed in the mouths

---

[74] The language of a new heaven and new earth is traditional (Isa 54:17; 66:22; 2 Pet 3:13), although AOW only mentions a new heaven (*1 Enoch* 91:16). However, it should be noted that Rev 21:1 and *1 Enoch* 91:16 are the only traditions that explicitly refer to the 'first' heaven. See Olson, *Enoch*, p. 222. The most important aspect here, however, is the order of events. See Charles, *Book of Enoch* (1893), pp. 260–5.

[75] Yarbro Collins, 'Revelation 18', p. 197.

of the kings of the earth, the merchants, and sailors.[76] However, the speaker is the same heavenly voice that calls the people of God to 'Come out'.[77] While the reported speech in these threnodies is not in the first person, it still possesses a theatrical quality in that it assumes the role of the speakers and portrays them in a stereotypical fashion.[78]

At the surface the laments are largely dependent on language and imagery from Isa 23 and Ezek 27, yet these traditions have been reshaped. Ruiz has already offered an analysis of the differences between the original context and the reformulation of language and imagery in Revelation 18 and thus there is no need to discuss every detail from a literary perspective.[79] However, the development of responses by the witnesses to Tyre's destruction into prophetic announcements of judgement in Revelation 18 is significant. In addition, the way in which traditions related to Tyre and Babylon in the prophetic tradition have been reshaped into this context (Rev 18) helps recover a certain theological understanding that goes beyond what we find in the biblical prophets. (1) The lament of the merchants and sailors in Ezek 27 does not include any formal announcements of judgement.[80] The entirety of the chapter has as its focus the wealth of Tyre gained through her trade networks with other nations. Her destruction is portrayed as a ship so laden with wealth and merchandise that she sinks into the heart of the sea (Ezek 27:27) and her excessive wealth is noted no fewer than five times (Ezek 27:12, 16, 18, 27, 33). (2) There is no explicit mention of God as the one who destroys her, though the east wind and the seas are certainly at his command (Ezek 27:26, 34), which is a common motif in Jewish tradition (Jonah 1:4, *1 Enoch* 101:6, Acts 27:24). (3) The text includes one single lament (Ezek 27:32–6) that is placed in the mouth of the sailors. Although the threnody refers to kings of the earth and merchants, the dirge is simply a summary of the greatness of Tyre's past wealth and power and a report of her now present disaster (Ezek 27:29–31).

---

[76] The participation of the kings in the destruction of the whore (Rev 17:16–17) and their lament over the destruction of Babylon (Rev 18:10) has caused some commentators to suggest that they reflect different groups. See Charles, *Revelation*, vol. II, pp. 100–1; Allo, *l'Apocalypse*, p. 292; Mounce, *Revelation*, p. 328. However, Ruiz is correct in pointing out the different backgrounds for each of these visions in which the same imagery was used. Thus, he states, 'we need not search for complete consistency where none was intended' (Ruiz, *Ezekiel in the Apocalypse*, p. 418).

[77] Lohmeyer, *Offenbarung*, p. 147; Fiorenza, *Vision*, p. 99; Boxall, *Revelation*, p. 256; Beale, *Revelation*, p. 905.

[78] See Holt and Clift, *Reporting Talk*, pp. 47, 273–87.

[79] Ruiz, *Ezekiel in the Apocalypse*, pp. 411–81.   [80] Block, *Ezekiel 25–48*, p. 53.

The lack of any formal announcements of judgement in Ezekiel 27 and the emphasis placed on the response of the eyewitnesses (Ezek 27:28–36) shows that the original text served to communicate the paradigmatic value of Tyre's experience to those who might be allured by her great wealth.[81] In that passage, the portrayal of Tyre is placed in a historical context that envisions the coming overthrow by Babylon and demonstrates God's sovereignty over the richest and most powerful kingdoms of the world, and effectively censures greed, pride, and arrogance in wealth. However, it also envisions a future restoration of the city in the present age (Isa 23:15–18).[82] This material has been reformulated in Revelation 18 in the following ways. (1) The single lament has been reshaped into three woe oracles of judgement. (2) The laments are expressed in language that places significantly more emphasis on the individual accumulation of wealth. Finally, (3) the author has placed the judgement of Babylon in an eschatological context of a final judgement with no hope of restoration.

Significant attention has been given to the form and function of the dirges as either a taunt song or funeral lament as well as the items included in the merchants' cargo list.[83] In light of the author's proclivity to use known forms of discourse to communicate to his readers/hearers, the focus of the present section will be the author's preference for using the more developed woe oracle in the speeches attributed to the kings and merchants and the significance of the passage (Rev 18:9–20) within the entirety of the chapter. The common characteristics of the three oracles include: (1) the phrase 'οὐαὶ οὐαί ἡ πόλις ἡ μεγάλη', Woe, woe to the great city, (2) a reference to judgement having occurred in one hour (μιᾷ ὥρᾳ), and (3) a reference to each speaker having accumulated wealth through association with Babylon.

Woe oracles are frequent among the OT prophets (Isa 3:11; 10;1, 5; Jer 22:13; 48:1; Ezek 13:3, 18; 34:2; Amos 5:18; 6:1). Westermann notes fifty-four woe oracles in the entirety of the Hebrew Bible.[84] Among the prophets, Isaiah has the highest percentage, accounting for twenty of these occurrences.[85] However, the *Epistle of Enoch* outnumbers the prophet Isaiah with thirty-two, a number that exceeds half of all occurrences in the Hebrew Bible.[86] In addition, thirty of these occur in a series of

---

[81] Zimmerli, *Ezekiel II*, p. 61; Block, *Ezekiel*, p. 87.

[82] Oswalt, *Isaiah 1–39*, p. 436; Brueggemann, *Isaiah 1–39*, p. 186.

[83] See Yarbro Collins, 'Revelation 18', pp. 185–204; Bauckham, *Climax of Prophecy*, pp. 338–83.

[84] Westermann, *Basic Forms*, p. 191.   [85] Whedbee, *Isaiah and Wisdom*, p. 80.

[86] Coughenour, 'Woe-Oracles', p. 192.

two to six collections of oracles (cf. *1 Enoch* 103:5, 8).[87] Both the OT prophets and the Enochic tradition follow a similar overall pattern that includes (1) an accusation and (2) a threat. It is a variation of the prophetic announcement of judgement, though the particular form grows out of the tradition of the funeral lament for the dead.[88] The reformulation of the funeral dirge into the woe oracle emphasizes that the judgement being announced is inescapable.[89]

It is important to note the thematic element of wealth in the woe oracles of our text, which finds a parallel in the prophetic tradition (Isa 5:8, 11, 22; Amos 6:1, 3–6). The prophets denounce the sumptuous living and greed of the leaders of Israel and anticipate the coming exile. John, however, has placed these woe oracles in an eschatological setting in which the rich enemies of God mourn the loss of their wealth and foresee their own destruction in the judgement of Babylon. In doing so, the author includes an accusation that refers to the opulence of the city and the wealth of her cohorts and the threat is spoken of as something that has been fulfilled. Thus, the woe oracles function in the same way that we find in the *Epistle*; they serve as a formal testimony that will be realized in the final judgement.

The kings of the earth, the merchants, and the shippers all mourn Babylon because they have lived luxuriously with her (Rev 18:9) and have become affluent by participating in the economic system (Rev 18:3). Their cries expose the devotion they had to the whore and the wealth she provided, while their fear demonstrates how quickly her judgement has happened. The suddenness with which the eschatological destruction takes place (*1 Enoch* 94:1, 6–7; 96:1; 98:6; 99:9) implies a degree of imminence; final judgement will overtake the wicked by surprise.[90] Twice in the Apocalypse John warns that Christ will come like a thief to those who are not awake (Rev 3:3; 16:15). In the latter reference, staying awake (γρηγορέω; cf. Rev 2:3) and being clothed are contrasted with being naked and exposed to shame, language that is directly associated with those who accumulate wealth in the seven messages (Rev 3:17). Their mourning is occasioned by the contrasting rejoicing in heaven (Rev 18:20), which also reflects a reshaping of prophetic language:[91]

---

[87] Aune, *Prophecy in Early Christianity*, p. 116.

[88] *TDOT*, vol. III, p. 362; Aune, *Prophecy in Early Christianity*, p. 96; Janzen, *Mourning Cry*, p. 83.

[89] *TDOT*, vol. III, p. 362.   [90] Stuckenbruck, *1 Enoch 91–108*, p. 251.

[91] Charles, *Revelation*, vol. I, pp. l–li.

> Then the heavens and the earth, and all that is in them, shall
> shout for joy over Babylon.   (Jer 51:48)

Jeremiah indicates that the entire universe will rejoice over Babylon's
destruction since God's plan has been fulfilled and the people who have
suffered under the social injustices of the Empire find resolution.[92] However, John has already precluded any possibility of rejoicing on the earth
in the fall of Satan (Rev 12:12) since the author understands he is living in the last days and the earth is irredeemable. Rather, this rejoicing
reflects the judgement of the rich enemy of God's people that persecuted
and killed them. Moreover, John does not describe Babylon in terms of
military or political power as much as he emphasizes her wealth, arrogance, and immorality in the sense that she lures humankind into the
trap of the pursuit of economic gain (cf. CD 4:16–18). While it is not
explicitly stated, the sharp distinction between the mourning of the merchants and the rejoicing in heaven gives the indication that at this point
the faithful no longer inhabit the earth. This does not mean that all of
them have been killed at some other point in the text since that would be
overly dependent on a chronological reading.[93] Rather, the author frames
the judgement scene in such a way that any time element is ambiguous. What is clear, however, is that at some point in the eschatological
age God will destroy the economic and political forces that dominate
the earth, while those who are associated with them through economic
participation, who also wield power over others, will be counted among
the wicked and destroyed. In that sense, the author has moved beyond
the function of woe oracles in the biblical prophets and employs them
in a similar fashion to the prophetic announcements on the rich in the
Epistle of Enoch. One wonders whether John means for this to be formal
testimony against his opponents and not just a pronouncement that makes
the marginalized and poor feel better. If it serves as formal testimony perhaps this is why the author warns against adding or subtracting from the
message.

---

[92] Beale, *Revelation*, p. 915 suggests that this, too, is the primary theme in the Apocalypse. Thus, John has reappropriated prophetic texts because the *Sitz im Leben* is similar
in each. While it is admitted that John does create a world where the faithful are in conflict with the rich and powerful, this does not mean that it reflects the concrete historical
circumstances of the recipients. Rather, John may be portraying what *should* be happening
and what is *going* to happen as opposed to what *is* happening.

[93] So Charles, *Revelation*, p. 96.

8.7   A theology of wealth in the Apocalypse

John states in unequivocal terms that faithfulness to God is incompatible with affluence in the present age. Yet, caution should be taken in assuming that his rejection of wealth is based solely on the idolatrous nature of the economic system of the Roman world. Several key features in John's theology of wealth suggest that however much language and imagery he borrowed from the prophetic tradition his world view differs from what we find in the Hebrew Bible. The following conclusions encourage us to consider how more recent interpretive traditions from the Second Temple period may have shaped the author's perspective on wealth in relation to the faithful and how they could have legitimized the perspective he imposed on his readers/hearers:

(1)   The author presupposes a postponement of the Deuteronomistic promise of material blessing into the coming age. The praise of poverty and calumniation of affluence in the seven messages, taken together with the denigration of economic participation and the judgement of the rich in chapter 18, makes it clear that wealth is not a feature of the present age for the faithful community. Rather, those who remain loyal to God and suffer can expect to be rewarded in the gold and jewel-laden new Jerusalem in the eschaton.

(2)   John's theological world view follows the pattern developed in the Second Temple period that views the faithful as poor while the wicked are associated with the rich. John's rejection of material blessing for the faithful arises from an already developed understanding that the last days are marked by an increasing desire for the accumulation of wealth among wicked humankind and an expectation of escalating hostility for the faithful. Apocalyptic traditions from the Second Temple period sought to explain the problem of theodicy faced by their communities by revealing the mystery of God in allowing the present atrocities to happen while he tests his people and allows the wicked to flourish. John, however, does not develop his symbolic universe in an effort to explain the present suffering of his community as much as he does to expose the incompatibility of the faithful with a lifestyle of wealth and luxury.

(3)   The author envisions the world in the present age as irretrievably evil and ruled temporarily by Satan. This follows the same pattern developed in the Second Temple period in which organized,

external forces deceive humankind and lure them into a life of affluence and away from worshipping God. For this reason, John categorically rejects participation in the economic system. This idea finds concrete expression in the Qumran community that sought to establish its own alternative system that rejected the individual accumulation of wealth. John, too, considers that the marginalized status of his readers/hearers in the Christian communities tangibly distinguishes them from the wicked outside world. This points back to Newsom's comments about apocalyptic discourse:

> apocalyptic is an 'outsider' discourse: not a language of the oppressed but a language of those who *elect* a stance of marginality and seek to use that marginal status to find a place in the cultural conversation.[94]

John's discourse is not about decrying the social injustice of the Roman Empire or any other world government. Rome is not the enemy of the church per se nor is this idea prevalent in early Christian tradition (cf. Matt 22:21; Luke 20:25; Rom 13; 1 Peter 2:13–17). John does not critique the Roman Empire with the hope of a new political power that rejects the imperial cults and idolatry. According to John's world view, the present age is completely irredeemable and not because of the Roman Empire, but because the eschatological age has been inaugurated and Satan and his angels have been cast down to the earth. There is no hope for the righteous in the present age apart from divine intervention in which Christ will vindicate the faithful poor and destroy the wicked rich.

The very nature of the eschatological age as John sees it is that people will seek affluence in order to find some sense of false security and establish their self-sufficiency. This pursuit of wealth bestows upon them the mark of Satan. The righteous, however, follow the example of the slaughtered Lamb and elect a position of marginalization in order to establish their identity visibly within the dominant discourse of power, greed, and luxurious living. Within this economy of faithfulness the poor become rich by remaining loyal to the Lamb and inheriting the gold and jewel-laden new Jerusalem. Correspondingly, the rich become poorer through their accumulation of wealth, since this alternative economic system of heaven finds its source of wealth in Christ and runs contrary to the evil earthly realm.

---

[94] Newsom, *Self as Symbolic Space*, p. 48 (italics added).

These conclusions make it possible to say that John was very much in conversation with traditions that were already circulating within the Second Temple period that allow for a rejection of wealth based not on socio-historical circumstances but on the already established paradigm that in the present age the faithful will be poor and the wicked will be rich. It is now necessary to distinguish the particular traditions that have most clearly shaped the author's world view and the implications that arise from the study.

9

CONCLUSIONS

The present study takes its point of departure in the Apocalypse of John. What does the language about wealth and poverty in the seven messages (Rev 2:9; 3:17) and other texts in the book (Rev 5:12; 13:16–17; 18) tell us about the author's ideal community of faith? In Part I the problem was delineated in a critical review of how scholars have attempted to deal with this language through either the social world of Roman Asia Minor or the author's use of the biblical prophets. This discussion demonstrated a further need to examine early Jewish traditions outside the Hebrew Bible. The emerging emphasis, then, was not on providing an analysis of how people lived in relation to riches and poverty in their socio-historical setting but what documents from the period reveal about attitudes towards affluence in relation to the faithful community. And so an attempt has been made to answer an ancillary question: to what degree can we say that John's portrayal of the faithful community is informed by Jewish traditions related to wealth in the Second Temple period?

Part II is limited to an analysis of Jewish literature from the Second Temple period that demonstrates a concern over wealth. In this discussion, the primary emphasis has fallen on apocalyptic traditions. In Part III, selected passages from the Apocalypse were investigated that revealed similarities with these apocalyptic traditions in both John's language of wealth and his theological perspective.

Despite the limited focus of the analysis, the Second Temple period provided a wide variety of documents through which to consider our question, so that we cannot expect that the author was in conversation with, or picked up on all of them. Rather, the analysis of selected passages in the Apocalypse heightened the distinction between many of these texts and John's perspective. For example, while John is clearly critical of wealth and urges the need for wisdom among his readers/hearers (Rev 13:18; 17:9), he does not do so in the same way as in documents such as *Aramaic Levi Document* or *Mûsār lᵉ Mēvîn*. That is to say, in these works the acquisition of wisdom is not necessary for the readers to acquire a future inheritance, nor is it the content or basis of that future reward. John's call for wisdom and discernment requires that his readers/hearers adopt his cosmological perspective on the world and, consequently, his idea of the faithful community.

The way wealth is treated in Ben Sira does not leave traces in the Apocalypse since here economic wellbeing can be a feature of the present age for one who is pious. While Ben Sira recognizes the social distinctions of the rich and poor and the disparity that exists even among the people of God, he maintains a theology of retribution. Likewise, Wisdom of Solomon, although in conversation with apocalyptic traditions in its economic characterization of the righteous and wicked and emphasis on the immortality of the soul, also anticipates material wealth for those who acquire wisdom. Book 3 of the *Sibylline Oracles* provides an anti-Roman polemic and critique of social injustices, albeit with an eye towards a correction of these inequities in the present age. However, these oracles lack any cosmological or eschatological concerns to the degree that we find in the Apocalypse. Thus, hardly any interest is shown for ethical behaviour or the impact of wealth on the pious. To be sure, the desire to have their circumstances reversed in the present age denotes an expectation that the Deuteronomistic promise has been delayed only because of the brutality and greed of the Roman Empire. A similar sentiment can be detected in *Pesher Habakkuk* from Qumran.

On the other hand, it is evident that certain traditions have fed and shaped the author's theological world view. While these are, to some degree, also found in the biblical prophets, it would be misleading to think that John is wholly dealing with the biblical tradition through exegetical and intertextual engagement. Rather, the evidence reveals an emphasis on the part of John on the irreversible, eschatological consequences of ethical behaviour directly related to wealth based on a certain cosmological and theological understanding, an emphasis that has close analogies in some Second Temple literature. This perspective is most extensively developed in the *Epistle of Enoch*, which seeks to provide an explanation for present circumstances in which the wicked are flourishing while the righteous suffer. This tradition directly challenges a theology of retribution by pushing the expectation of blessing for the righteous into the eschaton.

The *Epistle* utilizes the prophetic woe oracle to provide formal, irreversible indictments against rich sinners, thus assuring them of their punishment. John likewise includes in the judgement of Babylon woe oracles placed in the mouths of her rich cohorts, which assumes the realization of the judgement promised in the Enochic tradition. Like the traditions preserved in the AOW and *War Scroll*, John anticipates a complete reversal of fortunes for the faithful when God intervenes in history to judge the wicked and vindicate the righteous. The later *Eschatological Admonition* further develops the idea that the truly faithful are marked by their complete rejection of material wealth in the present age (*1 Enoch* 108:8–15). This tradition, which was appended to the *Epistle of Enoch* and *Birth of Noah* late in the first century CE, exhorts readers to voluntary suffering and poverty as the visible marks of those who love God and love heaven more than their life in this world (*1 Enoch* 108:8; cf. Rev 12:11).

It is possible to suggest that the author's cosmological understanding has also been shaped by traditions reflected in the Enochic texts. The BOW first develops the idea that the spirits of the bastard offspring are active on the earth to wreak havoc on humankind until the final judgement. Later tradition placed these spirit beings under the direct control of Satan on the earth (*Jub.* 10:11–12). Other texts portray the Belial figure as the demonic ruler of the present age and the eschatological adversary who raises up an army to fight against the faithful and God in the final decisive battle on earth (1QM 1:13; 13:2; cf. Rev 19:19; 20:8–9). *Damascus Document* and *Community Rule* also portray Belial as one who has rule over the present eschatological age (CD 4:13; 4:15–18; 1QS 1:18; 2:19; 4Q510 1:5–7) who seeks to distract humankind from worshipping God through the trap of accumulating wealth (CD 4:14–18; cf. Rev 13:16–17).

While John stands within the trajectory of such a tradition, he does not attribute all of humankind's faults to the influence of these cosmic forces but holds them accountable for their decisions through calls to repentance and separation (Rev 2:5, 16, 21–22; 3:3, 19; 18:4). This is the same approach taken in the *Epistle of Enoch*, as that in which the determinism of the BOW is reversed by attributing the cause of sin to humankind (*1 Enoch* 98:4–5). This cosmological perspective assumes the universe should be marked by wickedness and hostility, even though many of his readers/hearers are not experiencing these circumstances. Thus, John's conversation with these traditions legitimizes his symbolic universe, a world that presupposes that the faithful can expect conflict and death while the affluent can anticipate judgement.

While only alluded to in the prophetic tradition, the identity of the wicked as the rich becomes categorical in the *Epistle*, an idea that is also evident in the Apocalypse. In the same prophetic style as the *Epistle*, John categorically associates affluence and the pursuit of riches with unfaithfulness. At the same time, while the *Epistle* seeks to provide an explanation for why the righteous suffer in light of their present

difficult circumstances, John, shaped by tradition-historical developments preserved in these texts, negates for the present the luxurious
living of some of his readers/hearers and aligns them with the wicked.
The later *Eschatological Admonition* and the *Similitudes* further develop
the idea of the wicked rich by establishing the identity of the righteous as
those who willingly reject affluence outright and claim this distinction as
a mark of their devotion to God. Thus, the most obvious conclusion is that
traditions preserved in these texts, as well as the Apocalypse, postpone
any expectation of material blessing reflected in the Deuteronomistic
scheme. In light of these findings it is possible to say, in answer to our
question, that, while there are no obvious or open citations of these texts,
ideas reflected in the *Epistle of Enoch* and the later Enochic traditions
have played a formative role in shaping the world through which John
legitimized the radical stance he imposed on his readers/hearers. In that
sense, the *Epistle* helps us read the Apocalypse, to some degree, from
such a vantage point.

Final reflections of the study arise from the conclusions provided
above and encourage us to consider further the implications of John's
contact with Jewish apocalyptic traditions. By utilizing extensive language and imagery from the prophetic tradition, John places himself in
line with the biblical prophets. Yet, his theological world view, through
which he reshapes prophetic language and imagery, and his willingness
to incorporate Enochic traditions into his visions alongside the biblical
prophets, places him within a trajectory of Jewish apocalyptic prophets
from the Second Temple period. This calls into question studies that seek
to describe the Apocalypse as modelled on classical prophecy.

More importantly, this encourages us to consider seriously John's view
of the Enochic tradition in relation to the biblical prophets. His communication is directed to the Christian communities and is designed to
transform their present perspective of the universe and ultimately to alter
their attitudes related to wealth. By casting his visions within a cosmological framework known to us through Enochic texts, and by conflating
the prophetic tradition, known to us from the Hebrew Bible, we can infer
that (1) John thought his audience would have been familiar with both the
biblical traditions as well as traditions preserved in the Enochic literature,
and (2) that he assumed his disclosures, on such a basis, would be effective in pressing his readers/hearers to change their present behaviour.
While the study has not suggested any degree of literary dependence
between the Apocalypse and the Enochic texts, we must keep in mind
that the latter was a growing literary tradition that was being copied and
developed well into the first century CE. Other NT writers assume many

of the traditions developed in the earliest Enochic texts (Matt 8:16, 28–32; 12:43; Luke 8:29–33), while others allude to it (1 Pet 3:19–20; 2 Pet 2:4; Jude 6) and even quote from it (Jude 14). Their later acceptance into the Ethiopic canon further encourages us to consider the degree to which early Christian communities were receiving these traditions and to what extent they were considered authoritative.

We must also consider what shape John's radical obedience may have taken in the life of these Christian communities. John's language functions to move his audience towards a radical obedience to God and withdrawal from the present economic system. How this manifests itself may be best understood when viewed alongside the concrete expression of the sectarian ideology evidenced in the Dead Sea community. The Damascus community and traditions reflected in the *Community Rule* do not reject the use of wealth in order to maintain their existence. This is evident in their possession of land, slaves, livestock, and the individual incomes of the members whereby they contributed their possessions communally. In this way, wealth could be managed by a relatively isolated community. What they reject is a world view that values a life of affluence, which, from their perspective, presents a rival devotion to the pursuit of riches that detracts from obedience to God. Thus, the handling of wealth and economic transactions presented a precarious set of circumstances through which much care and deliberation was necessary. Likewise, John is moving his audience to a greater degree of discernment in how they negotiate wealth and whether their commitment is to God or the pursuit of wealth. Agreement with John would ultimately mean some degree of sectarian separation that would probably result in persecution from those actively involved in the present economic system. By taking greater care in economic relations and rejecting participation to the degree that one is pursuing wealth, the faithful can be distinguished visibly from the dominant discourse as the poor and marginalized, which, in John's world view marks them as the faithful.

One additional reflection should point out that the present study has also been limited to wealth in the Apocalypse while other NT texts that deal with the subject are deliberately absent. However, based on the conclusions we have formulated, a brief comparison may help to emphasize how John's perspective is quite different from that of other NT writers. For example, John does not allow for the diversity in the Corinthian correspondence in which the language of rich and poor functions to encourage giving to others in need (2 Cor 8:9–12). For Paul, the metaphorical use of the terms rich and poor refer to Christ's generosity in laying down his life for others so that they might become the people of God (rich). Paul does not relate this to the question of future reward and, more importantly, he does not critique the obvious abundance (περίσσευμα) of some of his recipients (2 Cor 8:14). Rather, like Ben Sira, who also sees the disparity among the faithful, he encourages voluntary giving to those less fortunate.

In addition, the gospel traditions recognize the inherent dangers of wealth in the present age (Matt 13:22; Mark 4:19; Luke 12:21; 18:22–3) and how devotion to possessions can distract one from commitment to God (Matt 6:24; Luke 16:13). However, the issue is left open and there are no radical calls for action concerning riches or economic withdrawal. Like other NT passages, the rich can coexist with the poor, and disparity in economic circumstances is tolerated (1 Tim 6:9–18). However, unlike the parable of the wheat and the tares (Matt 13:24–30), in which the faithful and the wicked are allowed to coexist until the Day of Judgement, John's sectarian world view does not allow for such blurred distinctions. His polarizing language demands that (a) the righteous be separated from the wicked, and that (b) this distinction becomes manifest in a tangible withdrawal from idolatrous economic structures.

For John, the reward of life with the Lamb and God in the new Jerusalem does not emerge from a superficial confession that visibly demonstrates a rival devotion to the pursuit of affluence in this age. Rather, it is only realized through radical obedience to God that follows the example of the Lamb who conquered through suffering and death. In other words, in John's alternative economic system, one's fate in the age to come is not determined so much by circumstances in the present eschatological age but by their responses to them.

BIBLIOGRAPHY

Achtemeier, P., 'Rev 5:1–14', *Int* 40 (1986), 284–5.

Aichele, G., and Phillips, G., 'Introduction: Exegesis, Eisegesis, Intergesis', *Semeia* 69/70 (1995), 7–18.

Aitken, J., 'Apocalyptic, Revelation, and Early Jewish Wisdom Literature', in P. Harland and R. Hayward (eds.), *New Heaven and New Earth Prophecy and the Millennium* (VTSup, 77; Leiden: Brill, 1999), pp. 181–93.

Alexander, P., 'The Redaction History of *Serekh Ha-Yahad*: A Proposal', *RevQ* 17 (1996), 437–56.

Alexander, P., and Vermès, G. (eds.), *Qumran Cave 4: XIX, Serek Ha-Yahad and Two Related Texts* (DJD, 26; Oxford: Clarendon Press, 1999).

Allo, E., *Saint Jean l'Apocalypse* (Paris: Gabalda, 1921).

Alon, G., *The Jews in their Land in the Talmudic Age: 70–640 CE* (Cambridge, MA: Harvard University Press, 1989).

Argal, R., *1 Enoch and Sirach: A Comparative Literary and Conceptual Analysis of the Themes of Revelation, Creation and Judgment* (Atlanta, GA: Scholars Press, 1995).

Asensio, V., 'Poverty and Wealth: Ben Sira's View of Possessions', in R. Egger-Wenzel and I. Krammer (eds.), *Der Einzelne und seine Gemeinschaft bei Ben Sira* (*BZAW*, 270; New York: de Gruyter, 1998), pp. 151–78.

Auffarth, C., and Stuckenbruck, L. (eds.), *The Fall of the Angels* (TBN, 6; Leiden: Brill, 2004).

Revelation 1–5 (WBC, 52a; Dallas: Word, 1997).

Revelation 6–16 (WBC, 52b; Dallas: Word, 1998).

Revelation 17–22 (WBC, 52c; Dallas: Word, 1998).

Prophecy in Early Christianity and the Ancient Mediterranean World (Grand Rapids, MI: Eerdmans, 1983).

Aune, D., *Apocalypticism, Prophecy and Magic in Early Christianity: Selected Essays* (*WUNT*, 199; Tübingen: Mohr Siebeck, 2006).

'The Apocalypse of John and the Problem of Genre', *Semeia* 36 (1986), 65–96.

'The Form and Function of the Proclamations to the Seven Churches (Revelation 2–3)', *NTS* 36 (1990), 182–204.

'The Influence of Roman Imperial Court Ceremonial on the Apocalypse of John', *BR* 28 (1983), 2–26.

Bachmann, M., 'Der erste apokalyptische Reiter und die Anlage des letzten Buches der Bibel', *Bib* 67 (1986), 240–75.

Bahktin, M. M., *The Dialogic Imagination: Four Essays by M. M. Bahktin* (UTPSS, 1; Austin: University of Texas Press, 1981).

Baillet, M., Milik, J. T., and de Vaux, R. (eds.), *Les 'Petites Grottes' de Qumrân* (DJD, 3; Oxford: Clarendon Press, 1962).

Balentine, S., and Barton, J. (eds.), *Language, Theology and the Bible: Essays in Honour of James Barr* (Oxford: Clarendon Press, 1994).

Barclay, J., 'Deviance and Apostasy: Some Applications of Deviance Theory to First-Century Judaism and Christianity', in P. Esler (ed.), *Modelling Early Christianity: Social-Scientific Studies of the New Testament in its Context* (London: Routledge, 1995), pp. 110–23.

Barr, D., *The Reality of Apocalypse: Rhetoric and Politics in the Book of Revelation* (SBLSS, 39; Atlanta, GA: Society of Biblical Literature, 2006).

Tales of the End: A Narrative Commentary on the Book of Revelation (Santa Rosa, CA: Polebridge Press, 1998).

Barrett, C., 'Gnosis and the Apocalypse of John', in A. Logan and A. Wedderburn (eds.), *The New Testament and Gnosis: Essays in Honour of Robert McL. Wilson* (Edinburgh: T & T Clark, 1983), pp. 125–37.

Barthélemy, D., and Milik, J. T., *Qumran Cave 1* (DJD 1; Oxford: Clarendon Press, 1955).

Bartlett, J., *Jews in the Hellenistic World: Josephus, Aristeas, the Sibylline Oracles, Eupolemus* (CCWJCW, 1.1; Cambridge University Press, 1985).

Barton, S., *Where Shall Wisdom be Found? Wisdom in the Bible, the Church, and the Contemporary World* (Edinburgh: T & T Clark, 1999).

Bate, H., *The Sibylline Oracles: Books III–V* (London: Macmillan, 1918).

Bauckham, R., *The Climax of Prophecy: Studies on the Book of Revelation* (Edinburgh: T & T Clark, 1993).

God Crucified: Monotheism and Christology in the New Testament (Didsbury Lectures; Carlisle: Paternoster, 1998).

The Theology of the Book of Revelation (New Testament Theology; Cambridge University Press, 1993).

Baumgarten, A., *The Flourishing of Jewish Sects in the Maccabean Era: An Interpretation* (JSJSup, 55; Leiden: Brill, 1997).

Baumgarten, J., *Qumran Cave 4: XIII: The Damascus Document (4Q266–273)* (DJD, 18; Oxford: Clarendon Press, 1996).

'The 'Sons of Dawn' in *CDC* 13:14–15 and the Ban on Commerce among the Essenes', *IEJ* 33 (1983), 81–5.

Beagley, A., *The 'Sitz im Leben' of the Apocaylpse with Particular Reference to the Role of the Church's Enemies* (BZNW, 50; Berlin: de Gruyter, 1987).

Beale, G. K., *The Book of Revelation: A Commentary on the Greek Text* (NIGTC; Grand Rapids, MI: Eerdmans, 1998).

John's Use of the Old Testament in Revelation (JSNTSup, 166; Sheffield: Academic Press, 1998).

The Use of Daniel in Jewish Apocalyptic Literature and in the Revelation of St John (New York University Press, 1984).

Beasley-Murray, G., 'Biblical Eschatology II: Apocalyptic Literature and the Book of Revelation', *EQ* 20 (1948), 272–82.

The Book of Revelation (NCBC; Grand Rapids, MI: Eerdmans, 1974).

Becker, H., *Outsiders: Studies in the Sociology of Deviance* (New York: Free Press, 1973).

Beckwith, I., *The Apocalypse of John: Studies in Introduction* (New York: Macmillan, 1919).

Beentjes, P., *The Book of Ben Sira in Hebrew* (VTSup, 68; Leiden: Brill, 1997).

— (ed.), *The Book of Ben Sira in Modern Research* (BZAW, 255; Berlin: de Gruyter, 1997).

— '"Full Wisdom is from the Lord." Sir 1:1–10 and its Place in Israel's Wisdom Literature', in Angelo Passaro and Bellia Giuseppe (eds.), *The Wisdom of Ben Sira: Studies on Tradition, Redaction, and Theology* (Berlin and New York: de Gruyter, 1998), pp. 139–54.

Beit-Arié, M., *The Makings of the Medieval Hebrew Book* (Jerusalem: Magnes Press, Hebrew University, 1993).

Ben-Hayyim, Z., *The Book of Ben Sira* (HDHL; Jerusalem: Academy of the Hebrew Language, 1973).

Berg, S., 'An Elite Group within the Yaḥad: Revisiting 1QS 8–9', in M. Thomas and B. Strawn (eds.), *Qumran Studies: New Approaches, New Questions* (Grand Rapids, MI: Eerdmans, 2007), pp. 161–77.

Berger, P., 'Kollyrium für die Blinden Augen', *NovTest* 27 (1985), 174–95.

Berges, U., and Hoppe, R., *Arm und Reich* (DNEBT, 10; Würzburg: Echter Verlag, 2009).

Beyer, K. (ed.), *Die aramäischen Texte Vom Toten Meer* (Göttingen: Vandenhoeck & Ruprecht, 1984).

Black, M., *The Scrolls and Christian Origins: Studies in the Jewish Background of the New Testament* (BJS, 48; Chico, CA: Scholars Press, 1983).

Black, M., in consultation with Vanderkam, J., *The Book of Enoch or 1 Enoch* (SVTP, 7; Leiden: Brill, 1985).

Blenkinsopp, J., *Isaiah 40–55* (Anchor Bible, 19a; New York: Doubleday, 2002).

Block, D., *Ezekiel 25–48* (NICOT; Grand Rapids, MI: Eerdmans, 1998).

Blomberg, C., *Neither Poverty nor Riches: A Biblical Theology of Possessions* (NSBT, 7; Grand Rapids, MI: Eerdmans, 1999).

Blount, B. K., *Revelation: A Commentary* (Louisville, Ky.: Westminster John Knox Press, 2009).

Boccaccini, G. (ed.), *Enoch and Qumran Origins: New Light on a Forgotten Connection* (Grand Rapids, MI: Eerdmans, 2005).

Bock, D., *Luke 9:51–24:53* (BECNT; Grand Rapids, MI: Baker Academic, 1996).

Boll, F., *Aus der Offenbarung Johannis* (Leipzig/Berlin: B. G. Teubner, 1914).

Boring, E., *Revelation* (Louisville, KY: John Knox Press, 1989).

Bosch, D., *Good News for the Poor, and the Rich: Perspectives from the Gospel of Luke* (Pretoria: C. B. Powell Bible Centre, 1993).

Bousset, W., *The Antichrist Legend: A Chapter in Christian and Jewish Folklore* (AARTTS, 24; Atlanta, GA: Scholars Press, 1999).

— 'Die Himmelsreise der Seele', *AR* 4 (1901), 136–69.

— *Die Offenbarung Johannnis*, 6th edn (KKNT, 16; Gottingen: Vandenhoeck & Ruprecht, 1906).

Boustan, R., and Reed, A. (eds.), *Heavenly Realms and Earthly Realities in Late Antique Religion* (Cambridge University Press, 2004).

Boxall, I., '"Jezebel" of Thyatira to John of Patmos', in Philip R. Davies (ed.), *Yours Faithfully: Virtual Letters from the Bible* (London: Equinox, 2004), 147–51.

— *The Revelation of Saint John* (BNTC, 18; New York: Hendrickson, 2007).

Brooke, G., 'The Kittim in the Qumran Pesherim', in L. Alexander (ed.), *Images of Empire* (JSOTSup, 122; Sheffield: JSOT Press, 1991), pp. 135–59.

Brownlee, W., *The Midrash Pesher of Habakkuk* (SBLMS, 24; Missoula, MT: Scholars Press, 1979).

'The Placarded Revelation of Habakkuk', *JBL* 82 (1963), 319–25.

'The Wicked Priest, the Man of Lies, and the Righteous Teacher – The Problem of Identity', *JQR* 73 (1982), 1–37.

Brueggemann, W., *Isaiah 1–39* (Louisville, KY: Westminster John Knox Press, 1998).

Buitenwerf, R., *Book III of the Sibylline Oracles and its Social Setting* (SVTP, 17; Leiden: Brill, 2003).

Bullard, R., and Hatton, H., *A Handbook on the Wisdom of Solomon* (UBSHS; New York: United Bible Societies, 2004).

Busch, P., *Der gefallene Drache: Mythenexegese am Beispiel von Apokalypse 12* (TANZ, 19; Tübingen: Francke Verlag, 1996).

Caird, G., *A Commentary on the Revelation of St John the Divine* (BNTC; London: Adam & Charles Black, 1966).

Campbell, J., Lyon, W., and Pietersen, L. (eds.), *New Directions in Qumran Studies* (LSTS, 52; London: T & T Clark, 2005).

Carson, D., and Williamson, H. (eds.), *It is Written: Scripture Citing Scripture* (Cambridge University Press, 1988).

Chalcraft, D. (ed.), *Sectarianism in Early Judaism: Sociological Advances* (London: Equinox, 2007).

Charles, R., *The Book of Enoch* (London: SPCK, 1917).

The Revelation of St John, 2 vols. (ICC; Edinburgh: T & T Clark, 1920).

Charlesworth, J. H., 'The Apocalypse of John: Its Theology and Impact on Subsequent Apocalypses', in *The New Testament Apocrypha and Pseudepigrapha: A Guide to Publications with Excurses on Apocalypses*, American Theological Library Association Bibliography Series 17 (Metuchen, NJ: Scarecrow Press, 1987), pp. 23–4.

The Hebrew Bible and Qumran (Richland Hills, TX.: BIBAL Press, 2000).

The Dead Sea Scrolls: Hebrew, Aramaic, and Greek Texts with English Translations, 6 vols. (Tübingen: J. C. B. Mohr, 1995).

(ed.), *Messiah: Developments in Earliest Judaism and Christianity* (Minneapolis: Fortress Press, 1992).

'Morphological and Philological Observations: Preparing the Critical Text and Translation of the *Serek Ha-Yahad*', in M. Wise (ed.), *Methods of Investigation of the Dead Sea Scrolls and the Khirbet Qumran Site: Present Realities and Future Prospects* (ANYAS, 722; New York: Academy of Sciences, 1994), pp. 271–8.

The New Testament Apocrypha and Pseudepigrapha: A Guide to Publications with Excurses on Apocalypses (Metuchen, NJ: Scarecrow Press, 1987).

The Old Testament Pseudepigrapha, 2 vols. (ABRL; New York: Doubleday, 1983).

Cheung, A., *Idol Food in Corinth: Jewish Background and Pauline Legacy* (JSNTSup, 176; Sheffield: Academic Press, 1999).

Chisholm, K., and Ferguson, J. (eds.), *Rome: The Augustan Age* (New York: Oxford University Press, 1984).

Clarke, E. (trans.), *Targum Pseudo-Jonathan: Deuteronomy* (TAB, 5b; College-ville, PA: Liturgical Press, 1998).

Cohen, S., *From the Maccabees to the Mishnah*, 2nd edn (Louisville, KY: John Knox Press, 2006).

'The Modern Study of Ancient Judaism', in S. J. D. Cohen and E. L. Greenstein (eds.), *The State of Jewish Studies* (Detroit, Mich.: Wayne State University Press, 1990), pp. 55–73.

Cohen, S., and Greenstein, E. (eds.), *The State of Jewish Studies* (Detroit, MI: Wayne State University Press, 1990).

Collins, John J., *Apocalypse: The Morphology of a Genre, Semeia*, 14 (Atlanta, GA: Society of Biblical Literature, 1979).

The Apocalyptic Imagination: An Introduction to Jewish Apocalyptic Litera-ture, 2nd edn (Grand Rapids, MI: Eerdmans, 1998).

Daniel (Hermeneia; Minneapolis, MN: Fortress Press, 1994).

Daniel: With an Introduction to Apocalyptic Literature (FOTL, 20; Grand Rapids, MI: Eerdmans, 1984).

'Forms of the Community in the Dead Sea Scrolls', in E. Tov, et al. (eds.), *Emanuel: Studies in the Hebrew Bible, the Septuagint, and the Dead Sea Scrolls in Honour of Emanuel Tov* (VTSup, 94; Leiden: Brill, 2003), pp. 97–111.

Jewish Wisdom in the Hellenistic Age (Edinburgh: T & T Clark, 1997).

'The Mysteries of God, Creation and Eschatology in 4QInstruction and the Wisdom of Solomon', in F. Martínez (ed.), *Wisdom and Apocalypticism in the Dead Sea Scrolls and in the Biblical Tradition* (BETL, 168; Leuven University Press, 2003), pp. 287–305.

'The Reinterpretation of Apocalyptic Traditions in the Wisdom of Solomon', in Angelo Passaro and Giussepe Bellia (eds), *The Book of Wisdom in Modern Research: Studies on Tradition, Redaction and Theology* (Berlin: de Gruyter, 2005), pp. 143–55.

Seers, Sibyls and Sages in Hellenistic-Roman Judaism (JSJSup, 54; Leiden: Brill, 1997).

The Sibylline Oracles of Egyptian Judaism (SBLDS, 13; Missoula, MT: Soci-ety of Biblical Literature for the Pseudepigrapha Group, 1974).

'Sibylline Oracles', in J. Charlesworth (ed.), *The Old Testament Pseude-pigrapha*, vol. 1 (ABRL; New York: Doubleday, 1983), pp. 317–47.

'The Son of Man in First-Century Judaism', *NTS* 38 (1992), 448–66.

'Wisdom Reconsidered, in Light of the Scrolls', *DSD* 4 (1997), 265–81.

Collins, John J., and Flint, P. (eds.), *The Book of Daniel: Composition and Reception*, 2 vols. (VTSup, 83; Leiden: Brill, 2001).

Collins, John J., et al. (eds.), *Sapiential Perspectives: Wisdom Literature in Light of the Dead Sea Scrolls* (STDJ, 51; Leiden: Brill, 2004).

Collins, M., *The Use of Sobriquets in the Qumran Dead Sea Scrolls* (LSTS, 67; London: T & T Clark, 2009).

Considine, J., 'The Rider on the White Horse', *CBQ* 6 (1944), 406–22.

Coughenour, R., 'The Woe-Oracles in Ethiopic Enoch', *JSJ* 9 (1978), 192–7.

Countryman, L., *The Rich Christian in the Church of the Early Empire: Contradictions and Accommodations* (New York: Edwin Mellen Press, 1980).

Court, J., *Myth and History in the Book of Revelation* (Atlanta, GA: John Knox Press, 1979).

Cowley, R., *The Traditional Interpretation of the Apocalypse of St John in the Ethiopian Orthodox Church* (Cambridge University Press, 1983).

Cross, F., 'The Development of Jewish Scripts', in G. Wright (ed.), *The Bible and the Ancient Near East* (New York: Doubleday, 1961), pp. 133–202.

Cryer, F., and Thompson, T. (eds.), *Qumran Between the Old and the New Testament* (JSOTSup, 290; Sheffield: Academic Press, 1998).

D'Arms, J., *Commerce and Social Standing in Ancient Rome* (Cambridge, MA: Harvard University Press, 1981).

Davies, P., *The Damascus Covenant: An Interpretation of the 'Damascus Document'* (JSOTSup, 25; Sheffield: JSOT Press, 1983).

Daniel (Sheffield: JSOT Press, 1985).

'A "Groningen" Hypothesis of Qumran Origins and Early History', *RevQ* 14 (1990), 521–41.

(ed.) *Faithfully Yours: Virtual Letters from the Bible* (London: Equinox, 2004).

Davies, P., and Halligan, J. (eds.), *Second Temple Studies III: Studies in Politics, Class and Material Culture* (JSOTSup, 340; Sheffield: Academic Press, 2002).

Davila, J., *The Provenance of the Pseudepigrapha: Jewish, Christian, or Other?* (JSJSup, 105; Leiden: Brill, 2005).

Davis, M., and Strawn, B. (eds.), *Qumran Studies: New Approaches, New Questions* (Grand Rapids, MI: Eerdmans, 2007).

Day, J., Gordon, R., and Williamson, H. (eds.), *Wisdom in Ancient Israel: Essays in Honour of J. A. Emerton* (Cambridge University Press, 1995).

de Jonge, M., *Pseudepigrapha of the Old Testament as Part of Christian Literature* (SVTP, 18; Leiden: Brill, 2003).

de Ste. Croix, G., *The Class Struggle in the Ancient Greek World: From the Archaic Age to the Arabic Conquests* (Ithaca, NY: Cornell University Press, 1981).

Dean-Otting, M., *Heavenly Journeys: A Study of the Motif in Hellenistic Jewish Literature* (JU, 8; Berlin: Peter Lang, 1984).

Delcor, M., et al. (eds.), *Mélanges bibliques et orienteaux en l'honneur de M. Mathias Delcor* (AOAT, 215; Kevelaer: Verlag Butzon & Bercker, 1985).

deSilva, D., 'The Revelation to John: A Case Study in Apocalyptic Propaganda and the Maintenance of Sectarian Identity', *SocAn* 53 (1992), 375–95.

Seeing Things John's Way: The Rhetoric of the Book of Revelation (Louisville, KY: Westminster John Knox Press, 2009).

Di Lella, A., 'Conservative and Progressive Theology: Sirach and Wisdom', *CBQ* 28 (1966), 139–46.

Dillman, A., *Das Buch Henoch* (Leipzig: F. C. W. Vogel, 1853).

Dimant, D., 'The Library of Qumran: Its Content and Character', in L. Schiffman, et al. (eds.) *The Dead Sea Scrolls: Fifty Years After their Discovery 1947–1997* (Jerusalem: Israel Exploration Society, 2000), pp. 170–6.

Dimant, D., and Schiffman, L. (eds.), *Time to Prepare the Way in the Wilderness* (STDJ, 16; Leiden: Brill, 1995).

Drawnel, H., *An Aramaic Wisdom Text from Qumran* (JSJSup, 86; Leiden: Brill, 2004).

Driver, G., 'The Number of the Beast', in *Bibel und Qumran* (Berlin, Evangelische Haupt-Bibelgesellschaft, 1968), pp. 75–81.

Duff, P., *Who Rides the Beast? Prophetic Rivalry and the Rhetoric of Crisis in the Churches of the Apocalypse* (Oxford University Press, 2001).

Duhaime, J., 'L'instruction sur les deux esprits et les interpolations dualistes à Qumran', *RevBib* 84 (1977), 572–94.

'The *War Scroll* from Qumran and the Greco-Roman Tactical Treatises', *RevQ* 13 (1988), 133–51.

Dunn, J., *The Parting of the Ways: Between Christianity and Judaism and their Significance for the Early Church*, 2nd edn (London: SCM Press, 2006).

Dupont-Sommer, A., *The Essene Writings from Qumran* (Gloucester: Peter Smith, 1973).

Egger-Wenzel, R., and Krammer, I. (eds.), *Der Einzelne und seine Gemeinschaft bei Ben Sira* (*BZAW*, 270; Berlin: de Gruyter, 1998).

Eisenmann R., and Wise, M., *The Dead Sea Scrolls Uncovered* (Rockport, MA: Element, 1992).

Elgvin, T., 'Admonition Texts from Qumran Cave 4', in M. Wise (ed.), *Methods of Investigation of the Dead Sea Scrolls and the Khirbet Qumran Site: Present Realities and Future Prospects* (ANYAS, 722; New York: Academy of Sciences, 1994), pp. 179–96.

'Jewish Christian Editing of the Old Testament Pseudepigrapha', in O. Skarsaune and R. Hvalvik (eds.), *Jewish Believers in Jesus* (Peabody, MA: Hendrickson, 2007), pp. 278–304.

'The Mystery to Come: Early Essene Theology of Revelation', in F. Cryer and T. Thompson (eds.), *Qumran Between the Old and the New Testament* (JSOTSup, 290; Sheffield: Academic Press, 1998), 113–50.

'Reconstruction of Sapiential Work A', *RevQ* 16 (1995), 559–80.

'Wisdom and Apocalypticism in the Early Second Century BCE – The Evidence of 4QInstruction', in L. H. Schiffman, E. Tov, and J. C. VanderKam, *The Dead Sea Scrolls, Fifty Years after their Discovery* (Jerusalem: Israel Exploration Society, 2000), p. 246.

Ellul, J., *Apocalypse: The Book of Revelation* (New York: Seabury Press, 1977).

Engel, H., *Das Buch der Weisheit* (NSKAT, 16; Stuttgart: Verlag Katholisches Bibelwerk GmbH, 1998).

Erikson, K., *Wayward Puritans: A Study in the Sociology of Deviance* (New York: Wiley, 1966).

Ernst, J., *Die Eschatologischen Gegenspieler in den Schriften des Neuen Testaments* (Regensburg: Pustet, 1967).

Eshel, H., *The Dead Sea Scrolls and the Hasmonean State* (SDSSRL; Grand Rapids, MI: Eerdmans, 2008).

Esler, P., *Modelling Early Christianity: Social-Scientific Studies of the New Testament in its Context* (London: Routledge, 1995).

Facsimiles of the Fragments Hitherto Recovered of the Book of Ecclesiasticus in Hebrew (Oxford University Press, 1901).

Falk, D., Martíne, F., and Schuller, E. (eds.), *Sapiential, Liturgical and Poetical Texts from Qumran* (STDJ, 35; Leiden: Brill, 2000).

Fanning, B., *Verbal Aspect in New Testament Greek* (Oxford: Clarendon Press, 1990).

Farrer, A., *A Rebirth of Images: The Making of St John's Apocalypse* (Westminster: Dacre Press, 1949).

The Revelation of St John the Divine: Commentary on the English Text (Oxford University Press, 1964).

Fee, G., *The First Epistle to the Corinthians* (NICNT; Grand Rapids, MI: Eerdmans, 1993).

Fekkes, J., *Isaiah and Prophetic Traditions in the Book of Revelation* (JSNTSup, 93; Sheffield: JSOT Press, 1994).

Finley, M., *The Ancient Economy* (London: Chatto & Windus, 1973).

Fiorenza, E., *The Apocalypse* (Chicago: Franciscan Herald Press, 1976).

'Apokalypsis and Propheteia', in J. Lambrecht (ed.), *L'Apocalypse johannique et l'Apocalyptique dans le Nouveau Testament* (BETL, 53; Leuven University Press, 1980), pp. 115–28.

The Book of Revelation: Justice and Judgment (Philadelphia, PA: Fortress Press, 1985).

Revelation: Vision of a Just World (Minneapolis, MN: Fortress Press, 1991).

Fitzmyer, J., *The Gospel According to Luke (X–XXIV): Introduction, Translation, and Notes* (Anchor Bible, 28a; New York: Doubleday, 1985).

Flusser, D., *Judaism of the Second Temple Period: Qumran and Apocalypticism* (Grand Rapids, MI: Eerdmans, 2007).

Fontenrose, J., *Python: A Study of Delphic Myth and its Origins* (Los Angeles: University of California Press, 1959).

Ford, J., *Revelation* (Anchor Bible, 38; Garden City, NY: Doubleday, 1965).

Forsyth, N., *The Old Enemy: Satan and the Combat Myth* (Princeton University Press, 1987).

Foster, G., 'Peasant Society and the Image of Limited Good', *AmAnth* 67 (1965), 293–315.

Foster, R., 'Shepherds, Sticks, and Social Destabilization: A Fresh Look at Zechariah 11:4–17', *JBL* 126 (2007), 735–53.

Fotopoulos, J., *Food Offered to Idols in Roman Corinth* (*WUNT* II; Tübingen: Mohr Siebeck, 2003).

Frank, T., *An Economic Survey of Ancient Rome*, 6 vols. (Baltimore, MD: Johns Hopkins Press, 1940).

Frey, J., 'Different Patterns of Dualistic Thought in the Qumran Library: Reflections on their Background and History', in M. Bernstein et al. (eds.), *Legal Texts and Legal Issues* (Leiden: Brill, 1997), pp. 275–335.

'Flesh and Spirit in the Palestinian Jewish Sapiential Tradition and in the Qumran Texts', in C. Hempel, et al. (eds.), *The Wisdom Texts from Qumran and the Development of Sapiential Thought* (BETL,159; Leuven University Press, 2002), pp. 368–404.

Friesen, S., *Imperial Cults and the Apocalypse of John: Reading Revelation in the Ruins* (Oxford University Press, 2001).

'Satan's Throne, Imperial Cults, and the Social Settings of Revelation', *JSNT* 27 (2005), 351–73.

Twice Neokoros: Ephesus, Asia, and the Cult of the Flavian Imperial Family (RGW, 116; Leiden: Brill, 1993).

Geffcken, J., *Komposition und Entstehungszeit der Oracula Sibyllina* (TUGAL, 23/1; Leipzig: J. C. Hinrichs, 1902).

Gilbert, M., 'Methodological and Hermeneutical Trends in Modern Exegesis on the Book of Ben Sira', in A. Passaro and G. Bellia (eds.), *The Wisdom of Ben Sira* (DCLS, 1; Berlin: de Gruyter, 2008), pp. 1–20.

Gillman, J., *Possessions and the Life of Faith: A Reading of Luke-Acts* (Collegeville, PA: Liturgical Press, 1991).

Ginzberg, L., *The Legends of the Jews*, 7 vols. (Philadelphia: Jewish Publication Society, 1937–66).

An Unknown Jewish Sect (New York: Jewish Theological Seminary of America, 1970).

Goff, M., 'Wisdom, Apocalypticism, and the Pedagogical Ethos of 4QInstruction', in B. Wright III and L. Mills (eds.), *Conflicted Boundaries in Wisdom and Apocalypticism* (SBLSS, 35; Atlanta, GA: SBL, 2005), pp. 57–67.

The Worldly and Heavenly Wisdom of 4QInstruction (STDJ, 50; Leiden: Brill, 2003).

Goldingay, J., *Daniel* (WBC, 30; Dallas, TX: Word Books, 1989).

González, J., *Faith and Wealth: A History of Early Christian Ideas on the Origin, Significance, and Use of Money* (San Francisco, CA: Harper & Row, 1990).

Gooder, P., *Only the Third Heaven? 2 Corinthians 12.1–10 and Heavenly Ascent* (LNTS, 313; London: T & T Clark, 2006).

Goranson, Stephen, 'Essene Polemic in the Apocalypse of John', in M. Bernstein, et al. (eds.), *Legal Texts and Legal Issues* (STDJ, 23; Leiden: Brill, 1997), pp. 453–60.

Gordon, C., 'Leviathan: Symbol of Evil', in A. Altmann (ed.), *Biblical Motifs: Origins and Transformations* (PLIAJS, 3; Cambridge, MA: Harvard University Press, 1966), pp. 1–10.

Goulder, M., 'The Apocalypse as an Annual Cycle of Prophecies', *NTS* 27 (1981), 342–67.

Grabbe, L., *Wisdom of Solomon* (GAP; Sheffield: Academic Press, 1997).

Gradl, H., *Zwischen Arm und Reich: das lukanische Doppelwerk in leserorientierter und textpragmatischer Perspektive* (Würzburg: Echter, 2005).

Green, W. S., 'Ancient Judaism: Contours and Complexity', in Samuel E. Balentine and James Barton (eds.), *Language, Theology, and the Bible: Essays in Honour of James Barr* (Oxford: Clarendon Press, 1994), pp. 293–310.

Greenfield J., and Stone, M., 'Remarks on the Aramaic Testament of Levi from the Geniza', *RevBib* 86 (1979), 214–30.

Greenfield, J., Stone, M. E., and Eshel, E. (eds.), *The Aramaic Levi Document: Edition, Translation and Commentary* (SVTP, 19; Leiden: Brill, 2004).

Grossfield, B., *The Targum Onqelos to Deuteronomy* (TAB, 9; Wilmington, NC: Michael Glazier Inc., 1988).

Gruenwald, I., *Apocalypticism and Merkavah Mysticism* (AGAJU, 14; Leiden: Brill, 1980).

Gunkel, H., *Schöpfung und Chaos in Urzeit und Endzeit*, 2nd edn (Göttingen: Vandenhoeck und Ruprecht, 1921).

Hahn, F., 'Die Sendschreiben der Johannesapokalypse. Ein Beitrag zur Bestimmung prophetischer Redeformen', in G. Jeremias, et al. (eds.), *Tradition und Glaube: Das frühe Christentum in seiner Umwelt* (Göttingen: Vandenhoeck & Ruprecht, 1971), pp. 357–94.

Hallévi, J., 'Recherches sur la langue de la rédaction primitive du livre d'Énoch', *JA* 6 (1867), 352–95.

Hanson, P. D., 'Apocalypse, Genre', 'Apocalypticism', *IBDSup* (1976), 27–34.
The Dawn of Apocalyptic (Philadelphia, PA: Fortress Press, 1979).

Harland, P., *Associations, Synagogues, and Congregations: Claiming a Place in Ancient Mediterranean Society* (Minneapolis, MN: Fortress Press, 2003).

Harrington, D., 'The *raz nihyeh* in a Qumran Wisdom Text (1Q26, 4Q215–418, 423)', *RevQ* 17 (1996), 549–53.
'Two Early Jewish Approaches to Wisdom: Sirach and Qumran Sapiential Work A', in *1996 Seminar Papers* (SBLSP, 35; Atlanta, GA: Scholars Press, 1996), pp. 123–32.
'Wisdom at Qumran', in E. Ulrich and J. Vanderkam (eds.), *The Community of the Renewed Covenant* (University of Notre Dame Press, 1994), pp. 137–52.
'The Wisdom of the Scribe According to Ben Sira', in G. Nickelsburg and J. Collins (eds.), *Ideal Figures in Ancient Judaism: Profiles and Paradigms* (SCSS, 12; Chico, CA: Scholars Press, 1980), pp. 181–8.
Wisdom Texts from Qumran (London: Routledge, 1996).

Harrington, W., *Revelation* (SPS, 16; Collegeville, PA: Liturgical Press, 1993).

Hayes, J., 'The Use of Oracles against Foreign Nations in Ancient Israel', *JBL* 87 (1968), 81–92.

Hellholm, D., 'The Problem of Apocalyptic Genre and the Apocalypse of John', *Semeia* 36 (1986), 13–64.

Hemer, C., *The Letters to the Seven Churches of Asia in their Local Setting* (JSNTSup, 11; Sheffield: JSOT Press, 1986).

Hempel, C., *The Laws of the Damascus Document: Sources, Tradition and Redaction* (STDJ, 29; Leiden: Brill, 1998).

Hempel, C., et al. (eds.), *The Wisdom Texts from Qumran and the Development of Sapiential Thought* (BETL, 159; Leuven University Press, 2002).

Hendricksen, W., *More than Conquerors: An Interpretation of the Book of Revelation*, 2nd edn (Grand Rapids, MI: Baker Books, 1940).

Hengel, M., *Judaism and Hellenism*, 2 vols. (Philadelphia, PA: Fortress Press, 1974).
Property and Riches in the Early Church: Aspects of a Social History of Early Christianity (London: SCM Press, 1974).

Hengstenberg, E., *The Revelation of St John* (Edinburgh: T & T Clark, 1851).

Heuver, G., *The Teachings of Jesus Concerning Wealth* (Chicago: Fleming H. Revell Company, 1903).

Hill, D., *New Testament Prophecy* (London: Marshall, Morgan & Scott, 1979).

Himmelfarb, M., *Ascent to Heaven in Jewish and Christian Apocalypses* (New York: Oxford University Press, 1993).

Hoffmann, M., *The Destroyer and the Lamb: The Relationship between Angelomorphic and Lamb Christology in the Book of Revelation* (*WUNT* II, 203; Tübingen: Mohr Siebeck, 2005).

Holladay, W., *Jeremiah 26–52*, 2 vols. (Hermeneia; Minneapolis, MN: Fortress Press, 1989).

Holland, D., et al. (eds.), *Identity and Agency in Cultural Worlds* (Cambridge, MA: Harvard University Press, 1998).

Holt, E., and Clift, R. (eds.), *Reporting Talk: Reported Speech in Interaction*, SIS 24 (Cambridge University Press, 2007).

Holtz, Traugott, *Die Christologie der Apokalypse des Johannes* (TUGAL, 85; Berlin: Akademie-Verlag, 1971).

Die Offenbarung des Johannes (NTD, 11; Göttingen: Vandenhoeck & Ruprecht, 2008).

Honeyman, A., 'Merismus in Biblical Hebrew', *JBL* 71 (1952), 11–18.

Hoppe, L., *There Shall Be No Poor Among You: Poverty in the Bible* (Nashville, TN: Abingdon Press, 2004).

Horbury, W., 'The Christian Use and the Jewish Origins of the Wisdom of Solomon', in J. Day, et al. (eds.), *Wisdom in Ancient Israel: Essays in Honour of J. A. Emerton* (Cambridge University Press, 1995), pp. 182–96.

Howard-Brook, W., and Gwyer, A. *Unveiling Empire: Reading Revelation Then and Now* (New York: Orbis Books, 1999).

Hultgren, S., *From the Damascus Covenant to the Covenant of the Community* (STDJ, 66; Leiden: Brill, 2007).

Humphrey, E., *The Ladies and the Cities* (JSPSup, 17; Sheffield: Academic Press, 1995).

Hurtado, L., 'Revelation 4–5 in Light of Jewish Apocalyptic Analogies', *JSNT* 25 (1985), 105–24.

Isaac, E., '(Ethiopic Apocalypse of) Enoch', in James H. Charlesworth (ed.), *The Old Testament Pseudepigrapha*, vol. 1, Anchor Bible Reference Library (New York: Doubleday, 1983), pp. 5–90.

Jackson, R., 'Eye Medicine in the Roman Empire', *ANRW* 37.3, Part 2, *Principat*, 33.1 (New York: de Gruyter, 1996), pp. 2228–51.

Janzen, W., *Mourning Cry and Woe Oracle* (BZAW, 125; Berlin: de Gruyter, 197).

Jastrow, M., *A Dictionary of the Targumim, the Talmud Babli and Yerushalmi, and the Midrashic Literature with an Index of Scriptural Quotations* (New York: Pardes Publishing House, 1950).

Jeffries, D., *Wisdom at Qumran: A Form–Critical Analysis of the Admonitions in 4QInstruction* (GDNES, 3; Piscataway, NJ: Gorgias Press, 2002).

Jenni, E., and Westermann, C., *Theological Lexicon of the Old Testament*, 3 vols. (Peabody, MA: Hendrickson, 1997).

Johns, L., 'The Dead Sea Scrolls and the Apocalypse of John', in J. Charlesworth (ed.), *The Bible and the Dead Sea Scrolls* (Waco, TX: Baylor University Press, 2006), vol. III, pp. 255–79.

The Lamb Christology of the Apocalypse of John (WUNT II, 167; Tübingen: Mohr Siebeck, 2003).

Jokiranta, J., '"Sectarianism" of the Qumran "Sect": Sociological Notes', *RevQ* 20 (2001), 223–39.

Jones, A., *The Roman Economy: Studies in Ancient Economy and Administrative History* (Oxford: Basil Blackwell, 1974).

Jones, B., *The Emperor Domitian* (London: Routledge, 1992).

Karrer, M., *Die Johannesoffenbarung als Brief* (FRLANT, 140; Göttingen: Vandenhoeck und Ruprecht, 1986).

Kelly, F., 'Poor and Rich in the Epistle of James', unpublished Ph.D. thesis, Temple University (1972).

Kerkeslager, A., 'Apollo, Greco-Roman Prophecy and the Rider on the White Horse in Rev 6:2', *JBL* 112 (1993), 116–21.

Kiddle, M., *The Revelation of St John* (MNTC; London: Hodder & Stoughton, 1952).

Kirby, J., 'The Rhetorical Situations of Revelation 1–3', *NTS* 34 (1988), 197–207.

Kirschenbaum, A., *Sons, Slaves, and Freedmen in Roman Commerce* (Washington, DC: Catholic University Press, 1987).

Kloppenberg, J., and Wilson, S. (eds.), *Voluntary Associations in the Graeco-Roman World* (London: Routledge, 1996).

Knibb, M., 'The Apocalypse of Weeks and the Epistle of Enoch', in G. Boccaccini (ed.), *Enoch and Qumran Origins: New Light on a Forgotten Connection* (Grand Rapids, MI: Eerdmans, 2005), pp. 213–19.

— *Essays on the Book of Enoch and Other Early Jewish Texts and Traditions* (SVTP, 22; Leiden: Brill, 2009).

— *The Ethiopic Book of Enoch: A New Edition in the Light of the Aramaic Dead Sea Fragments*, 2 vols. (Oxford: Clarendon Press, 1978).

— *The Qumran Community* (CCWJCW, 2; Cambridge University Press, 1987).

Koch, K., *The Rediscovery of Apocalyptic* (Naperville, IL: A. R. Allenson, 1972).

Kolarcik, M., *The Ambiguity of Death in the Book of Wisdom 1–6* (Analecta Biblica, 127; Rome: Editrice Pontificio Istituto Biblico, 1991).

Kosmala, H., 'The Three Nets of Belial', *ASTI* 4 (1965), 91–113.

Köstenberger, A., 'The Use of Scripture in the Pastoral and General Epistles and the Book of Revelation', in S. Porter (ed.), *Hearing the Old Testament in the New Testament* (MNTS; Grand Rapids, MI: Eerdmans, 2006), pp. 230–54.

Kraft, H., *Die Offenbarung des Johannes* (HNT, 16a; Tübingen: J. C. B. Mohr, 1974).

Kraybill, J., *Imperial Cult and Commerce in John's Apocalypse* (JSNTSup, 132; Sheffield: Academic Press, 1996).

Krüger, U., *Der Jakobusbrief als prophetische Kritik der Reichen* (BVB, 12; Münster: Lit, 2005).

Kuhn, H., *Enderwartung und gegenwärtiges Heil* (SUNT, 4; Göttingen: Vandenhoeck & Ruprecht, 1966).

Ladd, G., *A Commentary on the Revelation of John* (Grand Rapids, MI: Eerdmans, 1972).

Lambronac'i, N., *Commentary on Wisdom of Solomon* (New York: Skewra Press, 2007).

Lanchester, H., 'The Sibylline Oracles', in R. Charles (ed.), *The Apocrypha and Pseudepigrapha of the Old Testament in English* (Oxford: Clarendon Press, 1965), vol. II, pp. 368–406.

Lange, A., 'In Diskussion mit dem Tempel: zur Auseinandersetzung zwischen Kohelet und weisheitlichen Kreisen am Jerusalemer Tempel', in A. Schoors (ed.), *Qohelet in the Context of Wisdom* (BETL, 136; Leuven University Press, 1998), pp. 113–59.

— *Weisheit und Prädestination* (STDJ, 18; Leiden: Brill, 1995).

— 'Widsom and Predestination in the Dead Sea Scrolls', *DSD* 2 (1995), 340–54.

Larson, M., *The Functions of Reported Speech in Discourse* (SILPL, 59; Dallas: SIL, 1978).

Lawrence, D., *Apocalypse* (London: Martin Secker, 1932).

Laws, S., *In the Light of the Lamb: Imagery, Parody, and Theology in the Apocalypse of John* (Wilmington, NC: M. Glazier, 1988).

Leaney, A., *The Rule of Qumran and its Meaning* (Philadelphia, PA: Westminster Press, 1966).

Lenski, R., *The Interpretation of St John's Revelation* (Columbus, OH: Lutheran Book Concern, 1935).

Licht, J., 'An Analysis of the Treatise on the Two Spirits in DSD', *ScripHier* 4 (1958), 88–100.

Lightfoot, J., *The Sibylline Oracles* (Oxford University Press, 2007).

Lim, T., 'The Wicked Priests of the Groningen Hypothesis', *JBL* 112 (1993), 415–25.

Lohmeyer, E., *Die Offenbarung des Johannes* (HNT, 16; Tübingen: J. C. B. Mohr, 1970).

Lohse, E., *Die Offenbarung des Johannes* (NTD, 11; Gottingen: Vandenhoeck & Ruprecht, 1966).

Lücke, F., *Versuch einer vollständigen Einleitung in die Offenbarung des Johannes oder allgemeine Untersuchung über die apokalyptische Litteratur überhaupt und die Apokalypse des Johannes insbesondere* (Bonn: E. Weber, 1848).

Lust, J., et al. (eds.), *A Greek–English Lexicon of the Septuagint* (Stuttgart: Deutsche Bibelgesellschaft, 2003).

Macaskill, G., *Revealed Wisdom and Inaugurated Eschatology in Ancient Judaism and Early Christianity* (JSJSup, 15; Leiden: Brill, 2007).

McKane, W., *Jeremiah*, 2 vols. (ICC; Edinburgh: T & T Clark, 1996).

MacMullen, R., *Roman Social Relations: 50 BC to AD 284* (New Haven, CT: Yale University Press, 1974).

McNamara, M., *Targum Neofiti 1: Deuteronomy* (TAB, 5a; Collegeville, PA: Liturgical Press, 1997).

Maier, G., *Reich und Arm: der Beitrag des Jakobusbriefes* (Giessen: Brunnen, 1980).

Maier, H., *Apocalypse Recalled: The Book of Revelation after Christendom* (Minneapolis, MN: Fortress Press, 2002).

Malherbe, A., *Social Aspects of Early Christianity*, 2nd edn (Philadelphia, PA: Fortress Press, 1983).

Malina, B., 'Limited Good and the Social World of Early Christianity', *BTB* 8 (1978), 162–76.

   The New Testament World: Insights from Cultural Anthropology, rev. edn (Louisville, KY: John Knox Press, 1993).

Malina, B., and Neyrey, J. , 'Conflict in Luke-Acts: Labelling and Deviance Theory', in J. Neyrey (ed.), *The Social World of Luke-Acts: Models for Interpretation* (Peabody, MA: Hendrickson, 1991), pp. 97–122.

Manson, T., *The Sayings of Jesus: As Recorded in the Gospels According to St Matthew and St Luke* (London: SCM Press, 1949).

Marshall, I., *The Gospel of Luke* (NIGTC, 3; Grand Rapids, MI: Eerdmans, 1978).

Martínez, F., 'Judas Macabeo Sacerdote Impío? Notas al margen de 1QpHab viii, 8–13', in A. Caquot, et al. (eds.), *Mélanges bibliques et orienteaux en l'honneur de M. Mathias Delcor* (Kevelaer: Verlag Butzon & Bercker, 1985), pp. 169–81.

Martone, C., 'Evil or Devil? Belial between the Bible and Qumran', *Henoch* 26 (2004), 115–27.

Maynard-Reid, P., *Poverty and Wealth in James* (Maryknoll, NY: Orbis Books, 1987).

Mazzaferri, F., *The Genre of the Book of Revelation from a Source-Critical Perspective* (*BZNW*, 54; Berlin: de Gruyter, 1989).

Mealand, D., *Poverty and Expectation in the Gospels* (London: SPCK, 1980).

Meeks, W., *The First Urban Christians: The Social World of the Apostle Paul*, 2nd edn (New Haven, CT: Yale University Press, 2003).

Meggitt, J., 'Meat Consumption and Social Conflict in Corinth', *JTS* 45 (1994), 137–41.

Meijer, F., and van Nijf, O., *Trade, Transport and Society in the Ancient World* (London: Routledge, 1992).

Metso, S., 'Constitutional Rules at Qumran', in P. Flint and J. Vanderkam (eds.), *The Dead Sea Scrolls after Fifty Years* (Leiden: Brill, 1999), pp. 186–210.

　The Serekh Texts (LSTS, 62; London: T & T Clark, 2007).

　'Shifts in Covenantal Discourse in Second Temple Judaism', in A. Voitila and J. Jokiranta (eds.), *Scripture in Transition* (JSJSup,126; Leiden: Brill, 2008), pp. 497–512.

　The Textual Development of the Qumran Community Rule (STDJ, 21; Leiden: Brill, 1997).

Metzger, J., *Consumption and Wealth in Luke's Travel Narrative* (Leiden: Brill, 2007).

Meyers, C., and Meyers, E., *Haggai, Zechariah 1–8* (Anchor Bible, 25b; New York: Doubleday, 1987).

　Zechariah 9–14 (Anchor Bible, 25c; New York: Doubleday, 1993).

Milik, J., *The Books of Enoch: Aramaic fragments of Qumrân Cave 4* (Oxford University Press, 1976).

　'Milkî-sedeq et Milkî-resa dans les anciens écrits juifs et chrétiens', *JJS* 22 (1972), 95–144.

　Ten Years of Discovery in the Wilderness of Judea (SBT, 26; London: SCM, 1959).

Minear, P., 'The Cosmology of the Apocalypse', in W. Klassen and G. Snyder (eds.), *Current Issues in New Testament Interpretation* (New York: Harper and Brothers, 1962), pp. 23–37.

Moffat, J., 'Hurt Not the Oil and the Wine', *Exp* 6 (1908), 359–69.

Montgomery, J. A., *Critical and Exegetical Commentary on the Book of Daniel* (ICC; Edinburgh: T & T Clark, 1959).

Morgan, R., and Barton, J., *Biblical Interpretation* (Oxford University Press, 1988).

Mott, S., 'The Power of Giving and Receiving: Reciprocity in Hellenistic Benevolence', in G. Hawthorne (ed.), *Current Issues in Biblical and Patristic Interpretation* (Grand Rapids, MI: Eerdmans, 1975), pp. 60–72.

Mounce, R., *The Book of Revelation* (NICNT; Grand Rapids, MI: Eerdmans, 1977).

Moyise, S., *The Old Testament in the Book of Revelation* (JSNTSup, 115; Sheffield Academic Press, 1995).

Müller, U., *Messias und Menschensohn in jüdischen Apokalypsen und in der Offenbarung des Johannes* (Gütersloh: Gütersloher Verlagshaus Gerd Mohn, 1972).

　Die Offenbarung des Johannes (OTNT, 19; Würzburg: Echter Verlag, 1984).

　Prophetie und Predigt im Neuen Testament (SNT, 10; Gütersloh: Gütersloher Verlagshaus Gerd Mohn, 1975).

Muraoka, T., *A Greek–English Lexicon of the Septuagint* (Louvain: Peeters, 2009).

Murphy, C., *Wealth in the Dead Sea Scrolls and in the Qumran Community* (STDJ, 40; Leiden: Brill, 2002).

Murphy-O'Conner, J., 'La Genèse littéraire de la règle de la communauté', *RB* 76 (1969), 528–49.

Neusner, J., *Ancient Judaism: Debates and Disputes* (BJS, 64; Chico, CA: Scholars Press, 1984).

Rabbinic Judaism: Structure and System (Minneapolis, MN: Fortress Press, 1995).

Newsom, C., 'The Development of 1 Enoch 6–19', *CBQ* 42 (1980), 310–29.

'"Sectually Explicit" Literature from Qumran', in W. Propp, et al. (eds.), *The Hebrew Bible and its Interpreters* (BJSUCSD, 1; Winona Lake, IN: Eisenbrauns, 1990), pp. 167–87.

The Self as Symbolic Space (STDJ, 52; Leiden: Brill, 2004).

Nickelsburg, G., 'Apocalyptic and Myth in 1 Enoch 6–11', *JBL* 96 (1977), 383–405.

A Commentary on the Book of 1 Enoch: Chapters 1–36; 81–108 (Hermeneia; Minneapolis, MN: Fortress Press, 2001).

Jewish Literature between the Bible and the Mishnah, 2nd edn (Minneapolis, MN: Fortress Press, 2005).

'Revisiting the Rich and the Poor in 1 Enoch 92–105 and the Gospel According to Luke', in *1998 Seminar Papers* (SBLSP, 37; Atlanta, GA: Scholars Press, 1998), pp. 579–605.

'Riches, the Rich, and God's Judgment in 1 Enoch 92–105 and the Gospel According to Luke', in J. Neusner and A. Avery-Peck (eds.), *George W. E. Nickelsburg in Perspective*, 2 vols. (JSJSup, 80; Leiden: Brill, 2003), pp. 521–46.

'Torah and the Deuteronomic Scheme in the Apocrypha and Pseudepigrapha: Variations on a Theme and Some Noteworthy Examples of its Absence', in D. Sänger and M. Konradt (eds.), *Das Gesetz im frühen Judentum und im Neuen Testament* (NTOA, 57; Göttingen: Vandenhoeck & Ruprecht, 2006), pp. 222–35.

Nikiprowetzky, V., *La Troisiéme Sibylle* (EJ, 9; Paris: Mouton, 1970).

Nilsson, M., *Geschichte der griechischen Religion* (HA, 2; Munich: Beck, 1950).

Nitzan, B., 'Benedictions and Instructions for the Eschatological Community (*11QBer; 4Q285*)', *RevQ* 16 (1993), 77–90.

Nwachukwu, O., *Beyond Vengeance and Protest: A Reflection on the Macarisms in Revelation* (Berlin: Peter Lang, 2005).

Olson, D., *Enoch: A New Translation* (North Richland Hills, TX: BIBAL Press, 2004).

'Recovering the Original Sequence of 1 Enoch 91–93', *JSP* 11 (1993), 69–91.

'Those Who Have Not Defiled Themselves with Women: Revelation 14:4 and the Book of Enoch', *CBQ* 59 (1997), 492–510.

Osborne, G., *Revelation* (BECNT; Grand Rapids, MI: Baker Academic, 2002).

Oswalt, J., *Book of Isaiah 1–39* (NICOT; Grand Rapids, MI: Eerdmans, 1966).

Park, H., *Finding Herem? A Study of Luke-Acts in Light of Herem* (LNTS, 357; London: T & T Clark, 2007).

Parke, H., *Sibyls and Sibylline Prophecy in Classical Antiquity* (CHCS; London: Routledge, 1988).

Parry, D., and Tov, E. (eds.), *The Dead Sea Scrolls Reader*, 6 vols. (Leiden: Brill, 2005).

Parry, J., and Bloch, M. (eds.), *Money and the Morality of Exchange* (Cambridge University Press, 1993).

Pass, H., and Arendzen, J., 'Fragment of an Aramaic Text of the Testament of Levi', *JQR* 12 (1900), 651–61.

Perdue, L. (ed.), *Scribes, Sages, and Seers* (FRLANT, 219; Göttingen: Vandenhoeck & Ruprecht, 2008).

Perry, J., *The Roman Collegia: The Modern Evolution of an Ancient Concept* (MSupHACA, 277; Leiden: Brill, 2006).

Perry, P., 'Critiquing the Excess of Empire: A *Synkrisis* of John of Patmos and Dio of Prusa', *JSNT* 29 (2007), 473–96.

Phillips, T., *Reading Issues of Wealth and Poverty in Luke-Acts* (Lewiston, ME: Edwin Mellen Press, 2001).

Pietersen, L., 'Despicable Deviants: Labelling Theory and the Polemic of the 'Pastorals'', *SocRel* 58 (1997), 343–52.

Pilgrim, W., *Good News to the Poor: Wealth and Poverty in Luke-Acts* (Minneapolis, MN: Augsburg Publishing House, 1981).

Pleins, J., 'Poverty in the Social World of the Wise', *JSOT* 37 (1987), 61–78.

Porten, B., and Yardeni, A. (trans.), *Textbook of Aramaic Documents from Ancient Egypt* (Winona Lake, IN: Eisenbrauns, 1986).

Porter, J., 'Intertextuality and the Discourse Community', *RhetRev* 5 (1986), 34–47.

Porter, P., *Metaphors and Monsters* (CBOTS, 20; Lund: CWK Gleerup, 1983).

Poulain, F., *Jésus et la richesse d'après Saint-Luc: étude exégétique* (Paris: Fischbacher, 1903).

Price, S., *Rituals and Power: The Roman Imperial Cult in Asia Minor* (Cambridge University Press, 1985).

Prigent, P., *Commentary on the Apocalypse of St John* (Tubingen: Mohr Siebeck, 2004).

Provan, I., 'Foul Spirits Fornication and Finance: Revelation 18 from an Old Testament Perspective', *JSNT* 64 (1996), 81–100.

Puech, É., 'The Book of Wisdom and the Dead Sea Scrolls: An Overview', in F. Reiterer and G. Bellia (eds.), *The Book of Wisdom in Modern Research* (DCLY; Berlin: de Gruyter, 2005), pp. 117–42.

   La croyance des Esséniens en la vie future: immortalité, résurrection, vie éternelle? (EB, 22; Paris: J. Gabalda, 1993).

Rabin, C., *The Zadokite Documents* (Oxford University Press, 1958).

Rae, J., and Kirby, J., 'Designing Contexts for Reporting Tactical Speech', in E. Holt and R. Clift (eds.), *Reporting Talk: Reported Speech in Interaction* (SIS, 24; Cambridge University Press, 2007), pp. 179–94.

Räisänen, H., 'The Nicolaitans: Apoc. 2; Acta 6', *ANRW* 26.2, Part 2. *Principat*, 26.2 (New York: de Gruyter, 1995), pp. 1602–44.

Ramsay, W., *The Letters to the Seven Churches of Asia and their Place in the Plan of the Apocalypse* (Grand Rapids, MI: Baker Book House, 1963).

Reed, A., 'Heavenly Ascent, Angelic Descent, and the Transmission of Knowledge in 1 Enoch 6–16', in R. Boustan and A. Reed (eds.), *Heavenly Realms and Earthly Realities in Late Antique Religion* (Cambridge University Press, 2004), pp. 47–66.

Regev, E., *Sectarianism in Qumran: A Cross-Cultural Perspective* (RS, 45; Berlin: de Gruyter, 2007).

'Wealth and Sectarianism: Comparing Qumranic and Early Christian Social Approaches', in F. Martínez (ed.), *Echoes from the Caves: Qumran and the New Testament* (STDJ, 85; Leiden: Brill, 2009), pp. 211–29.

Rey, J., *4QInstruction: sagesse et eschatology* (STDJ, 81; Leiden: Brill, 2009).

Rissi, M., 'Rider on the White Horse', *Int* 18 (1964), 407–18.

Zeit und Geschichte in der Offenbarung des Johannesapokalypse (ATANT, 46; Zurich: Zwingli, 1965).

Roloff, J., *The Revelation of John* (Minneapolis, MN: Fortress Press, 1993).

Rostovtzeff, M., *The Social and Economic History of the Roman Empire* (Oxford: Clarendon Press, 1926).

Rowland, C., *The Open Heaven* (New York: Crossroad, 1982).

Revelation (Epworth Commentaries; London: Epworth Press, 1993).

Royalty Jr, R., *The Streets of Heaven* (Macon, GA: Mercer University Press, 1998).

Ruiz, J.-P., *Ezekiel in the Apocalypse* (EUS, 376; Frankfurt: Peter Lang, 1989).

Saffrey, H., 'Relire L'Apocalypse à Patmos', *RevBib* 82 (1975), 385–417.

Sanders, E., *Paul and Palestinian Judaism* (Philadelphia, PA: Fortress Press, 1977).

Sarason, R. S., 'Response', in P. J. D. Cohen and E. L. Greenstein, (eds.), *The State of Jewish Studies* (Detroit, Mich.: Wayne State University Press, 1990). pp. 74–9.

Schechter, S., *Documents of Jewish Sectaries* (Cambridge University Press, 1970).

Schechter, S., and Taylor, C., *Facsimiles of the Fragments Hitherto Recovered of the Book of Ecclesiasticus in Hebrew* (London: 1901).

Schiffman, L., *The Eschatological Community of the Dead Sea Scrolls* (SBLMS, 38; Atlanta, GA: Scholars Press, 1989).

The Halakhah at Qumran (Leiden: E. J. Brill, 1975).

'Jewish Sectarianism in the Second Temple Period', in R. Jospe and S. Wagner (eds.), *Great Schisms in Jewish History* (New York: Ktav, 1981), pp. 1–46.

'Legislation Concerning Relations with Non-Jews in the *Zadokite Fragments* and in Tannaitic Literature', *RevQ* 11 (1984), 379–89.

Sectarian Law in the Dead Sea Scrolls (BJS, 33; Chico, CA: Scholars Press, 1983).

Understanding Second Temple Judaism and Rabbinic Judaism (New York: Ktav, 2003).

Schiffman, L., and Vanderkam, J. (eds.), *Encyclopedia of the Dead Sea Scrolls*, 2 vols. (Oxford University Press, 2000).

Schmidt, T., *Hostility to Wealth in the Synoptic Gospels* (JSNTSup, 15; Sheffield: JSOT Press, 1987).

Schneemelcher, W. (ed.), *New Testament Apocrypha II* rev. edn. (Westminster: John Knox Press, 1992).

Schofield, A., *From Qumran to the Yahad* (STDJ, 77; Leiden: Brill, 2009).

Schürer, E., *The History of the Jewish People in the Age of Jesus Christ (175 BC–AD 135)* (Edinburgh: T & T Clark, 1986).

Schuller, E., 'Hodayot', in E. G. Chazon, et al. (eds.), *QumranCave 4.XX. Poetical and Liturgical Texts, Part 2* (DJD XXIX; Oxford: Clarendon Press, 1999).

Schultz, B., *Conquering the World: The War Scroll (1QM) Reconsidered* (STDJ, 76; Leiden: Brill, 2009).

Schur, E., *The Politics of Deviance: Stigma Contests and the Uses of Power* (Edgewood Cliffs, NJ: Prentice Hall, 1980).

Scoggins, R., *Sirach* (GAP; Sheffield: Academic Press, 1998).

Segal, A., 'Heavenly Ascent in Hellenistic Judaism, Early Christianity and their Environment', *ANRW* 23.2, Part 2, *Principat*, 23.2 (New York: de Gruyter, 1980), pp. 1333–94.

Skehan, P., and Di Lella, A., *The Wisdom of Ben Sira* (Anchor Bible, 39; New York: Doubleday, 1987).

Smalley, S., *The Revelation to John* (Downers Grove, IL: Intervarsity Press, 2005).

Smith, M., 'The Dead Sea Sect in Relation to Ancient Judaism', *NTS* 7 (1961), 347–60.

Smith, R. L., *Micah–Malachi* (WBC, 32; Waco, TX: Word Books, 1984).

Southern, P., *Domitian: Tragic Tyrant* (London: Routledge, 1997).

Speiser, E., 'The Hebrew Origin of the First Part of the Book of Wisdom', *JQR* 14 (1923–4), 455–82.

Spitta, F., *Die Offenbarung des Johannes* (Halle: Waisenhaus, 1889).

Stanford, T., 'Their Eyes They Have Closed? A Literary and Social-Historical Study of the Representation in Luke-Acts of High and Low Status, Wealth and Destitution', unpublished Ph.D. thesis, University of Newcastle (2004).

Stegemann, H., 'Die Bedeutung der Qumranfunde für die Erforschung der Apoka-lyptik', in D. Hellholm (ed.), *Apocalypticism in the Mediterranean World and the Near East* (Tübingen: J. C. B. Mohr, 1983), pp. 495–530.

  The Library of Qumran: On the Essenes, Qumran, John the Baptist, and Jesus (Grand Rapids, MI: Eerdmans, 1998).

Stegemann, H., and Schuller, E., *1QHodayot^a with Incorporation of 1QHodayot^b and 4QHodayot^{a-f}* (DJD XL; Oxford University Press, 2009).

Steudel, A., 'God and Belial', in L. Schiffman, et al. (eds.), *The Dead Sea Scrolls: Fifty Years after their Discovery* (Jerusalem: Israel Exploration Society, in collaboration with the Shrine of the Book, Israel Museum, 2000), pp. 332–40.

Stevenson, G., 'Conceptual Background to Golden Crown Imagery in the Apoc-alypse of John', *JBL* 114 (1995), 257–72.

Stone, M., 'Apocalyptic Literature', in M. Stone (ed.), *Jewish Writings of the Second Temple Period* (CRINT, 2; Philadelphia, PA: Fortress Press, 1984), pp. 383–441.

  'The Book of Enoch and Judaism in the Third Century BCE', *CBQ* 40 (1978), 479–92.

Stone, M., and Greenfield, J., 'The Fifth and Sixth Manuscript of *Aramaic Levi Document* from Cave 4 at Qumran (4QLevie aram and 4QLevif aram)', *Le Muséon* 110 (1997), 271–92.

  'The First Manuscript of *Aramaic Levi Document* from Cave 4 at Qumran (4QLevia aram)', *Le Muséon* 107 (1994), 257–81.

'The Second Manuscript of *Aramaic Levi Document* from Cave 4 at Qumran (4QLevib aram)', *Le Muséon* 109 (1996), 1–15.

'The Third and Fourth Manuscript of *Aramaic Levi Document* from Cave 4 at Qumran (4QLevic aram and 4QLevid aram)', *Le Muséon* 109 (1996), 245–59.

Strugnell, J., 'The Sapiential Work 4Q415 ff. and Pre-Qumranic Works from Qumran: Lexical Considerations', in D. Parry and E. Ulrich (eds.), *The Provo International Conference on the Dead Sea Scrolls* (STDJ, 30; Leiden: Brill, 1999), pp. 595–608.

Strugnell, J., et al. (eds.), *Qumran Cave 4 XXXIV: Sapiential Texts, Part 2: 4QInstruction (Mûsar le Mevîn): 4Q415 ff* (DJD, 34; Oxford: Clarendon Press, 1999).

Stuckenbruck, L., *1 Enoch 91–108* (CEJL; Berlin: de Gruyter, 2007).

Angel Veneration and Christology (WUNT II, 70; Tübingen: J. C. B. Mohr, 1995).

'"Angels" and "God": Exploring the Limits of Early Jewish Monotheism', in L. Stuckenbruck and W. North (eds.), *Exploring Early Jewish and Christian Monotheism* (London: T & T Clark, 2004), pp. 45–70.

The Book of Giants from Qumran (TSAJ, 63; Tübingen: Mohr Siebeck, 1997).

'The Formation and Re-Formation of Daniel in the Dead Sea Scrolls', in J. Charlesworth (ed.), *The Bible and the Dead Sea Scrolls: Scripture and the Scrolls* (SPSJCO, 1; Waco, TX: Baylor University Press, 2006), pp. 101–30.

'Temporal Shifts from Text to Interpretation: Concerning the Use of the Perfect and Imperfect in the *Habakkuk Pesher* (1QpHab)', in M. Davis and B. Strawn (eds.), *Qumran Studies: New Approaches, New Questions* (Grand Rapids, MI: Eerdmans, 2007), pp. 124–49.

'Wisdom and Holiness at Qumran: Strategies for Dealing with Sin in the *Community Rule*', in S. Barton (ed.), *Where Shall Wisdom be Found?* (Edinburgh: T & T Clark, 1999), pp. 47–60.

Suter, D., *Tradition and Composition in the Parables of Enoch* (SBLDS, 47; Missoula, MT: Scholars Press, 1979).

Swete, H., *The Apocalypse of St John* (London: Macmillan, 1911).

Takatemjen, A., *The Banquet is Ready: Rich and Poor in the Parables of Luke* (Delhi: ISPCK, 2003).

Talmon, S., *The Book of Ben Sira: Text, Concordance and an Analysis of the Vocabulary* (Jerusalem: The Academy of Hebrew Language and the Shrine of the Book, 1973).

The Internal Diversification of Judaism in the Second Temple Period', in S. Talmon (ed.), *Jewish Civilization in the Hellenistic-Roman Period* (Sheffield: JSOT Press, 1991), pp. 16–43.

Jewish Civilization in the Hellenistic-Roman Period (JSPSup, 10; Sheffield: JSOT Press, 1991).

Theissen, G., *The Social Setting of Pauline Christianity* (Philadelphia, PA: Fortress Press, 1982).

Thompson, J. A., 'Eye Paint', in George A. Buttrick (ed.), *Interpreter's Dictionary of the Bible*, vol. 2 (New York: Abingdon Press, 1961), pp. 202–3.

Thompson, L., *The Book of Revelation: Apocalypse and Empire* (Oxford University Press, 1990).

Tigchelaar, E., 'The Addressees of 4QInstruction', in D. Falk, et al. (eds.), *Sapiential, Liturgical and Poetical Texts from Qumran* (STDJ, 35; Leiden: Brill, 2000), pp. 62–75.

'Spiritual People', 'Fleshly Spirit' and 'Vision of Meditation': Reflections on 4QInstruction and 1 Corinthians', in F. Martínez (ed.), *Echoes from the Caves: Qumran and the New Testament* (STDJ, 44; Leiden: Brill, 2009), pp. 103–18.

'"These are the Names of the Spirits of . . .": A Preliminary Edition of *4QCatalogue of Spirits (4Q230)* and New Manuscript Evidence for the *Two Spirits Treatise (4Q257 and 1Q29a)*', *RevQ* 21 (2004), 531–47.

To Increase Learning for the Understanding Ones (STDJ, 44; Leiden: Brill, 2001).

Trever, J., *Scrolls from Qumran Cave I: The Great Isaiah Scroll, The Order of the Community, The Pesher to Habakkuk* (Jerusalem: The Albright Institute of Archeological Research and the Shrine of the Book, 1972).

Trudinger, L., 'Some Observations Concerning the Text of the Old Testament in the Book of Revelation', *JTS* (1966), 82–8.

Tucker, G., *Form Criticism of the Old Testament* (GBSOTS; Philadelphia, PA: Fortress Press, 1976).

Ulrich, J., 'Euseb, *HistEccl* III, 14–20 und die Frage nach der Christienverfolgung unter Domitian', *ZNW* 87 (1996), 269–89.

van der Waal, C., *Openbaring van Jezus Christus: Inleiding en Vertaling* (Groningen: De Vuurbaak, 1971).

van der Woude, A., 'Wicked Priest or Wicked Priests? Reflections on the Identification of the Wicked Priest in the Habakkuk Commentary', *JJS* 33 (1982), 349–59.

van Unnik, W., 'A Formula Describing Prophecy', *NTS* 9 (1962–3), 85–94.

Vanderkam, J., *Enoch and the Growth of an Apocalyptic Tradition* (CBQMS, 16; Washington, DC: Catholic Biblical Association of America, 1984).

Textual and Historical Studies in the Book of Jubilees (HSM, 41; Missoula, MT: Scholars Press, 1977).

Vanhoye, A., 'L'Utilisation du livre d'Ézéchiel dans l'Apocalypse', *Biblica* 43 (1962), 436–76.

Vanni, U., 'Il terzo "sigillo" dell'Apocalisse (Rev 6:5–6): simbolo dell'ingiustizia sociale?', *Gregorianum* 59 (1978), 691–719.

Vermès, G., *The Dead Sea Scrolls: Qumran in Perspective*, rev. edn (London: SCM Press, 1994).

Scripture and Tradition in Judaism: Haggadic Studies (SPB, 4; Leiden: Brill, 1961).

Verner, D., *The Household of God: The Social World of the Pastoral Epistles* (SBLDS, 71; Chico, CA: Scholars Press, 1983).

von der Osten-Sacken, P., *Gott und Belial* (SUNT, 6; Göttingen: Vandenhoeck and Ruprecht, 1969).

von Focke, F., *Die entstehung der Weisheit Salomos* (Göttingen: Vandenhoeck & Ruprecht, 1913).

von Schlatter, A., *Das alte Testament in der johanneischen Apokalypse* (BFCT, 16.6; Gütersloh: Bertelsmann, 1912).

von Siegfried, W. (ed.), *Bibel und Qumran* (Berlin: Evangelische Haupt- Bibelgesellschaft, 1968).

Wacholder, B., *The Dawn of Qumran: The Sectarian Torah and the Teacher of Righteousness* (MHUC, 8; Cincinnati, OH: Hebrew Union College Press, 1983).

Ward, G., *Christ and Culture* (Oxford: Blackwell Publishing, 2005).

Wassen, C., and Jokiranta, J., 'Groups in Tension: Sectarianism in the Rule of the Community and the Damascus Document', in David Chalcraft (ed.), *Sectarianism in Early Judaism: Sociological Advances* (London: Equinox, 2007), pp. 206–45.

Weinfeld, M., *Deuteronomy and the Deuteronomic School* (Oxford: Clarendon Press, 1972).

Weiss, J., *Die Offenbarung des Johannes* (Göttingen: Vandenhoeck & Ruprecht, 1904).

Westermann, C., *Basic Forms of Prophetic Speech* (Louisville, KY: John Knox Press, 1991).

Whealen, J., 'New Patches on an Old Garment: The Book of Revelation', *BTB* 11 (1981), 54–9.

Whedbee, J., *Isaiah and Wisdom* (Nashville, TN: Abingdon Press, 1971).

Wheeler, S., *Wealth as Peril and Obligation: The New Testament on Possessions* (Grand Rapids, MI: Eerdmans, 1995).

Whitney, K., *Two Strange Beasts: Leviathan and Behemoth in Second Temple and Early Rabbinic Judaism* (HSM, 63; Winona Lake, IN: Eisenbrauns, 2006).

Whybray, R., *The Book of Proverbs* (CBCOT; Cambridge University Press, 1972).

Wiersbicka, A., 'The Semantics of Direct and Indirect Discourse', *Papers in Linguistics* 7 (1974), 273–87.

Wikenhauser, A., *Introduction to the New Testament* (New York: Herder and Herder, 1963).

Wilken, R., *The Christians as the Romans Saw Them* (New Haven, CT: Yale University Press, 1984).

Williams, D., 'The Date of Ecclesiasticus', *VTest* 44 (1994), pp. 563–6.

Willis, W., *Idol Meat in Corinth* (SBLDS, 68; Chico, CA: Scholars Press, 1985).

Wilson, J., 'The Problem of the Domitianic Date of Revelation', *NTS* 39 (1993), pp. 587–95.

Winston, D., 'A Century of Research on the Book of Wisdom', in F. Reiterer and G. Bellia (eds.), *The Book of Wisdom in Modern Research* (DCLY; Berlin: de Gruyter, 2005), pp. 1–18.

The Wisdom of Solomon (Anchor Bible, 43; Garden City, NY: Doubleday, 1979).

Wise, M., Abegg, M., and Cook, E., *The Dead Sea Scrolls: A New Translation*, rev. edn (San Francisco: Harper, 2005).

Witherington III, B., 'Not so Idol Thoughts about εἰδωλόθυτος', *TynBul* 44 (1993), 237–54.

Revelation (Cambridge University Press, 2003).

Wold, B., 'Metaphorical Poverty in *Mûsār lĕ Mēvîn*', *JJS* 58 (2007), 140–53.

Women, Men and Angels (*WUNT* II, 201; Tübingen: Mohr Siebeck, 2005).

Wright III, B., 'The Discourses of Riches and Poverty in the Book of Ben Sira', in *1998 Seminar Papers* (Atlanta, GA: Scholars Press, 1998), pp. 559–78.

No Small Difference: Sirach's Relationship to its Hebrew Parent Text (SBLSCSS, 26; Atlanta, GA: Scholars Press, 1989).

Praise Israel for Wisdom and Instruction (JSJSup, 131; Leiden: Brill, 2008).

Wright III, B., and Camp, C., 'Who Has Been Tested by Gold and Found Perfect? Ben Sira's Discourse of Riches and Poverty', *Henoch* 23 (2001), 153–74.

Yadin, Y., *The Ben Sira Scroll from Masada* (Jerusalem: Israel Exploration Society, 1965).

The Scroll of the War of the Sons of Light against the Sons of Darkness (Oxford University Press, 1962).

Yarbro Collins, A., *The Apocalypse* (NTM, 22; Wilmington, NC: Michael Glazier, 1979).

The Combat Myth in the Book of Revelation (Missoula, MT: Scholars Press, 1976).

Crisis and Catharsis: The Power of the Apocalypse (Philadelphia, PA: Westminster Press, 1984).

'Insiders and Outsiders in the Book of Revelation', in J. Neusner, et al. (eds.), *To See Ourselves as Others See Us: Christians, Jews, 'Others' in Late Antiquity* (SPSHS, 9; Chico, CA: Scholars Press), pp. 187–218.

'Persecution and Vengeance in the Book of Revelation', in D. Hellholm (ed.), *Apocalypticism in the Mediterranean World and the Near East* (Tübingen: J. C. B. Mohr, 1983), pp. 729–49.

'The Political Perspective to the Revelation of John', *JBL* 96 (1977), 241–56.

'Revelation 18: Taunt Song or Dirge?' in J. Lambrecht (ed.), *L'Apocalypse johannique et l'Apocalyptique dans le Nouveau Testament* (BETL, 53; Leuven University Press, 1980), pp. 185–204.

'Review of *The Use of Daniel in Jewish Apocalyptic Literature and the Revelation of St John*, by G. K. Beale', *JBL* 105 (1986), 734–5.

'Women's History and the Book of Revelation' in K. Richards (ed.), *1987 Seminar Papers* (SBLSPS, 26; Atlanta, GA: Scholars Press, 1987), pp. 80–91.

Yoshiko Reed, A., *Fallen Angels and the History of Judaism and Christianity: The Reception of Enochic Literature* (Cambridge University Press, 2005).

Zahn, T., *Die Offenbarung des Johannes*, 2 vols. (Leipzig: A. Deichert, 1924–6).

Zimmerli, W., *Ezekiel II: A Commentary on the Book of the Prophet Ezekiel Chapters 25–48* (Hermeneia; Minneapolis, MN: Fortress Press, 1983).

Zsengellér, J., 'Does Wisdom Come from the Temple?', in G. Xeravits and J. Zsengellér (eds.), *Studies in the Book of Ben Sira* (JSJSup, 127; Leiden: Brill, 2008), pp. 135–49.

INDEX OF PASSAGES

Genesis
  5:22, 132
  5:24, 132
  14:21–4, 106
  23:6–16, 106
  23:16, 89, 206
  27:40, 181
  34:10, 89
  34:21, 89
  37:18, 89
  37:28, 206
  42:34, 89

Exodus
  3:7, 64
  15:11, 194
  30:15, 65
  41:31, 64

Leviticus
  13:37, 179
  14:21, 65
  19:9–10, 135
  19:19, 88
  19:35, 135
  19:35–6, 180
  19:35–7, 74
  22:10–16, 106
  22:16, 106
  23:22, 135
  26:22–6, 176
  26:26, 180
  27:28, 95
  27:28–9, 83
  27:29, 95
  27:33, 83

Numbers
  14:18, 95
  19:2, 181

Deuteronomy
  5:21, 109
  6:5, 84, 102
  7:26, 95
  8:7–10, 54
  8:12–16, 111
  8:16, 36
  8:16–18, 75
  8:17, 56, 157
  8:17–19, 53
  8:18, 73
  10:12, 84
  10:22, 84
  11:13, 84
  11:13–14, 54
  13:17, 95
  15:11, 55, 67
  15:17–18, 69
  15:7–8, 66
  15:7–11, 67
  16:13, 64
  17:14, 129
  17:17, 69
  19:1, 129
  19:14, 135
  21:3, 181
  22:5, 57
  22:9, 88
  24:12–15, 67
  24:19, 135
  25:9, 51
  25:13–16, 74
  25:14, 74
  25:15, 74, 135
  26:1, 129
  26:7, 64
  27:17, 135
  27:19, 95
  27:25, 76
  28:2–14, 54

Deuteronomy (*cont.*)
28:3–11, 36
28:4, 91
28:8, 111
28:12, 48
28:13, 60
28:15–68, 54
28:16, 45
28:25–6, 60
28:27, 91
28:28–9, 164
28:29, 60
28:33, 60
28:35, 91
28:38–42, 60
28:44, 60
28:44–5, 60
28:48, 60, 164
28:51, 60
28:62, 60
28:64–6, 60
28–31, 60
30:16, 91
30:20, 91
31:29, 108
32:23–4, 176, 179
32:24, 85
32:36, 73
32:39, 91
32:5, 108

Joshua
1:8, 87
6:18, 95
7:13, 95

Judges
6:15, 65

Ruth
4:11, 51

1 Samuel
2:35, 51

2 Samuel
7:27, 51

1 Kings
3:5–15, 125
9:27, 205
10:15, 206
10:28, 89, 206
11:38, 51

2 Kings
6:25, 182
7:1, 182
14:26, 64

1 Chronicles
17:10, 51
17:25, 51

2 Chronicles
1:7–12, 125
1:16, 89, 206
9:9–14, 181
9:14, 89
10:4, 181

Job
1:6–7, 191
6:2, 181
8:13–14, 52
10:15, 64
15:31, 52
20:19, 47
22:23, 51
22:23–5, 52
23:10, 165
24:4, 64
24:9, 64
24:14, 64
28:12–19, 44
29:12, 64
30:16, 64
30:27, 64
31:6, 181
31:23–8, 52
34:19, 61
34:28, 64
36:8, 64
36:15, 64
36:21, 64
39:10, 181
40:15–41:34, 192
40:30, 94
41:2–3, 194

Psalms
1:2, 87
2:3, 181
9:21, 64
10:1–4, 123
10:13, 55, 162
12:5, 118
17:14, 47
22:24, 64

34:6, 118
34:10, 194
35:25, 55, 162
37:1, 77
44:13, 84
49:5–6, 77
49:6, 52
52:7, 52
62:10, 47, 52
62:9, 181
70:5, 118
70:19, 194
72:12, 118
73:3, 77
73:3–19, 77
74:21, 118
86:1, 118
106:20, 83, 116
112:5, 194
119:36, 99
127:1, 51

Proverbs
1:5, 43
3:5, 44
3:14, 89
3:27, 72
3:31, 77
3:33, 74
4:5, 43
4:7, 43
6:1–5, 82
8:10–11, 44
10:15, 54, 61
10:22, 54
11:1, 74, 180,
    187
11:4, 124
11:15, 82
11:16, 47
11:28, 52
12:7, 74
13:20, 201
14:1, 51
14:11, 74
14:20, 54, 61
14:24, 54
15:15, 64
15:27, 99
15:32, 43
16:11, 180, 187
16:16, 43, 44
17:3, 165
17:16, 43

17:18, 82
18:11, 61
18:15, 43
18:23, 61
19:8, 43
20:1, 73
20:10, 180, 187
20:15, 44
20:16, 82
20:23, 74, 180,
    187
21:17, 73, 183
22:2, 61
22:4, 54
22:7, 61
22:16, 61
22:22, 64
22:26, 82
23:4–5, 76
23:5, 56
23:20–1, 73
23:23, 43
23:34, 205
24:1, 77
24:3, 51
24:12, 55, 162
24:19, 77
27:13, 82
27:21, 165
28:11, 61
28:16, 47, 99
28:20, 76
28:24, 201
30:14, 64
31:3–5, 73
31:5, 64
31:9, 64
31:14, 89
31:18, 89
31:20, 64
31:24, 94

Qoheleth
2:24, 123
3:13, 123
5:11, 76
5:12, 61
5:18, 123
6:2, 109
7:7, 76
8:15, 123
9:10, 78
10:6, 61
10:20, 61

Canticles
  1:5–6, 179
  5:11, 179

Isaiah
  1:4, 108
  1:23, 76
  3:11, 213
  3:12, 47
  3:14, 64
  3:15, 61
  3:16–24, 46
  5:8, 214
  5:11, 214
  5:18, 181
  5:22, 214
  6:9–10, 164
  9:4, 181
  10:1, 213
  10:2, 47, 61, 64, 95
  10:4, 73
  10:5, 213
  10:12, 68
  10:13, 4
  10:13–23, 198, 207
  10:27, 181
  14:17, 73
  14:25, 181
  20:4, 164
  22:2–3, 89
  22:8, 89, 206
  22:13, 123
  22:15–17, 211
  22:15–18, 213
  22:17, 203
  22:17–18, 204
  22:18, 89, 206
  22:23, 4
  24:17, 97
  29:9–10, 164
  29:15, 55, 162
  32:1–3, 164
  40:12, 181
  40:15, 181
  45:14, 89, 160
  46:3, 164
  46:6, 180, 181
  46:8, 55, 162
  46:15, 89
  46:47, 198
  48:10, 165
  48:20, 199
  52:11, 199

  54:17, 211
  58:9, 99
  66:22, 211

Jeremiah
  2:11, 83, 116
  2:23, 55, 162
  2:34, 61
  2:35, 55
  3:8–9, 47
  5:5, 61, 181
  5:27, 47
  6:13, 99
  9:7, 165
  9:23, 52, 61
  9:23–4, 56
  13:22, 47, 55, 162
  13:27, 47
  14:12, 179
  14:18, 89
  17:11, 47
  18:9, 51
  21:9, 179
  21:13, 55, 162
  22:13, 51, 213
  22:17, 109
  24:10, 179
  25:15–17, 203
  27:8, 179, 181
  27:13, 179
  27:44, 194
  28:14, 181
  29:17–18, 179
  30:8, 181
  30:16, 115
  31:28, 51
  32:10, 180
  32:24, 179
  32:36, 179
  38:2, 179
  42:13–14, 55, 162
  42:17, 179
  42:22, 179
  44:13, 179
  44:46–51, 207
  48:1, 213
  48:7, 52
  49:4, 52
  50:8, 199
  50:29, 210
  50:50–1, 4, 198
  51:6, 199
  51:7, 203, 211

51:13, 47
51:45, 199
51:48, 215

Lamentations
4:13, 61

Ezekiel
1:18, 169
2:8–3:3, 175
4:16, 180
5:16–17, 179
6:11, 179
12:16, 179
13:3, 213
13:18, 213
14:21, 176, 179
16:32, 47
16:36–7, 164
16:49, 61
17:4, 94
18:19, 162
18:25, 55
22:5, 47
22:9, 47
23:12, 89, 206, 212
23:12–24, 204
23:12–34, 203
23:12–36, 75
23:12–38, 206, 211
23:16, 89, 212
23:18, 89, 212
23:21, 89
23:25–31, 207
23:26, 212
23:26–7, 198
23:27, 4, 212
23:28–36, 213
23:29, 164
23:29–31, 212
23:32–6, 212
23:33, 203, 212
23:34, 212
23:36, 89
23:37, 47
23:38, 206
23:40, 46
23:40–2, 46
33:31, 109
34:2, 213
34:27, 181
38:16, 89
39:10, 115

44:29, 95
45:9–10, 180
48:14, 83

Daniel
5:27, 181
7:1–8, 193
7:4–7, 193
7:10, 160
7:18, 136
7:22, 136
7:23, 193
7:27, 136
8:10, 190
10:14, 175
10:21, 175
11:35, 165
11:40–12:3, 111
12:2, 23
12:3, 122
12:4, 159, 175, 181
12:9, 175

Hosea
2:3, 164
3:1, 47
4:7, 83
4:12, 47
4:15, 47
12:7, 74, 94, 162
12:8–9, 56, 180
12:9, 162

Amos
2:6–7, 61
4:1, 47, 61
5:11, 54
5:11–12, 61
5:18, 213
6:1, 213, 214
6:3–6, 214
6:6, 54
7:16, 55, 162
8:4, 61
8:4–6, 74, 180
8:6, 61
9:11, 51

Obadiah
13, 47

Jonah
1:1–16, 206
1:4, 212

Jonah (*cont.*)
  1:5, 58, 205
  1:7–10, 205
  1:14–16, 205

Micah
  6:11, 180
  6:12, 61

Nahum
  3:5, 164
  3:16, 206

Habakkuk
  2:4, 61
  2:5, 113, 114
  2:6, 47, 55
  2:9, 99
  3:14, 61

Zephaniah
  1:9, 47
  1:11, 94
  3:9, 181

Zechariah
  1:8–11, 175
  3:1, 191
  6:1–8, 175
  7:9–10, 61
  11:4–5, 94
  11:5, 162
  11:7, 93
  11:11, 93
  13:7, 93
  13:9, 165

Malachi
  1:4, 55
  2:17, 55
  3:2–3, 165
  3:5, 47
  3:8, 55

Matthew
  3:9, 55
  5:36, 179
  5:44–6, 210
  6:21, 209
  6:24, 224
  8:16, 223
  8:28–32, 223
  12:43, 223
  13:9–13, 196

13:22, 224
13:24–30, 224
18:22–3, 224
21:12, 187
22:21, 217
24:7–12, 159, 181
24:38, 188
25:9, 187

Mark
  4:9–11, 196
  4:19, 224
  11:15, 187
  12:40, 95
  13:19, 159, 181

Luke
  3:8, 55
  3:14, 47
  6:27–35, 210
  8:8–10, 196
  8:29–33, 223
  10:18, 191
  12:16–21, 69
  12:19, 162
  12:21, 224
  16:13, 131, 224
  17:28, 187
  18:11–12, 109, 117
  19:2–8, 147
  20:25, 217
  20:47, 95
  21:23, 159, 181

John
  8:52, 55

Acts
  2:23, 197
  4:34–5:2, 147
  16:14, 17, 147
  16:14–15, 150
  27:18–19, 205
  27:24, 212
  27:38, 205

Romans
  2:2, 55
  12:1–7, 16
  12:13, 217
  12:17–20, 210
  16:1–15, 147
  16:23, 147

1 Corinthians
  5:7, 173
  8:4, 154
  12:1–10, 168
  16:2, 147
  16:19, 147

2 Corinthians
  3:3, 179
  8:9–12, 223
  8:14, 224
  11:12–15, 148

1 Thessalonians
  5:15, 210

1 Timothy
  6:6–10, 156
  6:9–18, 224
  6:17, 17

2 Timothy
  3:1–4, 159

Titus
  1:11, 148
  1:13, 148
  3:11, 148

Philemon
  1–11, 147

James
  2:6, 47
  4:13, 162

1 Peter
  1:6–9, 165
  1:19, 173
  1:20, 197
  2:13–17, 217
  2:17, 16
  3:9, 210
  3:19–20, 223
  5:13, 199

2 Peter
  2:1, 148
  2:4, 223
  2:15, 3, 153
  3:13, 211

1 John
  4:1, 148

2 John
  12, 179

3 John
  13, 179

Jude
  6, 223
  11, 3, 153
  13, 191
  14, 223

Revelation (Apocalypse of John)
  1, 27
  1:1–3, 145
  1:1–6, 145
  1:3, 209
  1:5, 172, 200, 204
  1:7–8, 145, 146
  1:7–12, 144
  1:8, 172
  1:9, 149, 174, 200
  1:9–3:22, 145
  1:12–16, 8
  1:12b–3:22, 145
  1:13, 8
  1:14–16, 173
  1:16, 157
  1:17–20, 146
  1:19, 145
  2:1, 172
  2:2, 148, 158
  2:3, 149
  2:4, 33
  2:5, 9, 33, 221
  2:5–6, 158
  2:7, 9, 149, 153, 177, 185
  2:8, 172
  2:9, 3, 6, 8, 13, 33, 47, 142, 149, 156,
        158, 160, 165, 186, 188, 197, 219
  2:9–10, 165, 200, 209
  2:10, 158, 160, 173, 174, 188
  2:10–11, 9
  2:11, 149, 153, 173, 177, 185
  2:12, 172
  2:13, 33, 149, 174, 200
  2:14, 3, 33, 155
  2:14–15, 153
  2:16, 9, 173, 174, 221
  2:16–17, 9
  2:17, 153, 177, 185
  2:18, 172
  2:19, 158
  2:20, 33, 155, 195, 208

Revelation (Apocalypse of John) (*cont.*)
  2:21, 150, 155
  2:21–2, 9, 221
  2:22, 149, 174, 208
  2:22–3, 3
  2:23, 158, 160, 173
  2:24, 149
  2:25, 9
  2:26, 153, 158, 177, 204
  2:28, 177
  2:29, 9, 185
  3:1, 172
  3:1–2, 158
  3:2, 214
  3:2–3, 9
  3:3, 9, 173, 174, 209, 214, 221
  3:4, 33
  3:4–5, 165
  3:5, 153, 173, 177
  3:6, 9, 185
  3:7, 172
  3:8, 33, 142, 158, 167, 210
  3:9, 8, 149, 158, 160, 174
  3:11, 9, 173
  3:12, 149, 153, 160, 171, 177
  3:13, 9, 185
  3:14, 172, 200
  3:15, 158
  3:17, 3, 8, 11, 13, 17, 55, 142, 160, 161,
    186, 188, 195, 197, 206, 214, 219
  3:17–18, 13, 33, 204
  3:17–19, 184
  3:18, 165, 173, 184, 206, 209
  3:19, 9, 165, 221
  3:20, 167
  3:21, 153, 160, 171, 174, 177
  3:22, 9, 185
  4:1–2, 168
  4:1–11, 22, 167, 168
  4:2–11, 8
  4:4, 165
  4:4–5, 27, 33, 167
  4:11, 149, 157, 171
  5:1, 172
  5:5, 149, 153, 160, 177
  5:5–6, 153
  5:6, 174, 177, 196
  5:6–7, 182
  5:9, 171, 196
  5:12, 142, 157, 170, 196, 219
  6:1, 172
  6:1–8, 22
  6:2, 149, 153, 196
  6:5, 142, 206

6:5–6, 162, 178
6:6, 182
6:8, 179
6:9, 11, 149, 199
6:10, 210
6:11, 149, 165
6:15, 158, 204, 209
7:9, 165
7:12, 157, 165
7:13–14, 165, 173
7:14, 173
7:15, 149
8:1–3, 201
8:8, 191
8:10, 191
9:1, 191
9:18–20, 174
9:20, 155, 158
9:20–1, 149, 201
9:21, 155
10:1, 191
11:2, 204
11:3, 11, 199
11:7, 11, 149, 153, 160, 174, 177, 199
11:7–10, 149, 189
11:17, 157
11:18, 204, 210
12:1–10, 177
12:1–17, 192
12:3, 193
12:4, 190, 191
12:5, 191, 204
12:7–12, 168
12:8, 190
12:9, 149, 155, 158, 191, 192, 208
12:10, 157, 191
12:11, 11, 149, 153, 160, 174, 177, 188,
    199, 209, 221
12:12, 158, 191, 206, 215
12:13, 191
12:17, 173
12:18, 192
12:18–13:18, 185
13, 27
13:1, 158, 206
13:1–18, 22, 192
13:2, 157, 193
13:2–3, 185
13:3, 202
13:5–6, 158
13:7, 149, 153, 160, 188
13:8, 27, 196, 203
13:9, 9, 185
13:9–10, 146

13:10, 174, 196
13:11, 185, 206
13:14, 149, 155, 177, 193, 208
13:14–17, 3
13:15, 174, 196
13:15–17, 209
13:16, 158, 186
13:16–17, 150, 155, 185, 188, 196, 200, 202, 206, 219, 221
13:16–18, 142
13:17, 13
13:18, 9, 219
14:3, 11, 199
14:4, 208
14:7, 9
14:8, 146, 149, 155, 203, 204, 207, 208, 211
14:8–10, 155
14:9, 186, 208
14:10, 203, 210
14:11, 186
14:13, 146, 149, 158, 174, 200, 208
14:14–15, 200
14:14–20, 173
15:1–4, 186
15:2, 149, 153, 160, 174, 186, 188
15:3, 158
15:3–4, 204
15:8, 157
16:2, 186
16:5, 174
16:9, 158, 174, 201
16:9–11, 149
16:11, 158, 174, 201
16:15, 146, 149, 173, 186, 209, 214
16:17, 25
16:21, 158
17, 27
17:1, 202
17:1–2, 155
17:2, 149, 155, 200, 202, 203, 204, 208
17:2–6, 3
17:3, 158
17:4, 155, 202, 203, 208
17:4–5, 155
17:5, 202
17:6, 11, 149, 199, 203, 208
17:6–7, 202
17:7, 202
17:8, 27, 196, 197, 202
17:9, 202, 219
17:13, 157
17:14, 149, 153

17:15–16, 155, 202
17:16–17, 212
17:17–18, 3, 8
17:18, 202, 204
18, 4
18:1–3, 198
18:1–19, 10
18:1–24, 22, 34
18:2, 202, 207, 211
18:2–3, 161, 198, 199, 203
18:3, 13, 47, 75, 146, 149, 155, 199, 200, 202, 204, 208, 214
18:3–4, 3
18:4, 4, 9, 11, 16, 21, 34, 150, 154, 163, 198, 200, 201, 202, 211, 221
18:4–5, 198
18:4–6, 210
18:4–20, 198
18:6, 158, 161, 173, 210
18:6–7, 209, 211
18:6–8, 198
18:7, 4, 13, 55, 157, 161, 162, 200, 202
18:8, 161, 202
18:9, 155, 157, 200, 202, 214
18:9–19, 146
18:9–20, 173, 198, 211, 213
18:10, 149, 161, 200, 202, 212
18:11, 75, 204
18:11–19, 204
18:12–13, 202
18:13, 162
18:15, 13, 75, 200, 204
18:16, 161, 202
18:17, 200
18:18, 202
18:19, 13, 161, 200, 204
18:20, 202, 214
18:21, 202
18:21–2, 210
18:21–4, 146, 161, 198
18:23, 3, 75, 204, 208, 209
18:24, 149, 202, 203
19:1, 157
19:2, 149, 155, 210
19:8, 158
19:9, 209
19:10, 25
19:11–21, 173
19:14, 165
19:15, 173, 174
19:18, 186
19:19, 221
19:20, 186, 208
19:21, 173, 174, 188

Revelation (Apocalypse of John) (*cont.*)
  20:2, 158, 191
  20:2–3, 168
  20:4, 11, 186, 188, 199, 211
  20:6, 149, 173, 209
  20:7, 191
  20:8–9, 221
  20:10, 158, 191
  20:11–12, 211
  20:12, 158, 160
  20:14, 149, 173
  20:15, 188, 203
  21:1, 211
  21:2, 149
  21:3–8, 146
  21:4, 173, 174
  21:7, 149, 153, 171, 173, 197
  21:8, 149, 155, 173, 188
  21:21–2, 8
  22:2–3, 33
  22:6–21, 145
  22:7, 146, 209
  22:9, 26
  22:12, 210
  22:12–14, 146
  22:14, 149, 165, 209
  22:15, 155
  22:17, 9
  22:18–20, 146
  22:19, 149

Deuterocanonical writings
1 Maccabees
  3:41, 205, 206
  8:1–3, 134
  8:18, 181
  8:31, 181
  12:35–13:49, 187
  13:41, 181
  14:41–3, 136

2 Maccabees
  1:35, 68
  3:9–12, 95
  3:10, 47
  3:61, 68
  4:10–17, 37
  4:28, 68
  6:18–20, 159
  7:1–42, 159
  8:34, 205, 206

Ben Sira (*Greek* Sirach)
  1:1–10, 64

2:2, 73
3:6–7:29, 63
3:14–18, 63
3:17, 65
3:21–2, 63
3:21–5, 64
3:28, 73
3:30, 67
4:1–6, 66, 68, 69, 72
4:4, 65
4:8, 72, 77, 124, 171, 187
4:21, 63
4:22–3, 63
5:1, 55, 69, 72, 162
5:1–2, 75
6:14, 65
7:18–19, 68
7:29–31, 64
8:1–2, 69, 79
8:1–7, 82
8:2, 61, 65, 85, 139, 163
8:12–13, 82
8:13, 82
8:14–20, 82
10:3–31, 70
10:13, 73
10:19–11:10, 63
10:22, 61
10:22–3, 79
10:22–4, 70, 139
10:23, 65
10:27, 65
10:30, 61, 65
10:30–1, 65
11:1, 65
11:14, 65, 73, 77
11:17, 66, 69, 72, 73, 77, 79
11:17–19, 162
11:18, 65
11:18–19, 55, 68, 77, 85, 163
11:21, 163
11:21–2, 66, 68, 76, 79
11:22, 72
12:14, 201
13:1–4, 71, 79
13:2, 65, 71
13:3, 65
13:4, 163
13:17–20, 71, 79
13:17–23, 65
13:18–23, 61
13:19, 65, 163
13:21–3, 70
13:22–3, 65

13:24, 65, 70, 79
14:3, 65
14:3–4, 68
14:5, 68
14:14–17, 78
14:16–17, 68, 79, 123
17:20–3, 67
18:3, 77
18:25, 73
18:30–19:1, 68, 73, 77
18:30–3, 69
19:1, 65
19:1–2, 85
20:22–3, 63
20:29, 164
25:14, 73
26:29, 205, 206
26:29–27:3, 74, 79
27:1, 68, 163
27:2, 89, 98, 187
28:19–20, 181
29:8–13, 68, 69
29:10–13, 67
29:14–20, 82
30:14, 65
30:16, 65
30:19, 65
31:1, 65
31:1–11, 75, 77, 79
31:3, 65
31:4, 65
31:8, 163
31:15, 68
31:24–32:7, 63
32:1, 65
32:12–33:8, 63
32:16–34:1, 63
33:27, 181
34:21–7, 47
34:25–7, 68
35:1–12, 64
35:21, 65
36:24–38:1, 63
37:11, 205, 206
37:11–12, 201
38:11, 65
38:19, 73
40:1, 181
40:9, 73
40:13, 124
40:18, 72, 79
40:23, 65
40:25–6, 72, 74, 79
41:1–3, 68, 78

41:16, 63
42:1–4, 180
42:4–5, 187
42:5, 68
44:6, 163
44:6–7, 78, 79
44:10–15, 78
44:44–5, 64
50:1–21, 63
51:23–5, 43
51:26, 181
51:27–8, 72

Tobit
    14:10–11, 68

Wisdom of Solomon
    1:16, 123, 138, 165, 182
    2:1–5, 123
    2:1–11, 55
    2:1–20, 162
    2:6–9, 124
    2:6–11, 122
    2:9, 124
    2:10, 124, 139
    2:10–20, 124
    2:21, 164
    2:22–4, 121
    3:1–6, 124
    3:5–6, 138, 165, 182
    3:7, 122
    3:8, 122, 136
    3:12–13, 124
    3:16, 124
    4:7, 122
    4:11–12, 124
    5:1–15, 129
    5:2–3, 123
    5:2–8, 139
    5:4–13, 162
    5:5, 122
    5:8, 123
    5:15–16, 121, 124, 138
    5:16, 122
    5:17–23, 121
    7:7b–14, 125
    8:11–18, 125
    8:5, 125
    10:9–11, 125
    14:6, 124
    14:6–13, 124
    14:14, 126
    15:10–14, 127
    15:12, 126

Old Testament Pseudepigrapha

Apocalypse of Abraham
  9–19, 168

Apocalypse of Elijah
  4:11, 191

Ascension of Isaiah
  3:4, 146
  4:1–14, 195
  4:6–9, 168

2 Baruch
  1:11, 168
  3:29, 168
  6:55, 168
  29:3–4, 193
  67:7, 199
  70:2–8, 182, 184
  70:3, 134

3 Baruch
  1:3, 146
  4:15, 146
  13:1, 179
  15:4, 146
  16:1, 146

1 Enoch
  5:4–5, 122
  7:2–6, 48
  8:1–2, 44, 46, 49, 57, 128
  8:2, 154
  8:4, 201
  9:1, 154
  9:2, 201
  9:8–9, 48
  9:9–10, 154
  9:10, 201
  10:4–13, 191
  10:7, 45
  10:9, 47
  10:9–10, 191
  10:12–13, 168
  11:1, 47, 138, 159
  11:1–2, 45
  12:1–36, 45
  12:4–7, 53
  12:5, 168, 191
  12:6, 48, 57, 191
  12:8–25, 168
  12:14, 168
  12:23, 169
  15:8–12, 45

  15:8–9, 47
  15:8–16:2, 191
  15:10, 168
  16:1–2, 45
  17:1–5, 169
  18:6–8, 169
  18:11–16, 191
  18:13, 191
  19:1, 47
  21:1–7, 191
  22:5, 201
  38:1–5, 127
  38:1–44:1, 126
  38:5, 129
  40:7, 191
  41:1, 181
  43:1–3, 191
  43:2–44:1, 191
  45:1–57:3, 126
  45:4, 129
  45:4–6, 129, 138, 159
  46:1–8, 174
  46:4, 127
  46:7–8, 127
  48:7, 129, 138, 139, 159
  48:9, 129
  50:1–51:5, 211
  52:7, 46
  52:7–8, 128
  53:2, 128
  54:6, 128, 138, 165, 181
  56:4, 138, 165, 181
  58:1–69:29, 126
  60:6–11, 45
  60:6–19, 45
  60:7–10, 193
  62:14–16, 129
  63:2, 128
  63:10, 128
  65:6–8, 46, 128
  69:26–9, 174
  81:1–2, 160
  81:1–3, 175
  85:3, 179
  86:1, 191
  86:1–4, 45
  86:2, 179
  88:1, 191
  88:1–3, 191
  89:9, 179
  89:32, 164
  89:41, 164
  89:41–9, 195
  89:44, 164

89:54, 164
90:6–7, 164
90:9, 164
90:9–12, 195
90:19, 211
90:20–1, 175
90:24, 191
90:26, 164
90:31–6, 164
91:5–7, 159
91:6, 181, 184
91:11, 135
91:11–17, 49
91:12, 91, 108, 211
91:12–13, 50, 57, 78, 136, 159
91:13, 51, 54, 56, 138
91:13–14, 211
91:15, 211
91:16, 211
92:1–5, 50
93:1–10, 49
93:2, 160, 175
93:8, 164
93:9–10, 57, 74, 135
93:9–11, 159
93:11–105:2, 50
94:1, 77, 126, 214
94:3, 202
94:6, 51
94:6–10, 77, 130, 154
94:6–11, 50
94:6–7, 77, 126, 214
94:6–9, 127
94:6–95:2, 47
94:6–100:6, 51
94:7, 46, 51, 67
94:7–9, 85
94:8, 67
94:8–9, 52
95:3, 211
95:4, 53
95:4–7, 47, 77, 130, 154
95:6, 77, 210
95:7, 124, 127, 129, 135, 211
96:1, 77, 126, 129, 211, 214
96:4, 53, 58, 60, 97, 123, 126, 135, 165
96:4–6, 67
96:4–8, 77, 130, 154
96:5, 50, 54, 124, 139
96:5–8, 127
96:6, 77
96:7, 53
96:8, 67, 124
97:3–5, 163, 201

97:3–10, 130, 154
97:4, 106, 128, 129, 154
97:7, 53
97:7–10, 77, 127
97:8–9, 74, 124, 128, 162
97:8–10, 9, 46, 47, 50, 55, 85, 171
97:10, 49, 77
98:2, 46, 128
98:2–3, 49, 56, 59, 74, 77, 124
98:2–99:2, 130, 154
98:4–5, 221
98:6, 126, 214
98:10, 53
98:11, 122
98:11–16, 77
98:12, 129, 206, 211
98:14, 206
99:1–2, 77
99:3–5, 159, 181, 184
99:4, 135
99:6, 46, 53, 128
99:8, 164
99:9, 77, 126, 214
99:11–13, 77
99:11–16, 47, 127, 130, 154
99:12, 180
99:13, 51
99:14, 122
99:16, 135
100:1–3, 181, 184
100:1–4, 159
100:2, 124
100:3, 208
100:4–9, 77
100:6, 49, 57, 123, 124
100:7–102:3, 51
100:7–9, 130, 154
100:10–13, 58
101:1–3, 58
101:3, 122
101:4–102:3, 130, 154, 206
101:4–5, 58
101:5, 205
101:6, 212
102:4–103:15, 165
102:4–104:8, 51
102:5–104:6, 165
102:6–8, 124, 162
102:6–11, 59
102:9, 54, 109, 127, 130, 154
102:9–10, 50, 74, 135
102:9–11, 77
103:1–2, 60
103:1–4, 175

1 Enoch (cont.)
103:2, 160
103:3–4, 60
103:5, 214
103:5–6, 59
103:5–8, 130, 154
103:8, 122, 214
103:9–11, 157
103:9–14, 60
104:1–3, 60
104:2, 122
104:5, 122
104:6, 60, 129, 139, 159, 163, 200, 202
104:7, 123, 126, 162
104:7–9, 130, 154
105:2, 122
106:9–107:1, 181
106:19, 160
106:19–107:1, 159, 175
108:1, 130
108:1–10, 130
108:3, 160
108:6–7, 74
108:7, 175
108:8, 160, 221
108:8–10, 200
108:8–15, 135, 159, 165, 221
108:10, 138, 139
108:10–12, 139
108:12, 138

2 Enoch
7:3–4, 190
18:3–5, 191
18:18–22, 168
29:4–6, 190, 191
31:3–4, 190
49:2, 181

2 Esdras 3–14 (*=4 Ezra*)
3:1–2, 199
3:34, 181
4:7–12, 168
4:36, 181
5:1–13, 182, 184
5:2, 159
5:10, 159
6:20–4, 182, 184
6:24, 134
6:49–52, 193
9:3, 134
9:3–4, 182, 184
10:12–13, 55
13:30–1, 134, 159, 182, 184

2 Esdras 15–16 (*=6 Ezra*)
15:46, 199
16:1, 199

Joseph and Asenath
10:9–11, 179

Jubilees
4:15, 45
4:18, 49
4:19, 51
7:29, 51
10:11–12, 221
10:17, 51
22:16, 201
23:16–21, 182, 184
23:30, 211
26:34, 181

3 Maccabees
4:9, 181

4 Maccabees
7:1, 205

Psalms of Solomon
2:22–35, 209
2:32, 209
5:4, 181
7:9, 181
13:2–3, 179
17:30, 181

Sibylline Oracles
2:56, 47
3:63–70, 195
3:162–95, 134
3:175–90, 112, 134, 154, 159,
    182
3:188–90, 171
3:189, 135
3:234–45, 135
3:237, 135
3:240, 135
3:241–5, 135
3:270–1, 135
3:350–3, 134
3:391, 181
3:448, 181
3:508, 181
3:537, 181
3:624, 135
3:635–43, 112, 134, 159, 182
3:762–808, 136

3:780–6, 136, 138, 159
4:87, 181
4:104, 181
5:3, 181
5:143, 199
5:159, 199
5:414–17, 136
8:126, 181
8:326, 181
11:67, 181
11:76, 181
11:217, 181
13:94, 181
14:308, 181

Testament of Job
4:3, 146
7:9, 146

Testament of Solomon
20:16, 191

Questions of Ezra
19–21, 168

Apocalypse of Ezekiel
2:1, 179

Testament of the Twelve Patriarchs
  Testament of Abraham
    8:1–12, 168
    8:5, 146
    12:8–18, 181
    13:9–10, 181
  Testament of Reuben
    1–6, 190
    5, 45
  Testament of Levi
    13:1–9, 43
    13:2–8, 168
  Testament of Naphtali
    3:5, 190

Life of Adam and Eve
12–16, 191
12–17, 190
22:2, 146
35:4–36:3, 179

Dead Sea Scrolls and related texts
Damascus Document
  CD
    1:9, 164
    2:14, 164

4:12–5:11, 114
4:11–18, 47
4:12–18, 138, 165, 181
4:12–19, 94
4:12b–19a, 96
4:13, 221
4:14–18, 221
4:14–19, 138, 184
4:15, 43
4:15–18, 221
4:16–18, 215
4:17–18, 114
4:19, 160
5:11–16, 96
6:11–18, 171
6:14–17, 94
6:14b–17a, 95
6:16–17, 47
6:21, 94, 95
7:13–15, 150
8:4–9, 47
8:7, 99
10:17–19, 99
10:18–19, 171
11:15, 99, 171
12:6–8, 99
12:8–10, 94
12:8–11, 187
13:11–16, 74
13:14–15, 98, 187
14:7, 112
14:14, 94, 95
14:20, 94, 97
16:2, 164
19:7–11, 93
19:9, 139, 187
19:9–13, 139
19:16–21, 47
19:19, 99
20:14, 149
20:6–7, 96
4Q266 9 iii:1, 187
4Q266 9 iii:1–4, 74
4Q267 9 iii:4, 94
4Q271 5 ii:2–4, 94

Community Rule (1QS)
1:1–10, 101
1:11–13, 102
1:18, 221
1:1a–2b, 105
1:2–3, 102
2:19, 221

1QS 3:13–4:26 (=*Two Spirits Treatise*)
  3:11–12, 107
  3:17–18, 90
  3:20, 90
  3:20–1, 105
  3:21–3, 90
  3:22–3, 105
  4:2, 105
  4:5, 106
  4:6, 105
  4:6–8, 91, 138
  4:7, 122
  4:9–11, 47
  4:11, 164
  4:12, 105
  4:20, 165
  4:24, 105
  4:26, 91
  5–7, 105
  5:14, 106
  5:14–15, 106
  5:14b–15a, 106
  5:14–20, 74
  5:15b–17a, 106
  5:20, 106
  6:13–23, 103
  6:13b–14, 103
  6:15–16, 103
  6:18–21a, 104
  6:19–20a, 104
  6:24–5, 109
  7:4–5, 110
  7:22–5, 107
  8–9, 105
  8:7, 160
  9:22b–23a, 107
  9:8b–9a, 105
  10:18–19, 47, 108, 138, 139, 160, 171
  11:1–2, 47
4Q256 18:5–6, 107
4Q256 18:6, 108
4Q258 8:6–7, 107
4Q260 4:6–7, 108, 139
4Q261 3:3, 109

Mûsār lᵉ Mēvîn
  4Q415 6:2, 85
  4Q416 2 i:10–12, 138
  4Q416 2 ii:4–7, 138
  4Q416 2 ii:4b–7a, 82
  4Q416 2 ii:6–7, 160
  4Q416 2 ii:17–18, 84, 89, 138, 160, 201
  4Q416 2 ii:20, 85

4Q416 2 iii:2, 85
4Q416 2 iii:2–7, 85, 138
4Q416 2 iii:4, 84
4Q416 2 iii:8, 85
4Q416 2 iii:9–14, 83, 122, 138
4Q416 2 iii:12, 85
4Q416 2 iii:19, 85
4Q417 1 i:6, 87
4Q417 1 i:13, 81
4Q417 1 i:16, 83
4Q417 2 i:9, 84
4Q417 2 i:10–12, 87, 138, 139, 160
4Q417 2 i:14–18, 81
4Q417 2 i:17, 89
4Q417 2 i:19, 126
4Q417 2 i:19–22, 86
4Q417 2 i:21–2, 138
4Q417 2 i:22, 84
4Q418 103 ii:6–9, 88, 201
4Q418 103 ii:9, 84
4Q418 127:3, 84
4Q418 81+81a:9, 87

Pesher Habakkuk (1QpHab)
  1:7–8, 47
  2:12, 112
  2:1–3, 149
  2:14, 112
  2:16, 112
  3:1–5, 134
  3:4, 112
  3:9, 112
  4:10, 112
  4:5, 112
  5:8, 154
  5:8a, 113
  5:10–11, 149
  5:12–6:8, 154
  6:1, 47, 112
  6:10, 112
  6:1–8, 134
  7:4–5, 149
  8:10–11, 160
  8:11–12, 47
  8:13b–19, 115
  8:7, 115
  8:15, 47
  8:3–13a, 113
  8:8–11, 116
  8:8–12, 164
  8:9–13, 138
  9:4–7, 47
  9:6–7, 134
  9:7, 112

9:9–10, 149
11:4–6, 149
11:6, 150
11:12–13, 114, 116
12:2–10, 115

Pesher Hosea
4Q166 2: 5–6, 164

War Scroll (1QM)
1:3, 150
1:11–12, 159, 181, 184
1:13, 221
12:12–14, 111, 159
12:14, 122
12:14–15, 136, 160
13:2, 221
14:7, 112
14:8–15, 165
16:11, 138, 160, 165, 181
16:15, 138, 160, 165, 181
17:1, 138, 160, 165, 181

1QHodayot^a (Thanksgiving Hymns)
4:29–36, 118
5:19, 117
5:20, 117
6:13, 117
6:13–16, 118
6:26, 117
6:31, 116, 138, 139, 160
6:32, 117
6:36, 117
7:22–3, 117, 138, 160
7:31, 117
7:31–2, 117
9:21–2, 122
9:32, 117
10:12, 117
10:15–16, 160, 165
10:32–4, 47, 117, 165
11:20–37, 122
12:41, 117
13:11, 117
13:28, 117
14:12, 117
14:15, 117
14:32–9, 122
15:12, 165
15:19, 117
15:29, 117
15:41, 117
17:25, 122
18:22–5, 47, 160

18:22–25a, 118
18:22–31, 139
18:25, 171
18:29–30, 118
18:29–31, 160
18:29b–31a 118
19:10–11, 122
23:28, 160, 165

4QHodayot^b
4Q428 11, 118
4Q428 3, 117

4QHodayot^f
4Q432 3–4, 117

Temple Scroll (11Q19)
11Q19 51:13–14, 164
11Q19 54:12, 138, 165, 181

2QSirach
2Q18 6:20–31, 63
2Q18 6:14–15, 63

11QWar Scroll
11Q14ii:7–14a, 111

1QBook of Giants
1Q23 9+14+15:2–5, 48

4QPsalms Pesher^a
4Q171 1 2ii:1, 179

4QCatena^a
4Q177 9:2, 138, 165, 182
4Q177 10 11:10, 138, 165, 182

4QEnoch^a *ar*
4Q201, 45

4QEnoch^b *ar*
4Q202, 45
4Q202 1 ii:28, 46
4Q202 i 6: 9, 48

4QEnoch Giants^a *ar*
4Q203 4:3–6, 48
4Q203 8:7–15, 48

4QEnoch^c *ar*
4Q204, 45, 50
4Q204 1 v:7, 47
4Q204 i 6:16, 48

4QEnoch^d ar
4Q205, 45

4QEnoch^e ar
4Q206, 45

4QEnoch^g ar
4Q212, 50
4Q212 1 iv:17, 50, 56

4QAramaic Levi
4Q213 i 1:19–ii 2:1, 43

Prayer of Nabonidus
4Q242 1 3:4, 150

4QWar Scroll
4Q285 8:4–12, 111
4Q285 10:3, 111

4QNon-Canonical Psalms^b
4Q381 46a+b:5, 165

4QApocryphon of Jeremiah
4Q390 2 i:8–10, 47

4QMMT^d
4Q397 14–21:5, 47

4QRitual of Purification
4Q414 2 ii 4:1, 165

4QBarkhi Nafshi
4Q434 1 i:7, 165

4QWords of the Luminaries^a
4Q504 1 2Riii:8, 179

4QSongs of the Sage^a
4Q510 1:5–7, 221

4QBeatitudes
4Q525, 44

4QEnoch Giants^b
4Q530 1:4, 201

4QEnoch Giants^c
4Q531 1:1–16, 48

XQpapEn ar, 45

Rabbinic literature
Targum
Num 24:14, 3, 153
Deut. 6:5, 102
2 Kings 9:30, 46
Jer. 4:30, 46
Jer. 51:7, 203
Hab. 3:2, 85, 97
Mic. 7:12–16, 97
Mic. 7:14, 85

Targum Pseudo-Jonathan
Gen 6:2, 45

m. 'Abot 5:19–22, 3,
153
b. 'Abod. Zar. 2b, 193
b. Ber. 61b, 102
b. Pes. 25a, 102
b. Sanh. 74a, 102
b. Sanh. 105a, 153
b. Šebu. 6b, 193
b. Yoma 82a, 102

Midr. Ps.
Psalm 19:15, 165

Midr. Rab.
Gen 44:17, 193
Gen 76:6, 193
Ex 15:6, 193
Lev 12:3, 165
Num 20:23, 3, 153
Deut 8:4, 165

Pesiq. Rab.
14:15, 193

Classical sources
Aristophanes
Ach., 625, 187

Cicero
Off., 1.150–1, 205

Clement
Quis div., 42, 149

Clement of Alexandria
Strom. 2.20, 152

Dio Chrysostom
Orat. 46.10–11, 184

Diodorus
   Bib. Hist., 10.34.12.1–5, 154

Euripides
   Andr., 301, 181
   Frag. 533.1, 179
   Frag., 475.1, 181
   Hel., 392, 181
   Ion, 629–630, 154
   Med., 242, 181

Eusebius
   Hist. eccl. 3.18, 149

Herodotus
   Hist. 4.114, 203
   Hist. 4.5.10, 181
   Hist. 8.20.6, 181
   Hist., 3.115, 170

Hesiod
   Op., 155, 179
   Op., 815, 181
   Scut., 142, 170

Hippocrates
   Progn 2, 180

Homer
   Epigr. 15.10, 170
   Il., 1.490, 187
   Il., 2.834, 179
   Il., 7.479, 180
   Il., 10.293, 181
   Il., 13.706, 181
   Il., 16.470, 181
   Il., 19.406, 181
   Il., 23.294, 181
   Od., 3.846, 181
   Od., 11.43, 180
   Od. 12.92, 179
   Od., 15.184, 181
   Od. 15.460, 170

Horace
   Saec. 3.6.29–32, 205

Irenaeus
   Haer., 1.26.3, 152

Jerome
   Hom. Matth. 7.51, 149
   Hom. Matth. 16.6, 149

Petronius
   Satyricon, 26–78, 205

Philostratus
   Vit. Apoll. 4.32, 205

Plato
   Leg., 6.849.D.1, 187
   Leg. 6.917–18, 187
   Leg., 6.930d, 203
   Symp., 207b, 203
   Resp. 2.371–372, 187

Pliny
   Nat. 4.69–70, 149
   Ps.-Clem. Hom. 8:11–15, 45

Sophocles
   Frag. 591.6, 181
   Oed., 29, 179
   Oed., 1278, 179

Strabo
   Georg. 8.6.20, 205
   Geogr. 15.3.19, 187

Tacitus
   Ann., 4.30, 149
   Ann., 15.44, 17

Tertullian
   Marc. 1.29, 152
   Praescr. 33, 152

Thucydides
   3.33, 149
   7.39.2.6, 187

Xenophon
   Anab., 1.5.5.8, 187
   Anab., 7.7.36, 157
   Hell., 2.4.17.2–5, 154

Philo and Josephus
Josephus
   Ant. 4:126–30, 3, 153
   J. W. 3.24.55–6, 154

Philo
   Cher. 32, 153
   Deus, 147, 154
   Hypoth., 7.8, 180
   Mos. 1:294–9, 3, 153
   Praem. 104, 125

Other

Aramaic Levi Document
  6:3, 44
  6:6–10, 44
  13:1, 44
  13:1–3, 44
  13:1–8, 44
  13:4, 168

13:10, 126
13:10–12, 43, 138
13:10–15, 84
13:11–12, 44
13:12, 126
13:12–14, 87
13:13, 126

INDEX OF AUTHORS AND TOPICS

144,000, the, 16, 208
  sealing of, 189

Abegg, M., 86
Abraham, 106
abundance, 118
adultery, 124, 208
adversary eschatological, 221
affluence. *See* wealth
afterlife, 123, 124, 138, 141
age
  future, 91, 119, 120, 165
  of wickedness, 96, 124
  present/eschatological, 88, 96, 97,
      112, 137, 142, 171, 174, 175, 189,
      193, 196, 197, 200, 201, 217,
      224
Aitken, J., 85
Alexander as name of honour, 152
Alexander Janneus, 123
Alexandria, 122
almsgiving, 67
altar, 154, 201
alternative society, 104
alternative world, 16
Angel of Darkness, 90
angels, 122, 179, 190, 191, 217
  as role models, 86
  fallen, 45, 47, 53, 138, 190, 191
  of retribution, 210
  offspring of, 45, 47, 53, 57, 191
angelus interpres, 202
Animal Apocalypse, 164, 179
antichrist figure, 177
antimony, 46
Antipas, 200
Apocalypse of Weeks
  eighth week, 52, 57, 61
  seventh week, 135
apocalypse(s)

genre of, 37
  Jewish, 137
  non-canonical, 28
apocalyptic, 121, 171
  discourse, 39, 183, 217
  idiom, 8, 20, 37, 142, 144
  literature, 37, 125, 134
  visions, 147, 167
apocalypticism, 37
apostate(s), 103, 107, 114
apostles, 210
Aramaic Levi Document, 42, 119, 219
Arendzen, J., 42
arrogance, 123, 163, 204, 213, 215
Asael, 44, 57, 128
Asensio, V., 77
Asia Minor, 21, 132, 147, 199, 219
assets
  communal, 94
  equal distribution of, 98
Assyria, 136
Astronomical Book, 47
Aune, David E., 24, 145, 152, 180, 182
authority, 148, 151, 158, 185, 193, 195
avarice. *See* greed

Babylon, 136, 155, 158, 161, 163, 176,
      199, 200, 201, 203, 209, 213
  destruction of, 143, 200, 204
  judgement of, 197, 202, 204, 214
  Rome, 4, 7
  sins of, 154
  the whore, 3
  wine of, 208
Balaam, 3, 150, 151, 152, 153, 154, 163
balancing scales, 33, 142, 162, 167, 175,
      181, 185, 206
banking, 161
barley, 181, 182
barter, 96, 98, 187

battle, 154, 221
  heavenly, 190
Bauckham, Richard, 19, 28, 173
Beale, G. K., 22, 24, 27, 172
beast, the, 153, 176
  mark of, 142, 185, 186, 188, 197, 200,
    203
  name of, 185
beasts, 155, 157, 158, 176, 179, 185, 189,
    192, 193, 194, 195, 196, 202
Belial, 96, 97, 119, 138, 221
  traps of, 96, 114
belief awareness attribution, 55
Berges, Ulrich, 6
Birth of Noah, 221
black
  bull-calf, 179
  horse, 179
Black, D., 48
blasphemy, 99
blessing
  future, 47, 61, 88, 91, 136, 171
  material, 31, 36, 53, 54, 62, 67, 77, 85,
    91, 118, 125, 142, 165, 216
  postponement of, 48, 77, 129, 138, 165,
    197
  promise of, 48, 50, 111, 125, 129, 141,
    165
blindness, 164
  metaphorical, 164
Blomberg, Craig, 5
blood, 202, 210
  of saints, 203
body, 168
book of life, 196, 197
Book of the Watchers, 44, 124
Book of Wisdom, 121
bottomless pit, 189
boundary, 135
  between rich and poor, 71
Boundary Shifters, 151
Boxall, Ian, 156, 182
bread, 183
Builders of the Wall, 151
building metaphor of, 51
Buitenwerf, R., 133
buying and selling, 74, 89, 96, 98, 106,
    119, 138, 142, 153, 185, 186, 187,
    188, 189, 206

Caesar, 176
Cain, 179
Cairo Genizah, 42, 63, 92
calf, 179

camps, 187
canon, Muratorian, 122
cargo list, 162, 183, 202, 213
catastrophe, 184
cattle, 179
chariot, 175
Charles, R. H., 29, 42, 152
children of darkness, 90
Christ
  as moral philosopher, 7
  image of, 177
  voice of, 182
church, 148, 151, 157, 161, 172, 217
class
  socio-economic, 147
Claudius, 17
Cleopatra, 133
Cohen, S., 36
collegia. See trade guilds
Collins, J. J., 133, 169
Combat Myth, 185, 189, 190, 191
commandments, 114
  of God, 116
commerce, 89, 180, 205
commercial agents, 108
commodities, 108
common fund, 94
communal property, 89
community
  boundaries, 106
  Damascus, 93, 94, 95, 101, 138, 187,
    223
  Enochic, 54
  faithful, 56, 62, 79, 93, 119, 137, 139,
    151, 155, 163, 175, 178, 188, 198,
    207, 219
  Qumran, 40, 80, 89, 90, 91, 120,
    217
Community Rule, 90, 91, 100, 105, 107,
    221
complacency, 160
compromise, 157
confession, 163, 224
conflict, 150, 174, 176, 178, 189, 191,
    196
  internal, 150
  political, 151
  theological, 148
conquering, 148, 152, 158, 171, 173, 177,
    188, 196, 197
conqueror
  messianic, 174
  military, 173
corruption, 184

cosmology, 38, 53, 97, 134, 141, 142, 185
cosmos, 168, 170
covenant, 117, 118
Cowley, R., 42
creatures
    living, 169, 175, 178, 182
    malevolent, 177
crisis, 150
    of persecution, 149
cross-dressers, 57
crown
    gold, 173, 177, 178, 188
    of glory, 91
cultural assimilation, 141, 163, 166
curse, covenant, 60
curse(s), Deuteronomistic, 59, 73, 84, 164

Damascus Document, 42, 97, 99, 103, 119,
    164, 187, 221
Day of Judgement, 57, 129, 224
Day of Vengeance, 108
death, 78, 79, 124, 149, 153, 158, 171,
    173, 174, 179, 180, 184, 188, 196,
    199, 209, 221, 224
    second, 173, 174, 188
debt, 87
deceiver, 192
deception, 178
deeds, 90, 160, 181, 210
defilement, 106, 114
desert, 105, 176
deSilva, David, 11
Destroyer
    Christ as, 173, 174, 184
destruction
    of rich, 139, 200
    sudden, 74, 77, 126, 214
deviance, 151
Devil, the, 158, 192
devotion
    to God, 87, 95, 107, 138, 195, 222
Di Lella, A., 73
Dimant, Devorah, 40
dirge, 212, 214
discipline, 165, 184
disobedience, 136, 164
divine passive, 178, 184
Domitian, 183
doom, 181, 191
door, 167
    open, 168, 171
dragon, 191, 194, 195, 209
Dragon, the, 153, 155, 157, 191, 192, 193
Drawnel, H., 43

dualism, 90, 93
Duff, Paul, 21

ear, 196
earth, 168, 190
    judgement of, 186
earth dwellers, 174, 194
economic
    participation, 156, 188, 192, 196, 202,
        203, 206, 208, 215
    system, 118, 156, 163, 165, 181, 182,
        183, 194, 196, 197, 202, 216
    transactions, 98, 180
    withdrawal, 89, 157, 223, 224
economic success, 3, 17, 19, 37, 69, 161,
    203, 207
elders, 169, 178
elect, 93
    status of, 82, 84
Elisha, 182
emperors, 145, 194
empire, 14, 192, 210, 215
    Roman, 21, 142, 149, 176, 181, 182,
        192, 193, 194, 199, 205, 217, 220
endurance, 148, 149, 200
Enoch, 126
    ascension of, 168
Ephesus, 161
Epistle of Enoch, 49, 71, 106, 119, 129,
    139, 164, 213, 221
Eschatological Admonition, 221
eschatology, 134
    apocalyptic, 121
    book of, 125
    inaugurated, 83, 84
eschaton, 97, 141, 210, 216
evil, 110, 124, 153, 179, 180, 181, 194,
    200, 202, 216
    origin of, 46
exile, 135, 136, 150, 214
    Babylonian, 135
Exodus, 173, 174

faithful, the, 53, 117, 142, 149, 171, 173,
    177, 187, 194, 196, 204
faithfulness, 118, 197
    and wealth, 102
    covenant, 52, 74, 95, 99
    reward for, 62, 124
    to God, 97, 98, 107, 114, 136
Fall of the Watchers, 33, 39, 44, 45, 57, 191
famine, 179, 180, 181, 182
farmer, 88
feast, 124

feet, 122, 174
Fekkes, J., 26, 173
fellowship
    communal, 110
festivals, 154, 157
    pagan, 156
Finley, M., 206
Fiorenza, E., 16, 17
fire, 170, 202
flood, 187
food, 89, 106, 110, 183
forehead, 155, 202
fornication, 44, 47, 154, 155, 156, 199,
    202, 203, 208
four horsemen, 167, 175, 179
fraud, 109
Friesen, Steven, 14, 15, 16, 21
funeral lament, 213

garments, 202
giants, 44
gifts, 164
    spiritual, 157
glory, 87, 91, 116
    crown of, 122
Goff, Matthew, 84, 85, 88
gold, 111, 128, 130, 133, 202
    refined, 124, 165
golden cup, 155, 202, 203
Goulder, M., 23
grain, 108, 180, 182, 184
greed, 3, 90, 95, 97, 109, 129, 135, 137,
    153, 205, 213, 214, 217, 220
guilt, 89, 93, 106, 123, 163
    by association, 128

Habakkuk, 112
Hades, 178, 179
hair, 179
harlotry, 44, 202, 204
Harrington, D., 80, 88
harvest, 88
Hayes, J., 207
heaven, 167, 190, 202, 210, 221
    silence in, 201
heavenly ascent, 47, 168, 170
heavenly journey, 81, 168
    Enoch's, 53
heavens, 168, 169
Hebrew Bible, 22, 151, 164, 180, 205,
    219
Hekhalot, 168
Hellenism, 131
Hengel, Martin, 5

herem, 83, 95
High Priest, 194
Himmelfarb, M., 168
Hodayot, 116, 117, 119
Hoffmann, M., 173
Holiness Code, 106
honesty, 187
honour, 31, 116
Hoppe, Leslie, 6
Hoppe, Rudolph, 6
horn, 178, 193
horse, 173, 175, 181
    black, 178, 179, 180
    red, 180
    white, 174, 177, 179, 196
horseman
    first, 177, 195
    fourth, 177, 180, 182
    second, 177
    third, 142, 162, 167, 175, 178, 180, 182,
        197
hostility, 150, 175, 196, 216, 221
hour of testing, 200
hunger, 176
Hymn of Praise, 108
Hymns of the Community, 116

identity, 94, 151, 217
idol worship, 128
idolatry, 217
idols, 46, 126, 128, 154
immorality, 215
immortality, 121, 138
imperial cults, 12, 21, 142, 149, 156, 166,
    194, 205, 217
imperial edicts, 145, 146
impurity, 106, 179
income, 94, 110
industry, 161
inheritance, 85, 87, 129, 160, 171,
    220
injustice, correction of, 115, 120, 128
intertextuality, 22, 24
irony, 183, 205
Isaac, E., 48
Israel, 164
    leadership of, 61

Jehoiakim, 51
Jerusalem, 199
jewels, 167, 169, 170
Jezebel, 3, 7, 21, 46, 147, 150, 151, 154,
    155, 161, 163, 166, 170, 174, 196,
    208, 209

children of, 173
teaching of, 155, 195, 204, 206, 208
Johns, Loren, 172
Jonah, 58
journey, other-worldly, 169
Judah, 172
judgement, 122, 179
final, 74, 123, 124, 134, 211
formal announcement of, 212, 213
great white throne, 181
prophetic announcement of, 56, 61, 161, 198, 207, 211, 212
just measurements, 135

kingdom, 136, 149, 193, 196
kings, 127, 129, 203, 213
of the earth, 129, 155, 157, 199, 202, 203, 204, 212, 214
Kittim, 111, 112, 113, 114, 115
knowledge, 81, 104, 117
Kraybill, J., 13, 204, 205

labelling theory, 151
lake of fire, 188
lamb, 195
paschal, 173, 174
Lamb, the, 153, 157, 167, 173, 174, 182, 184, 188, 195
and wealth, 142
conquering, 177
followers of, 197
loyalty to, 15, 190, 196
marriage supper of, 209
slaughtered, 14, 171, 173, 174, 175, 188, 189, 217
vision of, 170
warrior, 173
lament, 212
land, 206, 209
possession of, 223
landowner, 88, 94
Lange, Armin, 40
Laodicea, 3, 6, 148, 160, 161, 167, 204
Leontopolis, 132
leopard, 193
limited good, 30
Lion, 193
of Judah, 172
livestock, 94, 139
loans, 87
lowly, the, 54
loyalty, 15

to God, 44, 96, 142, 194, 197
to the beast, 186
lukewarm, 163, 188, 195
luxury, 84, 85, 118, 188, 199, 201, 204, 216

Macedonia, 134
magistrates, 145
magnates, 209
Man of Lies, 151, 164
marketplace, 154, 187
martyrdom, 172, 174
Masada, 63
Maskil, 102, 108
Mazzaferri, F., 26
meals
communal, 110
pure, 110
meat, sacrificial, 7, 154
mediation, 146
Men of the Pit, 107, 108
merchandise, 89, 187, 212
merchants, 155, 162, 198, 199, 203, 204, 205, 206, 209, 211, 212, 213, 215
shippers, 10, 75, 204
Messiah, of Aaron, 93
metallurgy, 44, 49, 128
Metso, S., 108
mighty, the, 127, 129
Milik, J. T., 48
mixture, 89
of property, 89, 107
of wealth, 103, 104
money, 118, 184
love of, 135
monotheism, 131, 172
Moses, 102
Mounce, R., 183
mourning, 214, 215
Moyise, Steve, 22
Murphy, Catherine, 29, 84, 85, 88, 93, 94, 106, 108, 109
Murphy-O'Conner, J., 108
Mûsār lᵉMēvîn, 91, 108, 119, 219
mystery
of God, 216
that is to be, 81
myth, 189, 191
Leviathan-Behemoth, 192
Python-Leto-Apollo, 190

nakedness, 164, 209, 214
nations, 122, 203, 204

needy, the, 94
neokoros, 161
Nero, 17
networks
  economic, 155
  social, 154
  trade, 166
new heavens, 211
new Jerusalem, 160, 171, 188, 209, 216, 217, 224
Newsom, Carol, 39, 100, 102, 116, 117, 217
Nickelsburg, G., 48, 51
Nicolaitans, the, 150, 152, 153, 154
Nicolaus, 152, 153
Noah, 131

obedience, 15, 36, 119, 130, 136, 141, 197, 199, 210, 223, 224
  covenant, 54, 56
  to God, 90, 99
offerings, 95
oil, 108, 182, 183
Olivet Discourse, 188
Olson, Daniel, 48
Ophir, gold of, 68
opponent, eschatological, 194
opponents of God, 163, 193
oppression, 46, 47, 51, 53, 89, 128, 130, 131, 137, 154, 181, 203
  economic, 94, 113
  foreign, 115
  of righteous, 67, 163
oppressors, 127
  rich, 132, 141, 159
oracles, 132
  salvation-judgement, 145, 161
Oracles against the Nations, 4, 198, 204, 207
Oracula Sibyllina. See Sibylline Oracles
origin of sin, 61
orphans, 95
Osborne, Grant, 182
outsiders, 93, 100, 118, 138, 163, 196
Overseer, the, 104
  of the camps, 98

Pass, H., 42
Patmos, 149, 150, 172, 173, 174
peace, 122, 136, 180
penal codes, 97

perceived crisis, 17
Pergamum, 161
persecution, 17, 117, 139, 149, 150, 157, 174, 176, 177, 188, 189, 192, 200, 203, 223
  Domitianic, 150
  Neronic, 150
perseverance, 131
persuasion, 172
pesher, 97, 113
Pesher Habakkuk, 112, 115, 120, 164, 220
Pesher Hosea, 164
pestilence, 176, 179
Philadelphia, 3, 8, 148, 157, 178, 184, 200
Philo, 133
philosophy
  Cynic, 8
  Stoic, 8
piety, 98, 109, 141
Plato, 187
plunder, 115
poor ones, the, 187
poor, the, 94, 183
  as faithful, 141, 171
  as label, 69
  as marginalized, 141
  as prey for the rich, 65
  as rich, 3
  as social class, 65
  attitudes about, 71
  of the flock, 93
  of the sheep, 93
  persecuted, 163
  righteous, 119
possessions, 48, 75, 88, 99, 106, 124, 162, 223, 224
  of giants, 49
  proper response to, 58, 59
poverty, 130, 142, 148, 156, 158, 164, 165, 171, 174, 189, 219
  literal, 88
  metaphorical, 89, 166
  praise of, 197
  threat of, 74
power, 128, 129, 155, 157, 163, 217
praise, 119
prayer, 201
precious stones, 111, 167, 169, 170
pride, 90, 109, 213
priest, 154
Prigent, Pierre, 29
primordial time, 191

Prince of Light, 90
prison, 158, 200
profit, 99, 204
progeny, 36, 43, 47, 57, 91
property, communal, 96, 109
prophecy, 144, 145
 Christian, 25
 classical, 26, 222
 predictive, 26
prophetic
 formula, 145
 messages, 145
 messenger, 146
 rivalry, 147, 150, 170
prophetic oath formula, 60
prophets, 210
 biblical, 52, 170, 201, 212, 219, 220,
  222
 Christian, 26, 145, 147
 false, 164
prostitute, 202
pseudonymity, 131
Pseudo-Solomon, 126
Ptolemies, 132
punishment, 106
pure drink, 104
purity meals, 104, 107

queen, 161
Qumran sectarianism, 6, 91, 119

Räisänen, H., 152, 153
Regev, Eyal, 6
regulations, 93, 99
 as boundary markers, 100
remnant, 93, 94, 119, 189, 199
repentance, 148, 150, 156, 157, 158, 162,
  164, 172, 178, 186, 209, 221
rest, 122
restoration, 135, 204, 213
resurrection, 209
reversal of fortunes, 57, 60, 61, 77, 78,
  115, 120, 124, 129, 137, 142, 159,
  174
reward, 111, 121, 129, 160
 future, 112, 131, 141, 220, 224
rich, the, 171, 183
 and covenant unfaithfulness, 56
 as dangerous, 69
 as label, 69
 as poor, 3
 as sinners, 72, 77
 as wicked, 79, 119
 denunciation of, 52, 56, 60, 74

fate of, 57, 59
riches. *See* wealth
righteous, the, 91, 164
 fate of, 126
 hope for, 91
 vindication of, 138
righteousness
 appearance of, 165
 rituals of exchange, 31
robe
 of honour, 91
 white, 173, 188
Roman army, 112
Rome, 176, 199
Rowland, C., 38, 176
royal edicts, 145, 146
Royalty, Robert, 7, 21, 147, 148, 151, 158,
  160, 169
Ruiz, Jean-Pierre, 25

Sabbath, 99
sackcloth, 179
sacred donations, 106
sailors, 58, 204, 205, 207, 211, 212
saints, 201, 202, 210
salvation, 160
 promised, 82
sarcasm, 183
Satan, 158, 188, 189, 190, 192, 194, 197,
  202, 203, 206, 208, 209, 216, 217,
  221
 downfall of, 189
 fall of, 191, 215
scribe, retainer class of, 70
scroll, seven-sealed, 172, 175, 207
sea, 185, 192, 193, 195, 206, 209,
  212
sea captains, 58
seafarers, 204, 205, 206
seal
 of God, 186
 third, 178
seals, 175, 182
secrets, 196
 of heaven, 47
sect, 116
sectarian, 102, 106, 148
 disputes, 151
 ideology, 189, 223
 separation, 88
 texts, 100
sectarianism, cosmopolitan, 20
sects, Jewish, 102
security, 196

seer, 168, 202
seers, 164
self-sufficiency, 161, 162, 163, 204, 217
separation, 199, 200, 221
seraphim, 169
serpent, 192
seven messages, 142, 145, 148, 150, 153,
    155, 161, 163, 166, 167, 171, 172,
    173, 174, 176, 177, 178, 184, 186,
    189, 196, 197, 204, 206, 209, 216,
    219
seven seals, 142, 178
    breaking of, 175, 178
sexual immorality, 47
shame, 116, 209, 214
sheep, 93, 164
shekel, 182
Shema, 102
Shemihazah, 44
Sheol, 60
shepherd, 94
    of the flock, 94
ship captain, 205
ship(s), 11, 58, 212
shippers, 214
shipping, 204
Sibylline Oracles, 112, 131, 220
silver, 111, 128, 130, 133
Similitudes, 126, 129, 222
sinners, 127, 142, 174, 188, 209
    association with, 58, 61, 73, 163,
        201
    fate of, 201
    rich, 61, 129, 130, 162, 163
Sirach, 63
Skehan, P., 73
slander, 158
slavery, 94, 108, 135
slaves, 162, 181
Smyrna, 3, 6, 8, 148, 156, 161, 178, 184,
    209
sobriquet, 152, 153, 154, 163
social injustice, 76, 150, 201, 217, 220
societies, 194
    agrarian, 30
soliloquy, 56
Solomon, 125, 134
Son of Man, 173, 174, 200
Sons of Dawn, 98
sons of light, 90
sons of the pit, 94
soul, 102, 162
    immortality of, 220
sovereignty, 161, 213

space, 192
speech, 161
    imputed, 4, 55, 56, 60, 68, 123, 139,
        148, 161, 162, 206, 212
    prophetic, 146, 151, 161, 198, 199, 201,
        207
spirit
    of falsehood, 164
    of truth, 90
    of wickedness, 90
status, 110
    economic, 98, 155
    marginal, 118, 139, 157
    of elect, 87, 91
storehouse, 48, 67, 87
strength, 102, 127, 196
Strugnell, J., 80, 88
Stuckenbruck, Loren, 51, 53, 172
suffering, 112, 130, 141, 148, 149, 150,
        154, 156, 158, 165, 171, 174, 177,
        200, 216, 224
    voluntary, 94, 139, 221
Summons to Flight, 198, 199, 201,
        202
surety, 82, 83, 84
sword, 173, 179
symbolic universe, 20, 216
synagogue, 8, 158
Synagogue of Satan, 8

tablets of heaven, 60
Tacitus, 17
Targums, 102
taunt song, 199, 202, 213
taxes, 113
Teacher of Righteousness, 117
teachers
    false, 148, 186
    rival, 150, 152, 170
teaching, false, 47, 154
Temple, 94, 95, 114, 128, 187
    leadership of, 95, 97, 115, 141
Testament of Levi, 43
testimony, 149, 201, 214
testing, 124, 131, 160, 165
the poor ones, 93, 119
theodicy, 53, 60, 76, 79, 141, 216
theology
    Deuteronomistic, 36, 53, 54, 59, 69, 73,
        79, 97, 119, 174, 197
    historical, 35
    of retribution, 37, 70, 77, 79, 137,
        220
thief, 209, 214

Thompson, Leonard, 21
throne, great white, 181
throne-room, 142, 167, 168, 171
  of God, 191
  report, 167
  vision, 167, 170, 173, 177, 189, 190,
    195
thrones, twenty-four, 169
Tigchelaar, E., 86
time, 192
Torah, 96, 118
  faithfulness to, 68
trade, 89, 96, 187, 188, 205
  maritime, 11
  networks, 10, 212
  slave, 162
trade guilds, 10, 14, 17, 21, 149, 156, 157,
    194, 205
tradition
  Deuteronomistic, 45, 53, 115
  Enochic, 64, 121, 154
  prophetic, 131, 141, 146, 169, 175,
    198
Trajan, 183
treasure, 43, 44, 55, 125, 162
truth, 117, 119
  council of, 117
Two Spirits Treatise, 105, 109, 164
two witnesses, 189
Tyre, 4, 99, 204, 213
  destruction of, 205, 212

underworld, 168, 179
universe, 168, 176, 181, 192

Vanhoye, A., 23
victory, 110, 153
violence, 47, 108, 128
virtue, 135, 158
vision, 142, 192, 194, 196, 198, 203
  of horsemen, 176
visionary world, 150
visions
  apocalyptic, 167
  heavenly, 167
visitation, 91, 121
  of God, 91

war, 153, 173, 178, 183, 192
  eschatological, 110, 120, 121, 122
  Ptolemaic, 112
  Seleucid, 112
War Scroll, 110, 115, 122, 220
warrior, 173, 177

Watchers, 44, 45, 46, 47, 49, 53, 124, 191
wealth, 3, 5, 8, 9, 10, 13, 15, 19, 25, 28, 30,
    43, 44, 47, 52, 53, 56, 57, 59, 60, 65,
    67, 68, 70, 71, 72, 73, 75, 77, 82, 83,
    84, 85, 86, 87, 88, 89, 94, 95, 96, 97,
    98, 99, 100, 101, 102, 103, 104, 105,
    106, 107, 108, 110, 111, 112, 113,
    114, 116, 117, 118, 122, 123, 166,
    184, 200, 203, 214, 219
  accumulation of, 5, 52, 67, 69, 98, 107,
    117, 118, 120, 137, 148, 155, 163,
    188, 196, 200, 202, 204, 206, 207,
    210, 211, 213, 216, 217
  as boundary marker, 96, 103, 104
  as God's favour, 37, 141
  commercial, 7
  critique of, 9, 32, 49, 142, 148, 181,
    197, 205, 209
  devotion to, 75, 76
  distribution of, 137
  imagery, 168, 169, 171, 198
  just, 71, 79, 136
  material, 50, 87, 139, 159, 171,
    221
  metaphorical, 126, 160, 166
  of outsiders, 98, 103
  precious gems, 20
  pursuit of, 44, 56, 76, 97, 113, 142, 217,
    223
  rejection of, 129, 131, 135, 139, 142,
    167, 189
  righteous, 50, 52
  theology of, 143
  unjust, 51, 56, 72, 74, 99, 108, 111, 115,
    120, 124, 162
Westermann, C., 213
wheat, 181, 182, 224
whore, 155, 176, 194, 199, 202, 203, 208,
    214
Wicked Priest, 114, 115, 116, 120
wicked, the, 91, 117, 164, 187
  destruction of, 188
  fate of, 126
wickedness, 115
  path of, 105
  spirit of, 108
widows, 95
wine, 108, 113, 122, 124, 182, 183, 199,
    202
  immoral, 155, 202, 203, 208
  metaphorical, 203
wisdom, 163
  acquisition of, 44, 125, 219
  as treasure, 43

wisdom (*cont.*)
  Enoch's, 47
  heavenly, 47
  hidden, 43, 64, 87
  mantic, 44, 132
  pursuit of, 89
Wisdom of Solomon, 121
witness, 154, 172, 199
woe oracles, 51, 59, 198, 213, 214,
  220
Wold, Benjamin, 85
works, 160, 173
world, foundation of, 196

world view, 163, 196, 197, 198, 200, 216,
  217, 220, 223
  apocalyptic, 141, 166
worship, 15, 119, 169, 186, 188, 193, 194
wrath, 199, 208

Yaḥad, 90, 101, 102, 103, 104, 106, 109,
  116, 119
  identity markers, 104
  leadership of, 103
Yarbro Collins, Adela, 17, 19, 183, 190,
  192
yoke, 181